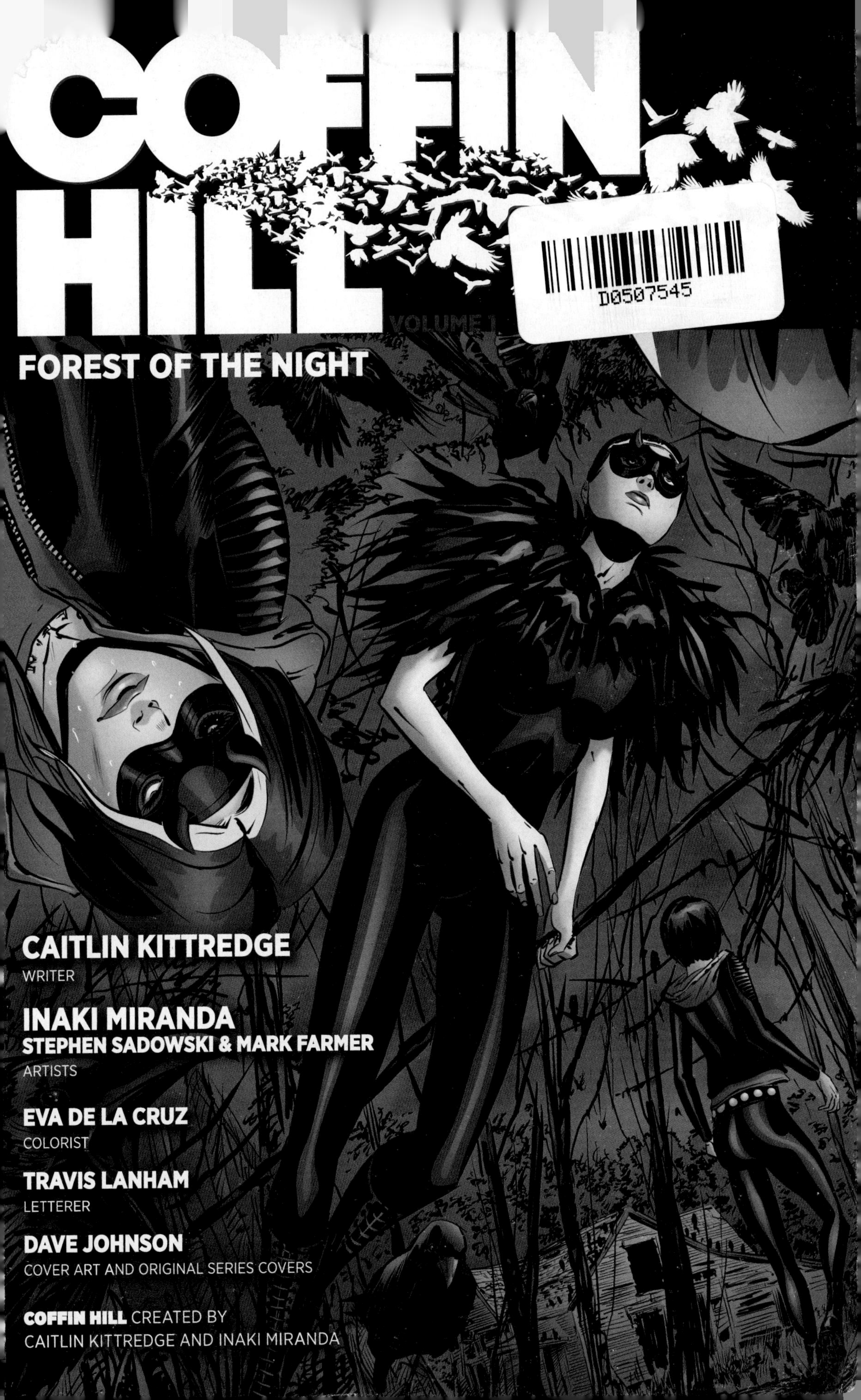

COFFIN HILL

VOLUME 1

FOREST OF THE NIGHT

CAITLIN KITTREDGE
WRITER

INAKI MIRANDA
STEPHEN SADOWSKI & MARK FARMER
ARTISTS

EVA DE LA CRUZ
COLORIST

TRAVIS LANHAM
LETTERER

DAVE JOHNSON
COVER ART AND ORIGINAL SERIES COVERS

COFFIN HILL CREATED BY
CAITLIN KITTREDGE AND INAKI MIRANDA

SHELLY BOND
EXECUTIVE EDITOR – VERTIGO AND EDITOR – ORIGINAL SERIES

GREGORY LOCKARD
ASSOCIATE EDITOR – ORIGINAL SERIES

SARA MILLER
ASSISTANT EDITOR – ORIGINAL SERIES

PETER HAMBOUSSI
EDITOR

ROBBIN BROSTERMAN
DESIGN DIRECTOR – BOOKS

CURTIS KING JR.
PUBLICATION DESIGN

HANK KANALZ
SENIOR VP – VERTIGO AND INTEGRATED PUBLISHING

DIANE NELSON
PRESIDENT

DAN DIDIO AND **JIM LEE**
CO-PUBLISHERS

GEOFF JOHNS
CHIEF CREATIVE OFFICER

JOHN ROOD
EXECUTIVE VP – SALES, MARKETING AND BUSINESS DEVELOPMENT

AMY GENKINS
SENIOR VP – BUSINESS AND LEGAL AFFAIRS

NAIRI GARDINER
SENIOR VP – FINANCE

JEFF BOISON
VP – PUBLISHING PLANNING

MARK CHIARELLO
VP – ART DIRECTION AND DESIGN

JOHN CUNNINGHAM
VP – MARKETING

TERRI CUNNINGHAM
VP – EDITORIAL ADMINISTRATION

ALISON GILL
SENIOR VP – MANUFACTURING AND OPERATIONS

JAY KOGAN
VP – BUSINESS AND LEGAL AFFAIRS, PUBLISHING

JACK MAHAN
VP – BUSINESS AFFAIRS, TALENT

NICK NAPOLITANO
VP – MANUFACTURING ADMINISTRATION

SUE POHJA
VP – BOOK SALES

COURTNEY SIMMONS
SENIOR VP – PUBLICITY

BOB WAYNE
SENIOR VP – SALES

LOGO DESIGN BY STEVE COOK

COFFIN HILL VOLUME ONE: FOREST OF THE NIGHT

PUBLISHED BY DC COMICS. COPYRIGHT © 2014 CAITLIN KITTREDGE AND INAKI MIRANDA. ALL RIGHTS RESERVED.

ORIGINALLY PUBLISHED IN SINGLE MAGAZINE FORM AS COFFIN HILL 1-7. COPYRIGHT © 2013, 2014 CAITLIN KITTREDGE AND INAKI MIRANDA. ALL RIGHTS RESERVED. ALL CHARACTERS, THEIR DISTINCTIVE LIKENESSES AND RELATED ELEMENTS FEATURED IN THIS PUBLICATION ARE TRADEMARKS OF DC COMICS. VERTIGO IS A TRADEMARK OF DC COMICS. THE STORIES, CHARACTERS AND INCIDENTS FEATURED IN THIS PUBLICATION ARE ENTIRELY FICTIONAL. DC COMICS DOES NOT READ OR ACCEPT UNSOLICITED SUBMISSIONS OF IDEAS, STORIES OR ARTWORK.

DC COMICS, 1700 BROADWAY, NEW YORK, NY 10019
A WARNER BROS. ENTERTAINMENT COMPANY
PRINTED IN THE USA. FIRST PRINTING.
ISBN: 978-1-4012-4887-1

Library of Congress Cataloging-in-Publication Data

Kittredge, Caitlin, author.
 Coffin Hill. Volume 1, Forest of the Night / Caitlin Kittredge ; [illustrated by] Inaki Miranda.
     pages cm
ISBN 978-1-4012-4887-1 (paperback)
1. Graphic novels. I. Miranda, Inaki, illustrator. II. Title. III. Title: Forest of the Night.
PN6728.C597K58 2014
741.5'973—dc23
                          2014000612

SUSTAINABLE FORESTRY INITIATIVE
Certified Chain of Custody
At Least 20% Certified Forest Content
www.sfiprogram.org
SFI-01042
APPLIES TO TEXT STOCK ONLY

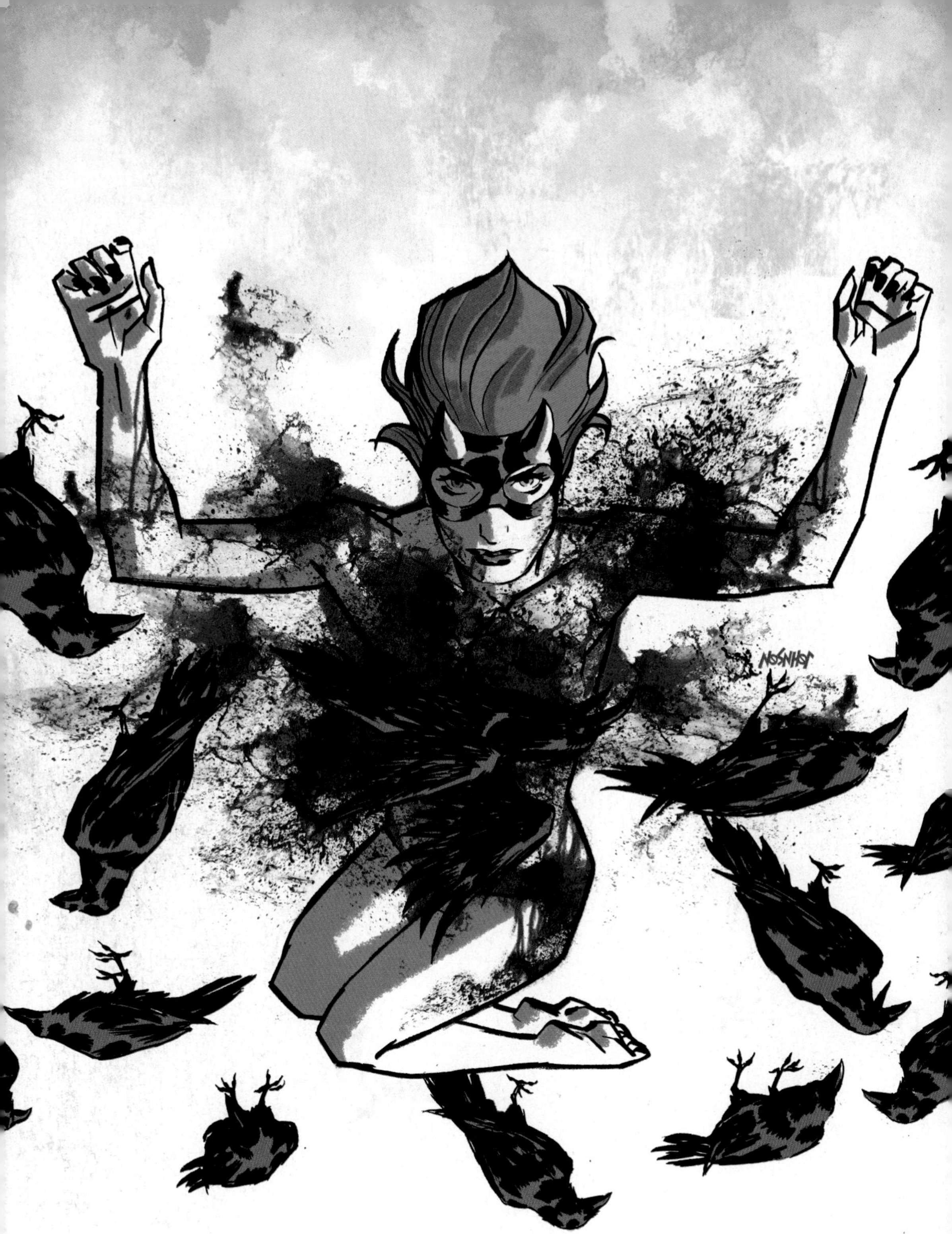

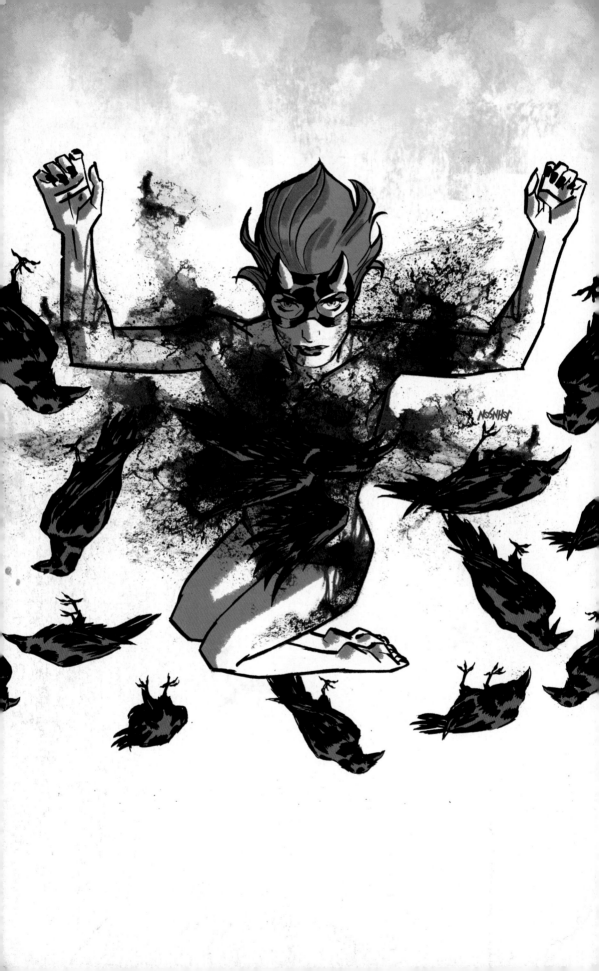

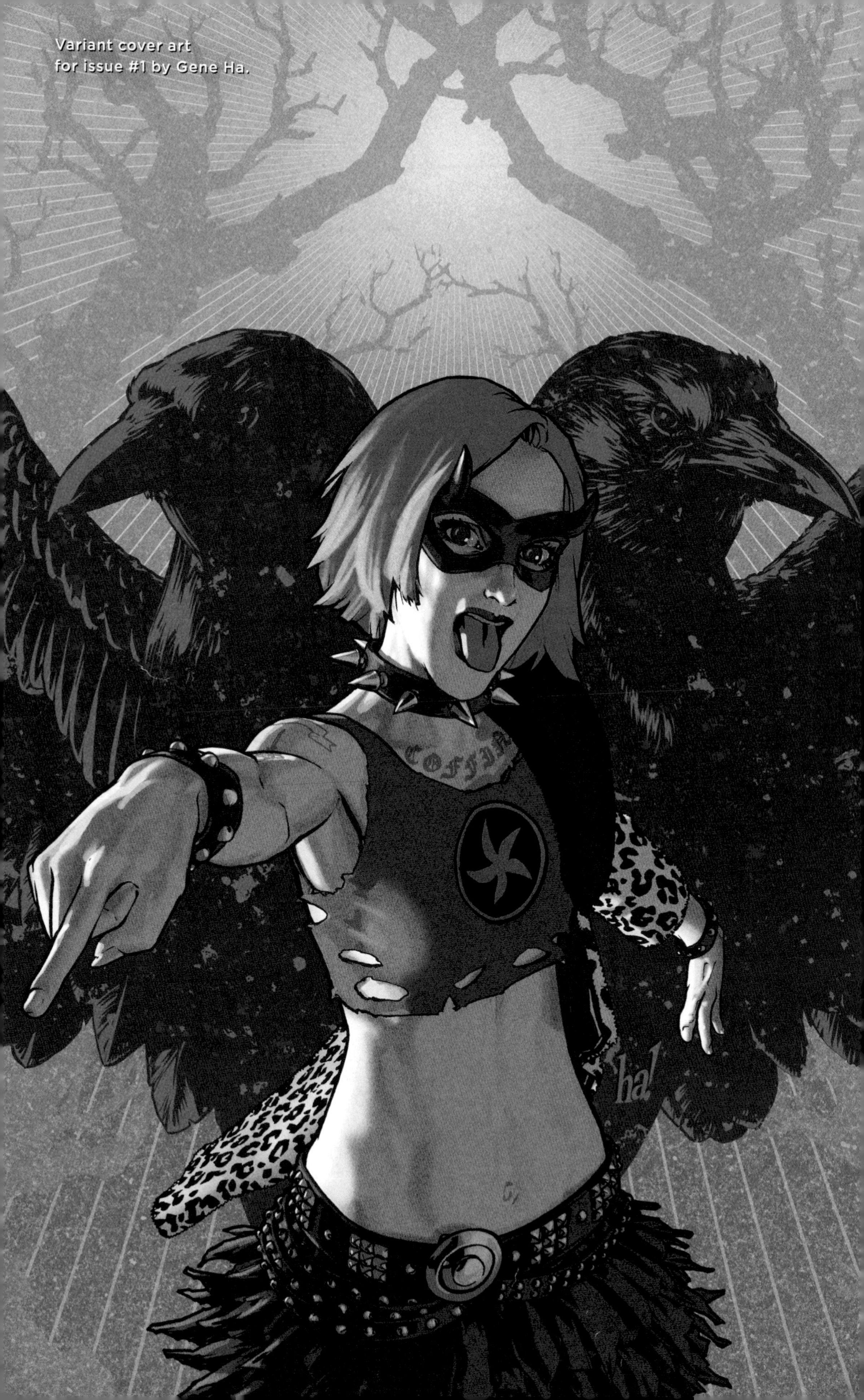
ha!

Variant cover art
for issue #1 by Gene Ha.

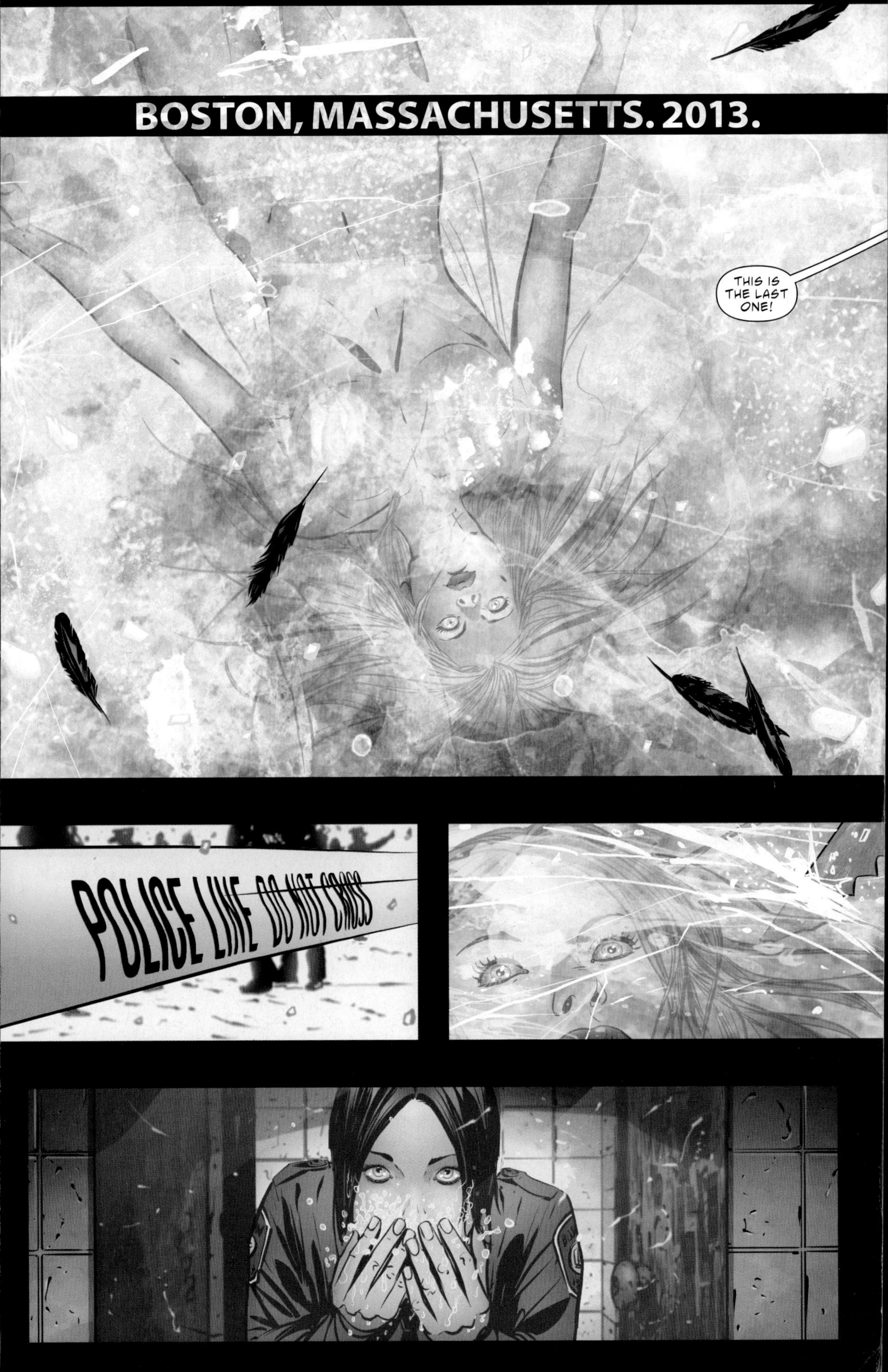
BOSTON, MASSACHUSETTS. 2013.
THIS IS THE LAST ONE!
POLICE LINE DO NOT CROSS

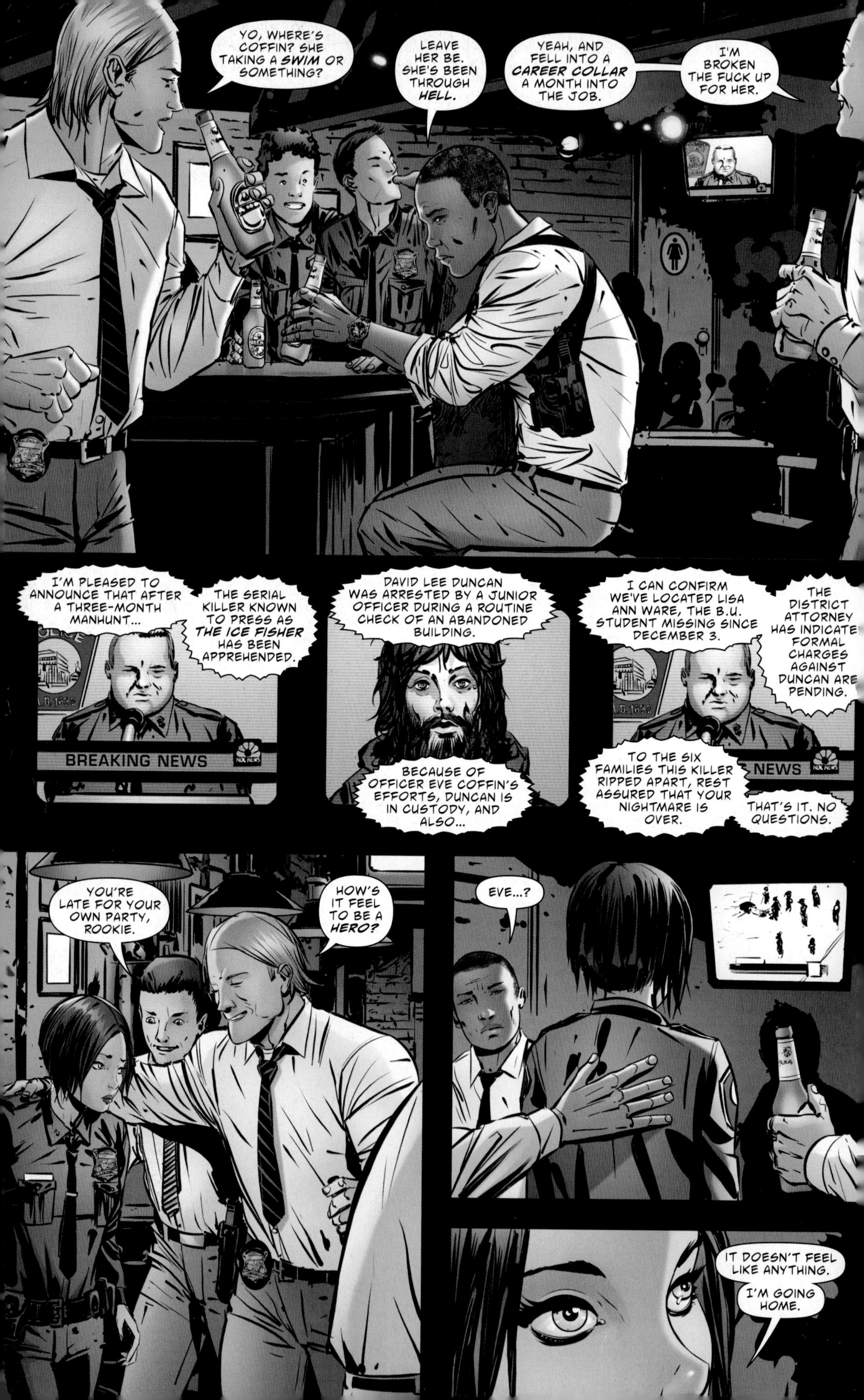
YO, WHERE'S COFFIN? SHE TAKING A SWIM OR SOMETHING?
LEAVE HER BE. SHE'S BEEN THROUGH HELL.
YEAH, AND FELL INTO A CAREER COLLAR A MONTH INTO THE JOB.
I'M BROKEN THE FUCK UP FOR HER.
I'M PLEASED TO ANNOUNCE THAT AFTER A THREE-MONTH MANHUNT...
THE SERIAL KILLER KNOWN TO PRESS AS THE ICE FISHER HAS BEEN APPREHENDED.
BREAKING NEWS
DAVID LEE DUNCAN WAS ARRESTED BY A JUNIOR OFFICER DURING A ROUTINE CHECK OF AN ABANDONED BUILDING.
BECAUSE OF OFFICER EVE COFFIN'S EFFORTS, DUNCAN IS IN CUSTODY, AND ALSO...
I CAN CONFIRM WE'VE LOCATED LISA ANN WARE, THE B.U. STUDENT MISSING SINCE DECEMBER 3.
THE DISTRICT ATTORNEY HAS INDICATE FORMAL CHARGES AGAINST DUNCAN ARE PENDING.
TO THE SIX FAMILIES THIS KILLER RIPPED APART, REST ASSURED THAT YOUR NIGHTMARE IS OVER.
THAT'S IT. NO QUESTIONS.
YOU'RE LATE FOR YOUR OWN PARTY, ROOKIE.
HOW'S IT FEEL TO BE A HERO?
EVE...?
IT DOESN'T FEEL LIKE ANYTHING.
I'M GOING HOME.

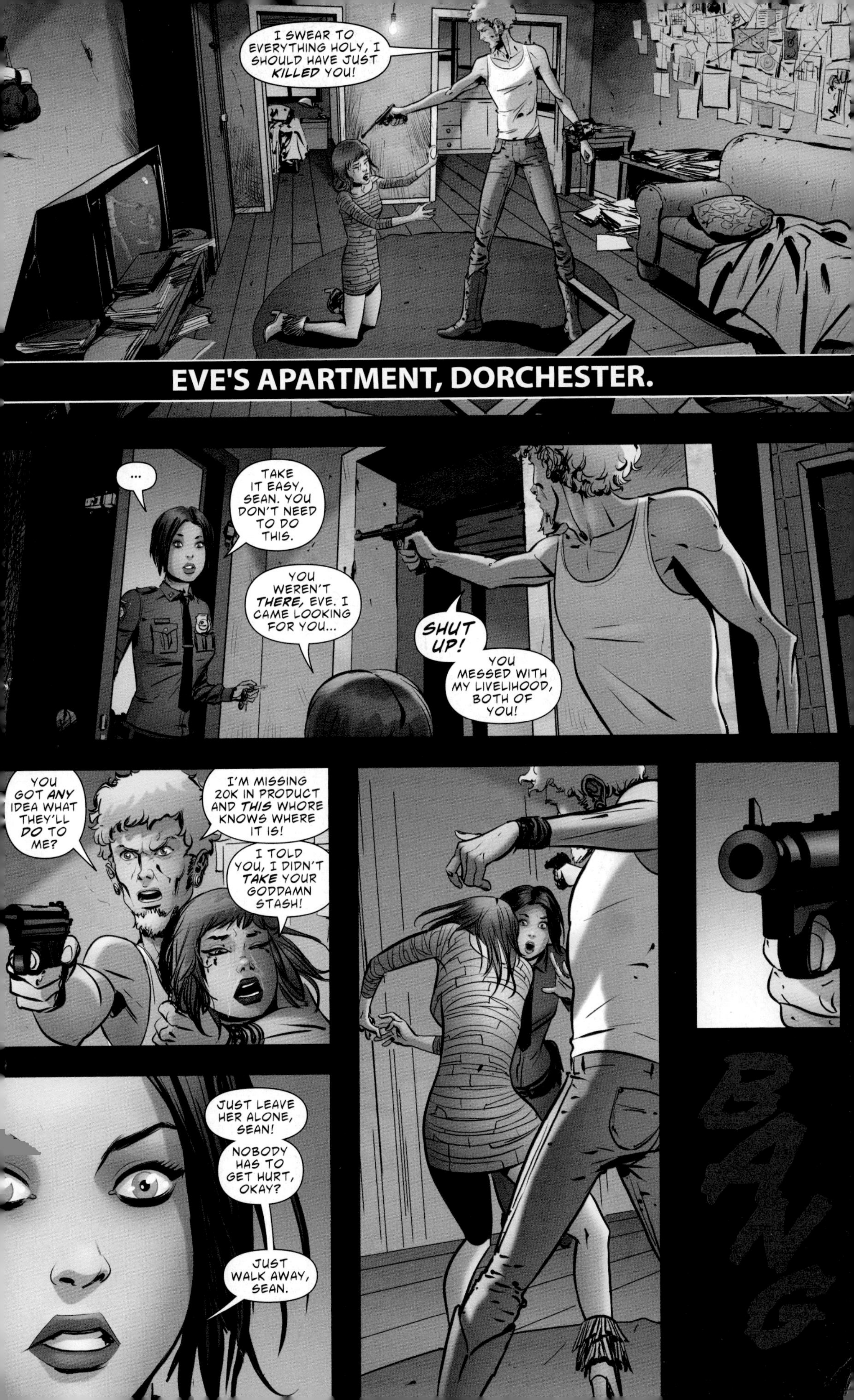
I SWEAR TO EVERYTHING HOLY, I SHOULD HAVE JUST KILLED YOU!
EVE'S APARTMENT, DORCHESTER.
...
TAKE IT EASY, SEAN. YOU DON'T NEED TO DO THIS.
YOU WEREN'T THERE, EVE. I CAME LOOKING FOR YOU...
SHUT UP!
YOU MESSED WITH MY LIVELIHOOD, BOTH OF YOU!
YOU GOT ANY IDEA WHAT THEY'LL DO TO ME?
I'M MISSING 20K IN PRODUCT AND THIS WHORE KNOWS WHERE IT IS!
I TOLD YOU, I DIDN'T TAKE YOUR GODDAMN STASH!
JUST LEAVE HER ALONE, SEAN!
NOBODY HAS TO GET HURT, OKAY?
JUST WALK AWAY, SEAN.
BANG

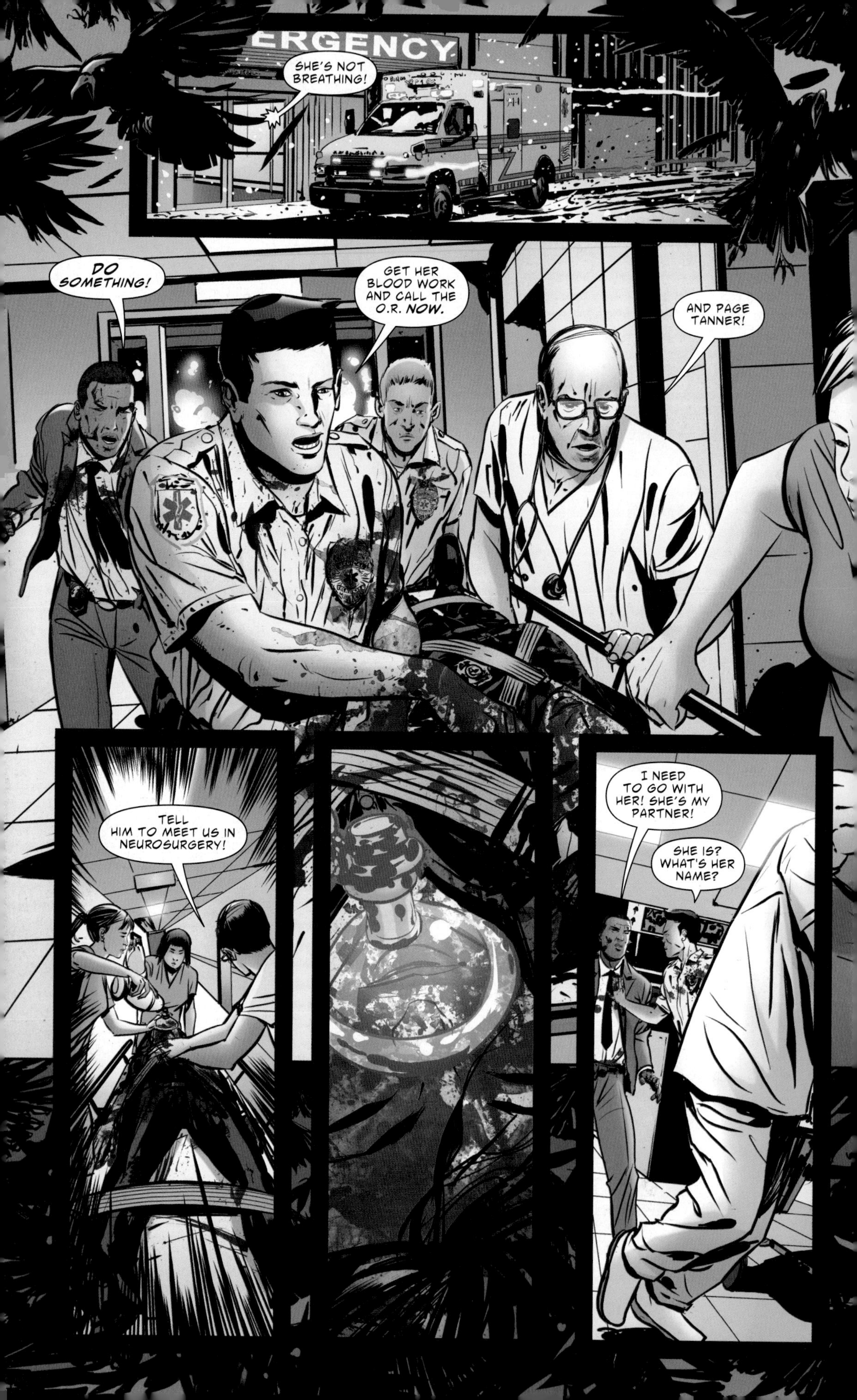
ERGENCY
SHE'S NOT BREATHING!
DO SOMETHING!
GET HER BLOOD WORK AND CALL THE O.R. NOW.
AND PAGE TANNER!
TELL HIM TO MEET US IN NEUROSURGERY!
I NEED TO GO WITH HER! SHE'S MY PARTNER!
SHE IS? WHAT'S HER NAME?

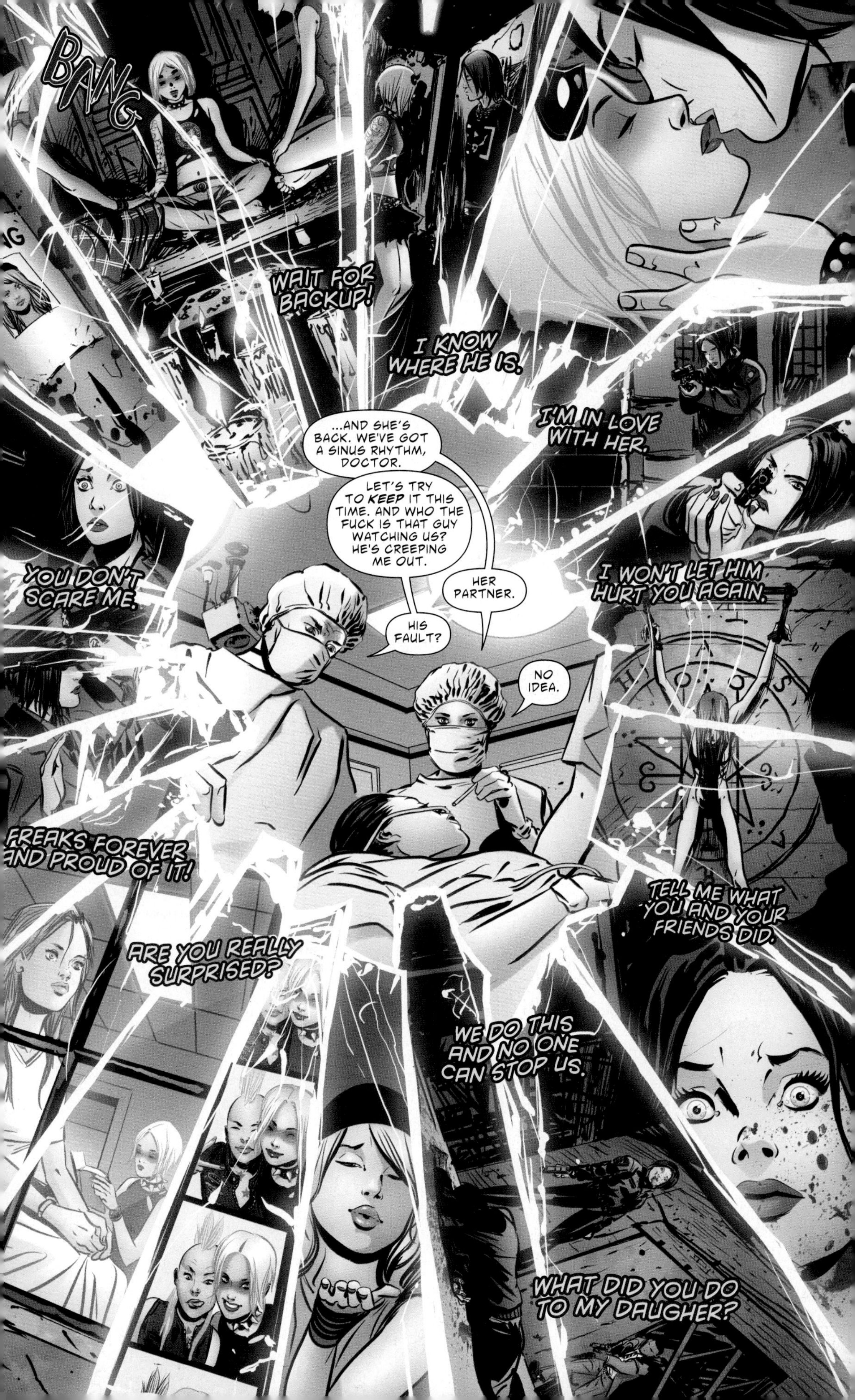
BANG
WAIT FOR BACKUP!
I KNOW WHERE HE IS.
I'M IN LOVE WITH HER.
...AND SHE'S BACK. WE'VE GOT A SINUS RHYTHM, DOCTOR.
LET'S TRY TO KEEP IT THIS TIME. AND WHO THE FUCK IS THAT GUY WATCHING US? HE'S CREEPING ME OUT.
HER PARTNER.
HIS FAULT?
NO IDEA.
YOU DON'T SCARE ME.
I WON'T LET HIM HURT YOU AGAIN.
FREAKS FOREVER AND PROUD OF IT!
TELL ME WHAT YOU AND YOUR FRIENDS DID.
ARE YOU REALLY SURPRISED?
WE DO THIS AND NO ONE CAN STOP US.
WHAT DID YOU DO TO MY DAUGHER?

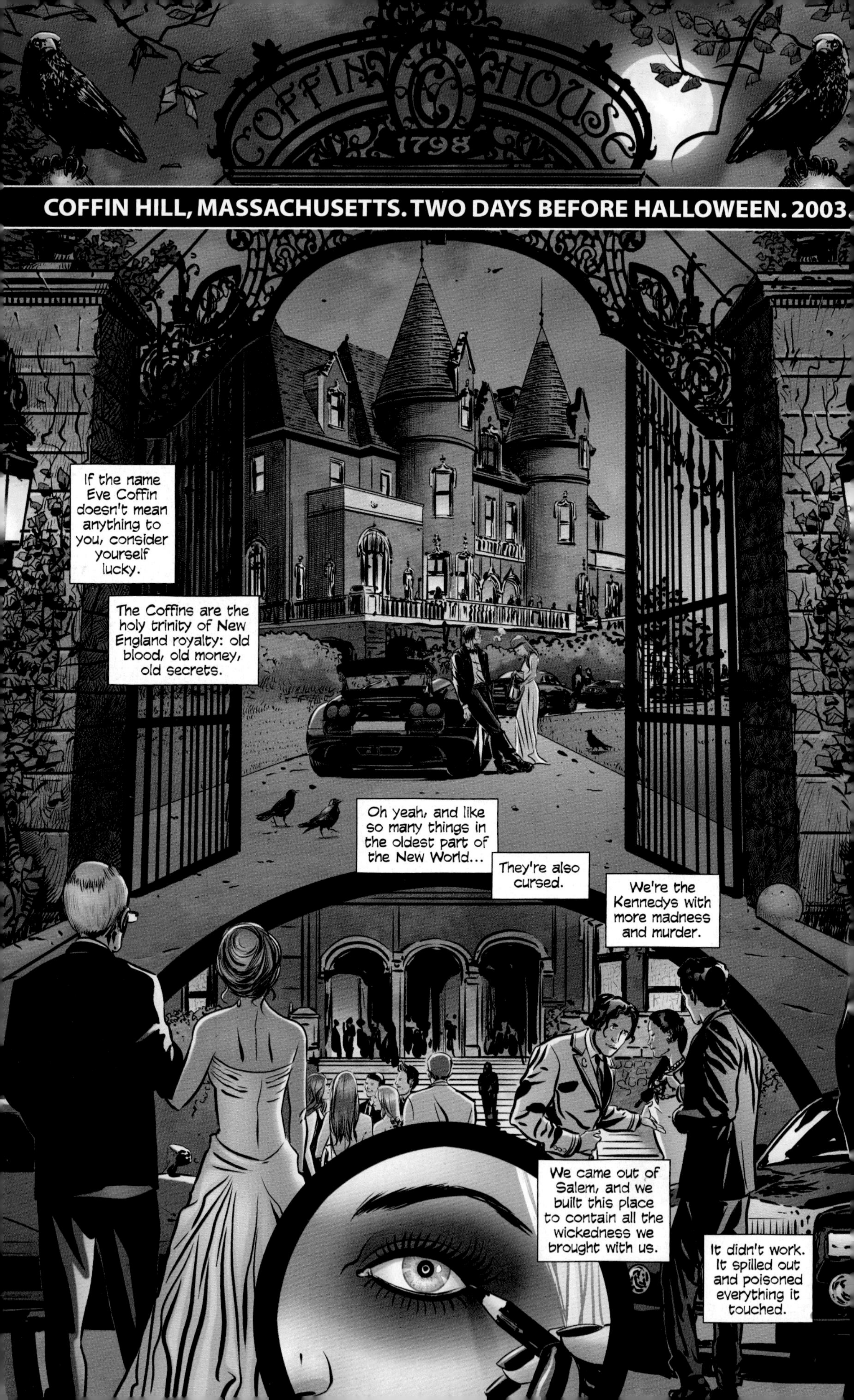
COFFIN HOUSE
1798
COFFIN HILL, MASSACHUSETTS. TWO DAYS BEFORE HALLOWEEN. 2003.
If the name Eve Coffin doesn't mean anything to you, consider yourself lucky.
The Coffins are the holy trinity of New England royalty: old blood, old money, old secrets.
Oh yeah, and like so many things in the oldest part of the New World...
They're also cursed.
We're the Kennedys with more madness and murder.
We came out of Salem, and we built this place to contain all the wickedness we brought with us.
It didn't work. It spilled out and poisoned everything it touched.

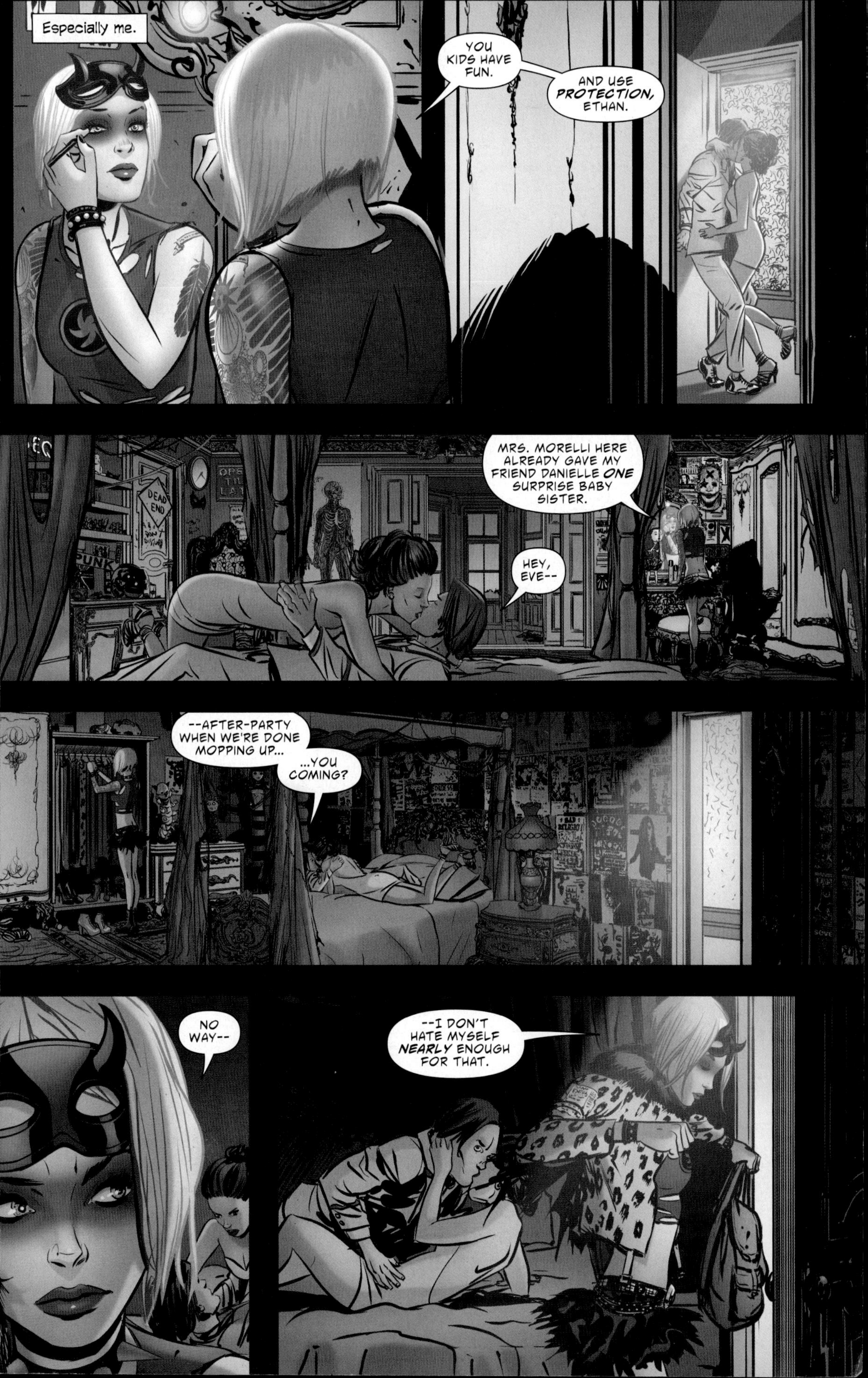
Especially me.
YOU KIDS HAVE FUN.
AND USE PROTECTION, ETHAN.
MRS. MORELLI HERE ALREADY GAVE MY FRIEND DANIELLE ONE SURPRISE BABY SISTER.
HEY, EVE--
--AFTER-PARTY WHEN WE'RE DONE MOPPING UP...
...YOU COMING?
NO WAY--
--I DON'T HATE MYSELF NEARLY ENOUGH FOR THAT.

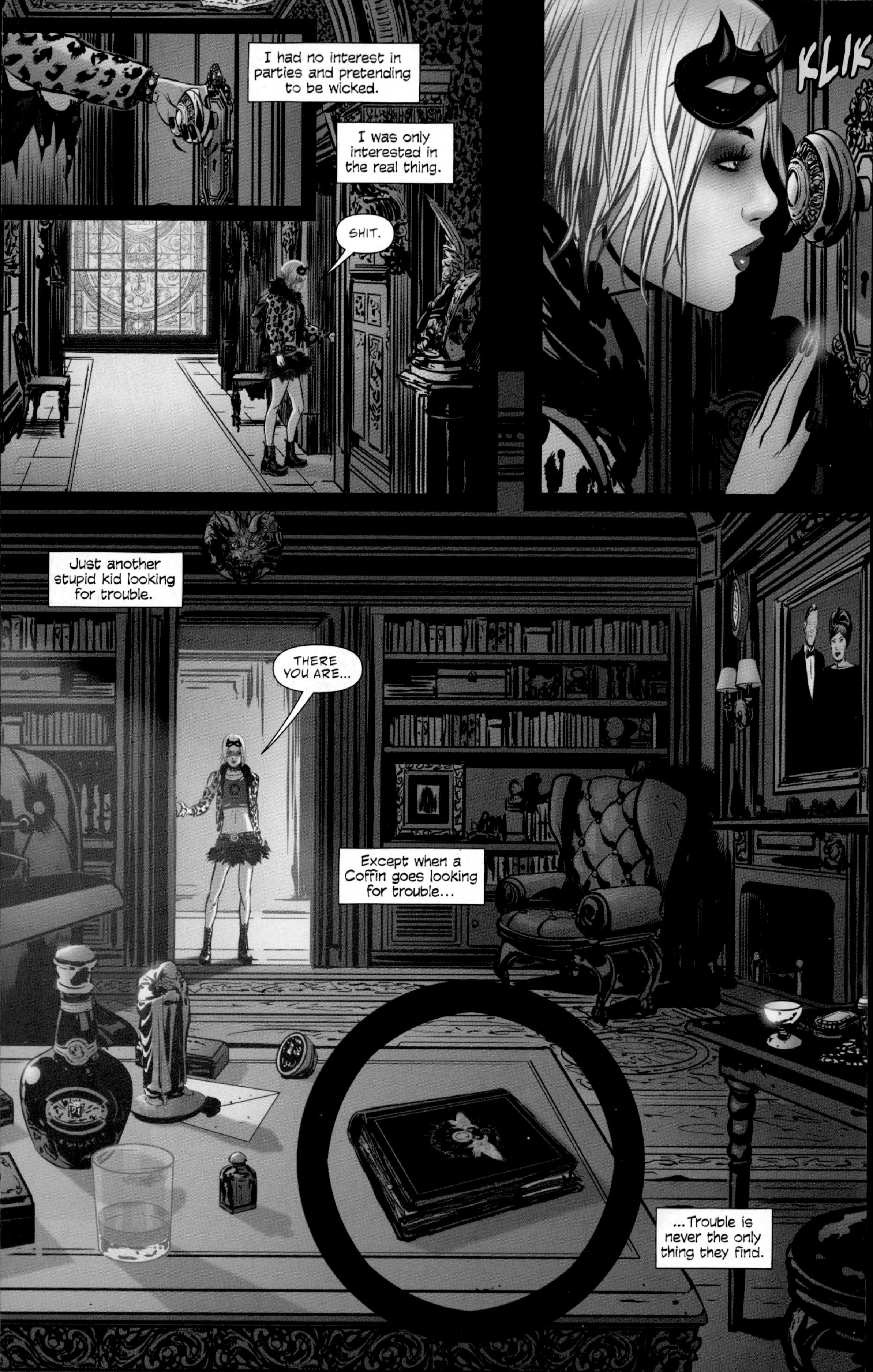
I had no interest in parties and pretending to be wicked.
I was only interested in the real thing.
SHIT.
KLIK
Just another stupid kid looking for trouble.
THERE YOU ARE...
Except when a Coffin goes looking for trouble...
...Trouble is never the only thing they find.

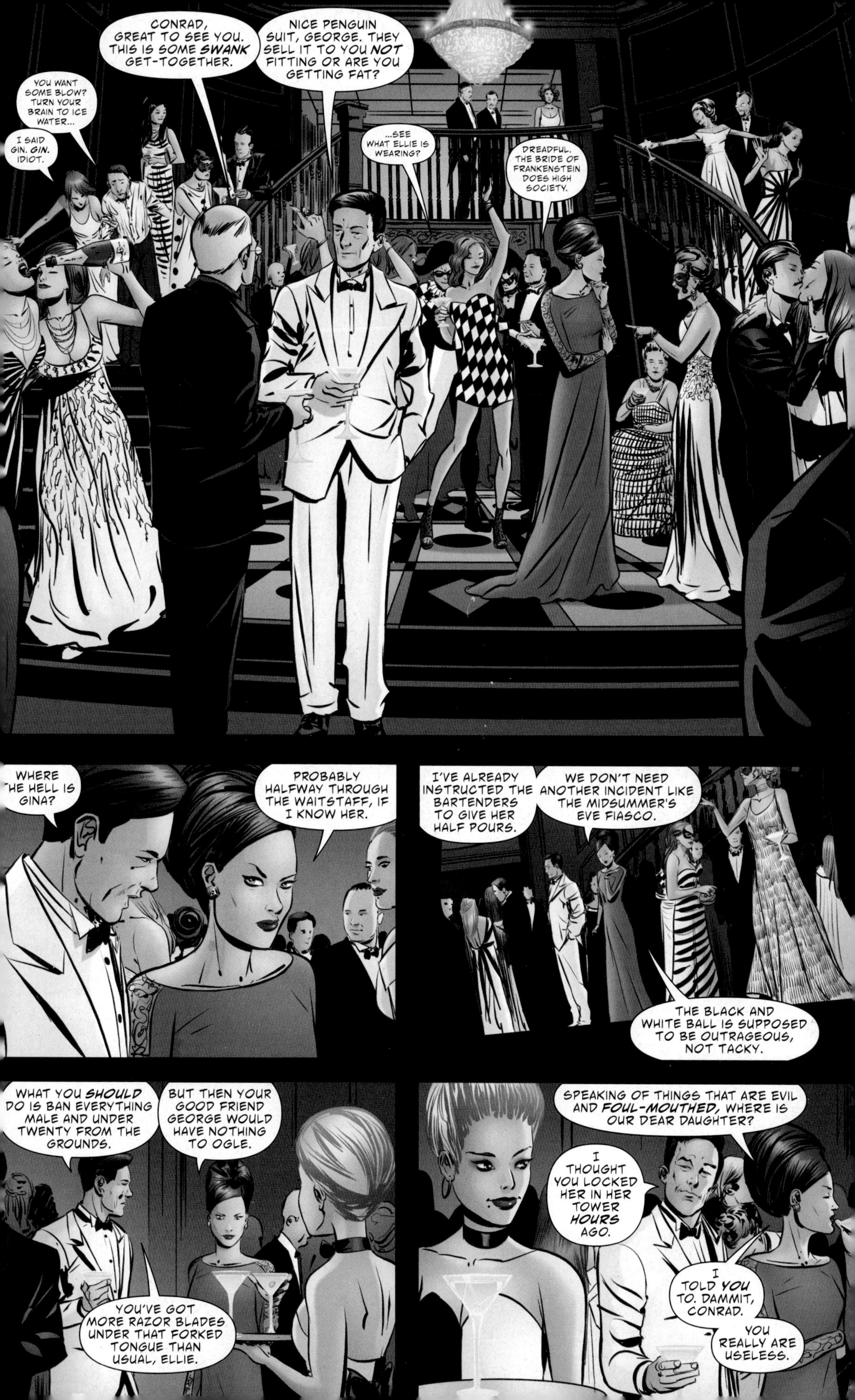

CONRAD, GREAT TO SEE YOU. THIS IS SOME SWANK GET-TOGETHER.
NICE PENGUIN SUIT, GEORGE. THEY SELL IT TO YOU NOT FITTING OR ARE YOU GETTING FAT?
YOU WANT SOME BLOW? TURN YOUR BRAIN TO ICE WATER...
I SAID GIN. GIN. IDIOT.
...SEE WHAT ELLIE IS WEARING?
DREADFUL. THE BRIDE OF FRANKENSTEIN DOES HIGH SOCIETY.
WHERE THE HELL IS GINA?
PROBABLY HALFWAY THROUGH THE WAITSTAFF, IF I KNOW HER.
I'VE ALREADY INSTRUCTED THE BARTENDERS TO GIVE HER HALF POURS.
WE DON'T NEED ANOTHER INCIDENT LIKE THE MIDSUMMER'S EVE FIASCO.
THE BLACK AND WHITE BALL IS SUPPOSED TO BE OUTRAGEOUS, NOT TACKY.
WHAT YOU SHOULD DO IS BAN EVERYTHING MALE AND UNDER TWENTY FROM THE GROUNDS.
BUT THEN YOUR GOOD FRIEND GEORGE WOULD HAVE NOTHING TO OGLE.
YOU'VE GOT MORE RAZOR BLADES UNDER THAT FORKED TONGUE THAN USUAL, ELLIE.
SPEAKING OF THINGS THAT ARE EVIL AND FOUL-MOUTHED, WHERE IS OUR DEAR DAUGHTER?
I THOUGHT YOU LOCKED HER IN HER TOWER HOURS AGO.
I TOLD YOU TO. DAMMIT, CONRAD.
YOU REALLY ARE USELESS.

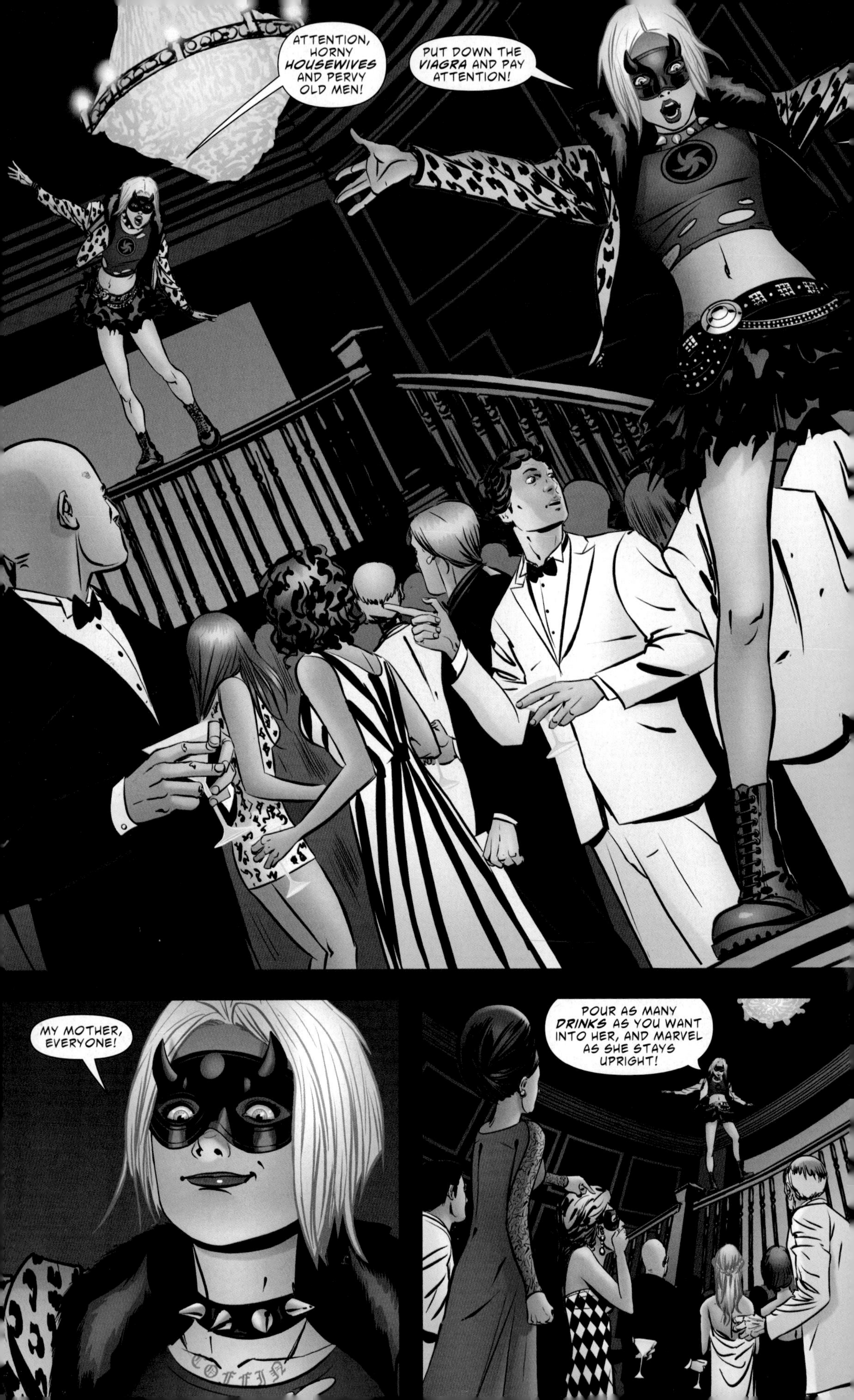
ATTENTION, HORNY *HOUSEWIVES* AND PERVY OLD MEN!
PUT DOWN THE *VIAGRA* AND PAY ATTENTION!
MY MOTHER, EVERYONE!
POUR AS MANY *DRINKS* AS YOU WANT INTO HER, AND MARVEL AS SHE STAYS UPRIGHT!

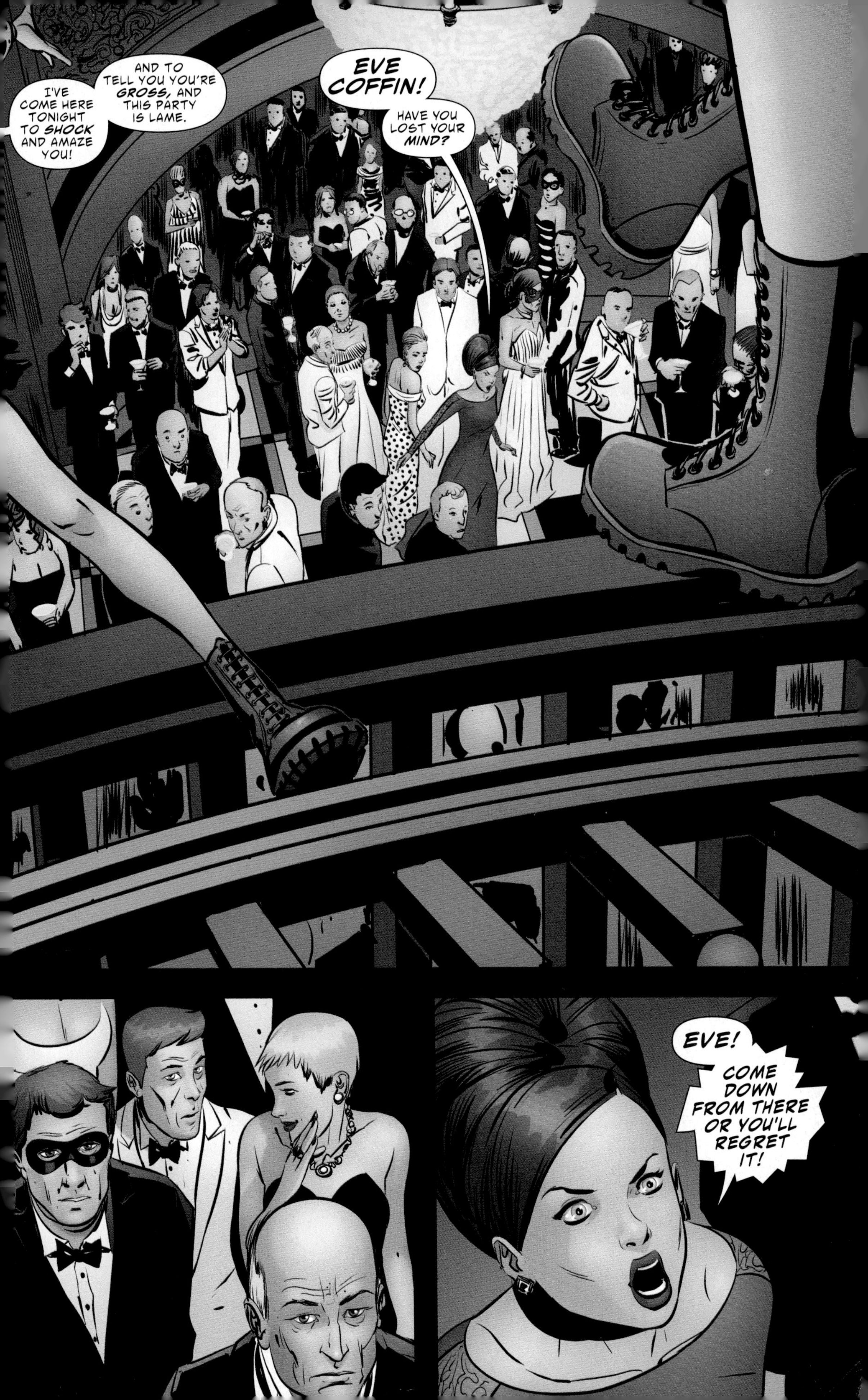
I'VE COME HERE TONIGHT TO SHOCK AND AMAZE YOU!
AND TO TELL YOU YOU'RE GROSS, AND THIS PARTY IS LAME.
EVE COFFIN!
HAVE YOU LOST YOUR MIND?
EVE!
COME DOWN FROM THERE OR YOU'LL REGRET IT!

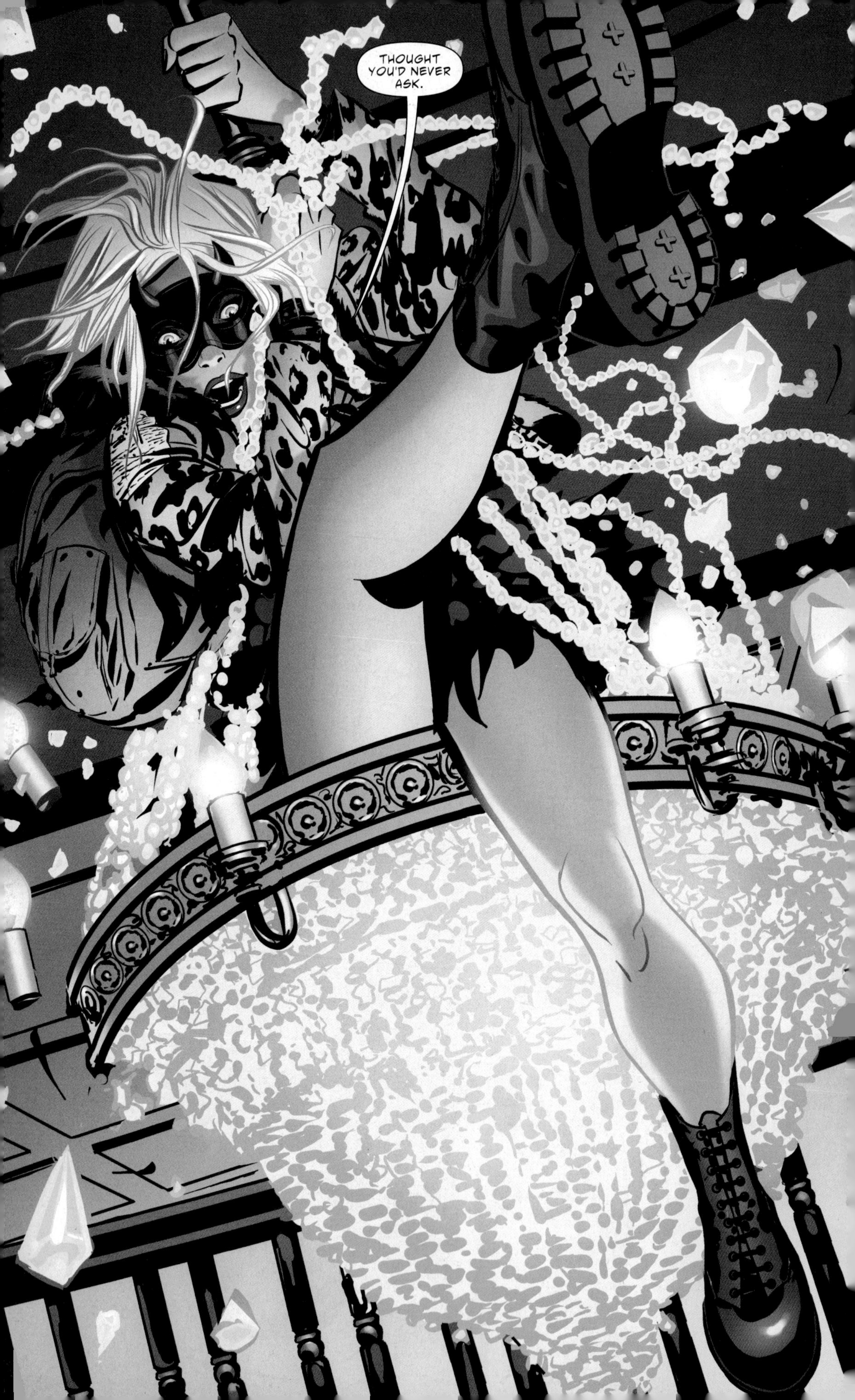
THOUGHT YOU'D NEVER ASK.

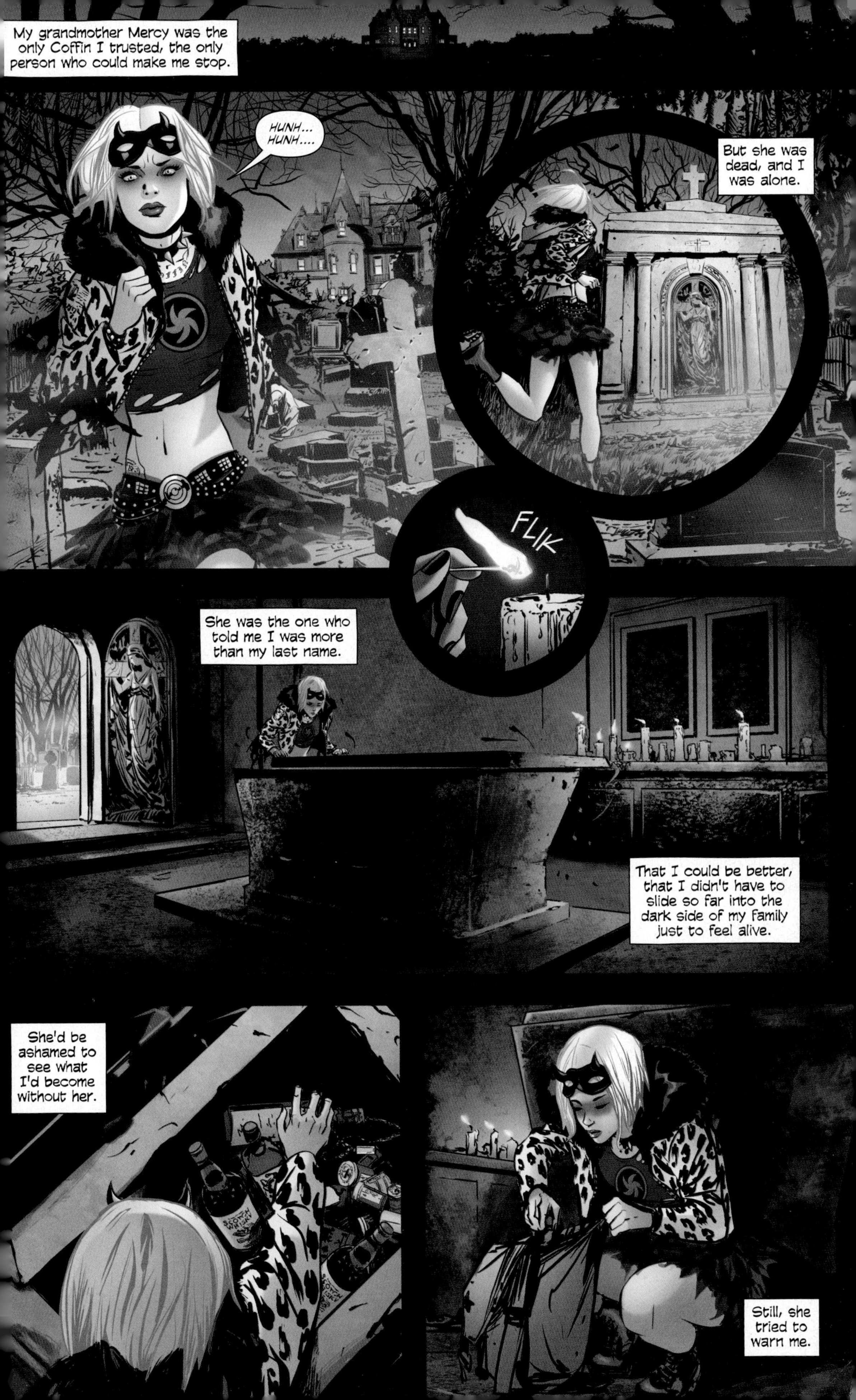
My grandmother Mercy was the only Coffin I trusted, the only person who could make me stop.
HUNH... HUNH....
But she was dead, and I was alone.
FLIK
She was the one who told me I was more than my last name.
That I could be better, that I didn't have to slide so far into the dark side of my family just to feel alive.
She'd be ashamed to see what I'd become without her.
Still, she tried to warn me.

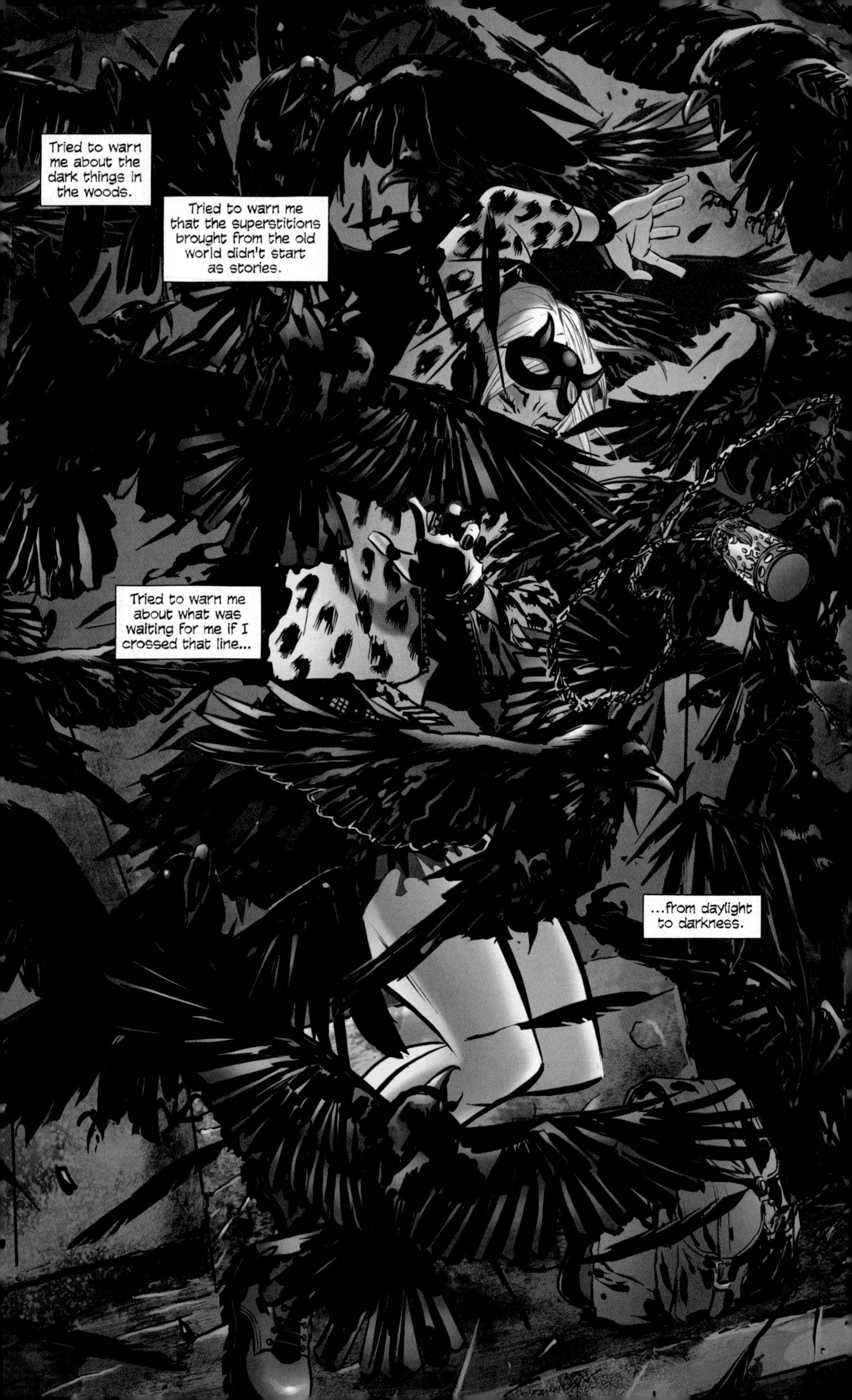
Tried to warn me about the dark things in the woods.
Tried to warn me that the superstitions brought from the old world didn't start as stories.
Tried to warn me about what was waiting for me if I crossed that line...
...from daylight to darkness.

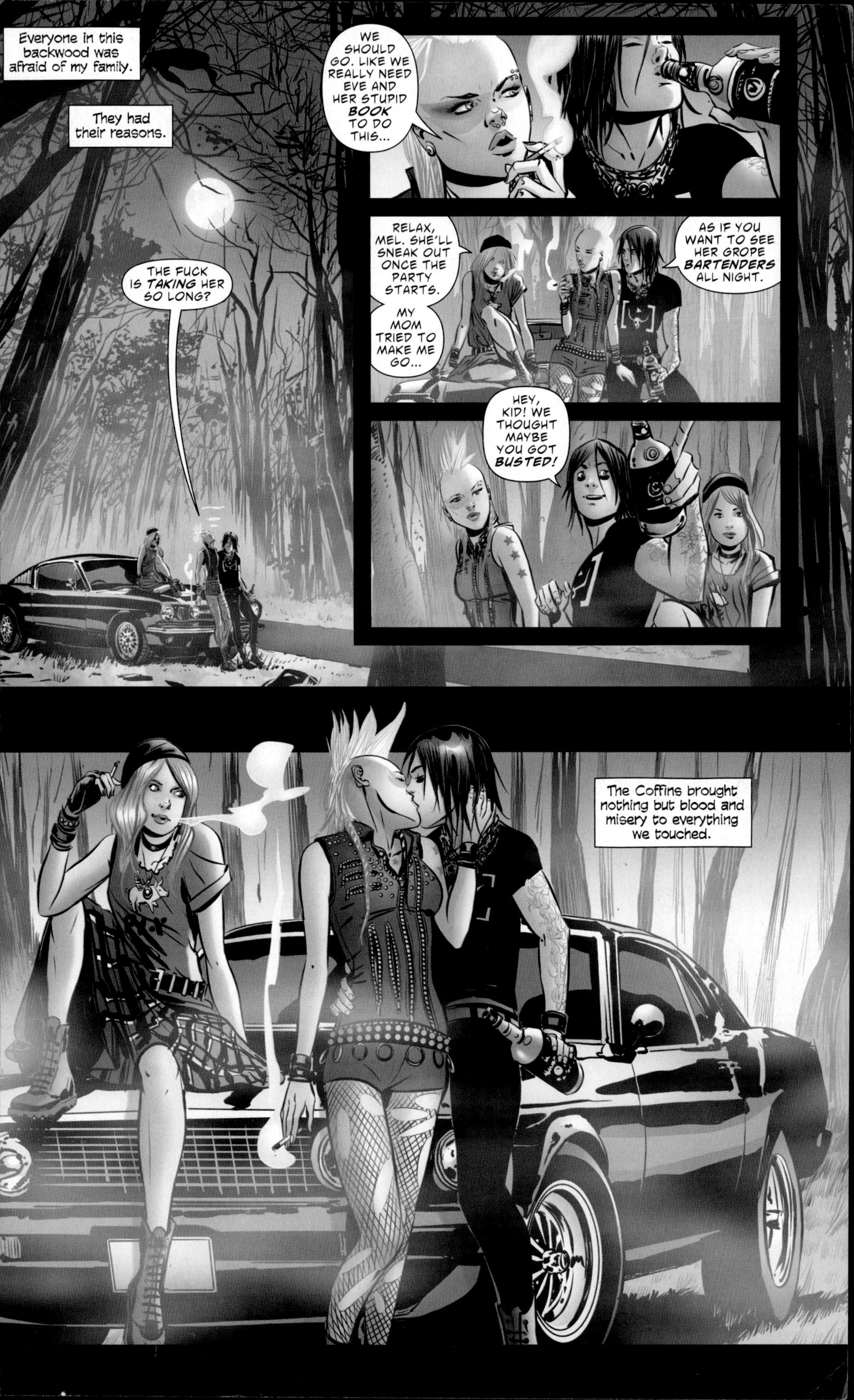
Everyone in this backwood was afraid of my family.
They had their reasons.
THE FUCK IS TAKING HER SO LONG?
WE SHOULD GO. LIKE WE REALLY NEED EVE AND HER STUPID BOOK TO DO THIS...
RELAX, MEL. SHE'LL SNEAK OUT ONCE THE PARTY STARTS.
AS IF YOU WANT TO SEE HER GROPE BARTENDERS ALL NIGHT.
MY MOM TRIED TO MAKE ME GO...
HEY, KID! WE THOUGHT MAYBE YOU GOT BUSTED!
The Coffins brought nothing but blood and misery to everything we touched.

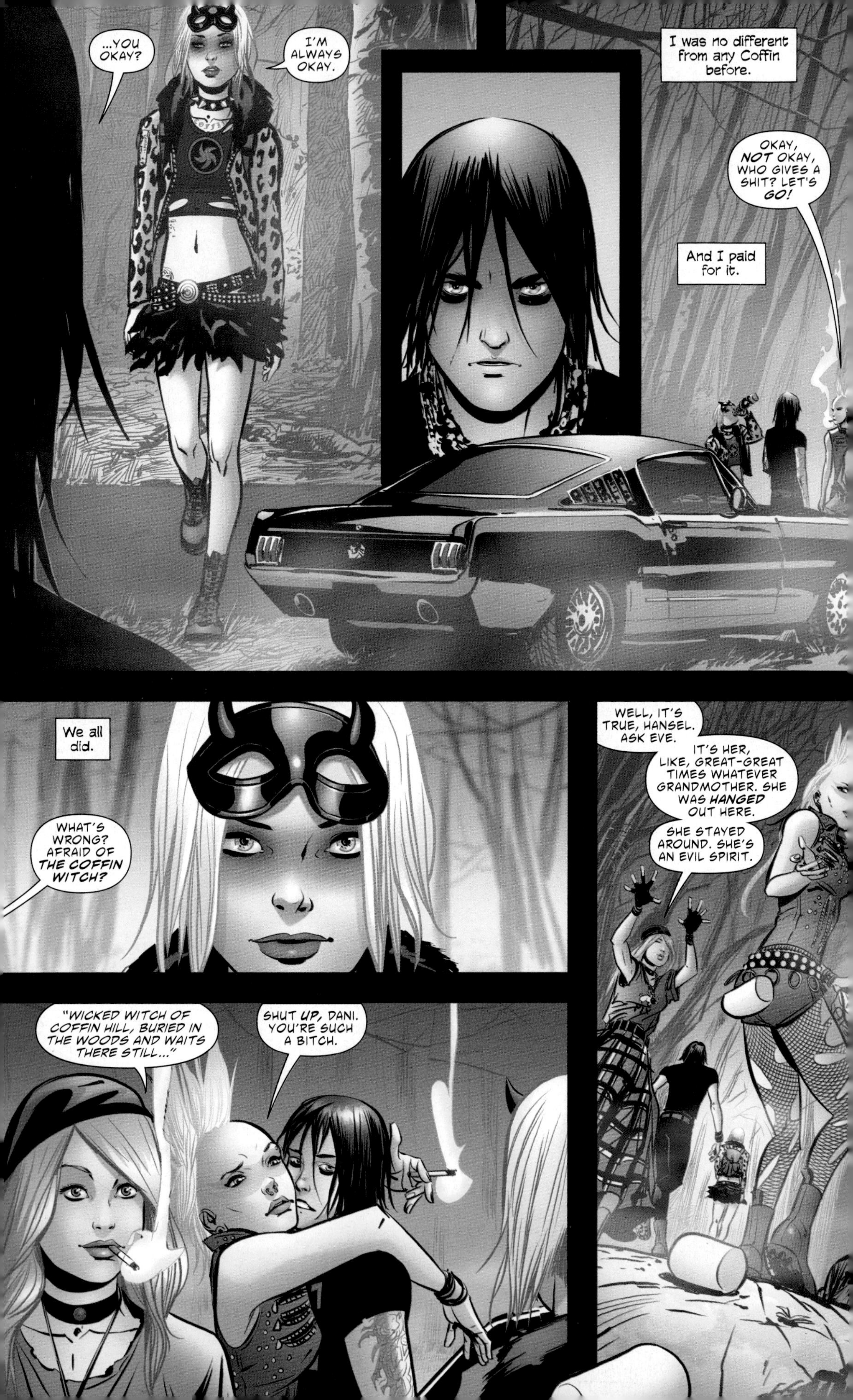

...YOU OKAY?
I'M ALWAYS OKAY.
I was no different from any Coffin before.
OKAY, NOT OKAY, WHO GIVES A SHIT? LET'S GO!
And I paid for it.
We all did.
WHAT'S WRONG? AFRAID OF THE COFFIN WITCH?
"WICKED WITCH OF COFFIN HILL, BURIED IN THE WOODS AND WAITS THERE STILL..."
SHUT UP, DANI. YOU'RE SUCH A BITCH.
WELL, IT'S TRUE, HANSEL. ASK EVE.
IT'S HER, LIKE, GREAT-GREAT TIMES WHATEVER GRANDMOTHER. SHE WAS HANGED OUT HERE.
SHE STAYED AROUND. SHE'S AN EVIL SPIRIT.

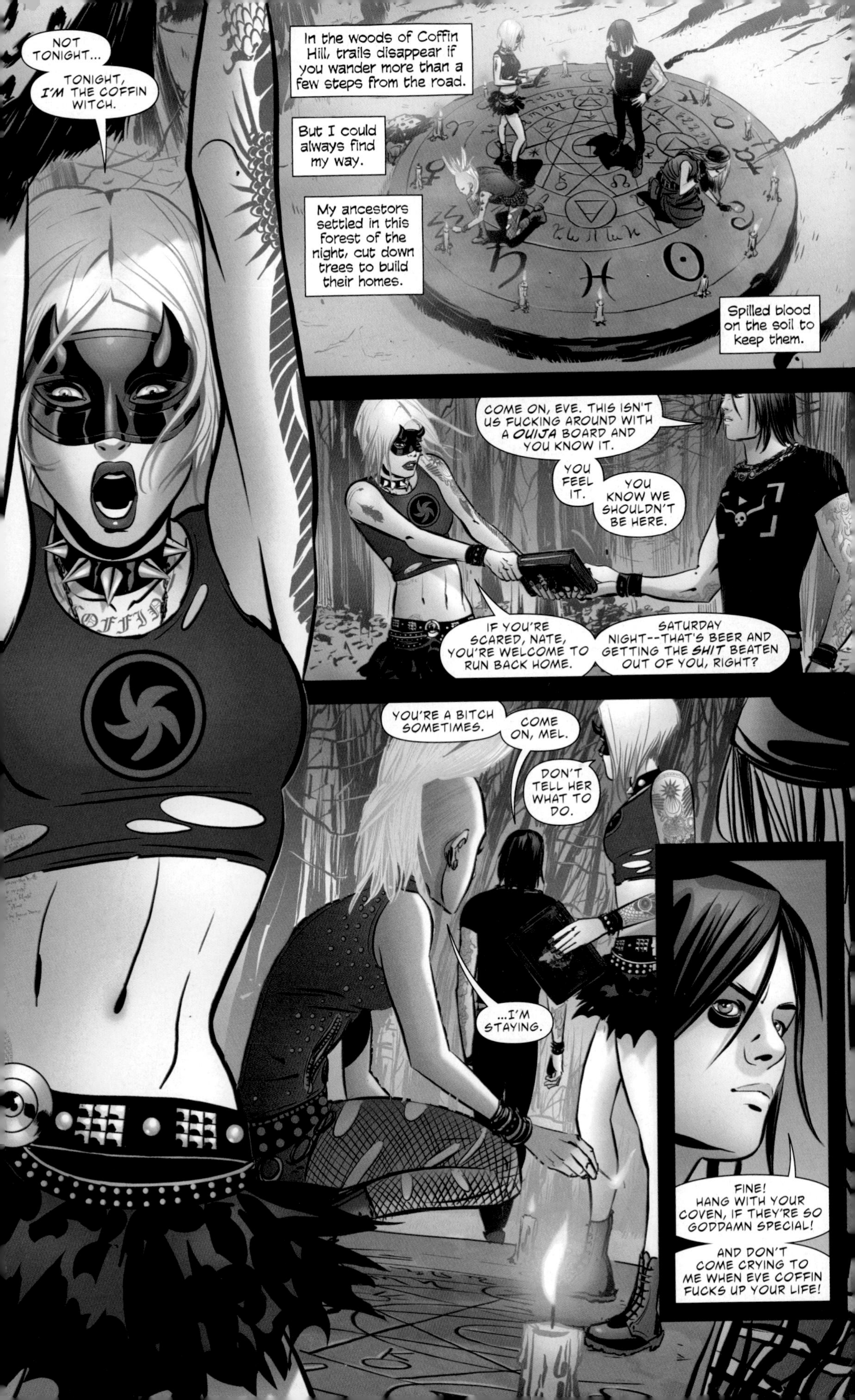

NOT TONIGHT...
TONIGHT, I'M THE COFFIN WITCH.
In the woods of Coffin Hill, trails disappear if you wander more than a few steps from the road.
But I could always find my way.
My ancestors settled in this forest of the night, cut down trees to build their homes.
Spilled blood on the soil to keep them.
COME ON, EVE. THIS ISN'T US FUCKING AROUND WITH A OUIJA BOARD AND YOU KNOW IT.
YOU FEEL IT.
YOU KNOW WE SHOULDN'T BE HERE.
IF YOU'RE SCARED, NATE, YOU'RE WELCOME TO RUN BACK HOME.
SATURDAY NIGHT--THAT'S BEER AND GETTING THE SHIT BEATEN OUT OF YOU, RIGHT?
YOU'RE A BITCH SOMETIMES.
COME ON, MEL.
DON'T TELL HER WHAT TO DO.
...I'M STAYING.
FINE! HANG WITH YOUR COVEN, IF THEY'RE SO GODDAMN SPECIAL!
AND DON'T COME CRYING TO ME WHEN EVE COFFIN FUCKS UP YOUR LIFE!

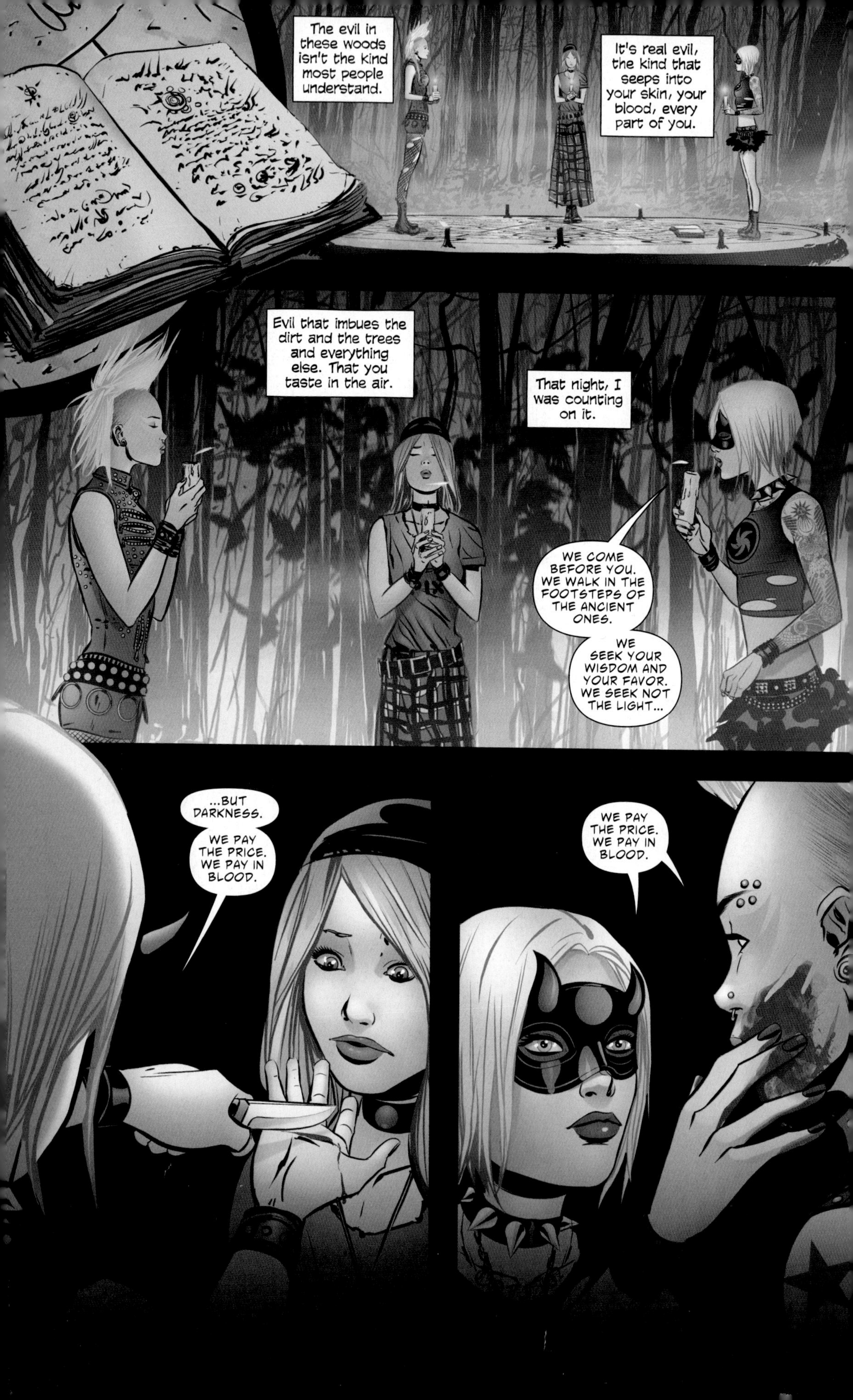
The evil in these woods isn't the kind most people understand.
It's real evil, the kind that seeps into your skin, your blood, every part of you.
Evil that imbues the dirt and the trees and everything else. That you taste in the air.
That night, I was counting on it.
WE COME BEFORE YOU. WE WALK IN THE FOOTSTEPS OF THE ANCIENT ONES.
WE SEEK YOUR WISDOM AND YOUR FAVOR. WE SEEK NOT THE LIGHT...
...BUT DARKNESS.
WE PAY THE PRICE. WE PAY IN BLOOD.
WE PAY THE PRICE. WE PAY IN BLOOD.

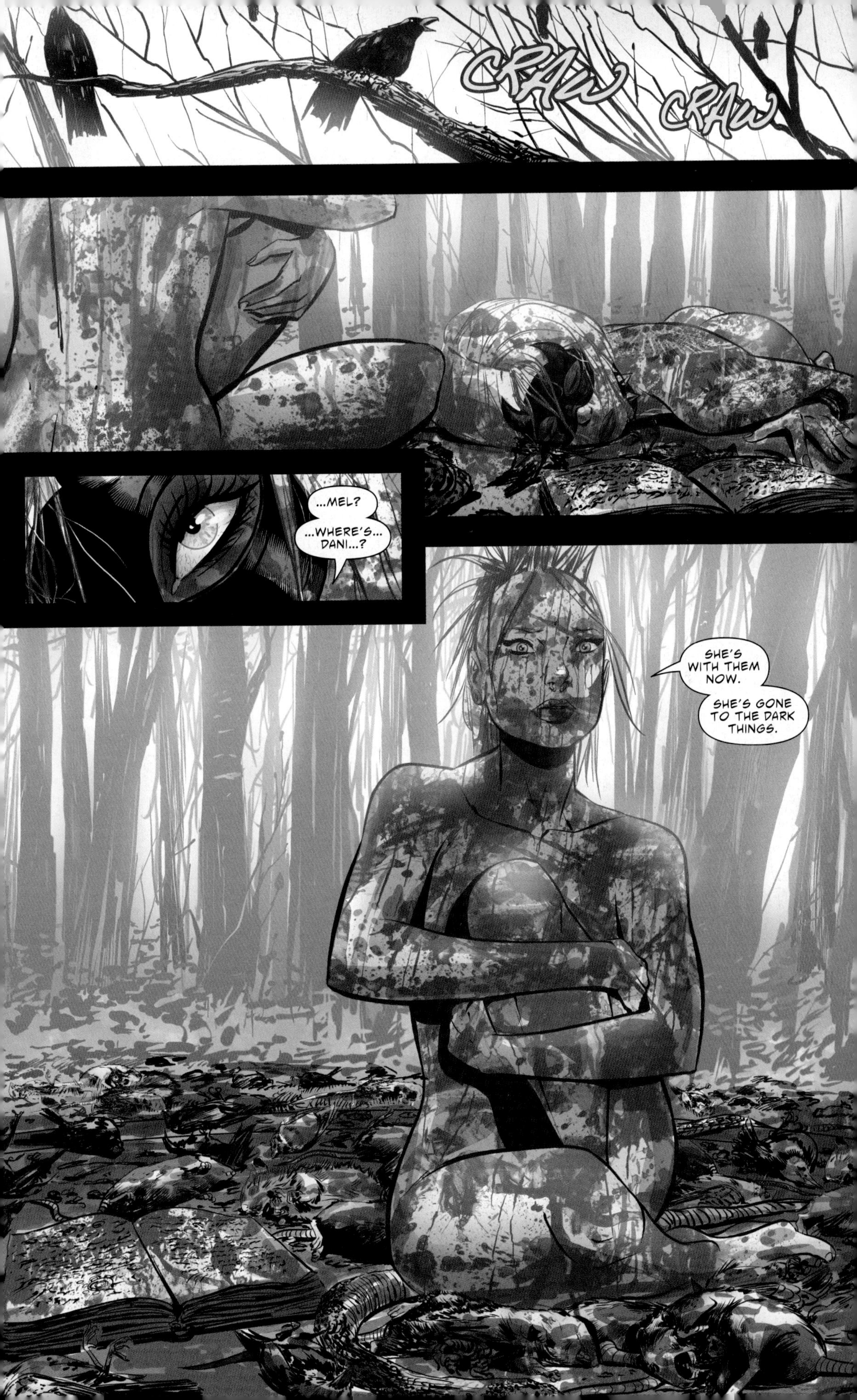
CRAW
CRAW
...MEL?
...WHERE'S... DANI...?
SHE'S WITH THEM NOW.
SHE'S GONE TO THE DARK THINGS.

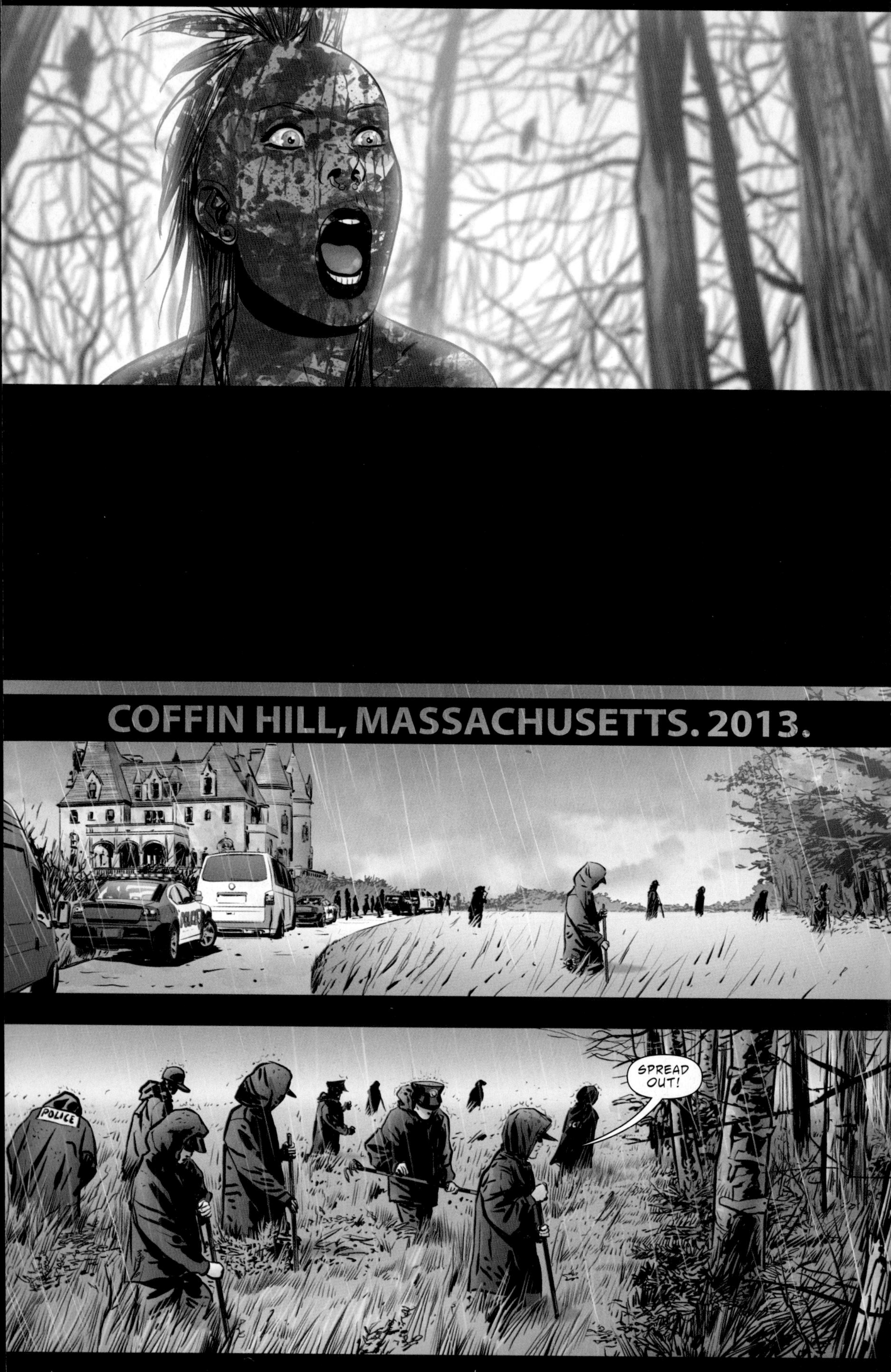
COFFIN HILL, MASSACHUSETTS. 2013.
POLICE
POLICE
SPREAD OUT!

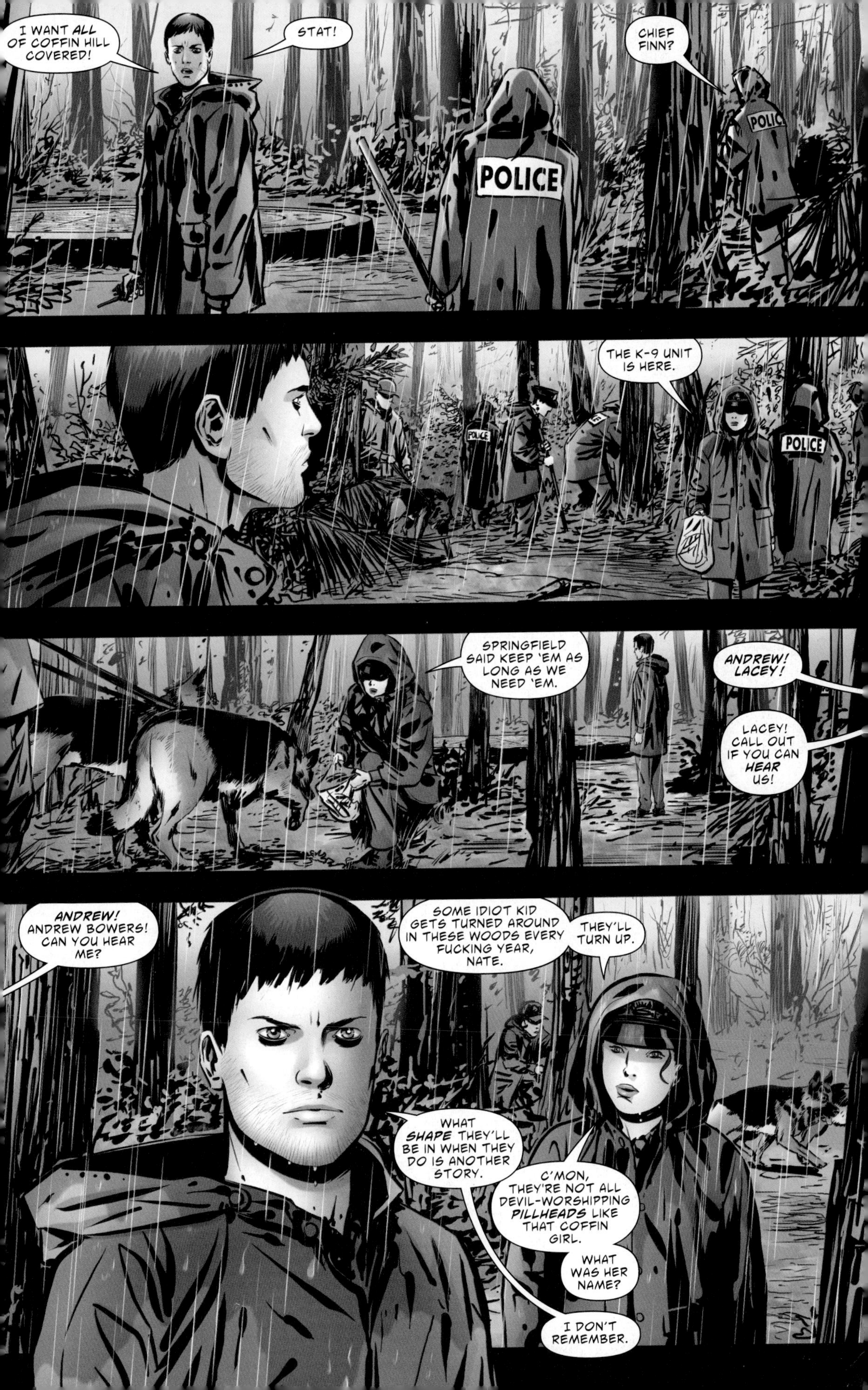

I WANT *ALL* OF COFFIN HILL COVERED!
STAT!
CHIEF FINN?
POLICE
POLIC
THE K-9 UNIT IS HERE.
POLICE
POLICE
SPRINGFIELD SAID KEEP 'EM AS LONG AS WE NEED 'EM.
ANDREW! LACEY!
LACEY! CALL OUT IF YOU CAN *HEAR* US!
ANDREW! ANDREW BOWERS! CAN YOU HEAR ME?
SOME IDIOT KID GETS TURNED AROUND IN THESE WOODS EVERY FUCKING YEAR, NATE.
THEY'LL TURN UP.
WHAT *SHAPE* THEY'LL BE IN WHEN THEY DO IS ANOTHER STORY.
C'MON, THEY'RE NOT ALL DEVIL-WORSHIPPING *PILLHEADS* LIKE THAT COFFIN GIRL.
WHAT WAS HER NAME?
I DON'T REMEMBER.

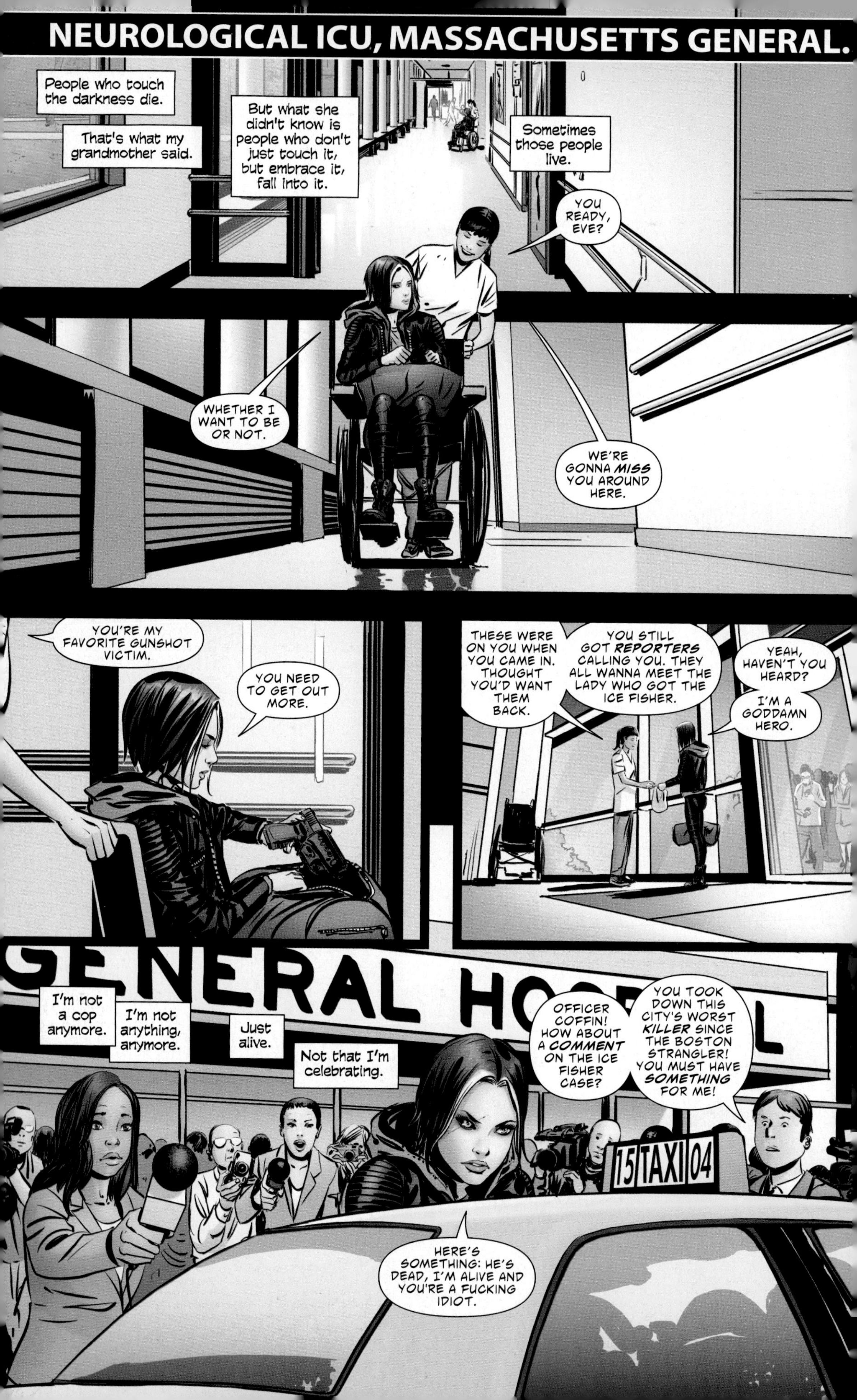
NEUROLOGICAL ICU, MASSACHUSETTS GENERAL.
People who touch the darkness die.
That's what my grandmother said.
But what she didn't know is people who don't just touch it, but embrace it, fall into it.
Sometimes those people live.
YOU READY, EVE?
WHETHER I WANT TO BE OR NOT.
WE'RE GONNA MISS YOU AROUND HERE.
YOU'RE MY FAVORITE GUNSHOT VICTIM.
YOU NEED TO GET OUT MORE.
THESE WERE ON YOU WHEN YOU CAME IN. THOUGHT YOU'D WANT THEM BACK.
YOU STILL GOT REPORTERS CALLING YOU. THEY ALL WANNA MEET THE LADY WHO GOT THE ICE FISHER.
YEAH, HAVEN'T YOU HEARD?
I'M A GODDAMN HERO.
GENERAL HO L
I'm not a cop anymore.
I'm not anything, anymore.
Just alive.
Not that I'm celebrating.
OFFICER COFFIN! HOW ABOUT A COMMENT ON THE ICE FISHER CASE?
YOU TOOK DOWN THIS CITY'S WORST KILLER SINCE THE BOSTON STRANGLER! YOU MUST HAVE SOMETHING FOR ME!
15 TAXI 04
HERE'S SOMETHING: HE'S DEAD, I'M ALIVE AND YOU'RE A FUCKING IDIOT.

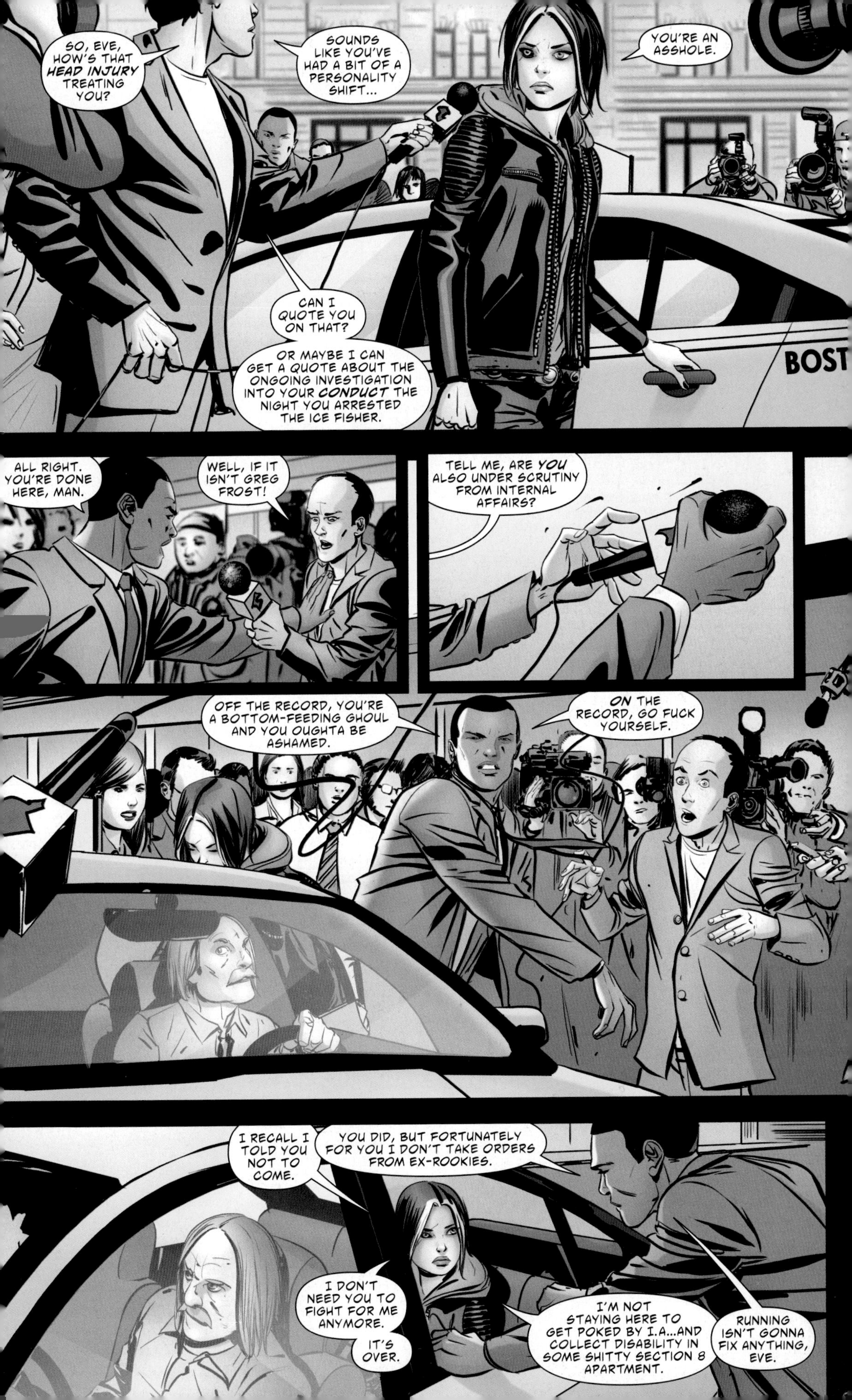
SO, EVE, HOW'S THAT HEAD INJURY TREATING YOU?
SOUNDS LIKE YOU'VE HAD A BIT OF A PERSONALITY SHIFT...
YOU'RE AN ASSHOLE.
CAN I QUOTE YOU ON THAT?
OR MAYBE I CAN GET A QUOTE ABOUT THE ONGOING INVESTIGATION INTO YOUR CONDUCT THE NIGHT YOU ARRESTED THE ICE FISHER.
BOST
ALL RIGHT. YOU'RE DONE HERE, MAN.
WELL, IF IT ISN'T GREG FROST!
TELL ME, ARE YOU ALSO UNDER SCRUTINY FROM INTERNAL AFFAIRS?
OFF THE RECORD, YOU'RE A BOTTOM-FEEDING GHOUL AND YOU OUGHTA BE ASHAMED.
ON THE RECORD, GO FUCK YOURSELF.
I RECALL I TOLD YOU NOT TO COME.
YOU DID, BUT FORTUNATELY FOR YOU I DON'T TAKE ORDERS FROM EX-ROOKIES.
I DON'T NEED YOU TO FIGHT FOR ME ANYMORE.
IT'S OVER.
I'M NOT STAYING HERE TO GET POKED BY I.A...AND COLLECT DISABILITY IN SOME SHITTY SECTION 8 APARTMENT.
RUNNING ISN'T GONNA FIX ANYTHING, EVE.

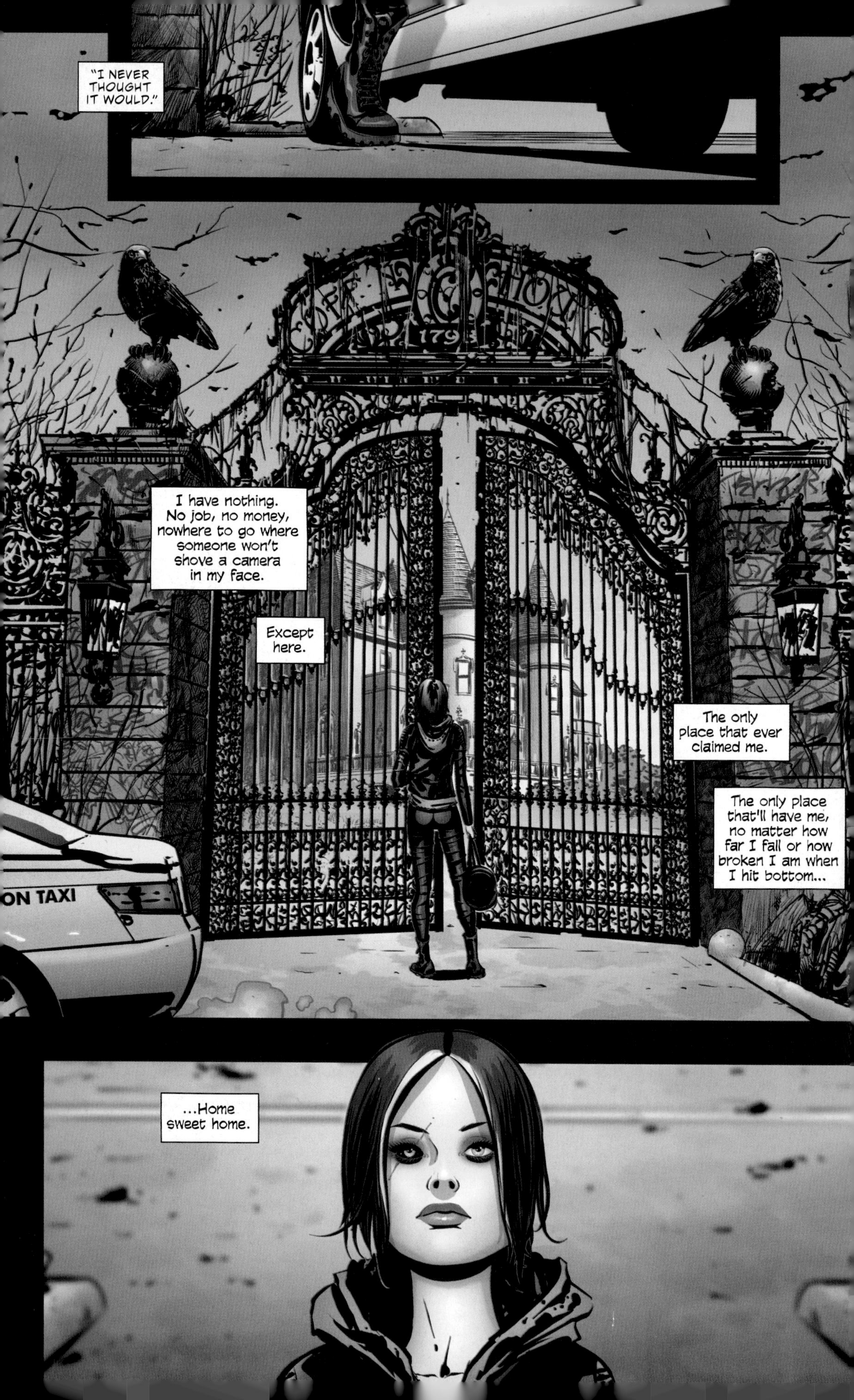
"I NEVER THOUGHT IT WOULD."
I have nothing. No job, no money, nowhere to go where someone won't shove a camera in my face.
Except here.
The only place that ever claimed me.
The only place that'll have me, no matter how far I fall or how broken I am when I hit bottom...
ON TAXI
...Home sweet home.

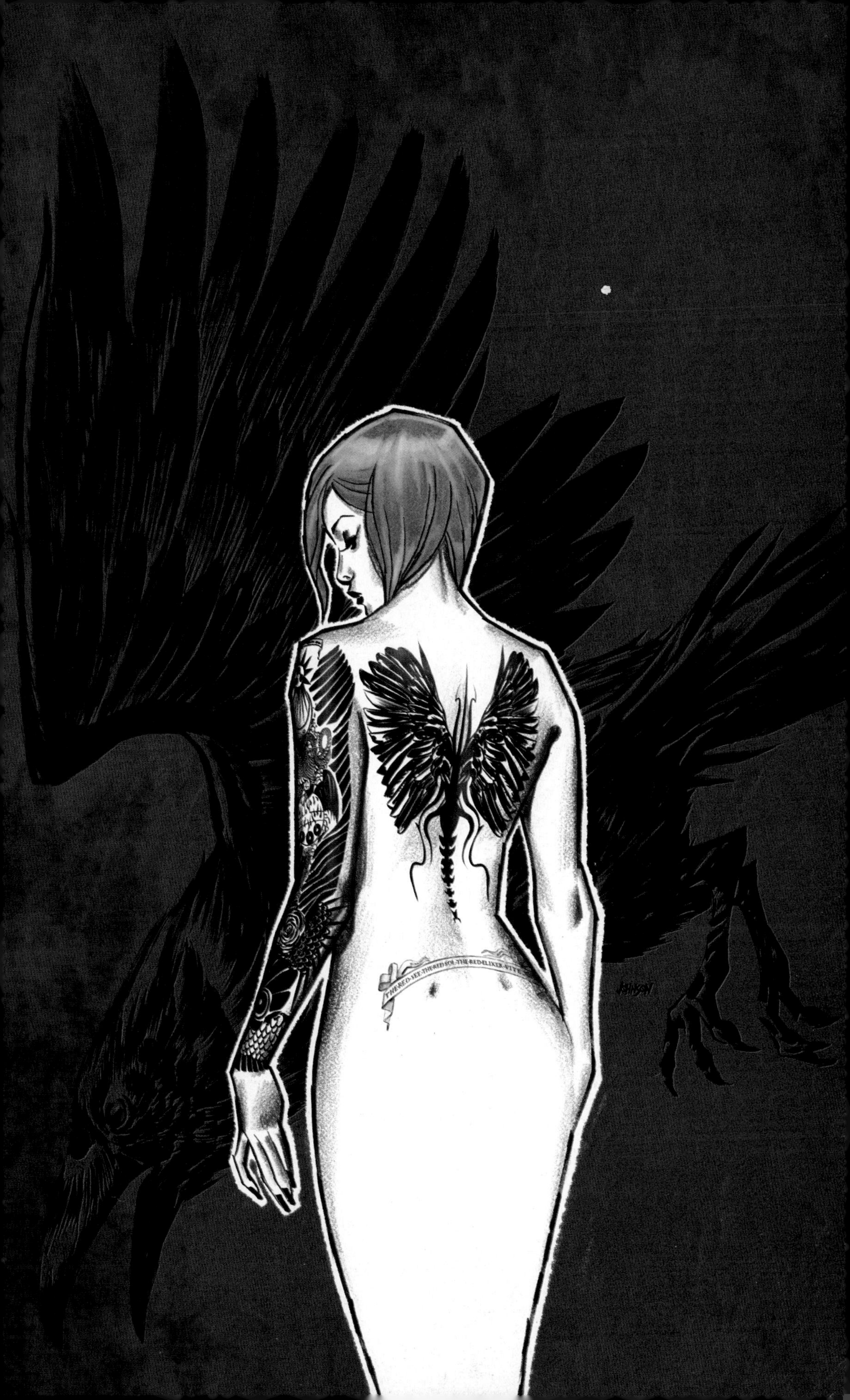
THE·RED·SEE·THE·RED·SOL·THE·RED·ELIXER·
JOHNSON

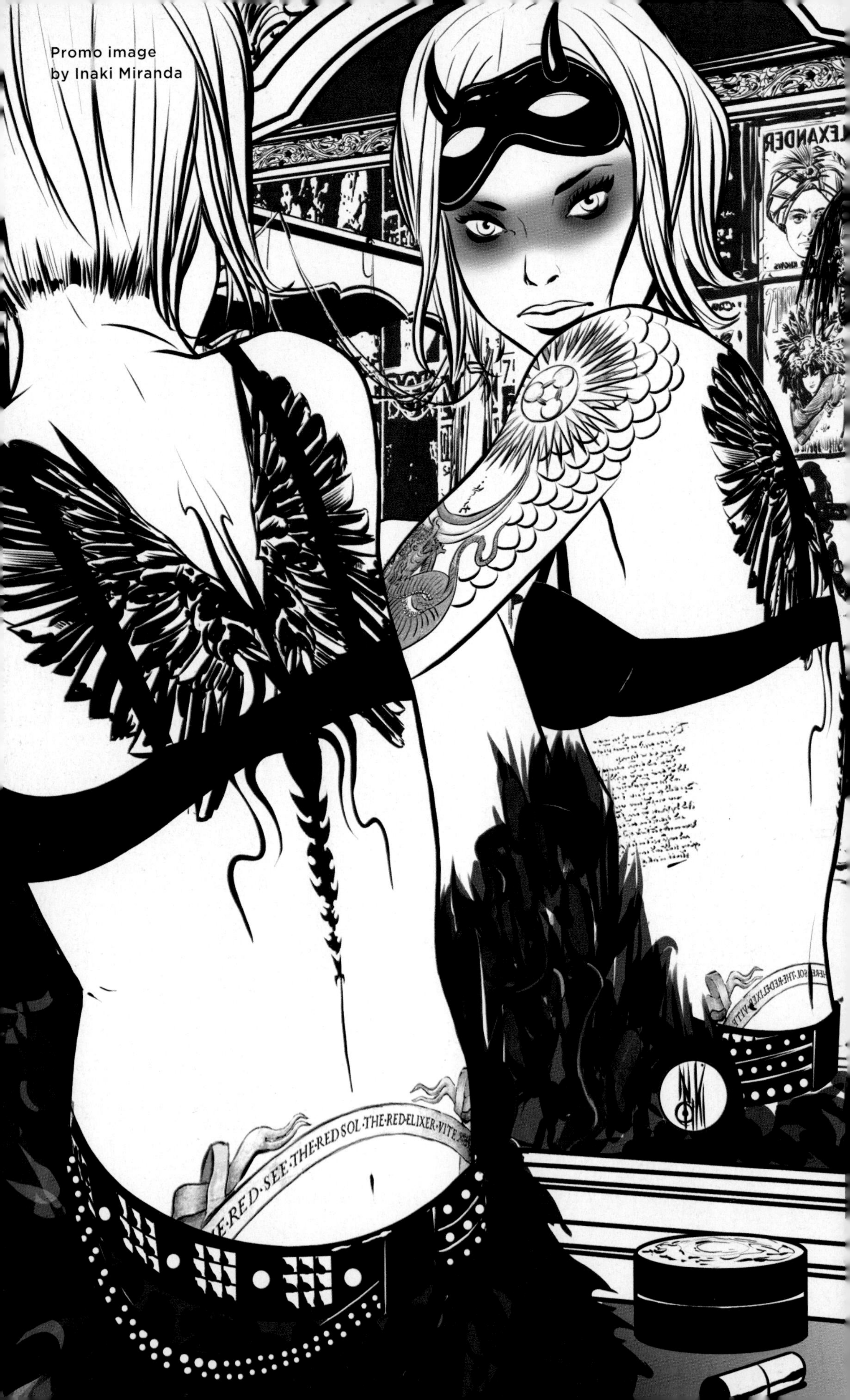
LEXANDER
E·RED·SEE·THE·RED SOL·THE·RED·ELIXER·VITE

Promo image
by Inaki Miranda

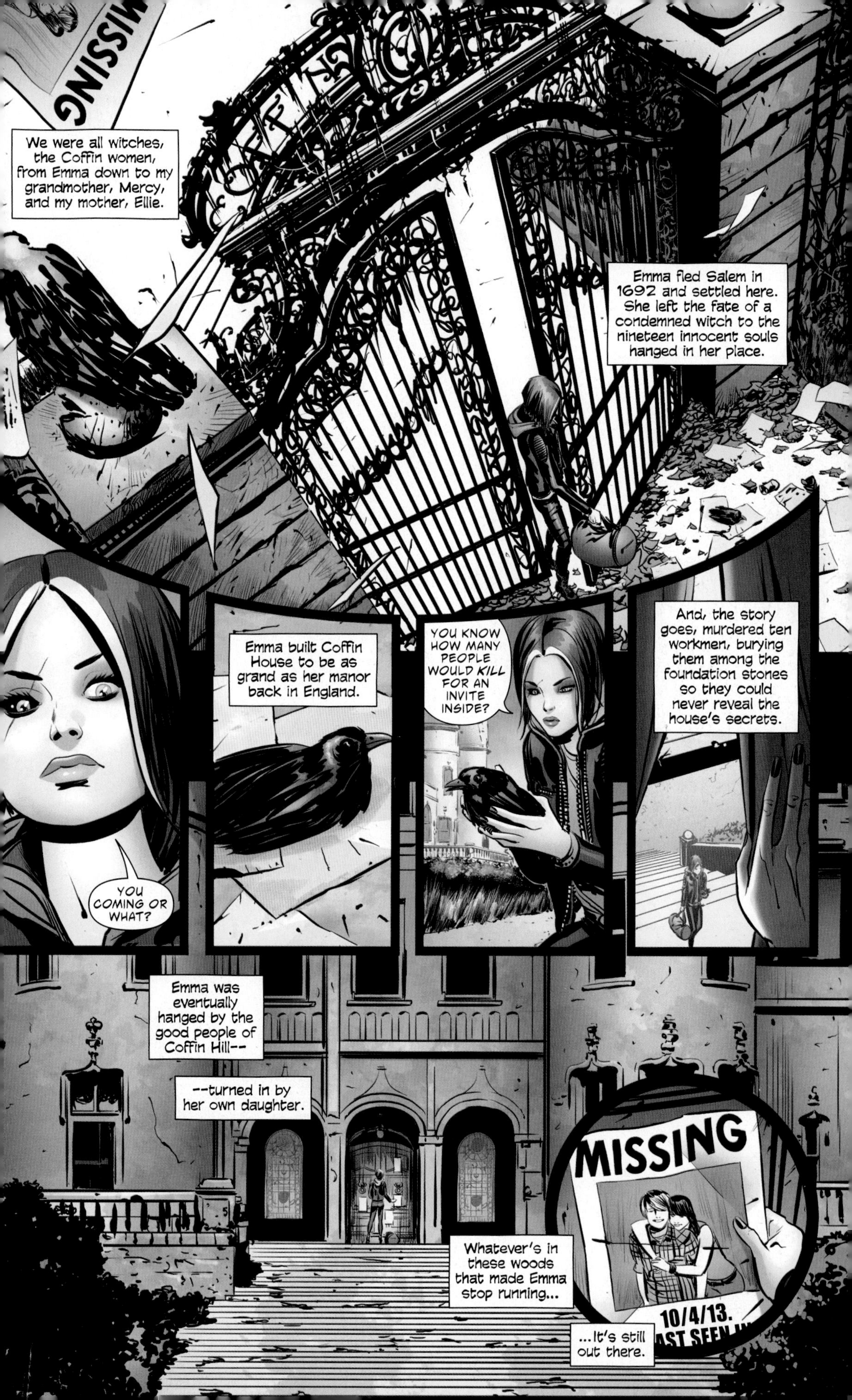

MISSING
1798
We were all witches, the Coffin women, from Emma down to my grandmother, Mercy, and my mother, Ellie.
Emma fled Salem in 1692 and settled here. She left the fate of a condemned witch to the nineteen innocent souls hanged in her place.
YOU COMING OR WHAT?
Emma built Coffin House to be as grand as her manor back in England.
YOU KNOW HOW MANY PEOPLE WOULD KILL FOR AN INVITE INSIDE?
And, the story goes, murdered ten workmen, burying them among the foundation stones so they could never reveal the house's secrets.
Emma was eventually hanged by the good people of Coffin Hill--
--turned in by her own daughter.
MISSING
Whatever's in these woods that made Emma stop running...
10/4/13.
...It's still out there.

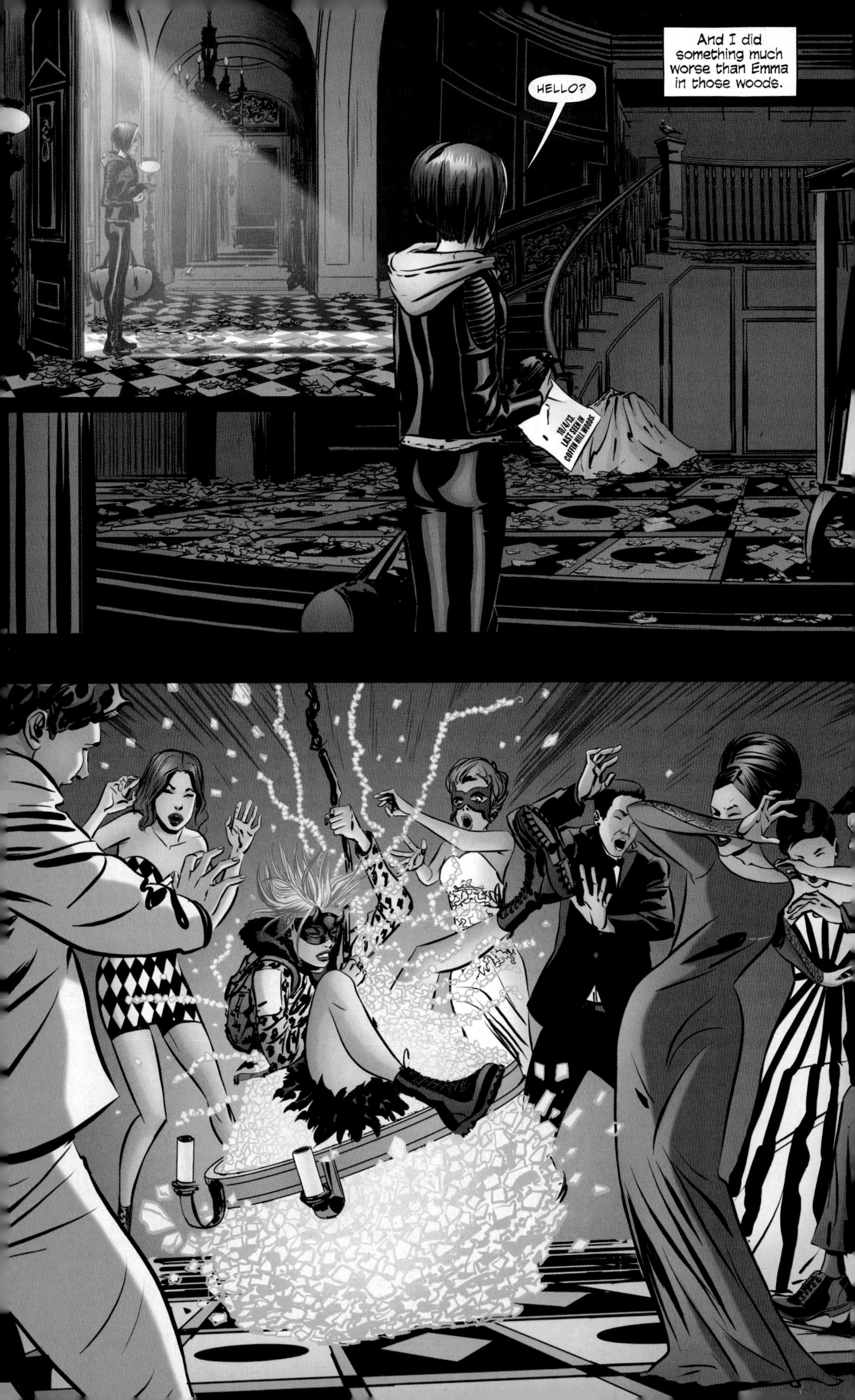
And I did something much worse than Emma in those woods.
HELLO?
10/4/13. LAST SEEN IN COFFIN HILL WOODS.

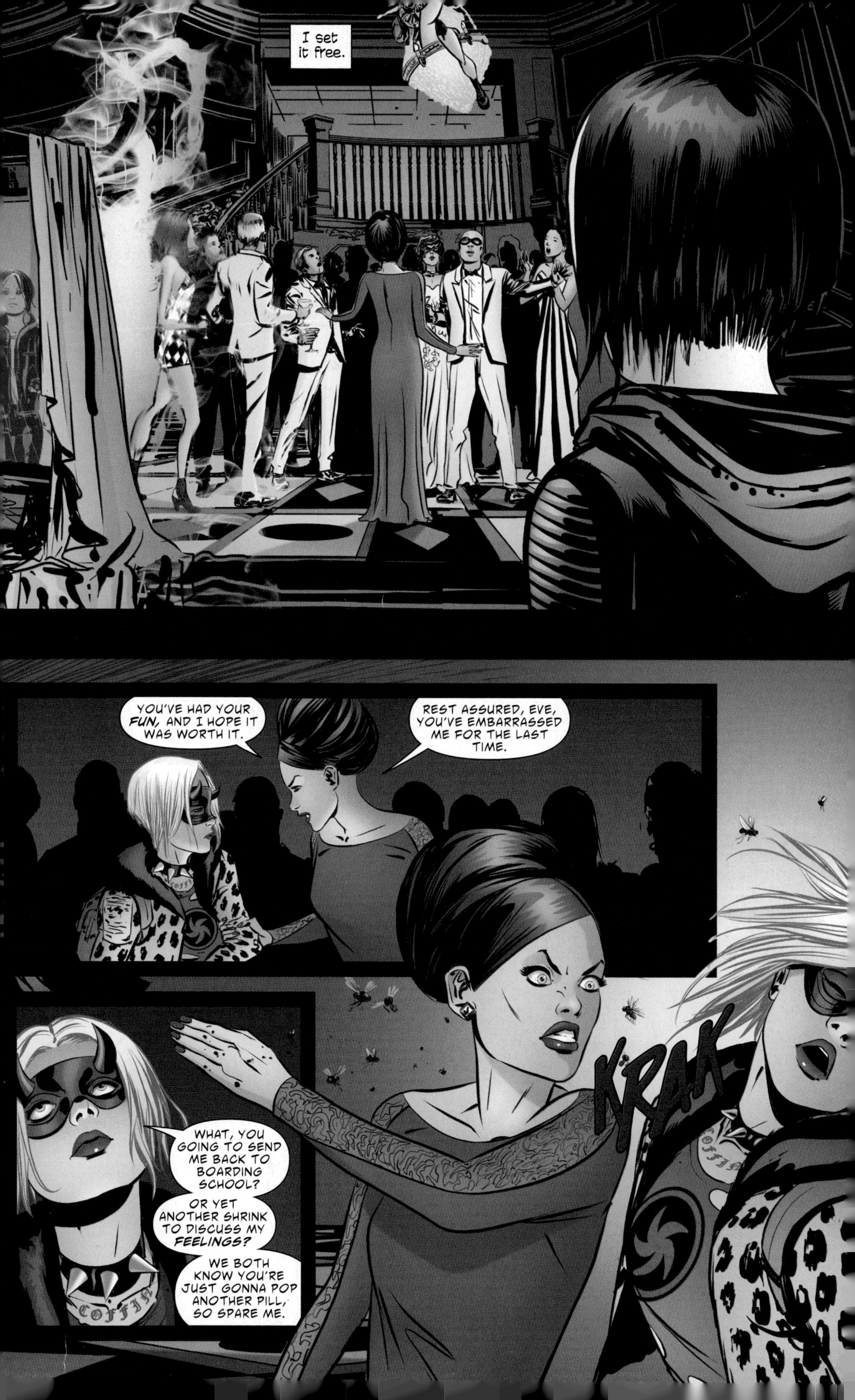
I set it free.
YOU'VE HAD YOUR FUN, AND I HOPE IT WAS WORTH IT.
REST ASSURED, EVE, YOU'VE EMBARRASSED ME FOR THE LAST TIME.
WHAT, YOU GOING TO SEND ME BACK TO BOARDING SCHOOL?
OR YET ANOTHER SHRINK TO DISCUSS MY FEELINGS?
WE BOTH KNOW YOU'RE JUST GONNA POP ANOTHER PILL, SO SPARE ME.
KRAK

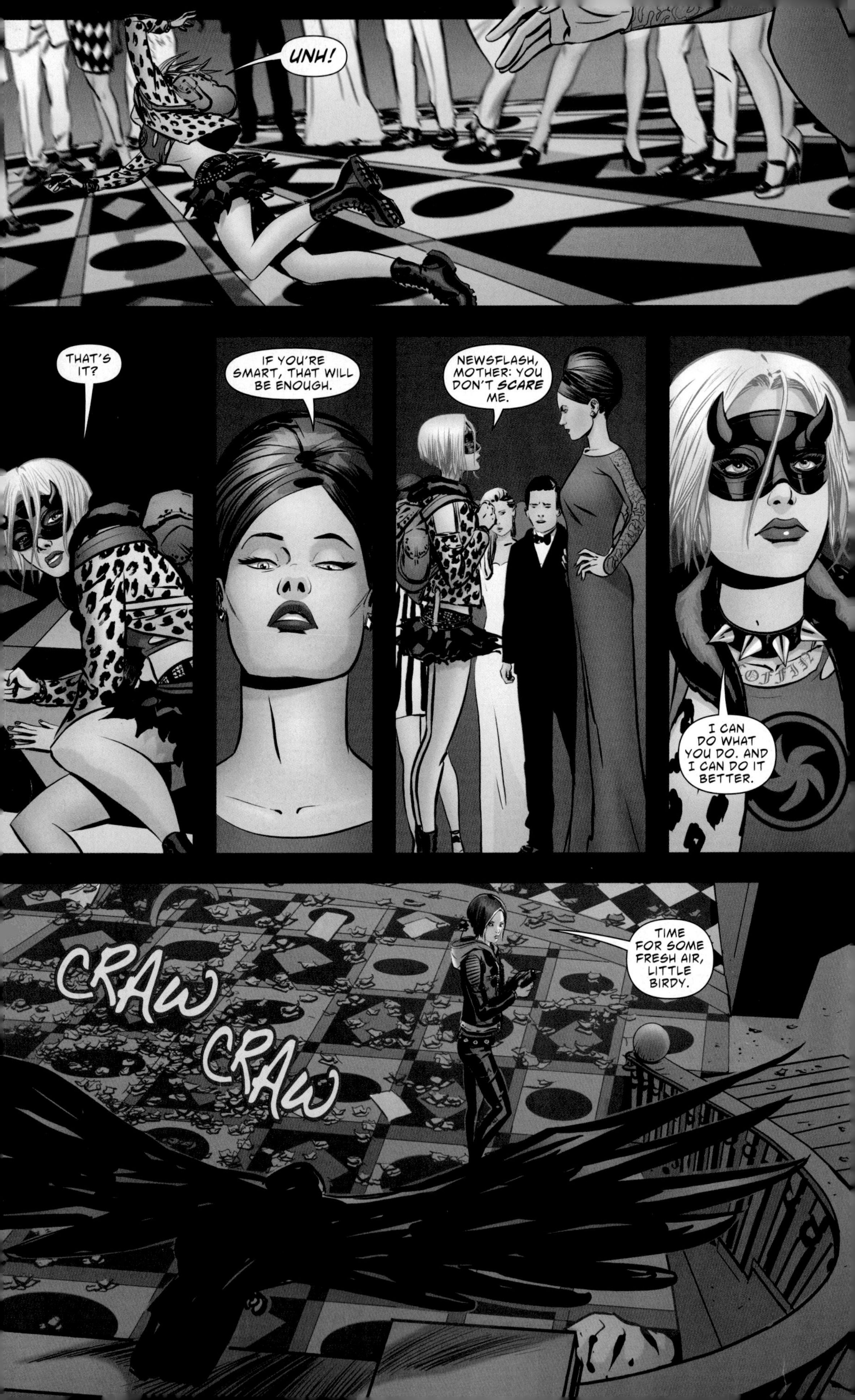
UNH!
THAT'S IT?
IF YOU'RE SMART, THAT WILL BE ENOUGH.
NEWSFLASH, MOTHER: YOU DON'T SCARE ME.
I CAN DO WHAT YOU DO. AND I CAN DO IT BETTER.
CRAW CRAW
TIME FOR SOME FRESH AIR, LITTLE BIRDY.

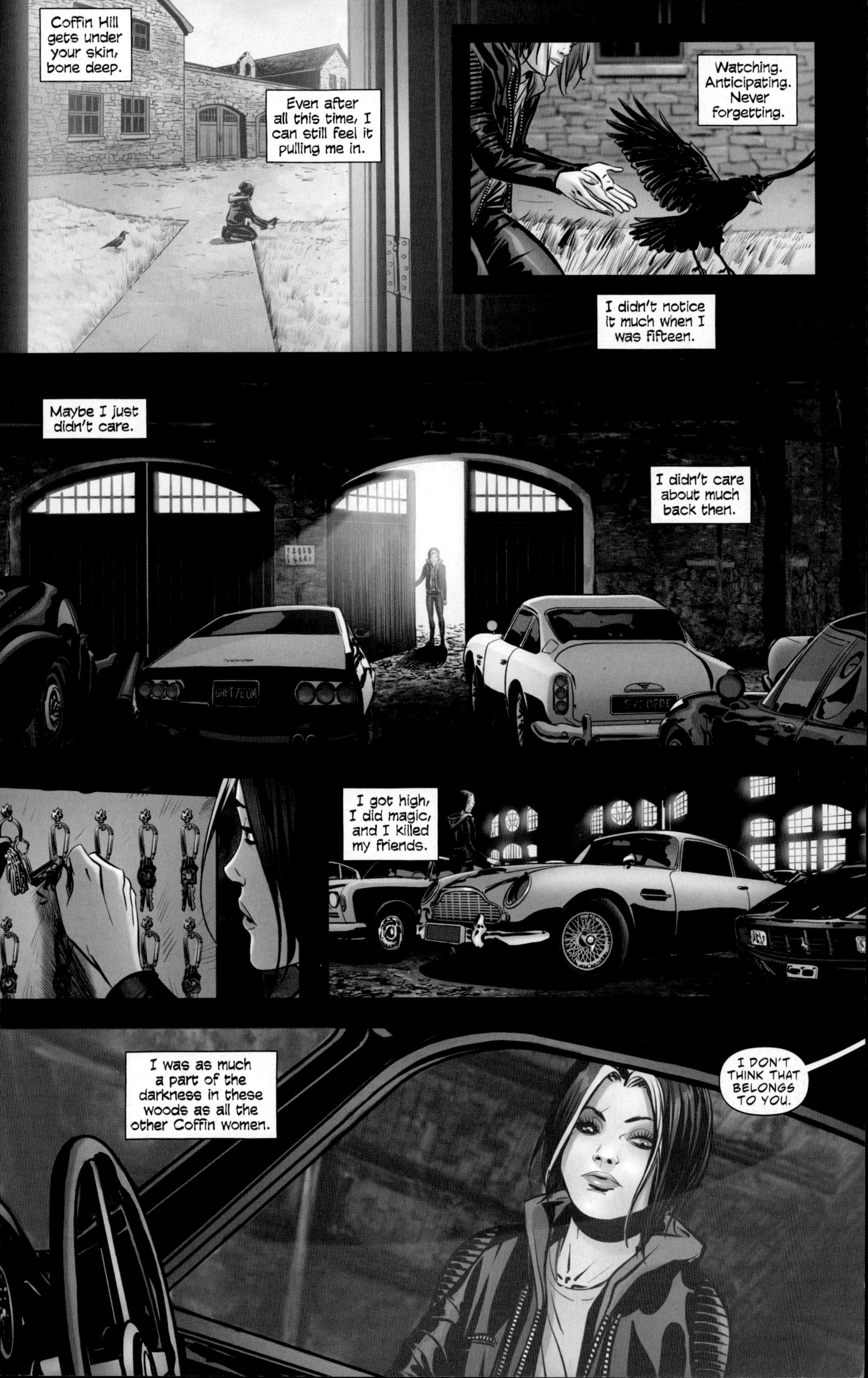
Coffin Hill gets under your skin, bone deep.
Even after all this time, I can still feel it pulling me in.
Watching. Anticipating. Never forgetting.
I didn't notice it much when I was fifteen.
Maybe I just didn't care.
I didn't care about much back then.
I got high, I did magic, and I killed my friends.
I was as much a part of the darkness in these woods as all the other Coffin women.
I DON'T THINK THAT BELONGS TO YOU.

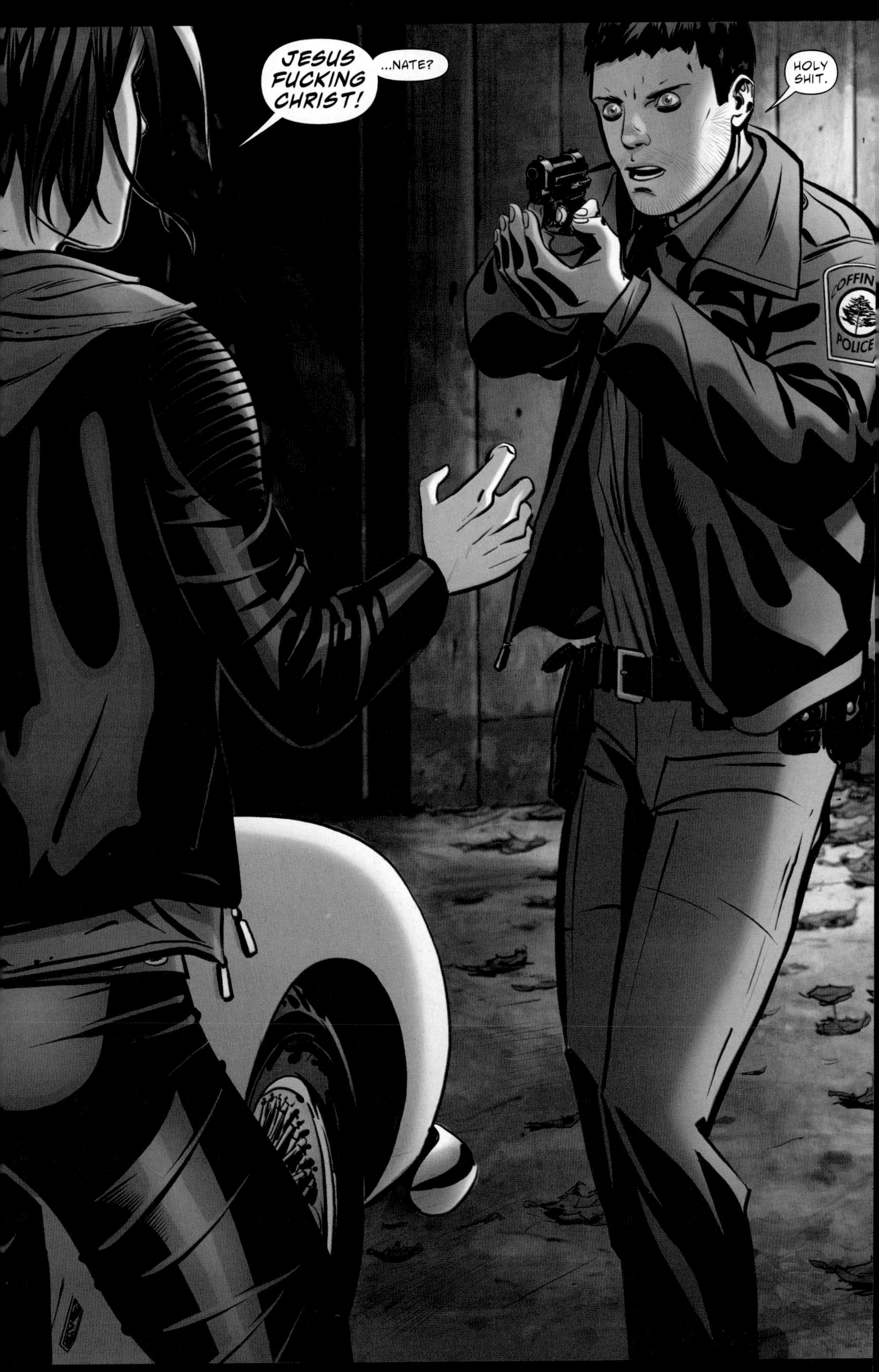
JESUS FUCKING CHRIST!
...NATE?
HOLY SHIT.
COFFIN POLICE

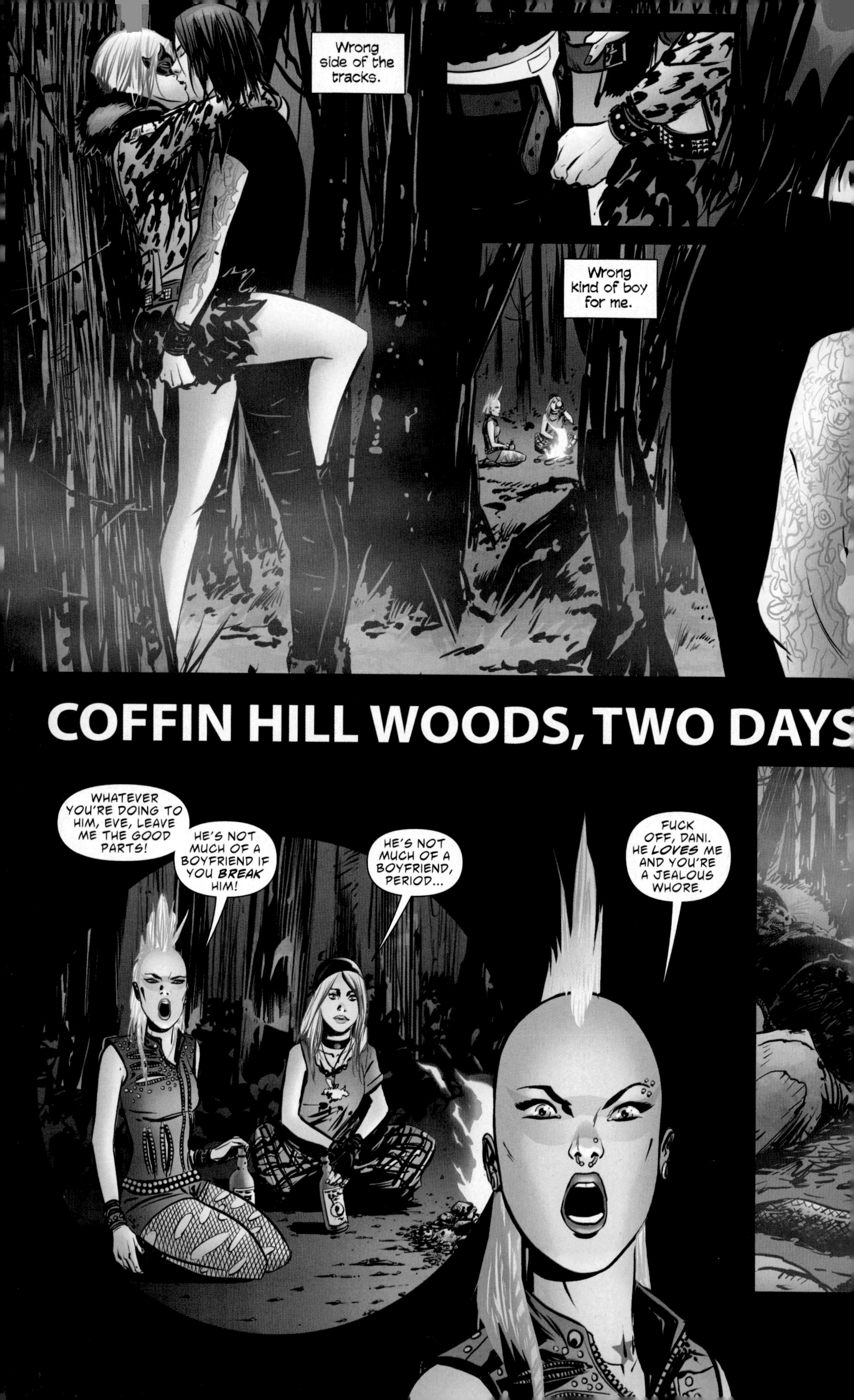
Wrong side of the tracks.
Wrong kind of boy for me.
COFFIN HILL WOODS, TWO DAYS
WHATEVER YOU'RE DOING TO HIM, EVE, LEAVE ME THE GOOD PARTS!
HE'S NOT MUCH OF A BOYFRIEND IF YOU BREAK HIM!
HE'S NOT MUCH OF A BOYFRIEND, PERIOD...
FUCK OFF, DANI. HE LOVES ME AND YOU'RE A JEALOUS WHORE.

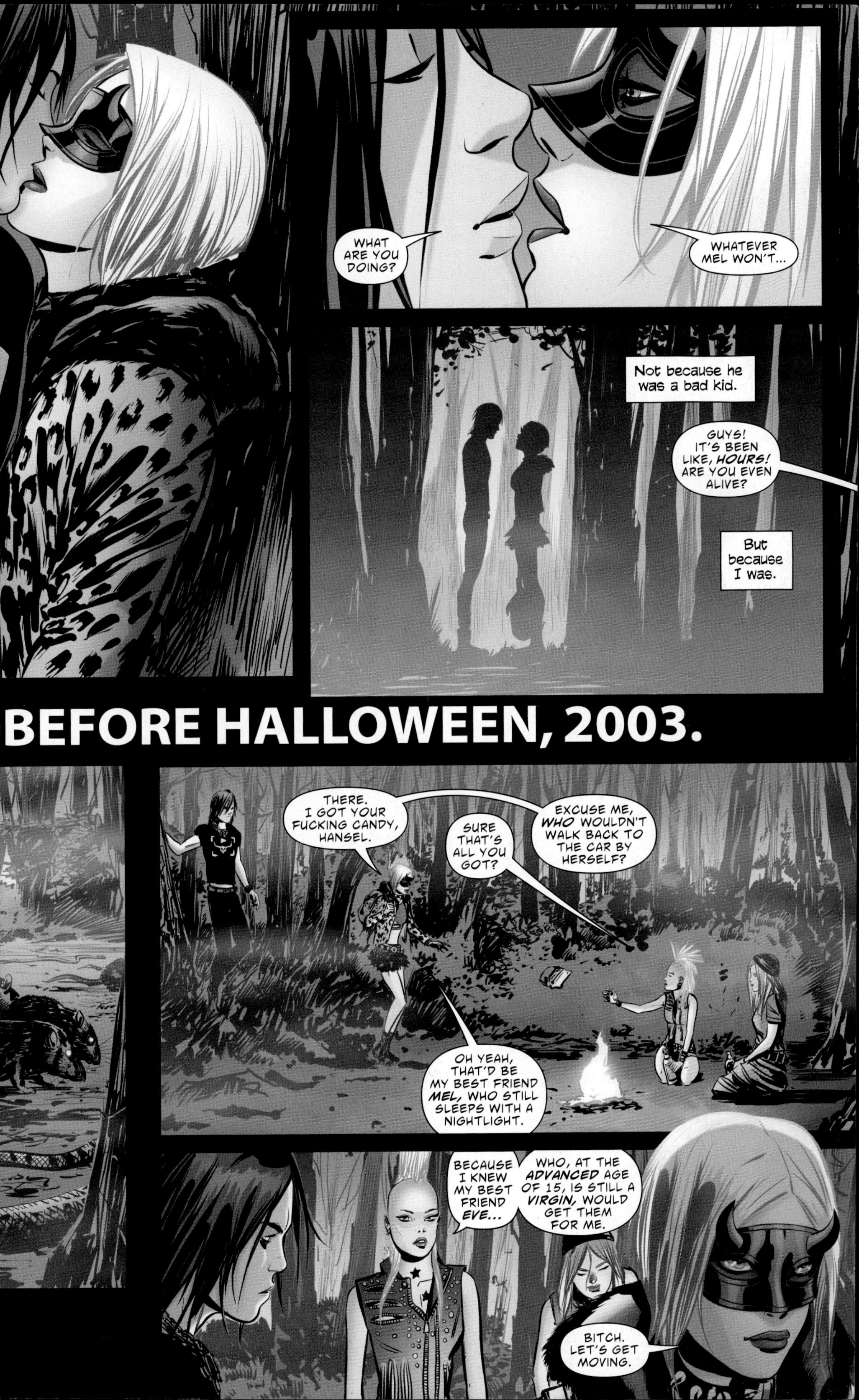
WHAT ARE YOU DOING?
WHATEVER MEL WON'T...
Not because he was a bad kid.
GUYS! IT'S BEEN LIKE, HOURS! ARE YOU EVEN ALIVE?
But because I was.
BEFORE HALLOWEEN, 2003.
THERE. I GOT YOUR FUCKING CANDY, HANSEL.
SURE THAT'S ALL YOU GOT?
EXCUSE ME, WHO WOULDN'T WALK BACK TO THE CAR BY HERSELF?
OH YEAH, THAT'D BE MY BEST FRIEND MEL, WHO STILL SLEEPS WITH A NIGHTLIGHT.
BECAUSE I KNEW MY BEST FRIEND EVE...
WHO, AT THE ADVANCED AGE OF 15, IS STILL A VIRGIN, WOULD GET THEM FOR ME.
BITCH. LET'S GET MOVING.

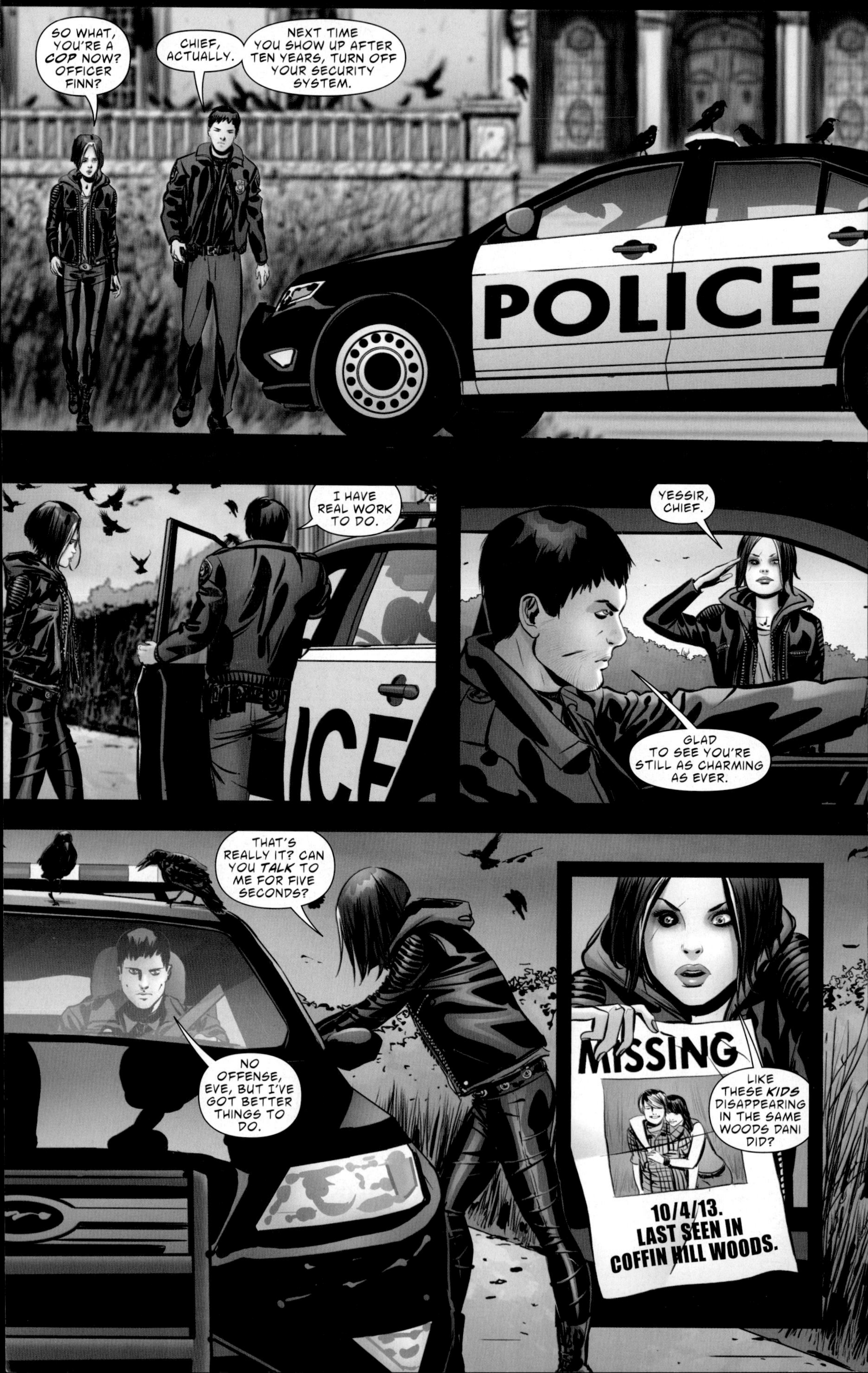
SO WHAT, YOU'RE A COP NOW? OFFICER FINN?
CHIEF, ACTUALLY.
NEXT TIME YOU SHOW UP AFTER TEN YEARS, TURN OFF YOUR SECURITY SYSTEM.
POLICE
I HAVE REAL WORK TO DO.
ICE
YESSIR, CHIEF.
GLAD TO SEE YOU'RE STILL AS CHARMING AS EVER.
THAT'S REALLY IT? CAN YOU TALK TO ME FOR FIVE SECONDS?
NO OFFENSE, EVE, BUT I'VE GOT BETTER THINGS TO DO.
MISSING
LIKE THESE KIDS DISAPPEARING IN THE SAME WOODS DANI DID?
10/4/13.
LAST SEEN IN
COFFIN HILL WOODS.

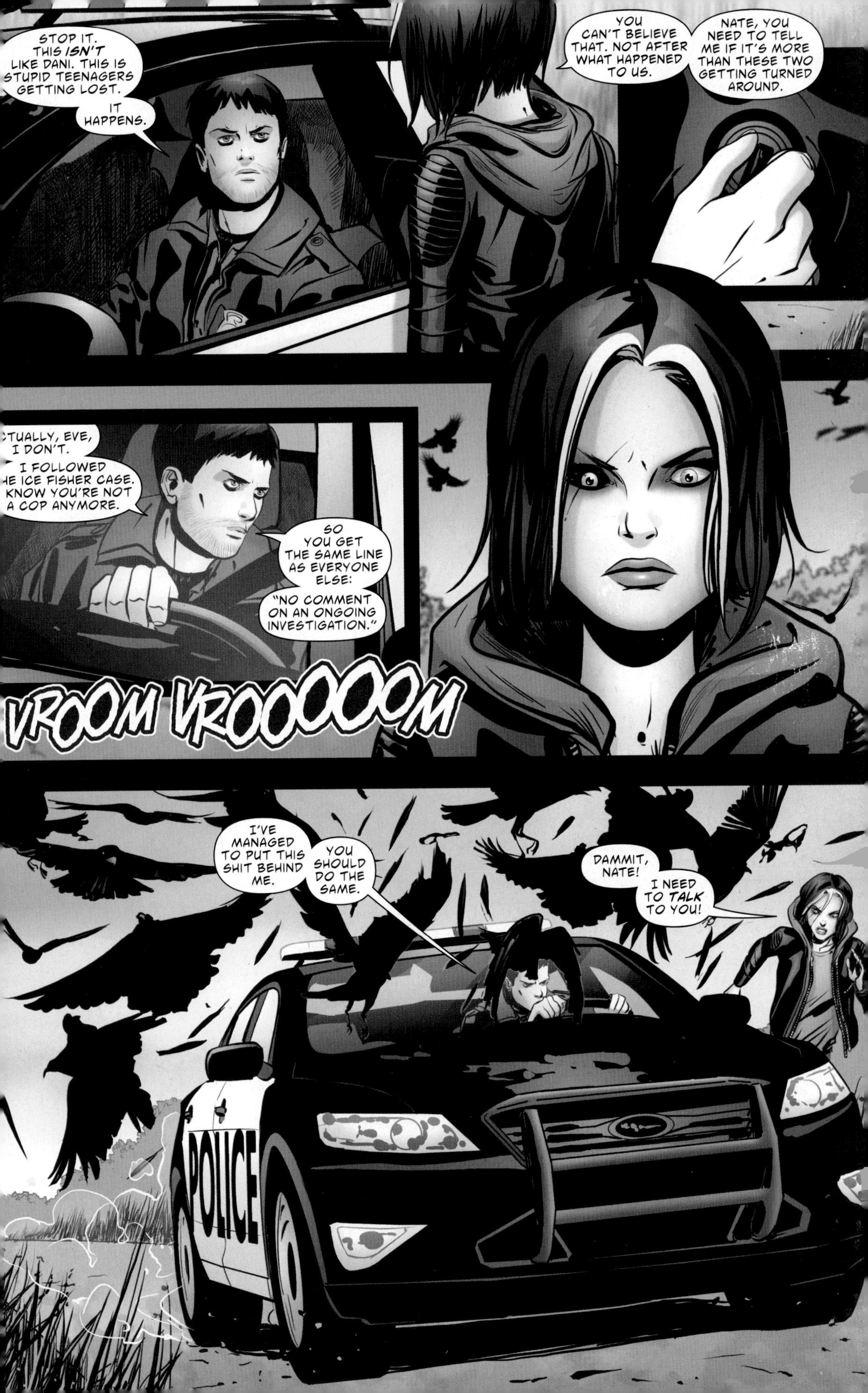

STOP IT. THIS ISN'T LIKE DANI. THIS IS STUPID TEENAGERS GETTING LOST.
IT HAPPENS.
YOU CAN'T BELIEVE THAT. NOT AFTER WHAT HAPPENED TO US.
NATE, YOU NEED TO TELL ME IF IT'S MORE THAN THESE TWO GETTING TURNED AROUND.
CTUALLY, EVE, I DON'T.
I FOLLOWED HE ICE FISHER CASE. KNOW YOU'RE NOT A COP ANYMORE.
SO YOU GET THE SAME LINE AS EVERYONE ELSE:
"NO COMMENT ON AN ONGOING INVESTIGATION."
VROOM VROOOOOOM
I'VE MANAGED TO PUT THIS SHIT BEHIND ME.
YOU SHOULD DO THE SAME.
DAMMIT, NATE!
I NEED TO TALK TO YOU!
POLICE

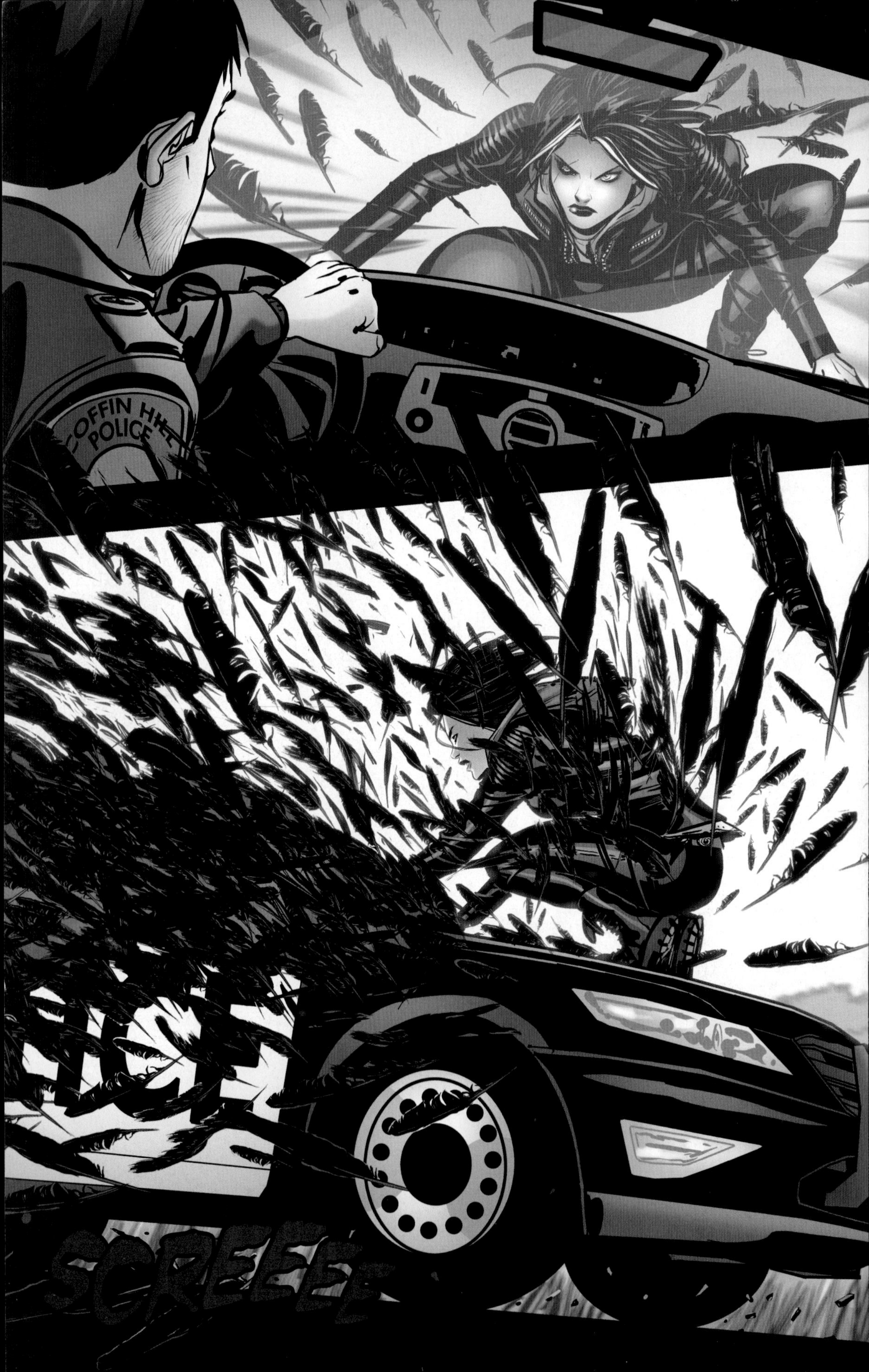
COFFIN HILL POLICE
SCREEEE

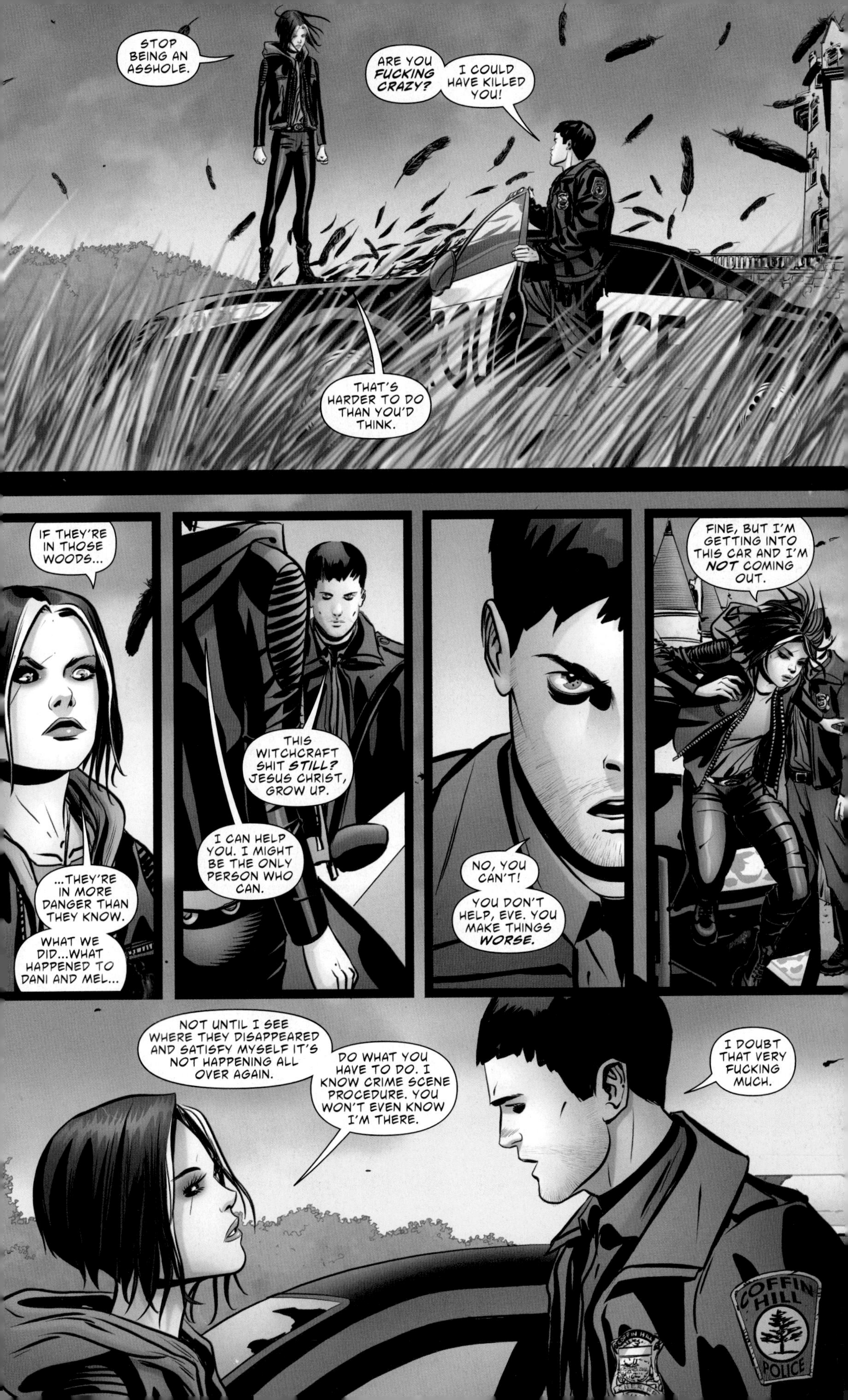
STOP BEING AN ASSHOLE.
ARE YOU FUCKING CRAZY?
I COULD HAVE KILLED YOU!
THAT'S HARDER TO DO THAN YOU'D THINK.
IF THEY'RE IN THOSE WOODS...
...THEY'RE IN MORE DANGER THAN THEY KNOW.
WHAT WE DID...WHAT HAPPENED TO DANI AND MEL...
THIS WITCHCRAFT SHIT STILL? JESUS CHRIST, GROW UP.
I CAN HELP YOU. I MIGHT BE THE ONLY PERSON WHO CAN.
NO, YOU CAN'T!
YOU DON'T HELP, EVE. YOU MAKE THINGS WORSE.
FINE, BUT I'M GETTING INTO THIS CAR AND I'M NOT COMING OUT.
NOT UNTIL I SEE WHERE THEY DISAPPEARED AND SATISFY MYSELF IT'S NOT HAPPENING ALL OVER AGAIN.
DO WHAT YOU HAVE TO DO. I KNOW CRIME SCENE PROCEDURE. YOU WON'T EVEN KNOW I'M THERE.
I DOUBT THAT VERY FUCKING MUCH.
COFFIN HILL POLICE

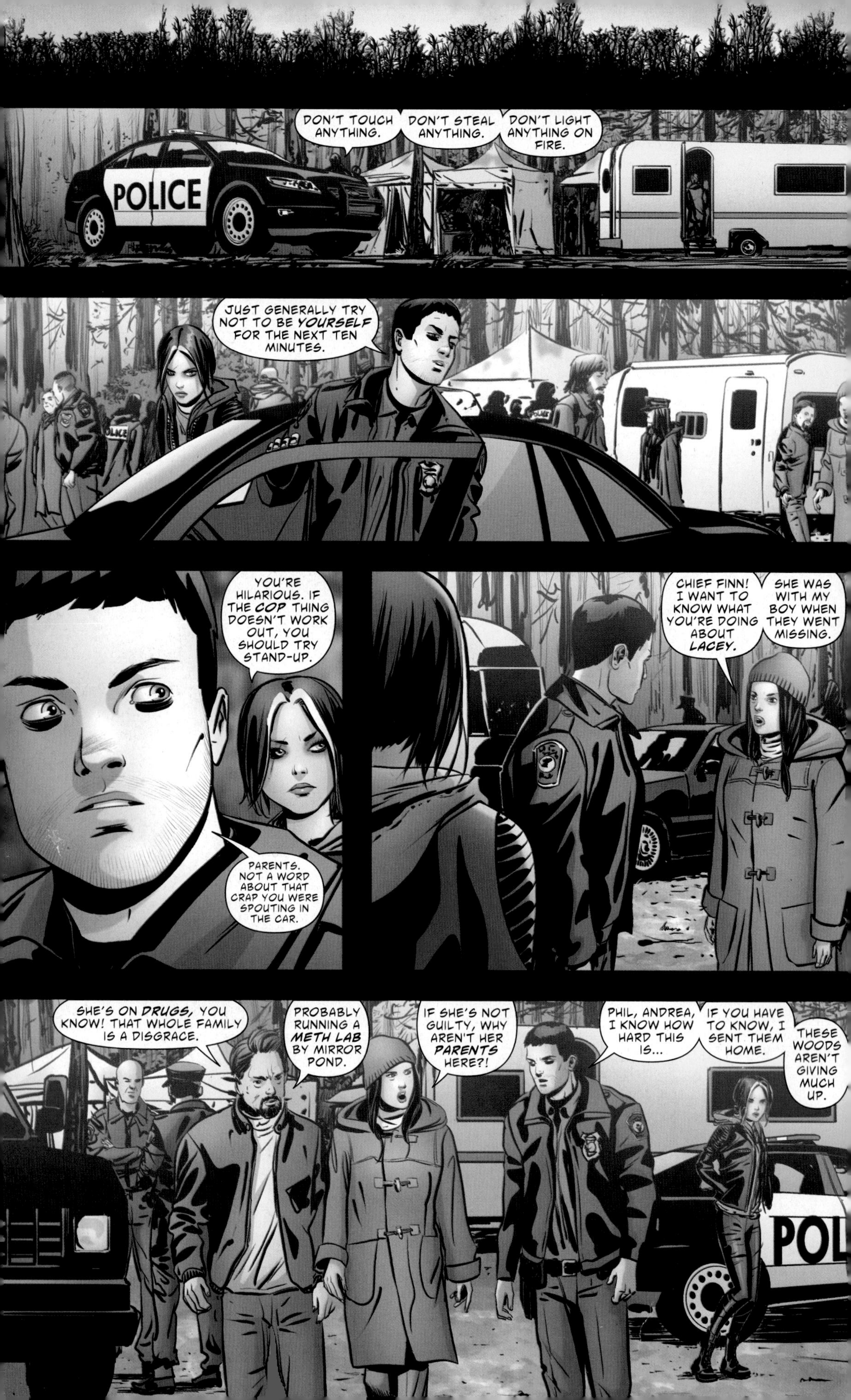

DON'T TOUCH ANYTHING.
DON'T STEAL ANYTHING.
DON'T LIGHT ANYTHING ON FIRE.
POLICE
JUST GENERALLY TRY NOT TO BE YOURSELF FOR THE NEXT TEN MINUTES.
YOU'RE HILARIOUS. IF THE COP THING DOESN'T WORK OUT, YOU SHOULD TRY STAND-UP.
PARENTS. NOT A WORD ABOUT THAT CRAP YOU WERE SPOUTING IN THE CAR.
CHIEF FINN! I WANT TO KNOW WHAT YOU'RE DOING ABOUT LACEY.
SHE WAS WITH MY BOY WHEN THEY WENT MISSING.
SHE'S ON DRUGS, YOU KNOW! THAT WHOLE FAMILY IS A DISGRACE.
PROBABLY RUNNING A METH LAB BY MIRROR POND.
IF SHE'S NOT GUILTY, WHY AREN'T HER PARENTS HERE?!
PHIL, ANDREA, I KNOW HOW HARD THIS IS...
IF YOU HAVE TO KNOW, I SENT THEM HOME.
THESE WOODS AREN'T GIVING MUCH UP.
POL

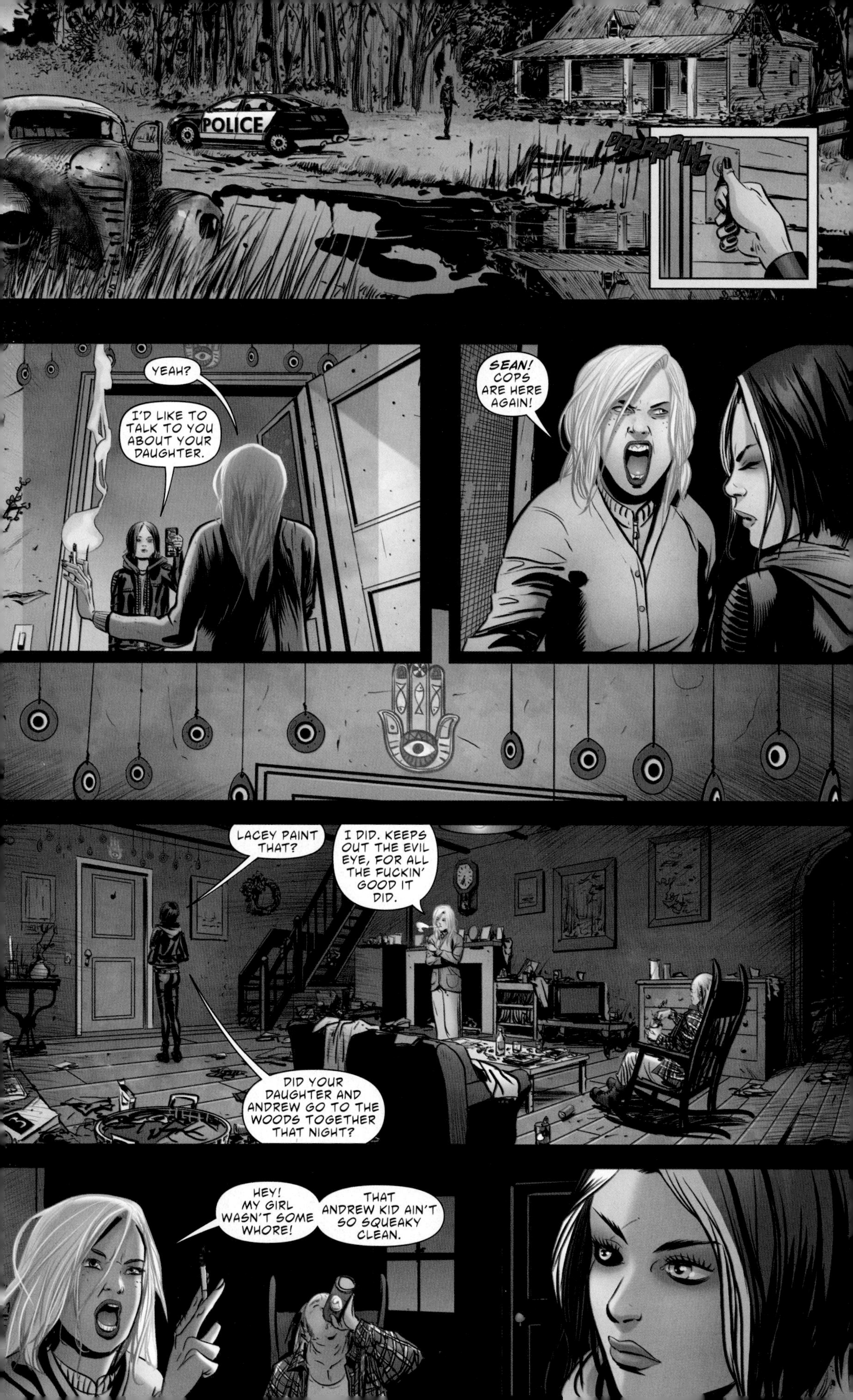
DRRRRRING
YEAH?
I'D LIKE TO TALK TO YOU ABOUT YOUR DAUGHTER.
SEAN! COPS ARE HERE AGAIN!
LACEY PAINT THAT?
I DID. KEEPS OUT THE EVIL EYE, FOR ALL THE FUCKIN' GOOD IT DID.
DID YOUR DAUGHTER AND ANDREW GO TO THE WOODS TOGETHER THAT NIGHT?
HEY! MY GIRL WASN'T SOME WHORE!
THAT ANDREW KID AIN'T SO SQUEAKY CLEAN.

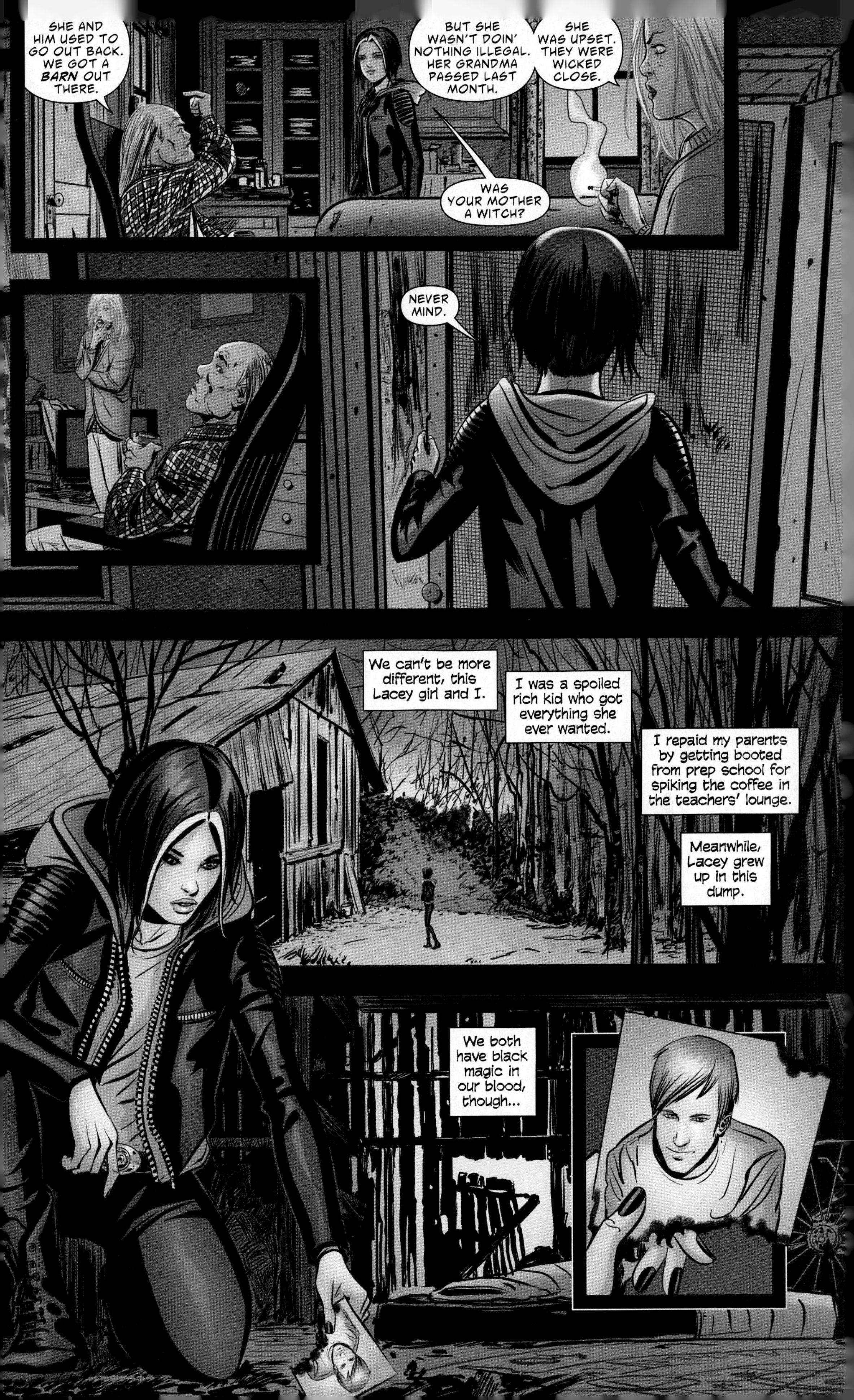
SHE AND HIM USED TO GO OUT BACK. WE GOT A BARN OUT THERE.
BUT SHE WASN'T DOIN' NOTHING ILLEGAL. HER GRANDMA PASSED LAST MONTH.
SHE WAS UPSET. THEY WERE WICKED CLOSE.
WAS YOUR MOTHER A WITCH?
NEVER MIND.
We can't be more different, this Lacey girl and I.
I was a spoiled rich kid who got everything she ever wanted.
I repaid my parents by getting booted from prep school for spiking the coffee in the teachers' lounge.
Meanwhile, Lacey grew up in this dump.
We both have black magic in our blood, though...

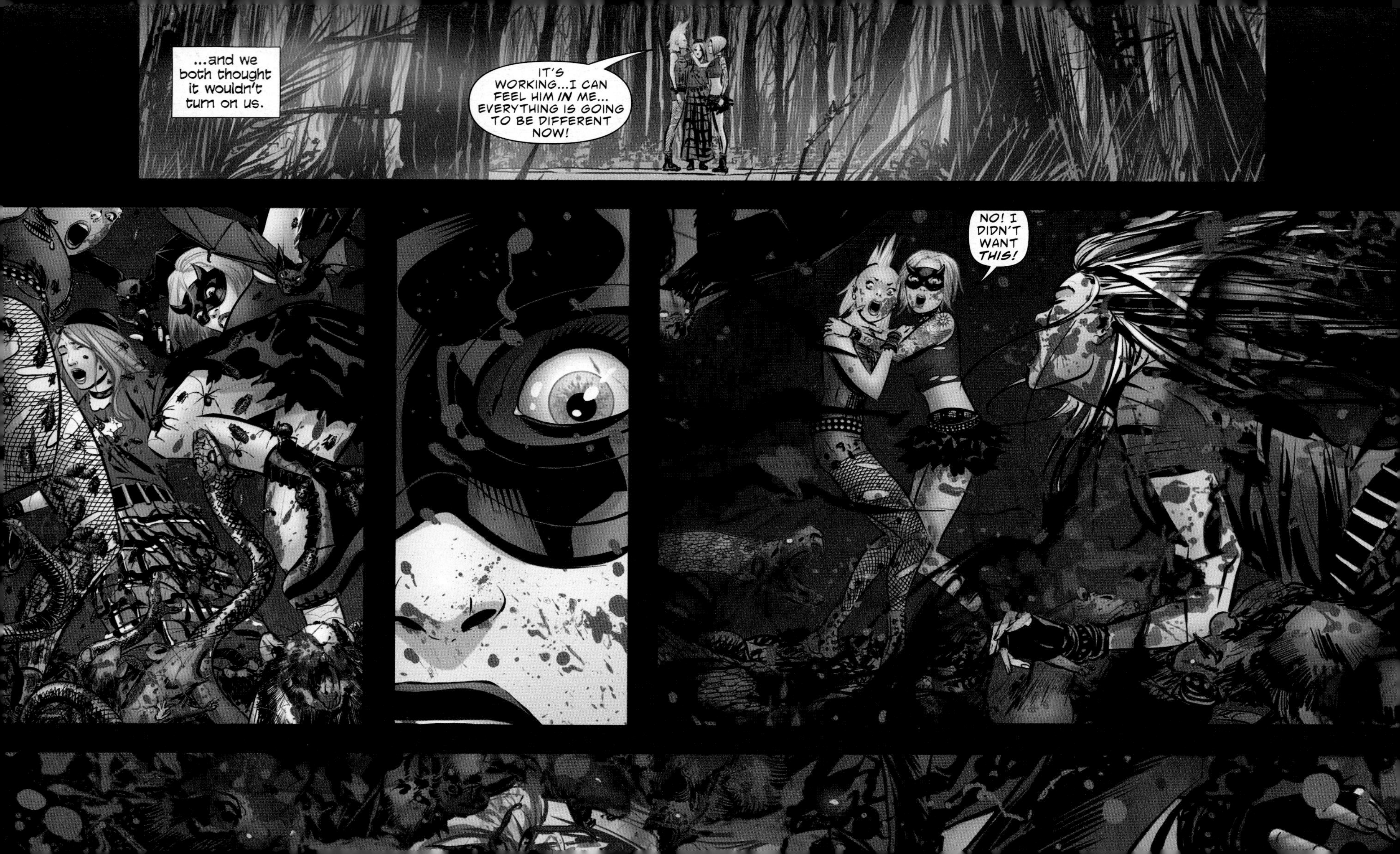

...and we both thought it wouldn't turn on us.
IT'S WORKING...I CAN FEEL HIM IN ME... EVERYTHING IS GOING TO BE DIFFERENT NOW!
NO! I DIDN'T WANT THIS!

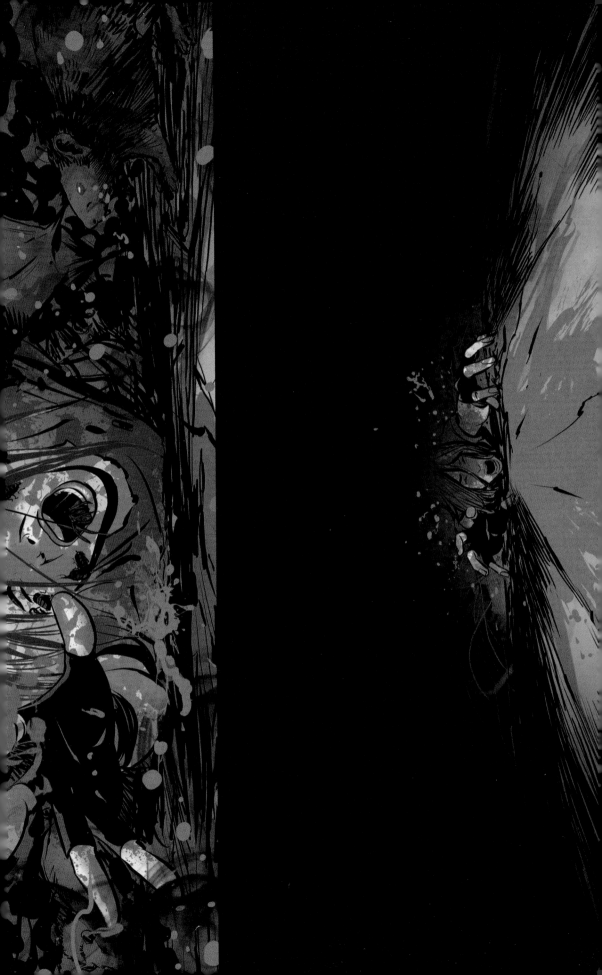

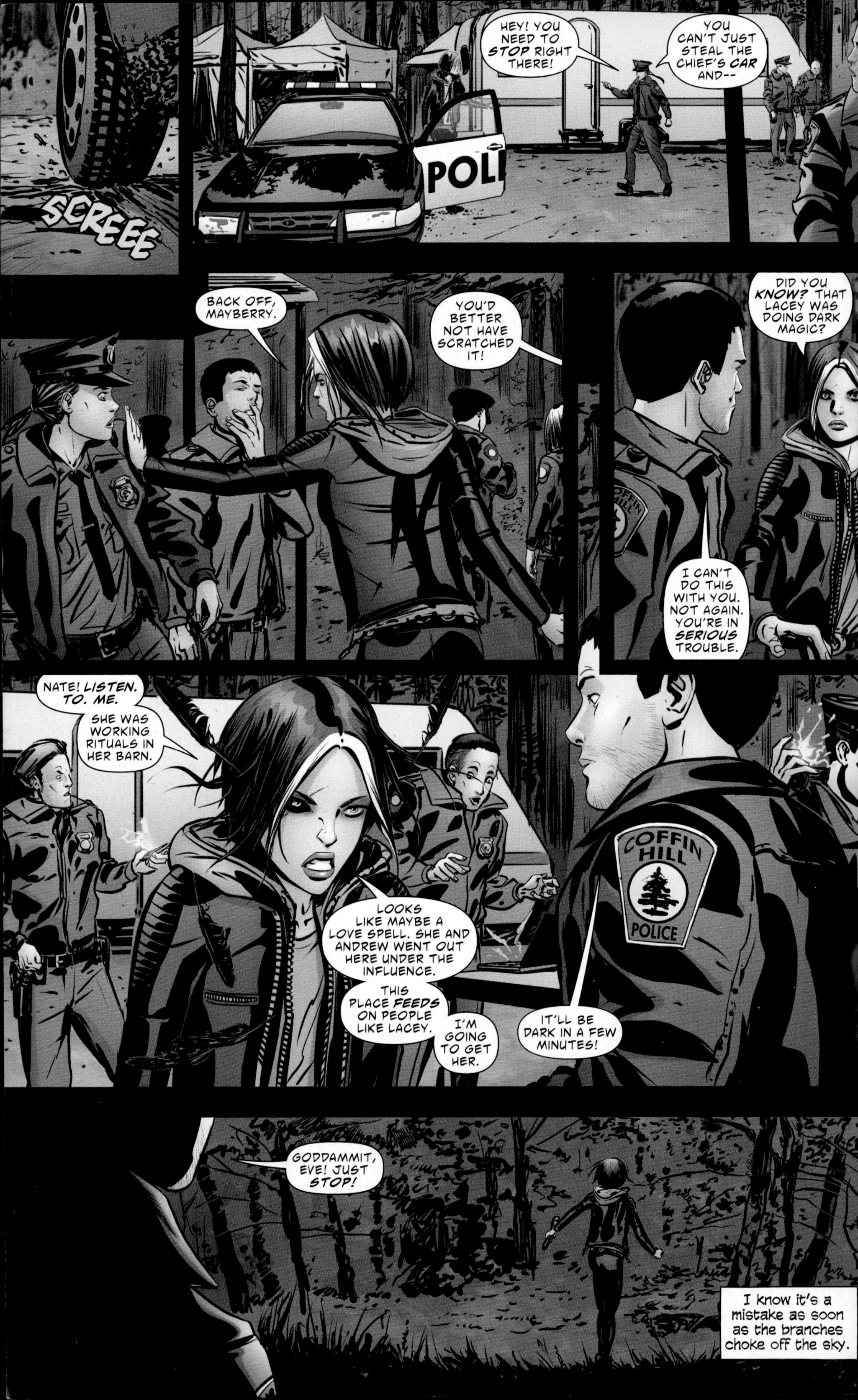
SCREEE
HEY! YOU NEED TO STOP RIGHT THERE!
YOU CAN'T JUST STEAL THE CHIEF'S CAR AND--
POLI
BACK OFF, MAYBERRY.
YOU'D BETTER NOT HAVE SCRATCHED IT!
DID YOU KNOW? THAT LACEY WAS DOING DARK MAGIC?
I CAN'T DO THIS WITH YOU. NOT AGAIN. YOU'RE IN SERIOUS TROUBLE.
NATE! LISTEN. TO. ME.
SHE WAS WORKING RITUALS IN HER BARN.
LOOKS LIKE MAYBE A LOVE SPELL. SHE AND ANDREW WENT OUT HERE UNDER THE INFLUENCE.
THIS PLACE FEEDS ON PEOPLE LIKE LACEY.
I'M GOING TO GET HER.
IT'LL BE DARK IN A FEW MINUTES!
COFFIN HILL POLICE
GODDAMMIT, EVE! JUST STOP!
I know it's a mistake as soon as the branches choke off the sky.

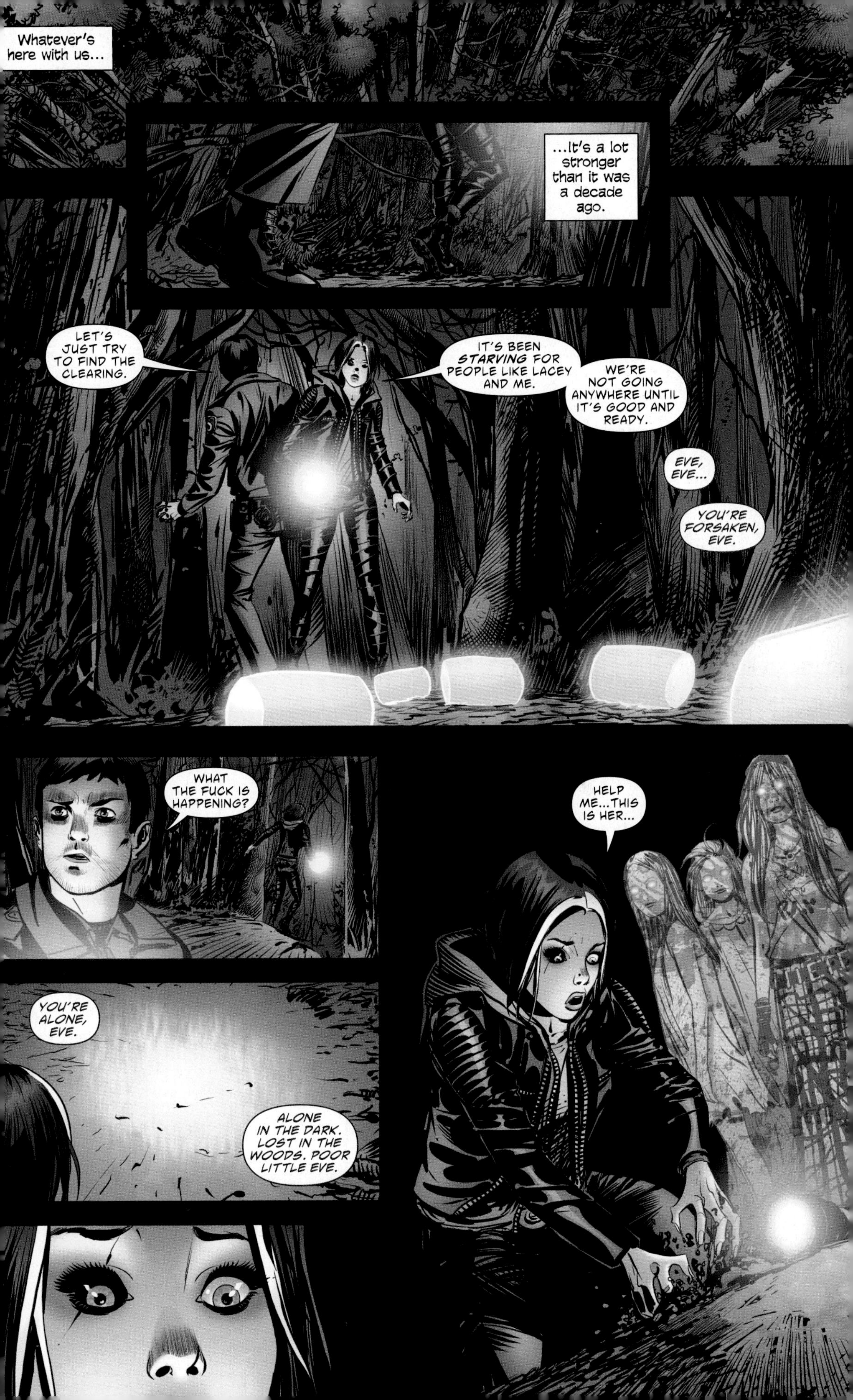

Whatever's here with us...
...It's a lot stronger than it was a decade ago.
LET'S JUST TRY TO FIND THE CLEARING.
IT'S BEEN *STARVING* FOR PEOPLE LIKE LACEY AND ME.
WE'RE NOT GOING ANYWHERE UNTIL IT'S GOOD AND READY.
EVE, EVE...
YOU'RE FORSAKEN, EVE.
WHAT THE FUCK IS HAPPENING?
HELP ME...THIS IS HER...
YOU'RE ALONE, EVE.
ALONE IN THE DARK. LOST IN THE WOODS. POOR LITTLE EVE.

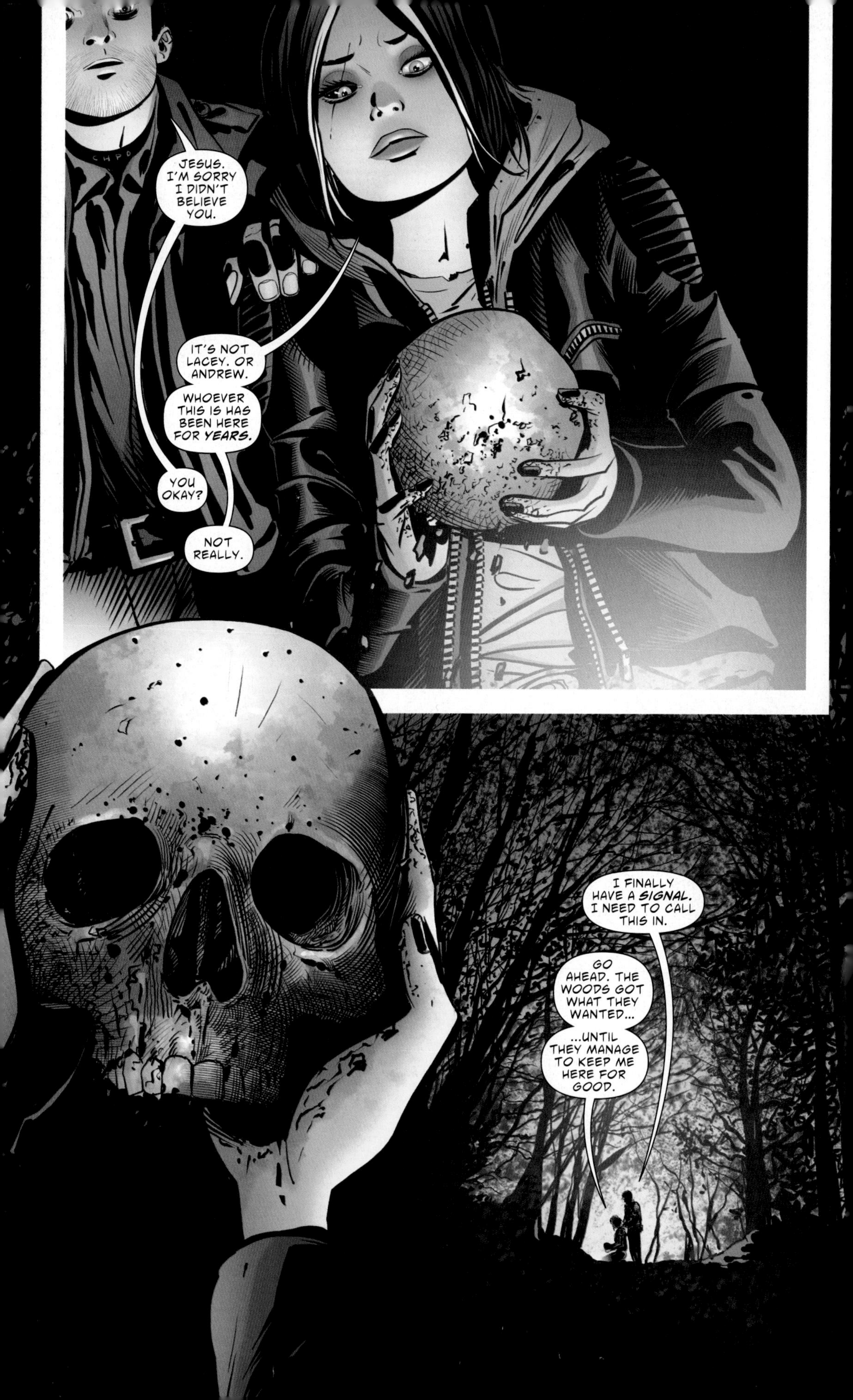
JESUS. I'M SORRY I DIDN'T BELIEVE YOU.
IT'S NOT LACEY. OR ANDREW.
WHOEVER THIS IS HAS BEEN HERE FOR YEARS.
YOU OKAY?
NOT REALLY.
I FINALLY HAVE A SIGNAL. I NEED TO CALL THIS IN.
GO AHEAD. THE WOODS GOT WHAT THEY WANTED...
...UNTIL THEY MANAGE TO KEEP ME HERE FOR GOOD.

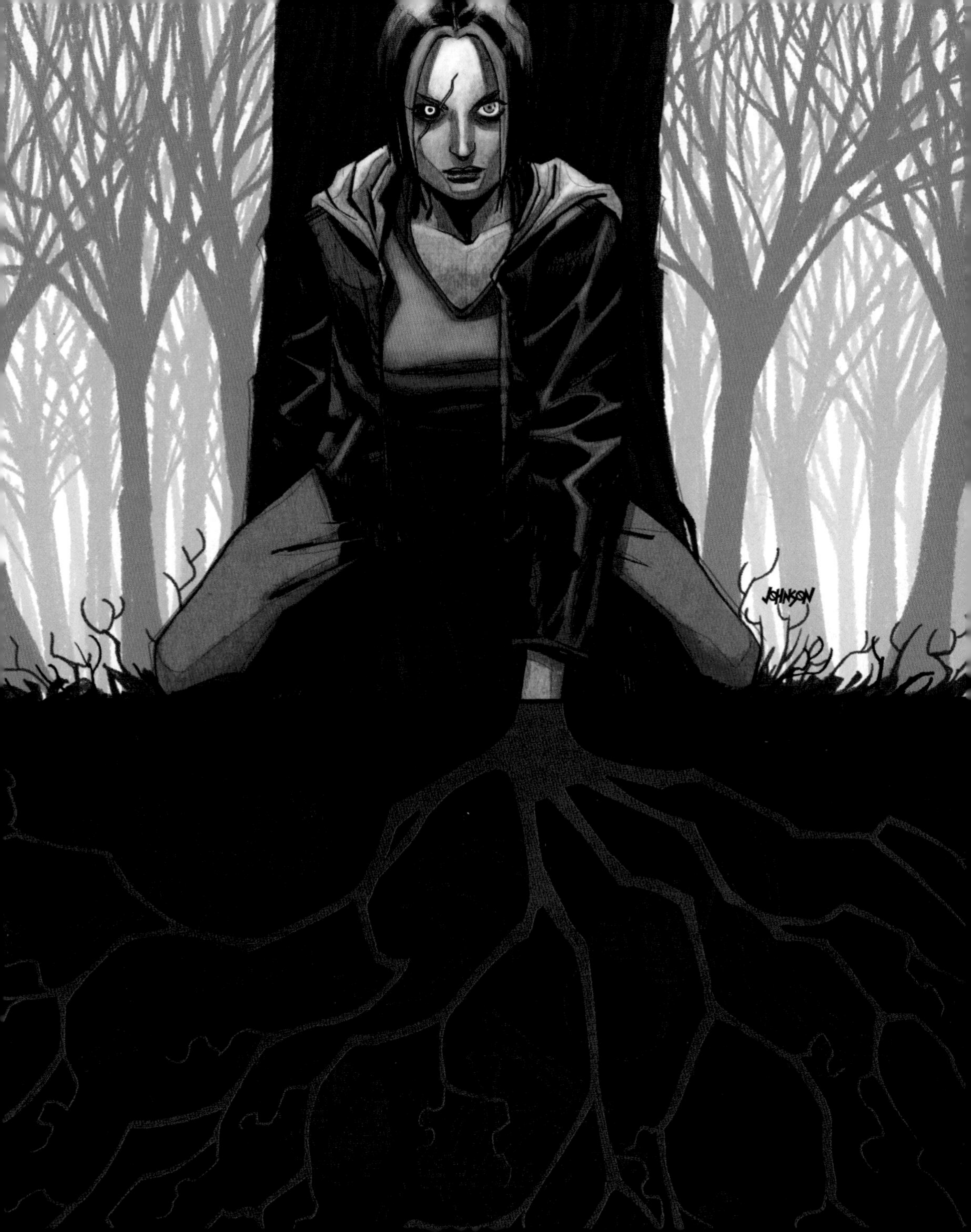
JOHNSON

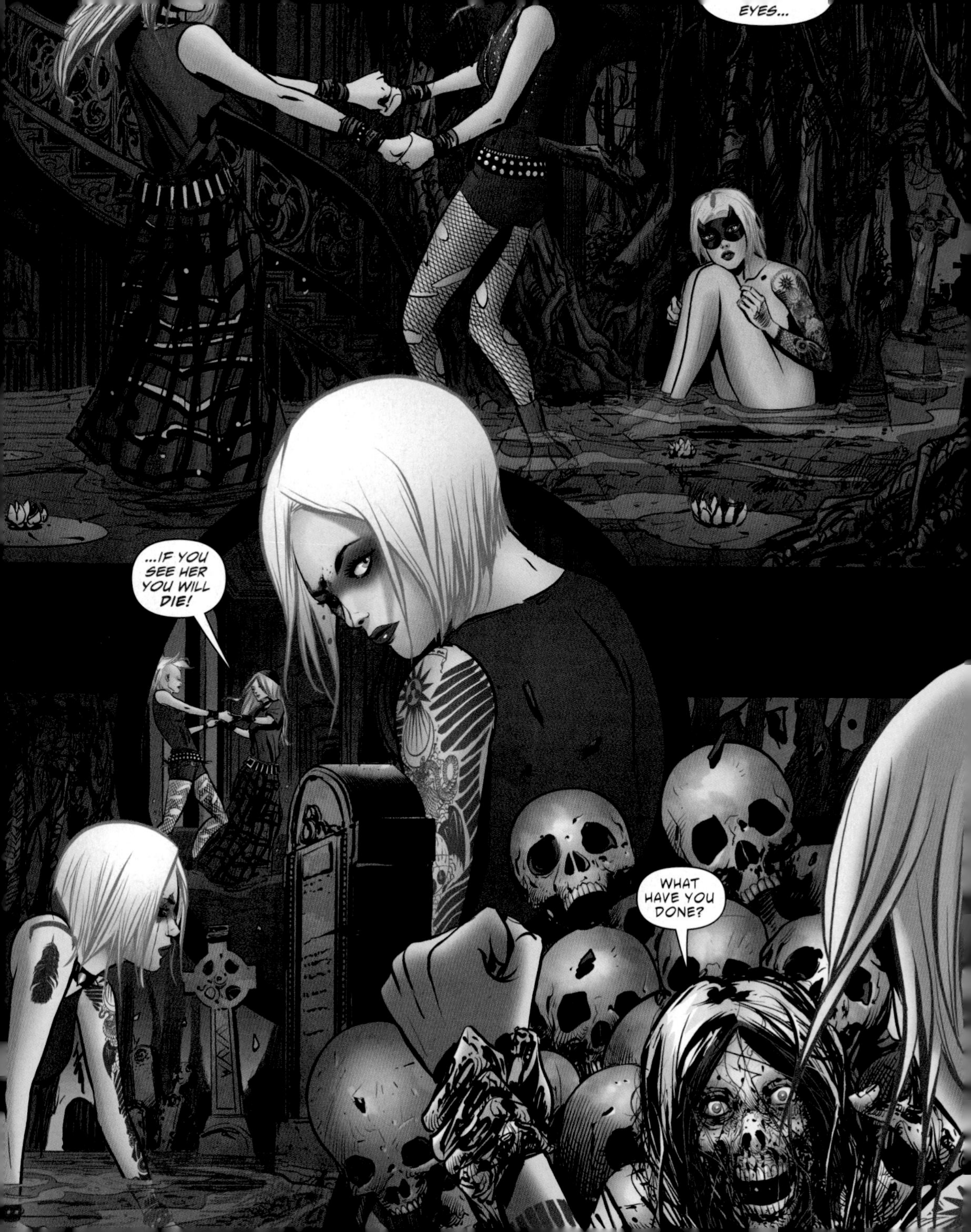
EYES...
...IF YOU SEE HER YOU WILL DIE!
WHAT HAVE YOU DONE?

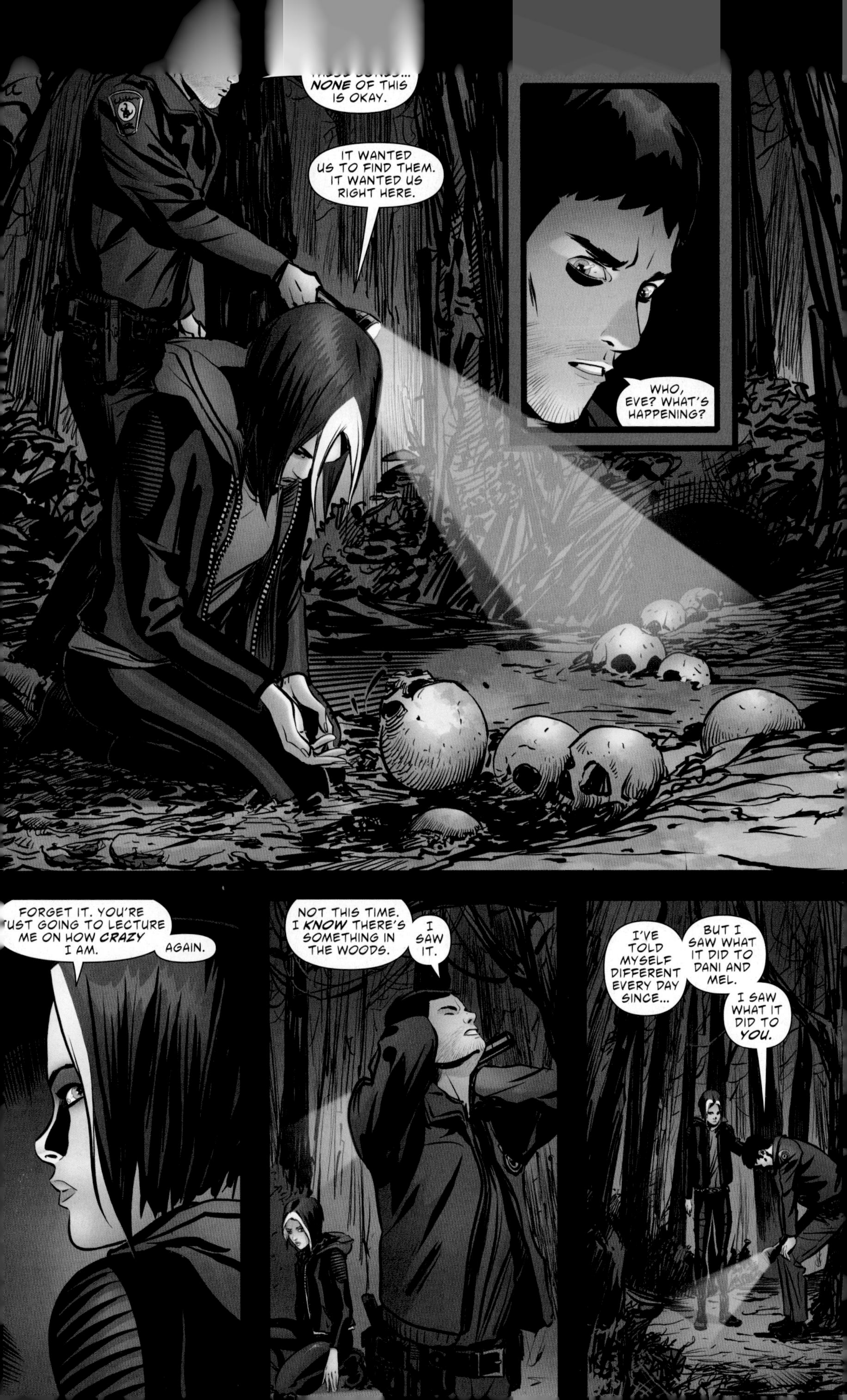
NONE OF THIS IS OKAY.
IT WANTED US TO FIND THEM. IT WANTED US RIGHT HERE.
WHO, EVE? WHAT'S HAPPENING?
FORGET IT. YOU'RE JUST GOING TO LECTURE ME ON HOW CRAZY I AM.
AGAIN.
NOT THIS TIME. I KNOW THERE'S SOMETHING IN THE WOODS.
I SAW IT.
I'VE TOLD MYSELF DIFFERENT EVERY DAY SINCE...
BUT I SAW WHAT IT DID TO DANI AND MEL.
I SAW WHAT IT DID TO YOU.

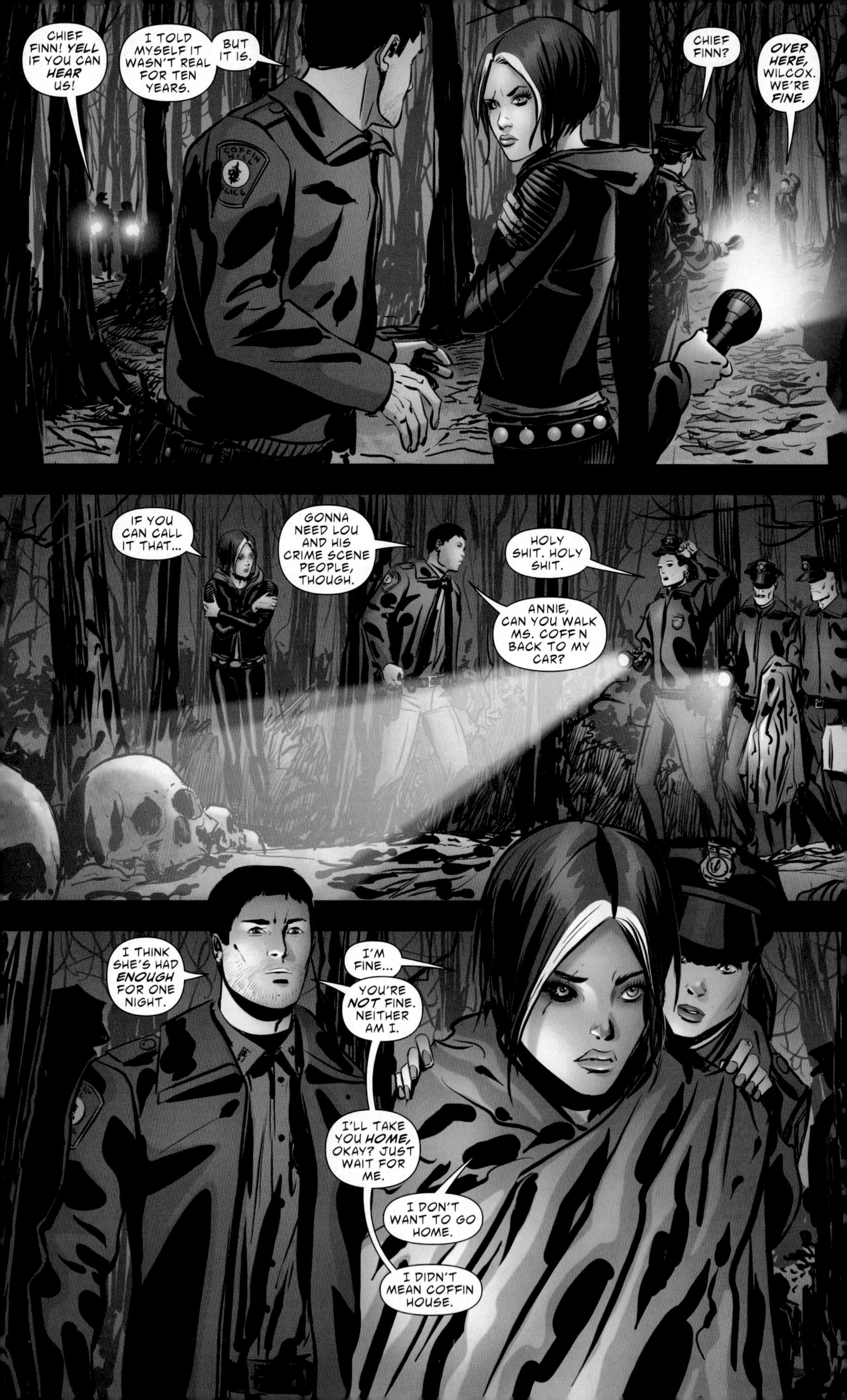
CHIEF FINN! YELL IF YOU CAN HEAR US!
I TOLD MYSELF IT WASN'T REAL FOR TEN YEARS.
BUT IT IS.
CHIEF FINN?
OVER HERE, WILCOX. WE'RE FINE.
IF YOU CAN CALL IT THAT...
GONNA NEED LOU AND HIS CRIME SCENE PEOPLE, THOUGH.
HOLY SHIT. HOLY SHIT.
ANNIE, CAN YOU WALK MS. COFF N BACK TO MY CAR?
I THINK SHE'S HAD ENOUGH FOR ONE NIGHT.
I'M FINE...
YOU'RE NOT FINE. NEITHER AM I.
I'LL TAKE YOU HOME, OKAY? JUST WAIT FOR ME.
I DON'T WANT TO GO HOME.
I DIDN'T MEAN COFFIN HOUSE.

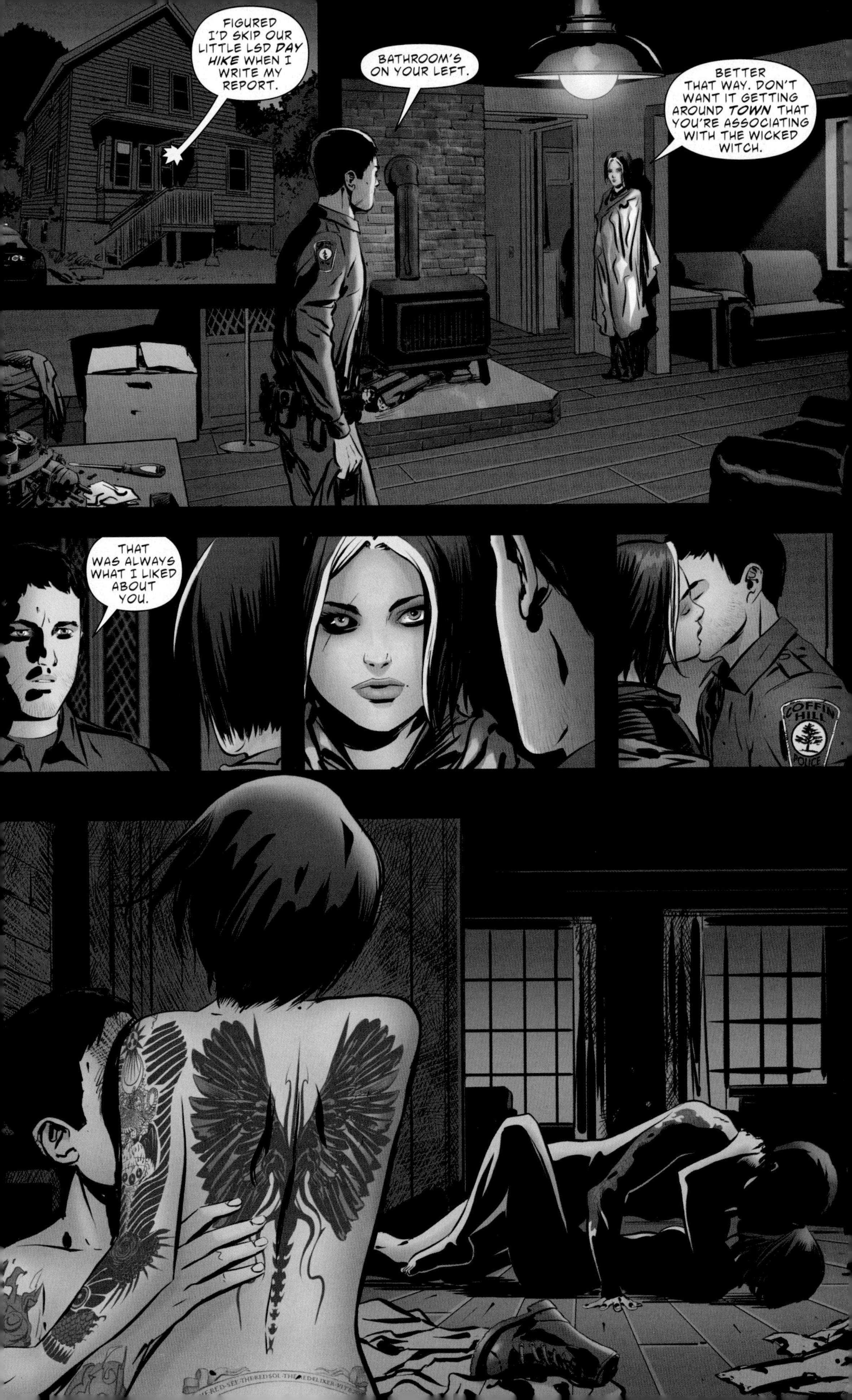
FIGURED I'D SKIP OUR LITTLE LSD DAY HIKE WHEN I WRITE MY REPORT.
BATHROOM'S ON YOUR LEFT.
BETTER THAT WAY. DON'T WANT IT GETTING AROUND TOWN THAT YOU'RE ASSOCIATING WITH THE WICKED WITCH.
THAT WAS ALWAYS WHAT I LIKED ABOUT YOU.
COFFIN HILL POLICE

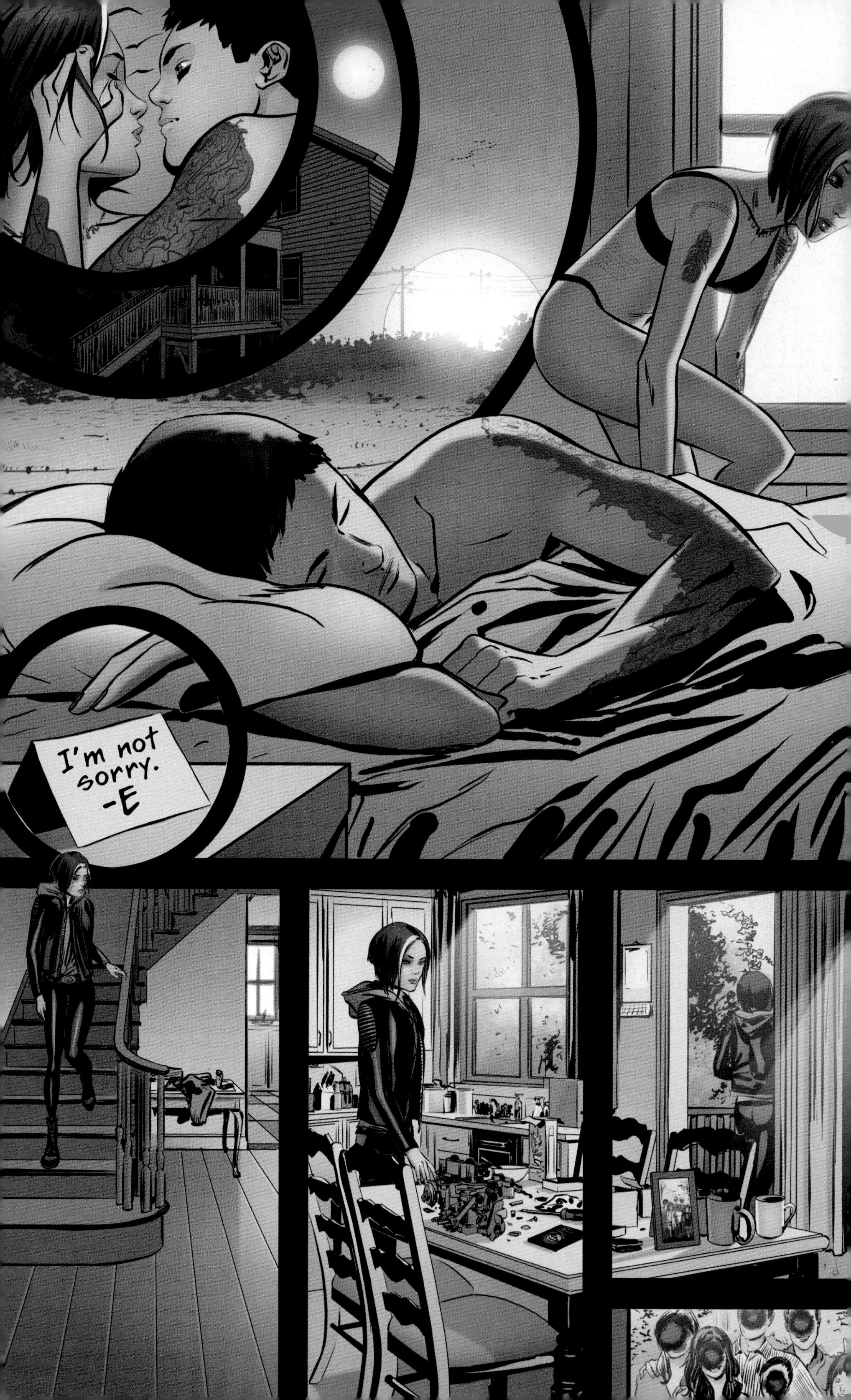
I'm not sorry.
-E

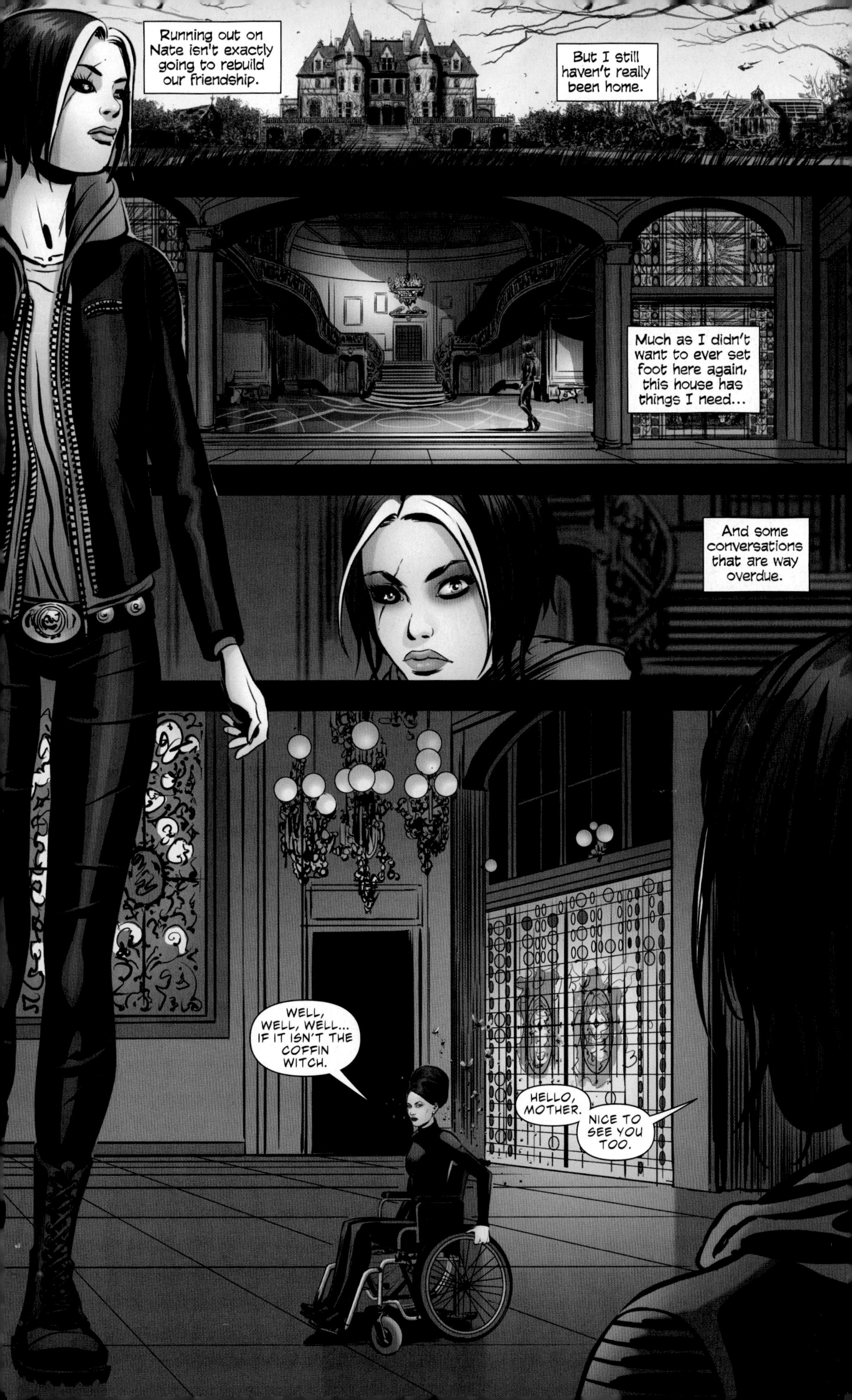
Running out on Nate isn't exactly going to rebuild our friendship.
But I still haven't really been home.
Much as I didn't want to ever set foot here again, this house has things I need...
And some conversations that are way overdue.
WELL, WELL, WELL... IF IT ISN'T THE COFFIN WITCH.
HELLO, MOTHER.
NICE TO SEE YOU TOO.

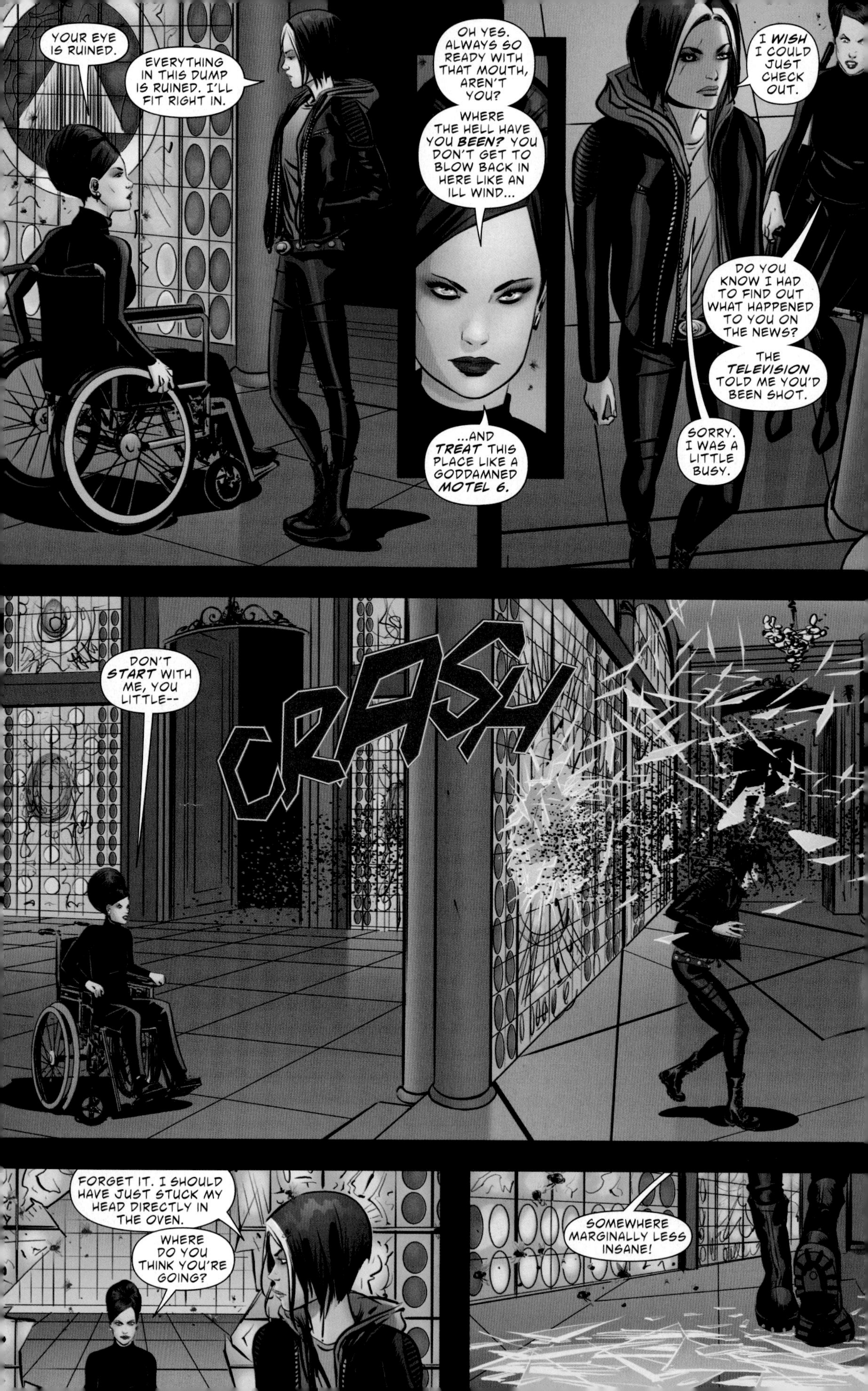
YOUR EYE IS RUINED.
EVERYTHING IN THIS DUMP IS RUINED. I'LL FIT RIGHT IN.
OH YES. ALWAYS SO READY WITH THAT MOUTH, AREN'T YOU?
WHERE THE HELL HAVE YOU BEEN? YOU DON'T GET TO BLOW BACK IN HERE LIKE AN ILL WIND...
...AND TREAT THIS PLACE LIKE A GODDAMNED MOTEL 6.
I WISH I COULD JUST CHECK OUT.
DO YOU KNOW I HAD TO FIND OUT WHAT HAPPENED TO YOU ON THE NEWS?
THE TELEVISION TOLD ME YOU'D BEEN SHOT.
SORRY. I WAS A LITTLE BUSY.
DON'T START WITH ME, YOU LITTLE--
CRASH
FORGET IT. I SHOULD HAVE JUST STUCK MY HEAD DIRECTLY IN THE OVEN.
WHERE DO YOU THINK YOU'RE GOING?
SOMEWHERE MARGINALLY LESS INSANE!

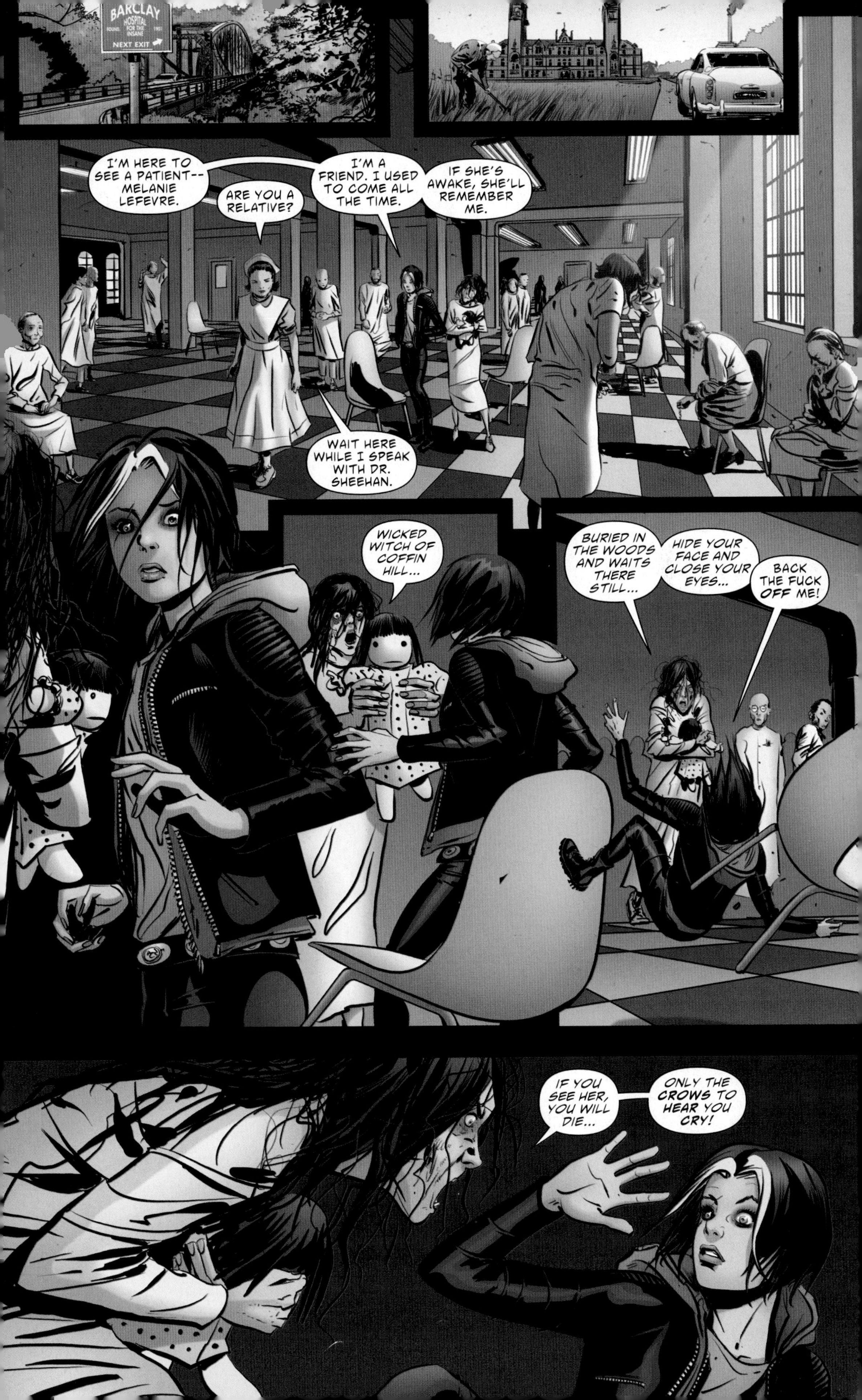
BARCLAY
HOSPITAL FOR THE INSANE
NEXT EXIT
I'M HERE TO SEE A PATIENT-- MELANIE LEFEVRE.
ARE YOU A RELATIVE?
I'M A FRIEND. I USED TO COME ALL THE TIME.
IF SHE'S AWAKE, SHE'LL REMEMBER ME.
WAIT HERE WHILE I SPEAK WITH DR. SHEEHAN.
WICKED WITCH OF COFFIN HILL...
BURIED IN THE WOODS AND WAITS THERE STILL...
HIDE YOUR FACE AND CLOSE YOUR EYES...
BACK THE FUCK OFF ME!
IF YOU SEE HER, YOU WILL DIE...
ONLY THE CROWS TO HEAR YOU CRY!

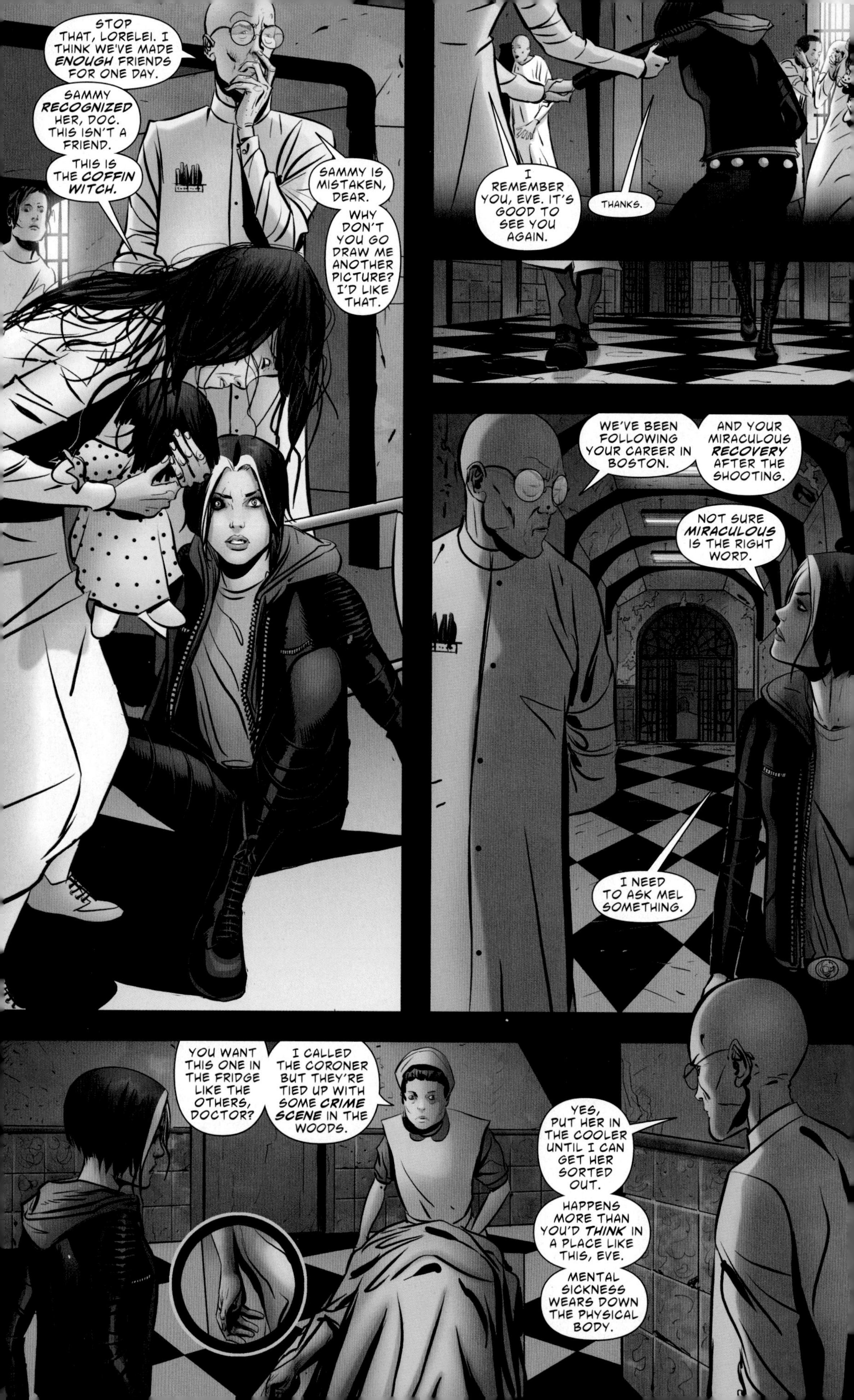

STOP THAT, LORELEI. I THINK WE'VE MADE ENOUGH FRIENDS FOR ONE DAY.
SAMMY RECOGNIZED HER, DOC. THIS ISN'T A FRIEND.
THIS IS THE COFFIN WITCH.
SAMMY IS MISTAKEN, DEAR.
WHY DON'T YOU GO DRAW ME ANOTHER PICTURE? I'D LIKE THAT.
I REMEMBER YOU, EVE. IT'S GOOD TO SEE YOU AGAIN.
THANKS.
WE'VE BEEN FOLLOWING YOUR CAREER IN BOSTON.
AND YOUR MIRACULOUS RECOVERY AFTER THE SHOOTING.
NOT SURE MIRACULOUS IS THE RIGHT WORD.
I NEED TO ASK MEL SOMETHING.
YOU WANT THIS ONE IN THE FRIDGE LIKE THE OTHERS, DOCTOR?
I CALLED THE CORONER BUT THEY'RE TIED UP WITH SOME CRIME SCENE IN THE WOODS.
YES, PUT HER IN THE COOLER UNTIL I CAN GET HER SORTED OUT.
HAPPENS MORE THAN YOU'D THINK IN A PLACE LIKE THIS, EVE.
MENTAL SICKNESS WEARS DOWN THE PHYSICAL BODY.

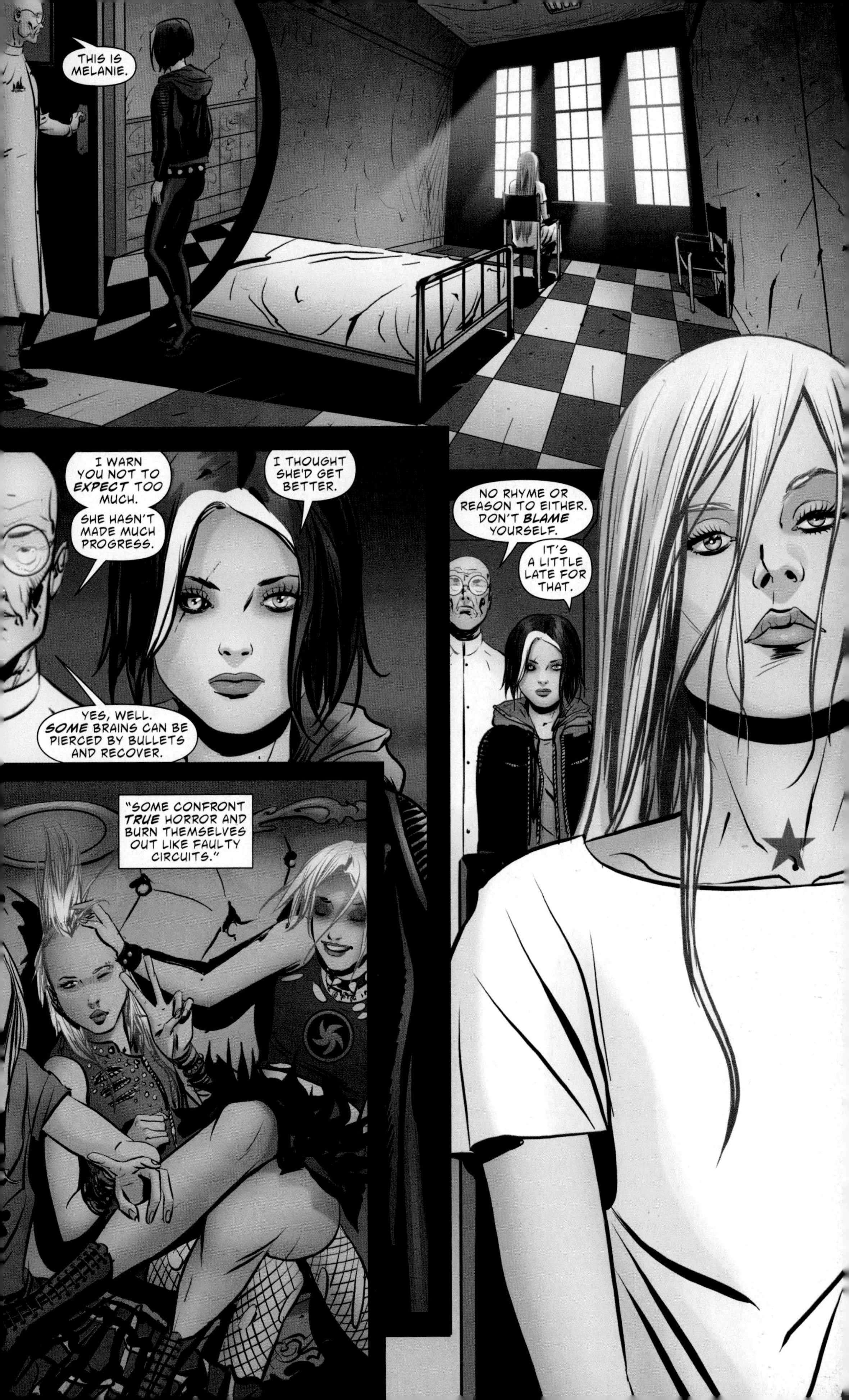
THIS IS MELANIE.
I WARN YOU NOT TO EXPECT TOO MUCH.
SHE HASN'T MADE MUCH PROGRESS.
I THOUGHT SHE'D GET BETTER.
YES, WELL. SOME BRAINS CAN BE PIERCED BY BULLETS AND RECOVER.
NO RHYME OR REASON TO EITHER. DON'T BLAME YOURSELF.
IT'S A LITTLE LATE FOR THAT.
"SOME CONFRONT TRUE HORROR AND BURN THEMSELVES OUT LIKE FAULTY CIRCUITS."

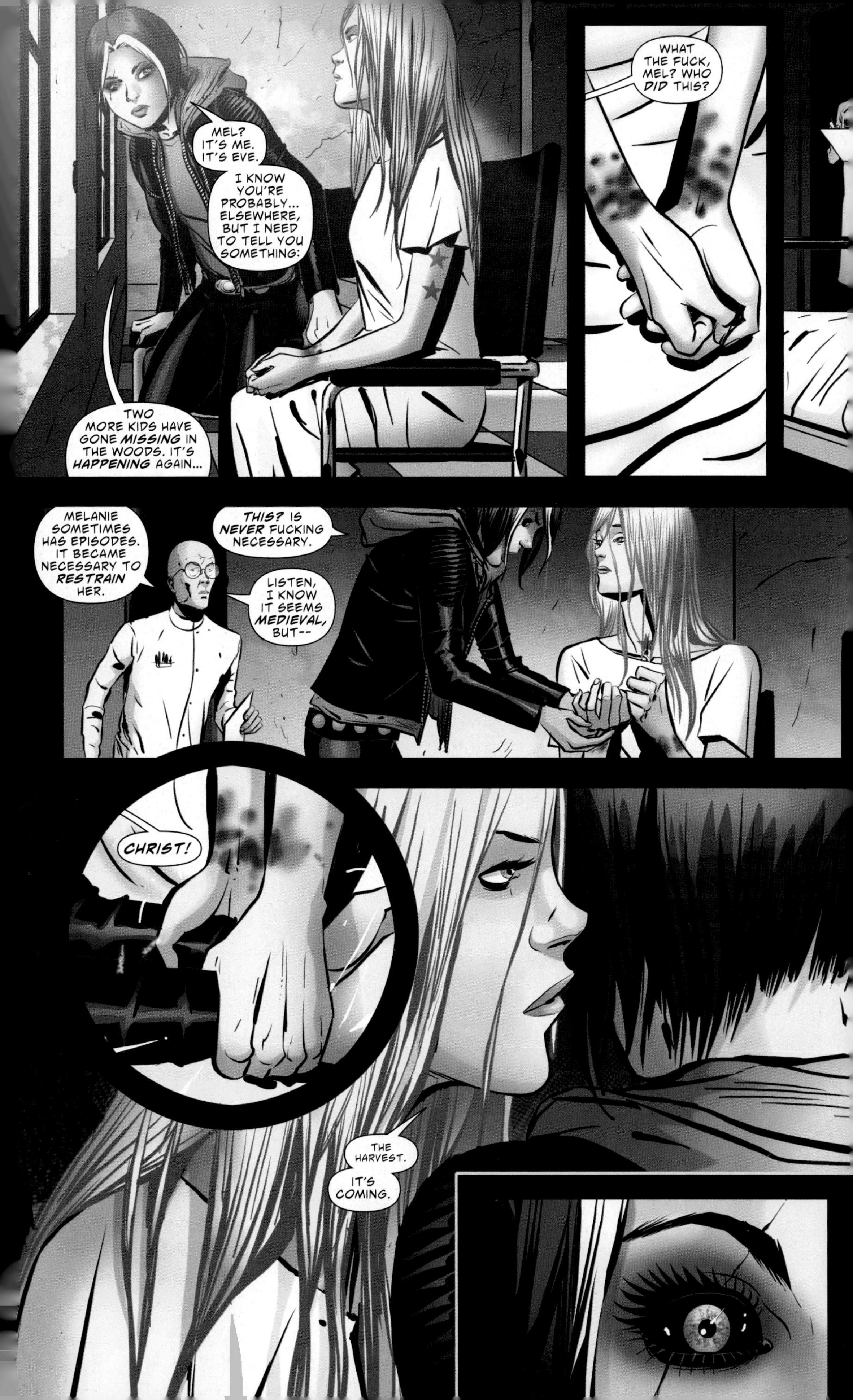
MEL? IT'S ME. IT'S EVE.
I KNOW YOU'RE PROBABLY... ELSEWHERE, BUT I NEED TO TELL YOU SOMETHING:
TWO MORE KIDS HAVE GONE MISSING IN THE WOODS. IT'S HAPPENING AGAIN...
WHAT THE FUCK, MEL? WHO DID THIS?
MELANIE SOMETIMES HAS EPISODES. IT BECAME NECESSARY TO RESTRAIN HER.
THIS? IS NEVER FUCKING NECESSARY.
LISTEN, I KNOW IT SEEMS MEDIEVAL, BUT--
CHRIST!
THE HARVEST.
IT'S COMING.

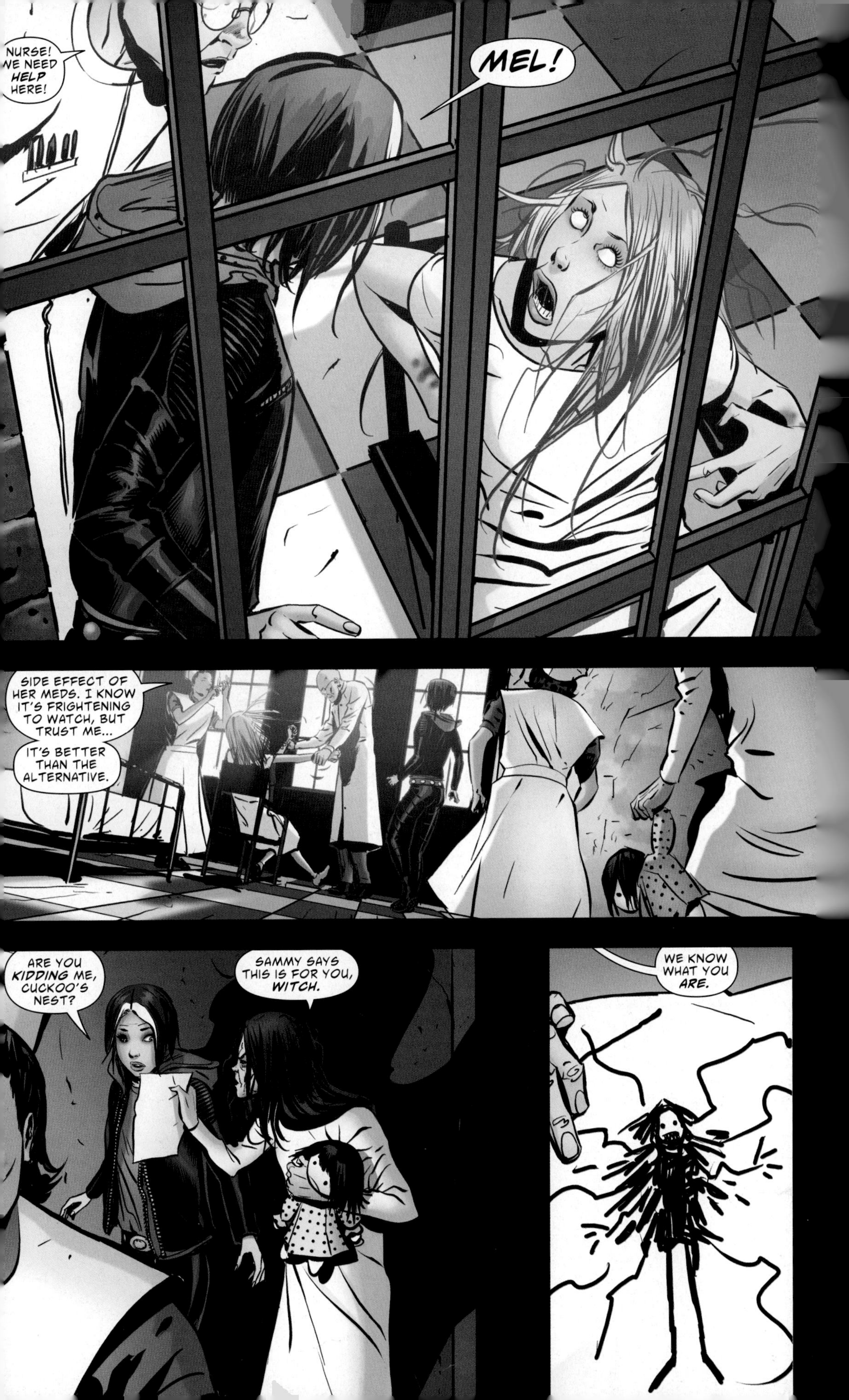
NURSE! WE NEED HELP HERE!
MEL!
SIDE EFFECT OF HER MEDS. I KNOW IT'S FRIGHTENING TO WATCH, BUT TRUST ME...
IT'S BETTER THAN THE ALTERNATIVE.
ARE YOU KIDDING ME, CUCKOO'S NEST?
SAMMY SAYS THIS IS FOR YOU, WITCH.
WE KNOW WHAT YOU ARE.

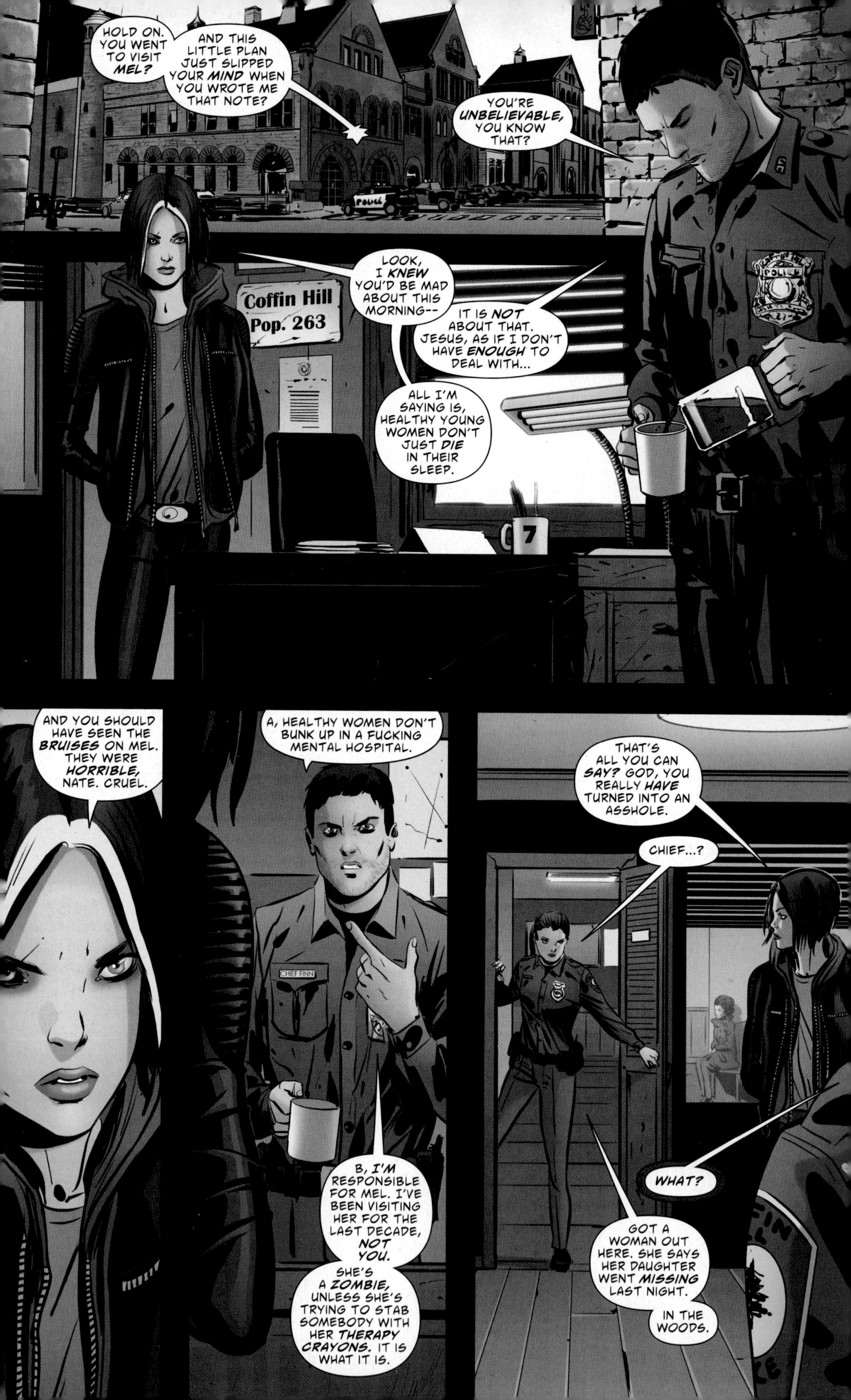
HOLD ON. YOU WENT TO VISIT MEL?
AND THIS LITTLE PLAN JUST SLIPPED YOUR MIND WHEN YOU WROTE ME THAT NOTE?
YOU'RE UNBELIEVABLE, YOU KNOW THAT?
Coffin Hill Pop. 263
LOOK, I KNEW YOU'D BE MAD ABOUT THIS MORNING--
IT IS NOT ABOUT THAT. JESUS, AS IF I DON'T HAVE ENOUGH TO DEAL WITH...
ALL I'M SAYING IS, HEALTHY YOUNG WOMEN DON'T JUST DIE IN THEIR SLEEP.
AND YOU SHOULD HAVE SEEN THE BRUISES ON MEL. THEY WERE HORRIBLE, NATE. CRUEL.
A, HEALTHY WOMEN DON'T BUNK UP IN A FUCKING MENTAL HOSPITAL.
CHIEF FINN
B, I'M RESPONSIBLE FOR MEL. I'VE BEEN VISITING HER FOR THE LAST DECADE, NOT YOU.
SHE'S A ZOMBIE, UNLESS SHE'S TRYING TO STAB SOMEBODY WITH HER THERAPY CRAYONS. IT IS WHAT IT IS.
THAT'S ALL YOU CAN SAY? GOD, YOU REALLY HAVE TURNED INTO AN ASSHOLE.
CHIEF...?
WHAT?
GOT A WOMAN OUT HERE. SHE SAYS HER DAUGHTER WENT MISSING LAST NIGHT.
IN THE WOODS.

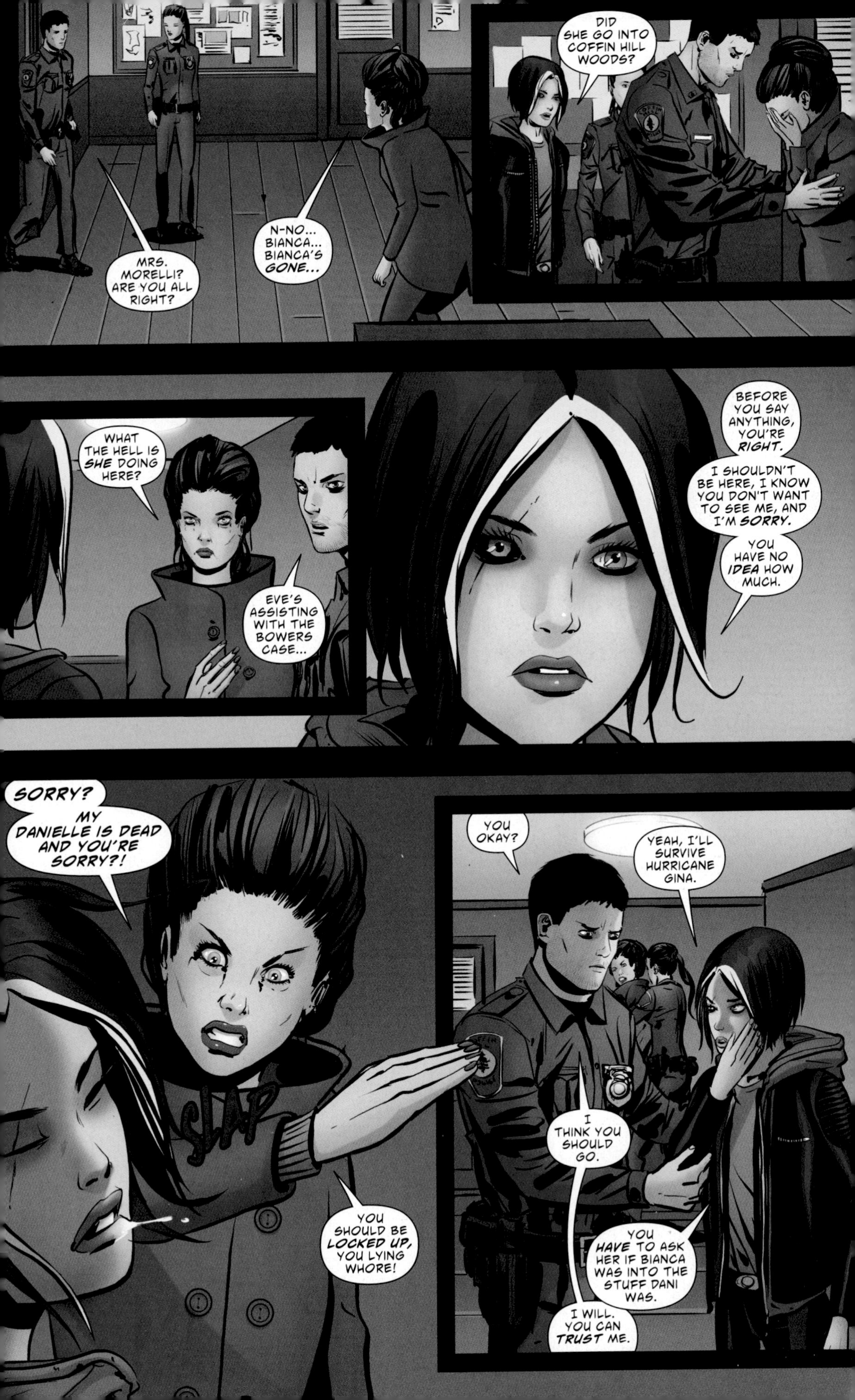
MRS. MORELLI? ARE YOU ALL RIGHT?
N-NO... BIANCA... BIANCA'S GONE...
DID SHE GO INTO COFFIN HILL WOODS?
WHAT THE HELL IS SHE DOING HERE?
EVE'S ASSISTING WITH THE BOWERS CASE...
BEFORE YOU SAY ANYTHING, YOU'RE RIGHT.
I SHOULDN'T BE HERE, I KNOW YOU DON'T WANT TO SEE ME, AND I'M SORRY.
YOU HAVE NO IDEA HOW MUCH.
SORRY?
MY DANIELLE IS DEAD AND YOU'RE SORRY?!
SLAP
YOU SHOULD BE LOCKED UP, YOU LYING WHORE!
YOU OKAY?
YEAH, I'LL SURVIVE HURRICANE GINA.
I THINK YOU SHOULD GO.
YOU HAVE TO ASK HER IF BIANCA WAS INTO THE STUFF DANI WAS.
I WILL. YOU CAN TRUST ME.

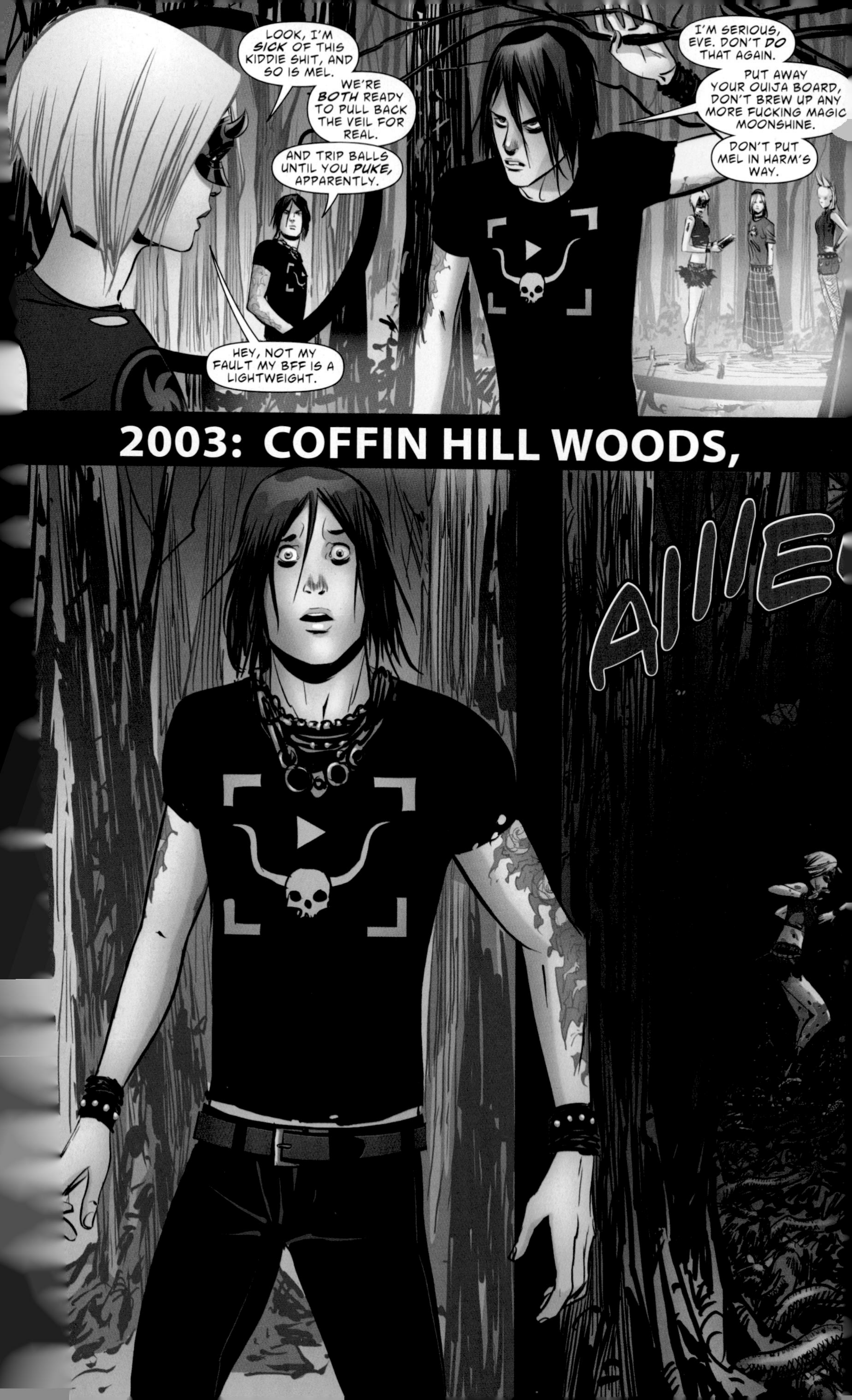
LOOK, I'M SICK OF THIS KIDDIE SHIT, AND SO IS MEL.
WE'RE BOTH READY TO PULL BACK THE VEIL FOR REAL.
AND TRIP BALLS UNTIL YOU PUKE, APPARENTLY.
HEY, NOT MY FAULT MY BFF IS A LIGHTWEIGHT.
I'M SERIOUS, EVE. DON'T DO THAT AGAIN.
PUT AWAY YOUR OUIJA BOARD, DON'T BREW UP ANY MORE FUCKING MAGIC MOONSHINE.
DON'T PUT MEL IN HARM'S WAY.
2003: COFFIN HILL WOODS,
AIIIEE

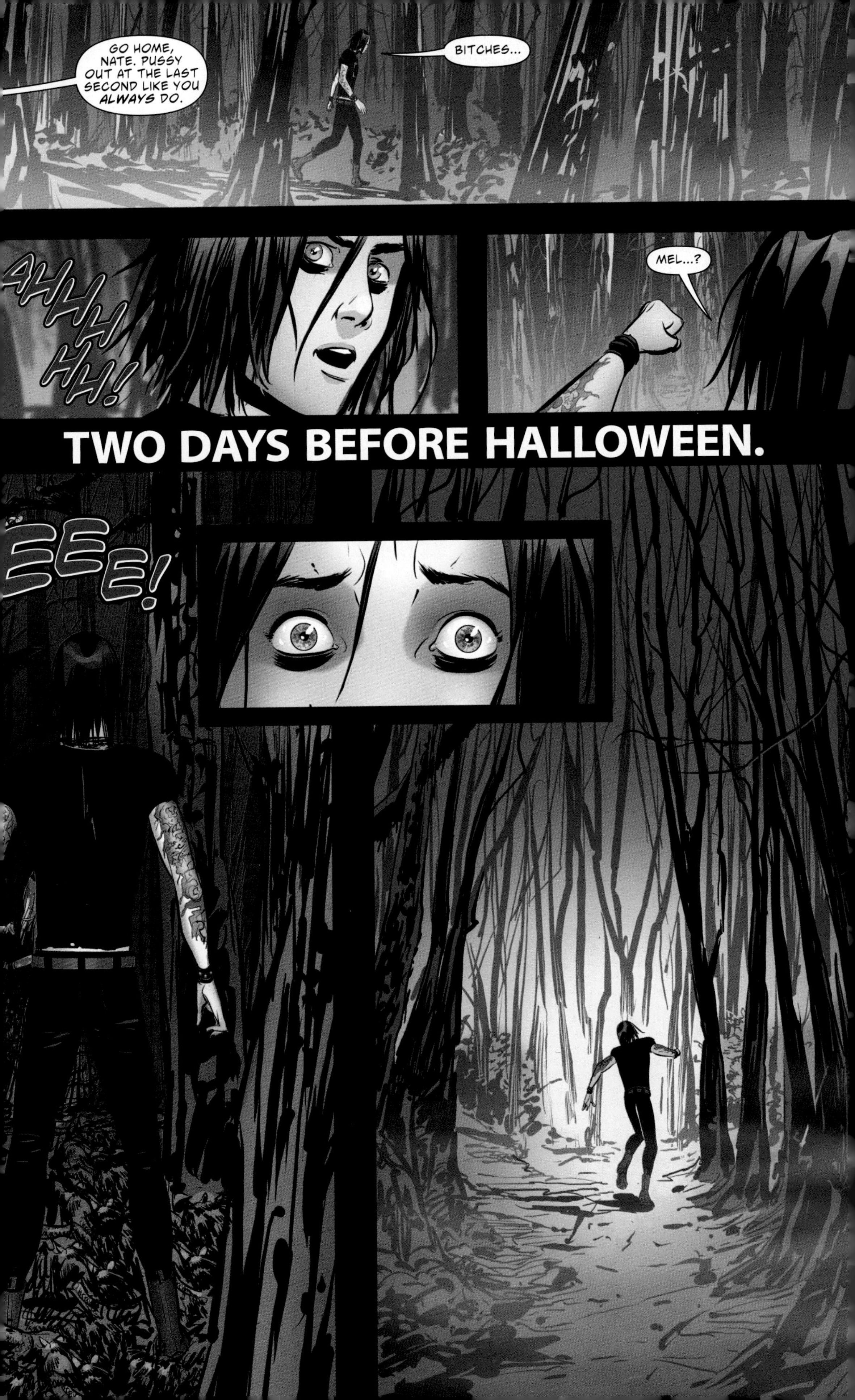
GO HOME, NATE. PUSSY OUT AT THE LAST SECOND LIKE YOU ALWAYS DO.
BITCHES...
AHHHHH!
MEL...?
TWO DAYS BEFORE HALLOWEEN.
EEEE!

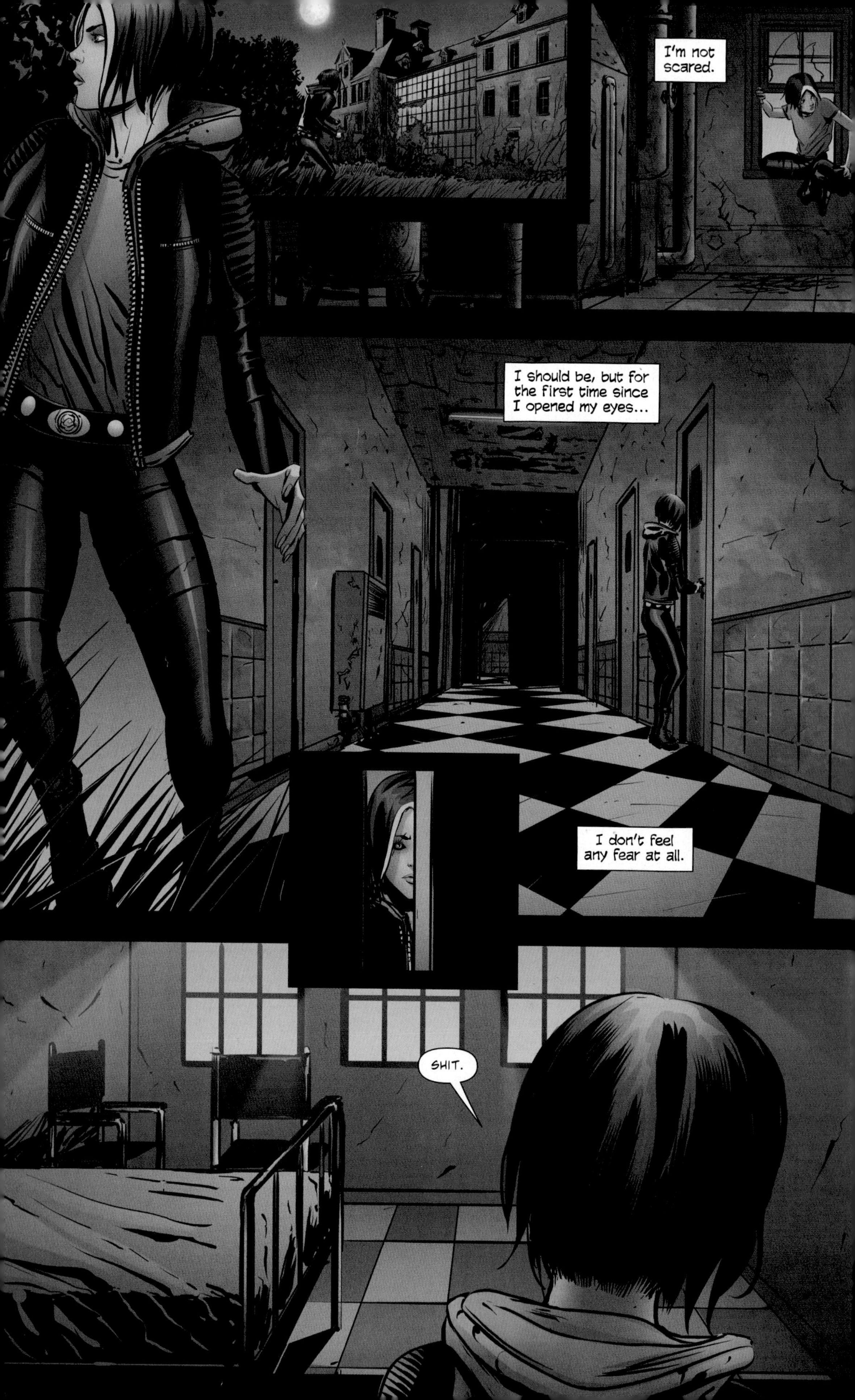
I'm not scared.
I should be, but for the first time since I opened my eyes...
I don't feel any fear at all.
SHIT.

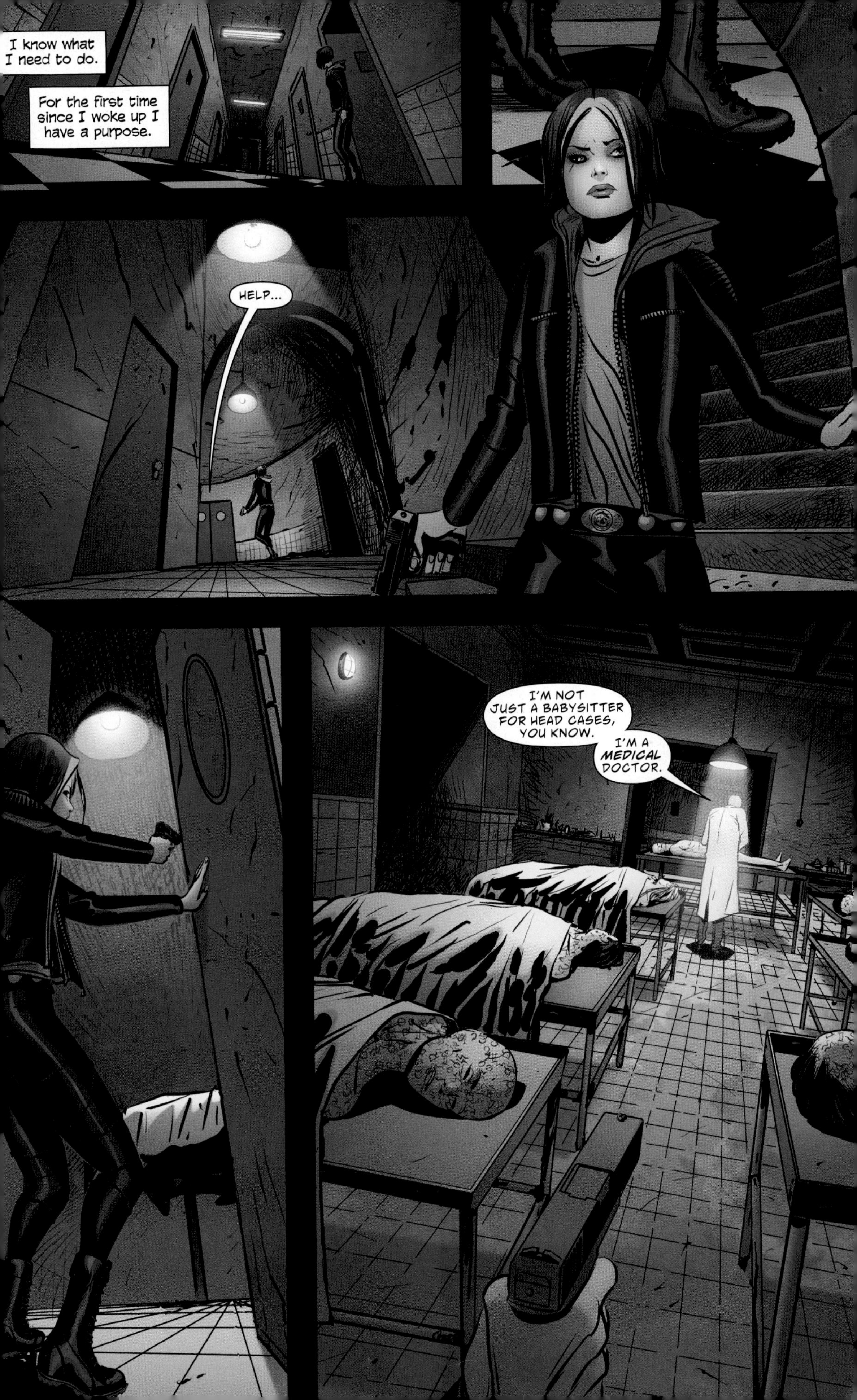

I know what I need to do.
For the first time since I woke up I have a purpose.
HELP...
I'M NOT JUST A BABYSITTER FOR HEAD CASES, YOU KNOW.
I'M A *MEDICAL* DOCTOR.

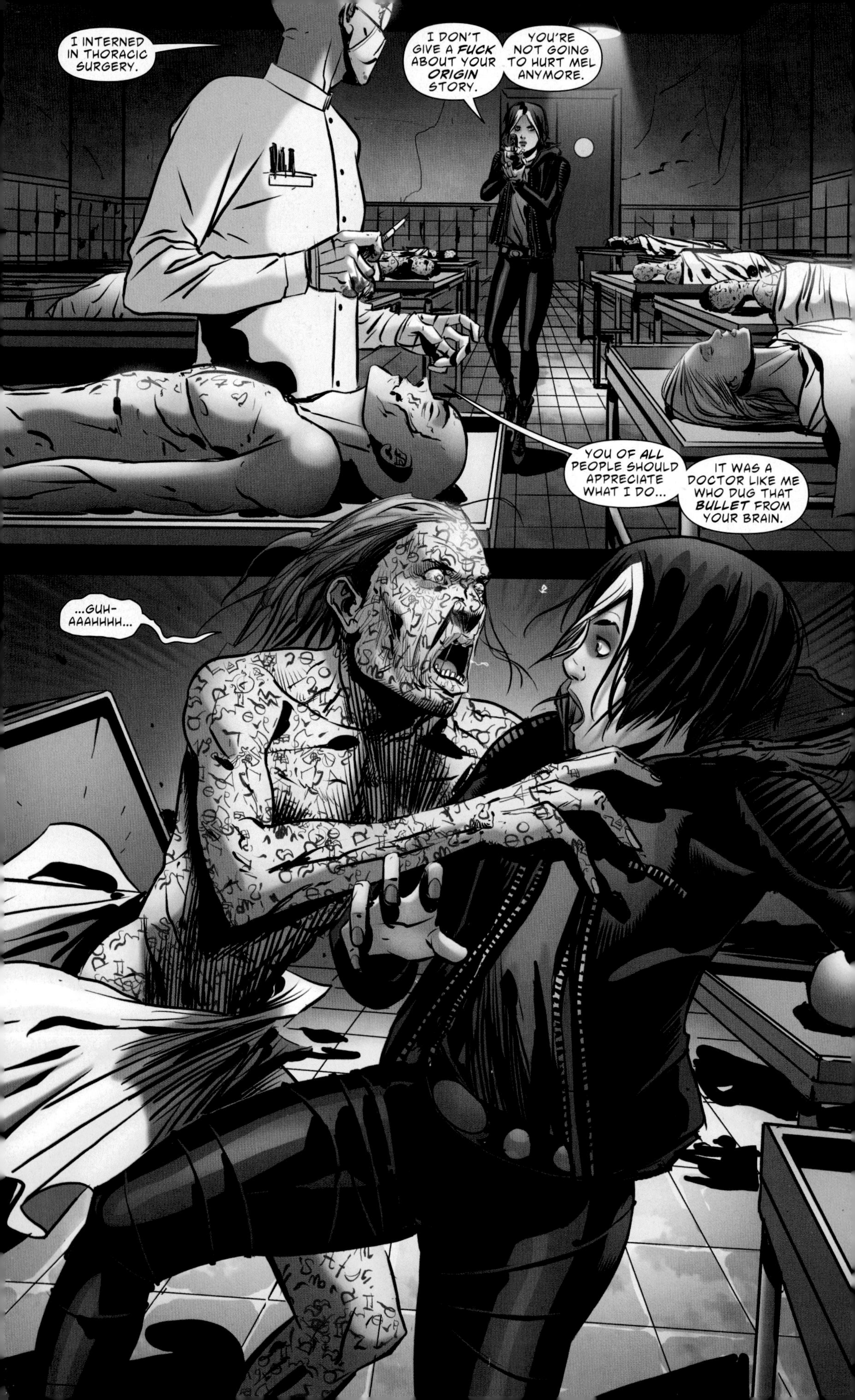
I INTERNED IN THORACIC SURGERY.
I DON'T GIVE A FUCK ABOUT YOUR ORIGIN STORY.
YOU'RE NOT GOING TO HURT MEL ANYMORE.
YOU OF ALL PEOPLE SHOULD APPRECIATE WHAT I DO...
IT WAS A DOCTOR LIKE ME WHO DUG THAT BULLET FROM YOUR BRAIN.
...GUH-AAAHHHH...

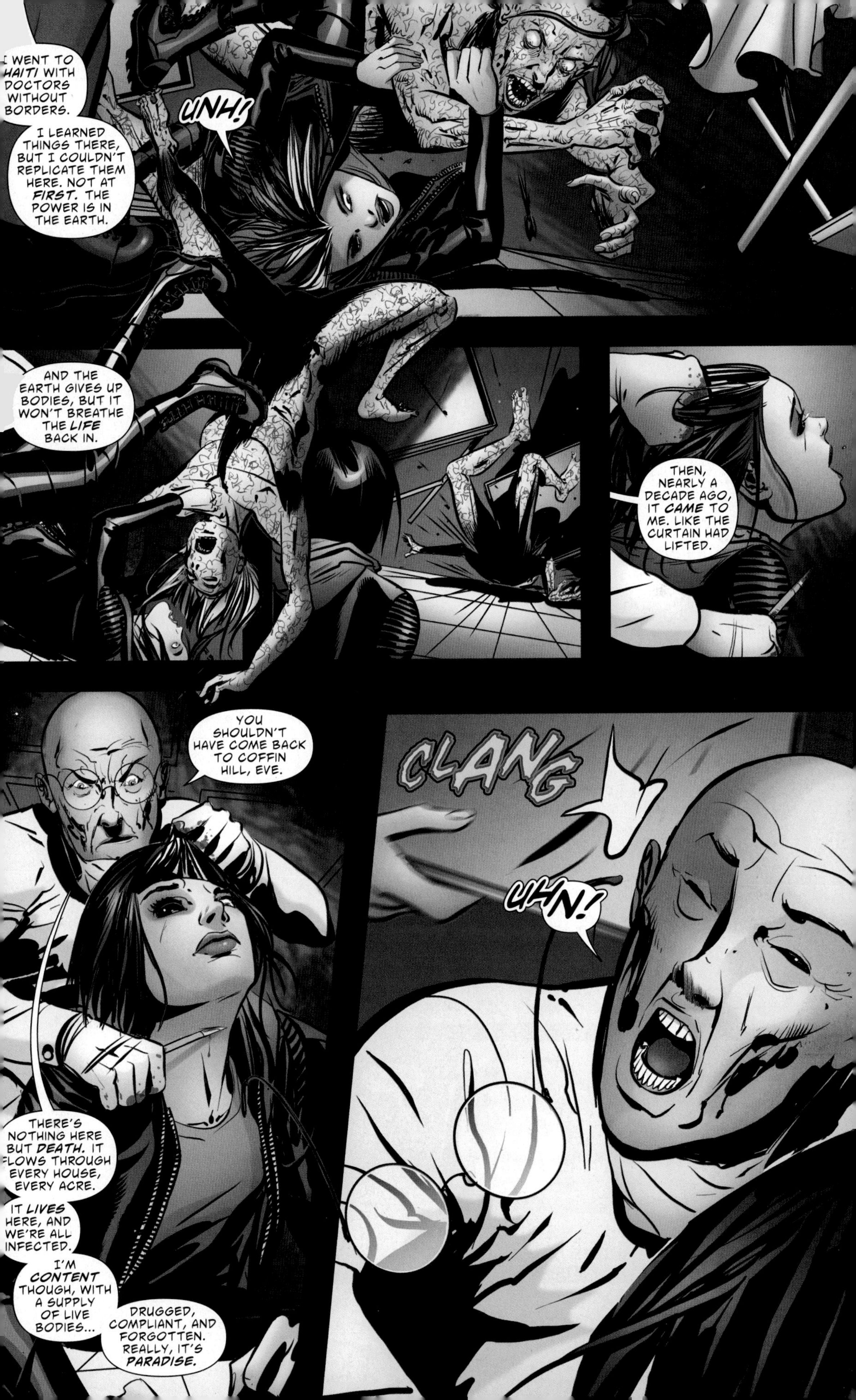
I WENT TO HAITI WITH DOCTORS WITHOUT BORDERS.
I LEARNED THINGS THERE, BUT I COULDN'T REPLICATE THEM HERE. NOT AT FIRST. THE POWER IS IN THE EARTH.
UNH!
AND THE EARTH GIVES UP BODIES, BUT IT WON'T BREATHE THE LIFE BACK IN.
THEN, NEARLY A DECADE AGO, IT CAME TO ME. LIKE THE CURTAIN HAD LIFTED.
YOU SHOULDN'T HAVE COME BACK TO COFFIN HILL, EVE.
THERE'S NOTHING HERE BUT DEATH. IT FLOWS THROUGH EVERY HOUSE, EVERY ACRE.
IT LIVES HERE, AND WE'RE ALL INFECTED.
I'M CONTENT THOUGH, WITH A SUPPLY OF LIVE BODIES...
DRUGGED, COMPLIANT, AND FORGOTTEN. REALLY, IT'S PARADISE.
CLANG
UHN!

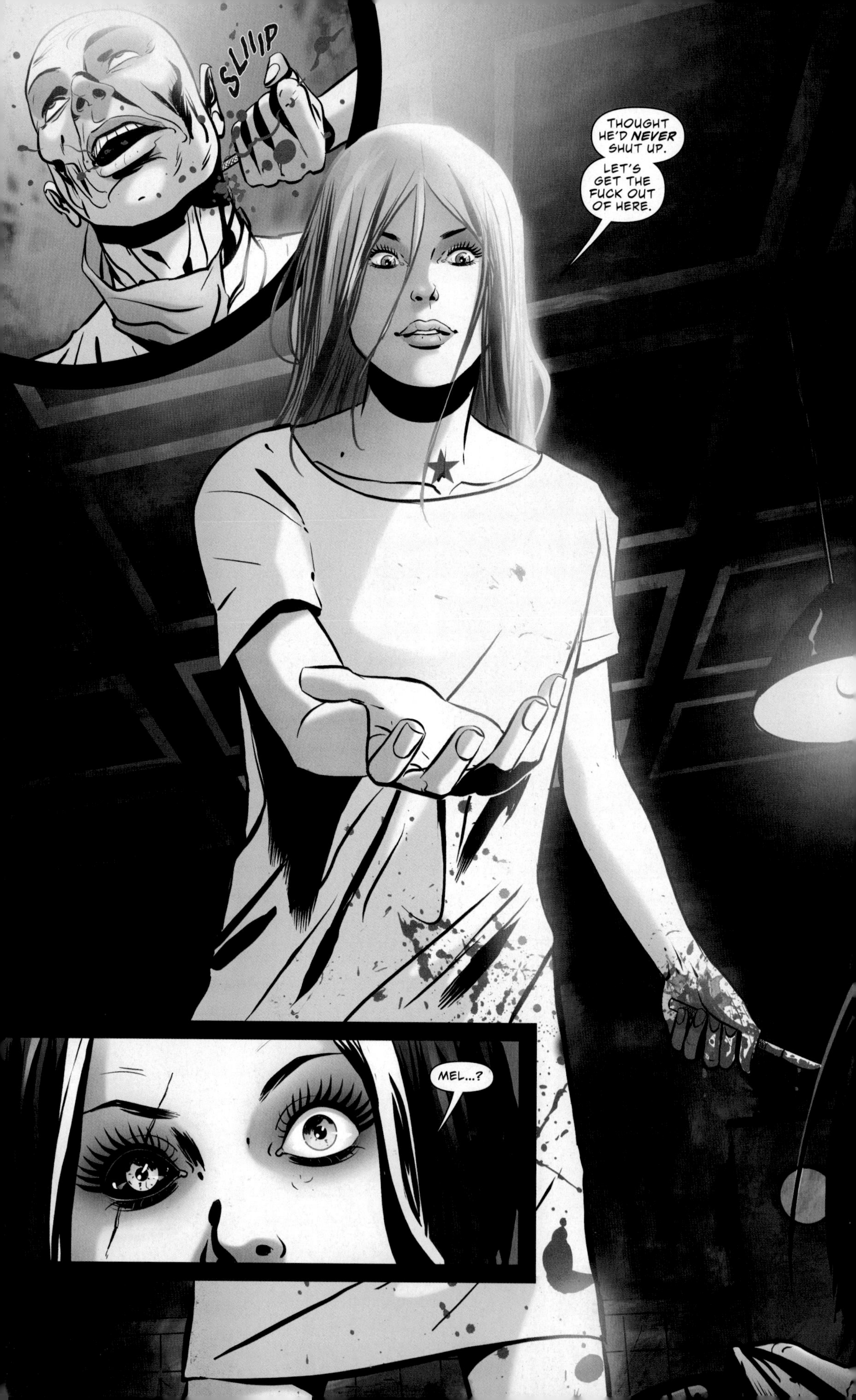
SLIIIP
THOUGHT HE'D NEVER SHUT UP.
LET'S GET THE FUCK OUT OF HERE.
MEL...?

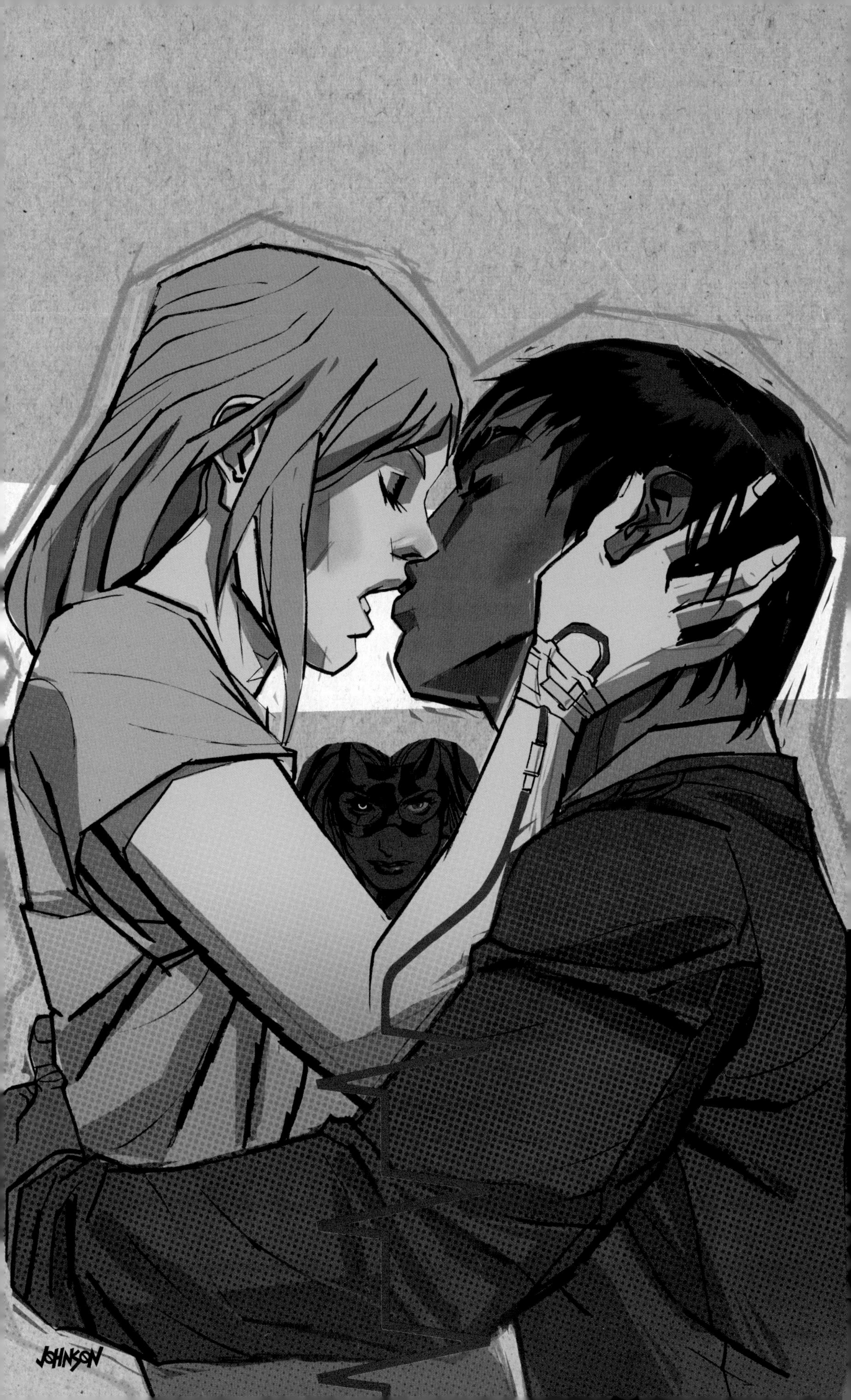
JOHNSON

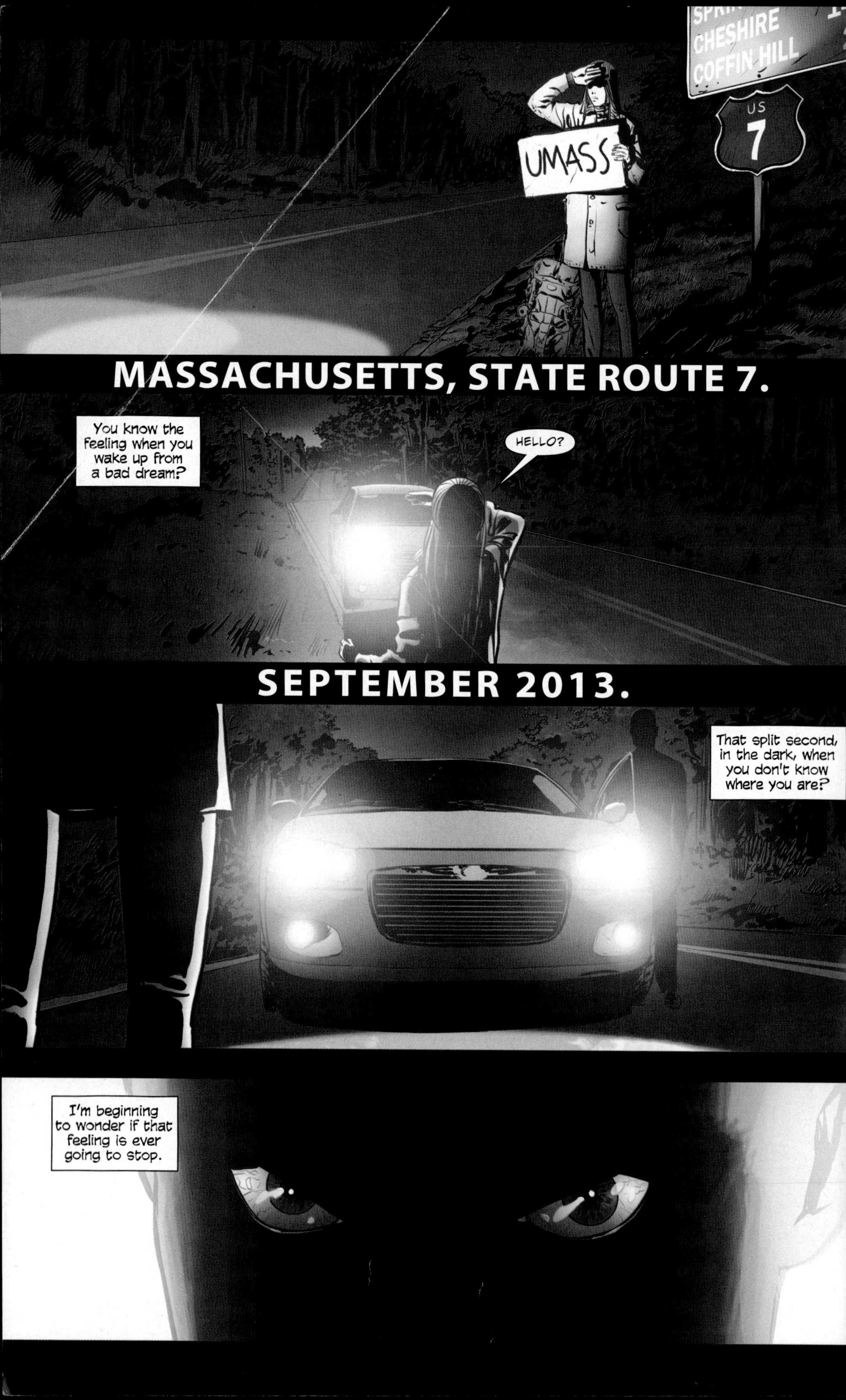
CHESHIRE
COFFIN HILL
US
7
UMASS
MASSACHUSETTS, STATE ROUTE 7.
You know the feeling when you wake up from a bad dream?
HELLO?
SEPTEMBER 2013.
That split second, in the dark, when you don't know where you are?
I'm beginning to wonder if that feeling is ever going to stop.

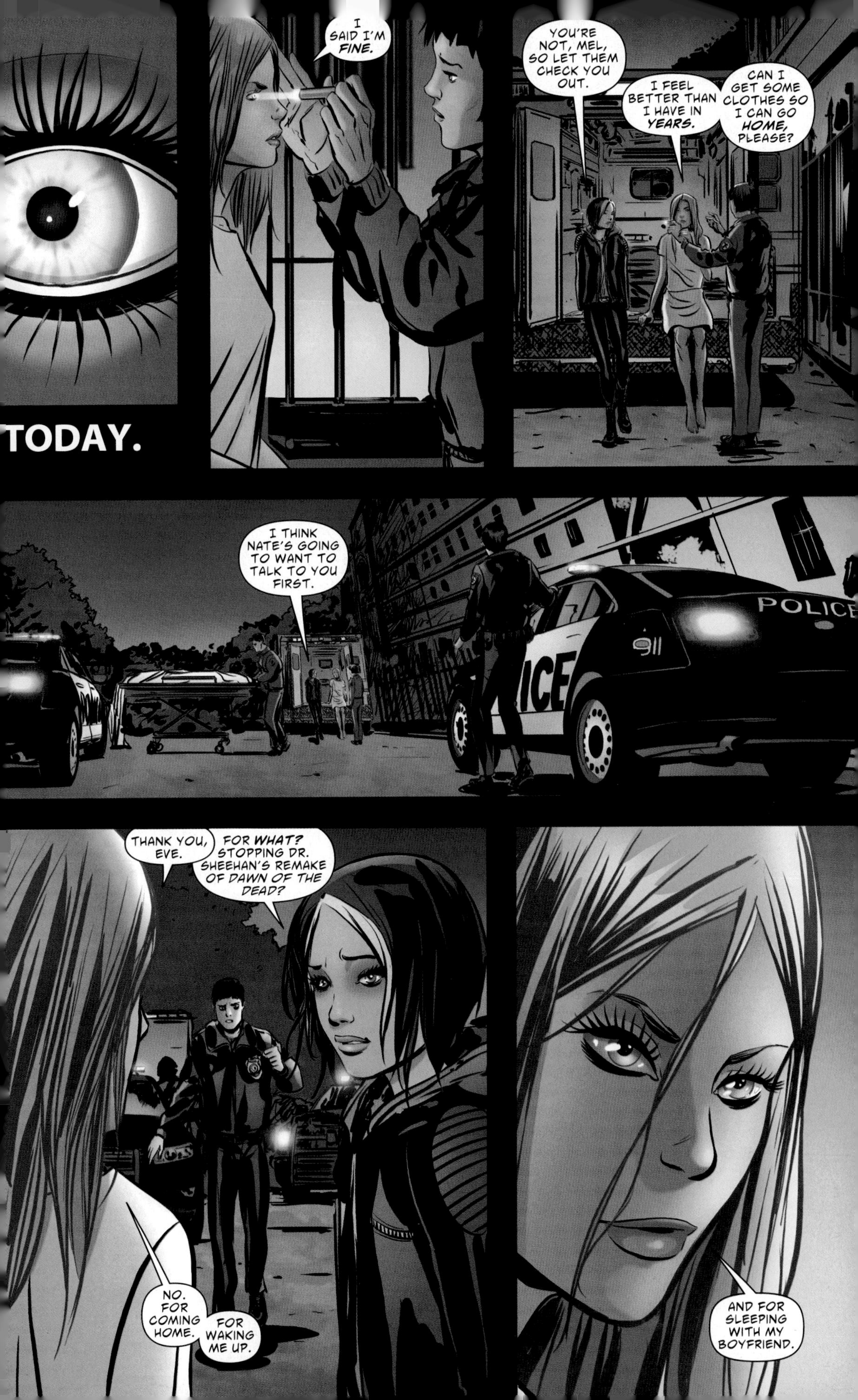

TODAY.
I SAID I'M FINE.
YOU'RE NOT, MEL, SO LET THEM CHECK YOU OUT.
I FEEL BETTER THAN I HAVE IN YEARS.
CAN I GET SOME CLOTHES SO I CAN GO HOME, PLEASE?
I THINK NATE'S GOING TO WANT TO TALK TO YOU FIRST.
POLICE
911
ICE
THANK YOU, EVE.
FOR WHAT? STOPPING DR. SHEEHAN'S REMAKE OF DAWN OF THE DEAD?
NO. FOR COMING HOME.
FOR WAKING ME UP.
AND FOR SLEEPING WITH MY BOYFRIEND.

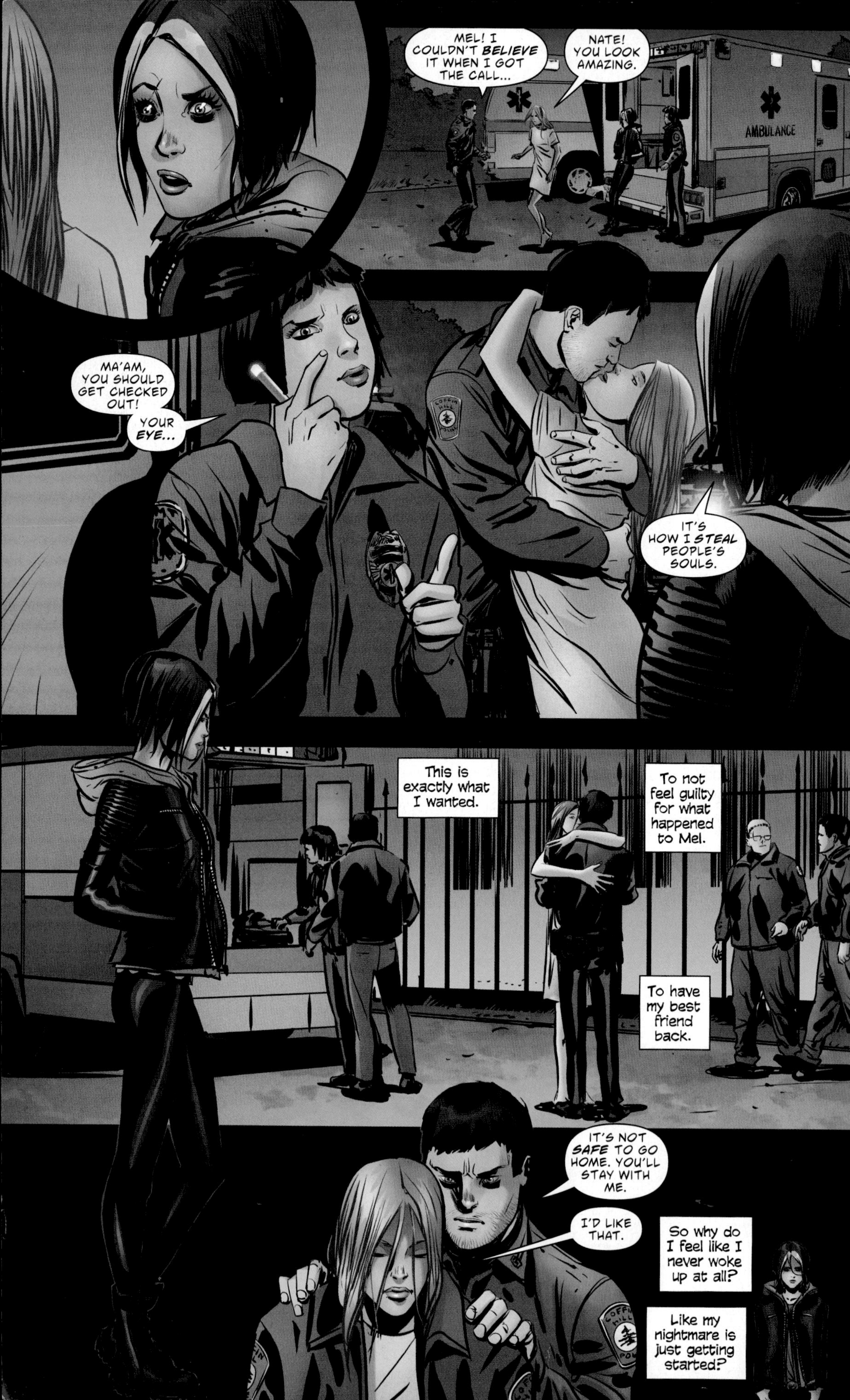
MEL! I COULDN'T BELIEVE IT WHEN I GOT THE CALL...
NATE! YOU LOOK AMAZING.
AMBULANCE
MA'AM, YOU SHOULD GET CHECKED OUT!
YOUR EYE...
IT'S HOW I STEAL PEOPLE'S SOULS.
This is exactly what I wanted.
To not feel guilty for what happened to Mel.
To have my best friend back.
IT'S NOT SAFE TO GO HOME. YOU'LL STAY WITH ME.
I'D LIKE THAT.
So why do I feel like I never woke up at all?
Like my nightmare is just getting started?

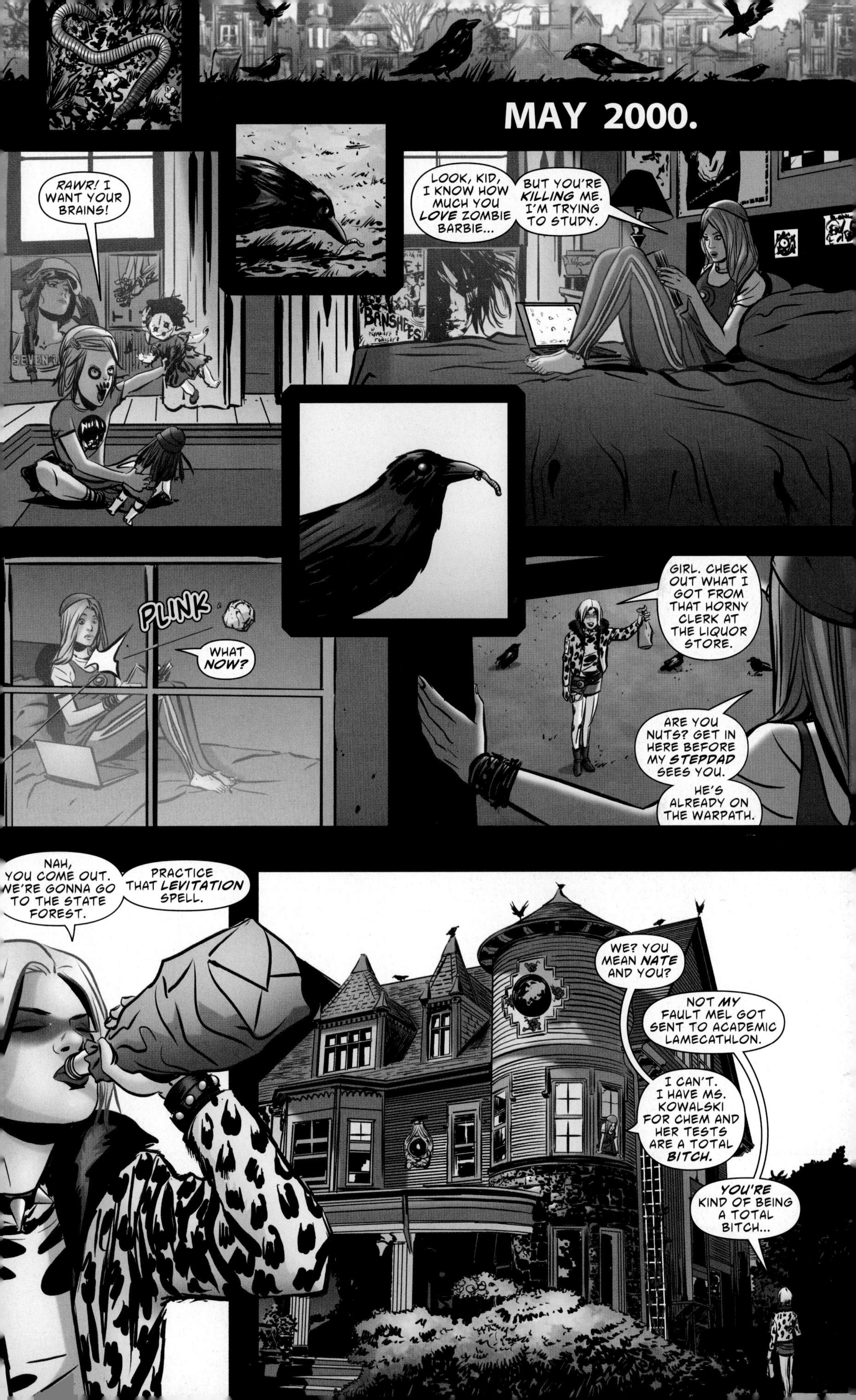
MAY 2000.
RAWR! I WANT YOUR BRAINS!
LOOK, KID, I KNOW HOW MUCH YOU LOVE ZOMBIE BARBIE...
BUT YOU'RE KILLING ME. I'M TRYING TO STUDY.
BANSHEES
PLINK
WHAT NOW?
GIRL. CHECK OUT WHAT I GOT FROM THAT HORNY CLERK AT THE LIQUOR STORE.
ARE YOU NUTS? GET IN HERE BEFORE MY STEPDAD SEES YOU.
HE'S ALREADY ON THE WARPATH.
NAH, YOU COME OUT. WE'RE GONNA GO TO THE STATE FOREST.
PRACTICE THAT LEVITATION SPELL.
WE? YOU MEAN NATE AND YOU?
NOT MY FAULT MEL GOT SENT TO ACADEMIC LAMECATHLON.
I CAN'T. I HAVE MS. KOWALSKI FOR CHEM AND HER TESTS ARE A TOTAL BITCH.
YOU'RE KIND OF BEING A TOTAL BITCH...

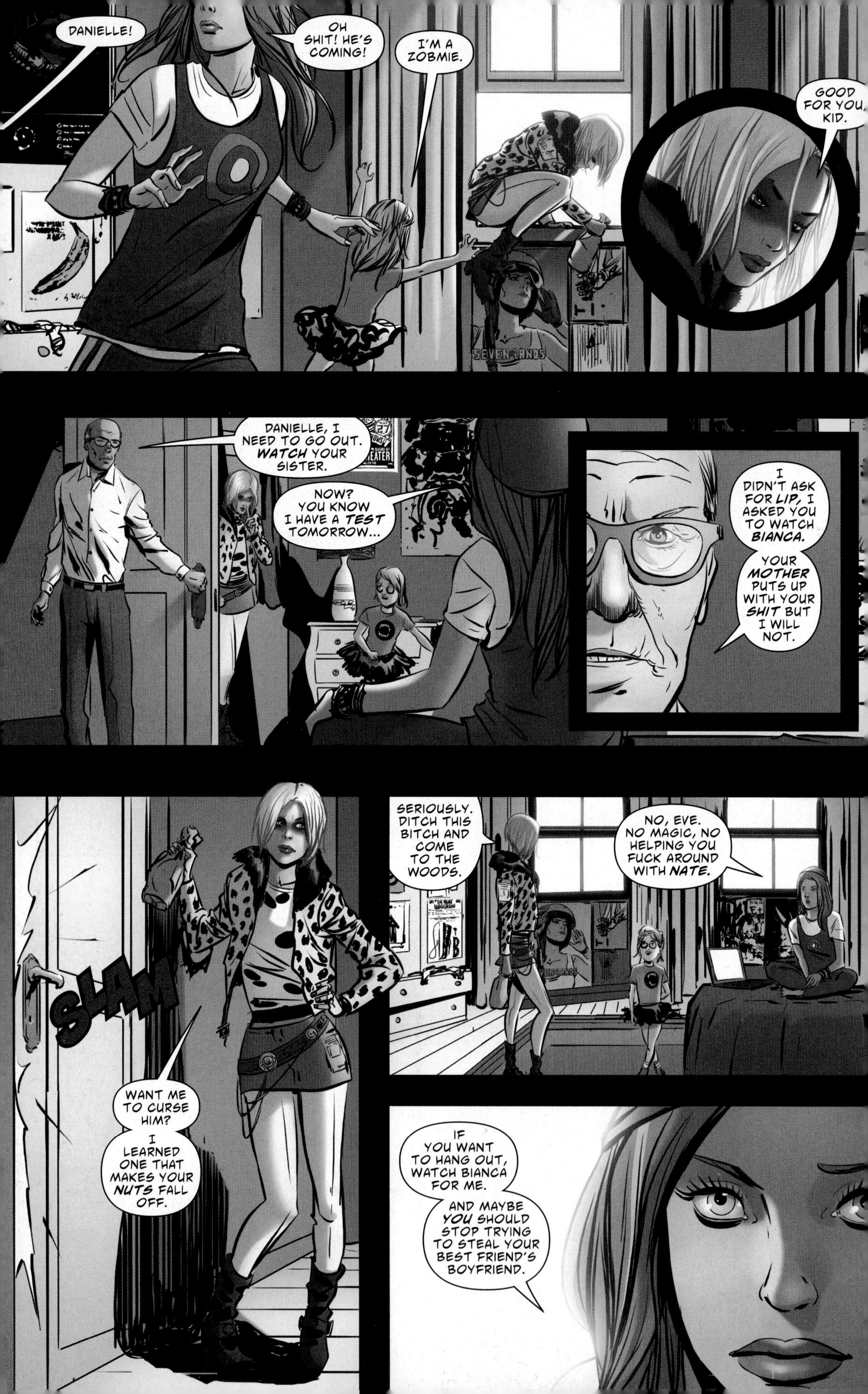
DANIELLE!
OH SHIT! HE'S COMING!
I'M A ZOBMIE.
GOOD FOR YOU, KID.
SEVEN LANDS
DANIELLE, I NEED TO GO OUT. WATCH YOUR SISTER.
NOW? YOU KNOW I HAVE A TEST TOMORROW...
I DIDN'T ASK FOR LIP, I ASKED YOU TO WATCH BIANCA.
YOUR MOTHER PUTS UP WITH YOUR SHIT BUT I WILL NOT.
SLAM
WANT ME TO CURSE HIM?
I LEARNED ONE THAT MAKES YOUR NUTS FALL OFF.
SERIOUSLY. DITCH THIS BITCH AND COME TO THE WOODS.
NO, EVE. NO MAGIC, NO HELPING YOU FUCK AROUND WITH NATE.
IF YOU WANT TO HANG OUT, WATCH BIANCA FOR ME.
AND MAYBE YOU SHOULD STOP TRYING TO STEAL YOUR BEST FRIEND'S BOYFRIEND.

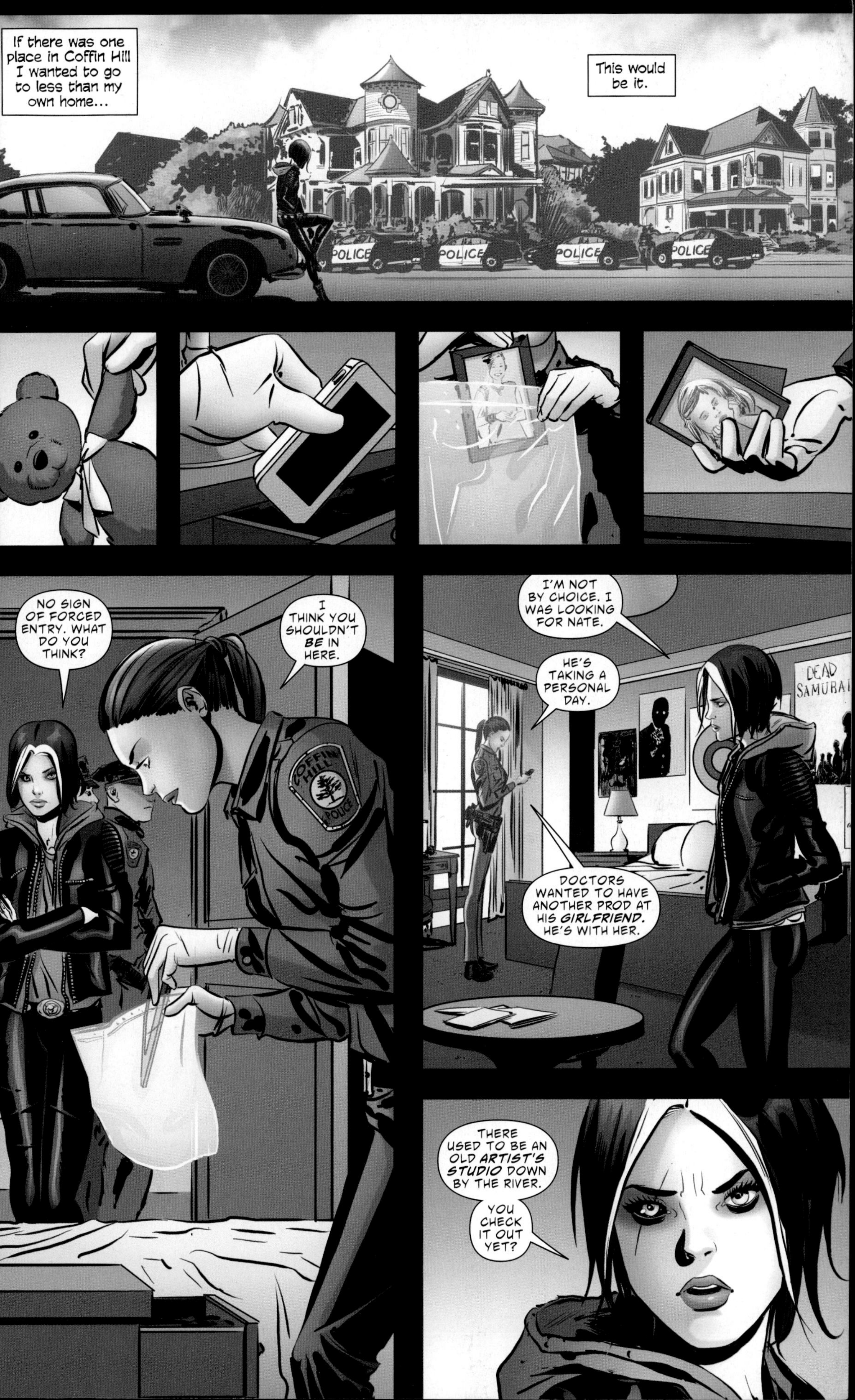
If there was one place in Coffin Hill I wanted to go to less than my own home...
This would be it.
POLICE
POLICE
POLICE
POLICE
NO SIGN OF FORCED ENTRY. WHAT DO YOU THINK?
I THINK YOU SHOULDN'T *BE* IN HERE.
COFFIN HILL POLICE
I'M NOT BY CHOICE. I WAS LOOKING FOR NATE.
HE'S TAKING A PERSONAL DAY.
DOCTORS WANTED TO HAVE ANOTHER PROD AT HIS *GIRLFRIEND*. HE'S WITH HER.
DEAD SAMURAI
THERE USED TO BE AN OLD *ARTIST'S STUDIO* DOWN BY THE RIVER.
YOU CHECK IT OUT YET?

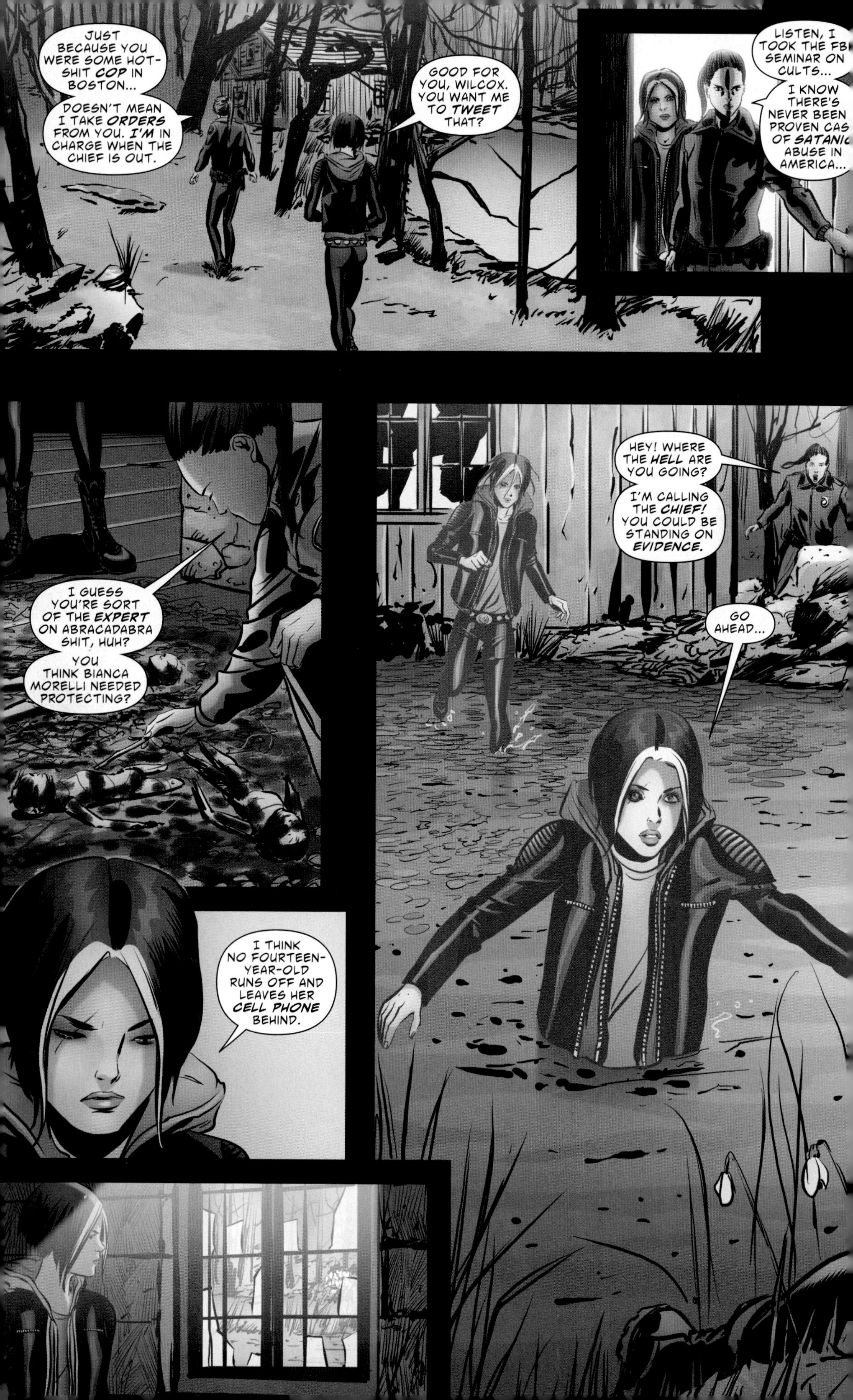
JUST BECAUSE YOU WERE SOME HOT-SHIT COP IN BOSTON...
DOESN'T MEAN I TAKE ORDERS FROM YOU. I'M IN CHARGE WHEN THE CHIEF IS OUT.
GOOD FOR YOU, WILCOX. YOU WANT ME TO TWEET THAT?
LISTEN, I TOOK THE FB SEMINAR ON CULTS...
I KNOW THERE'S NEVER BEEN PROVEN CAS OF SATANIC ABUSE IN AMERICA...
I GUESS YOU'RE SORT OF THE EXPERT ON ABRACADABRA SHIT, HUH?
YOU THINK BIANCA MORELLI NEEDED PROTECTING?
I THINK NO FOURTEEN-YEAR-OLD RUNS OFF AND LEAVES HER CELL PHONE BEHIND.
HEY! WHERE THE HELL ARE YOU GOING?
I'M CALLING THE CHIEF! YOU COULD BE STANDING ON EVIDENCE.
GO AHEAD...

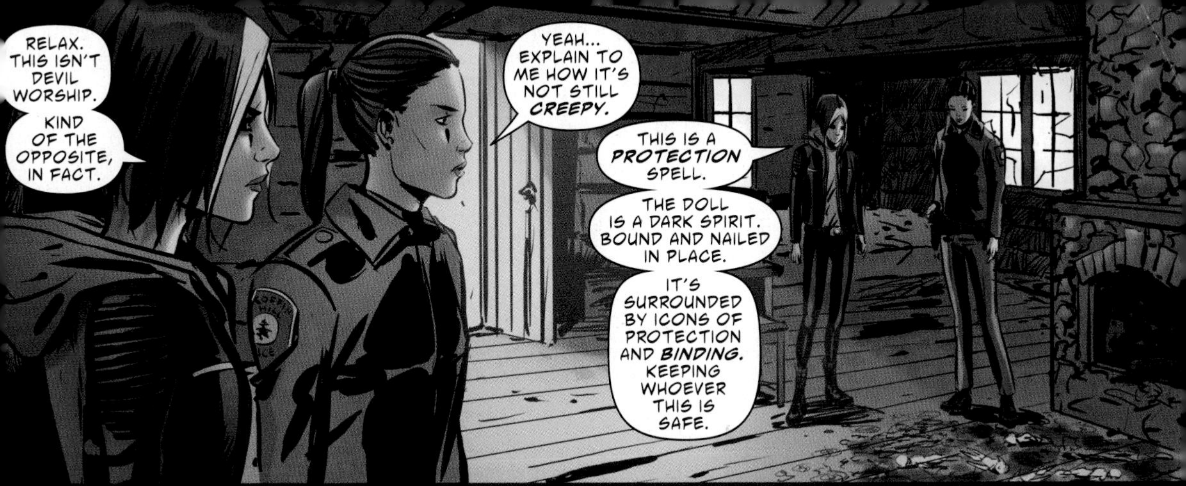
RELAX. THIS ISN'T DEVIL WORSHIP.
KIND OF THE OPPOSITE, IN FACT.
YEAH... EXPLAIN TO ME HOW IT'S NOT STILL CREEPY.
THIS IS A PROTECTION SPELL.
THE DOLL IS A DARK SPIRIT. BOUND AND NAILED IN PLACE.
IT'S SURROUNDED BY ICONS OF PROTECTION AND BINDING. KEEPING WHOEVER THIS IS SAFE.

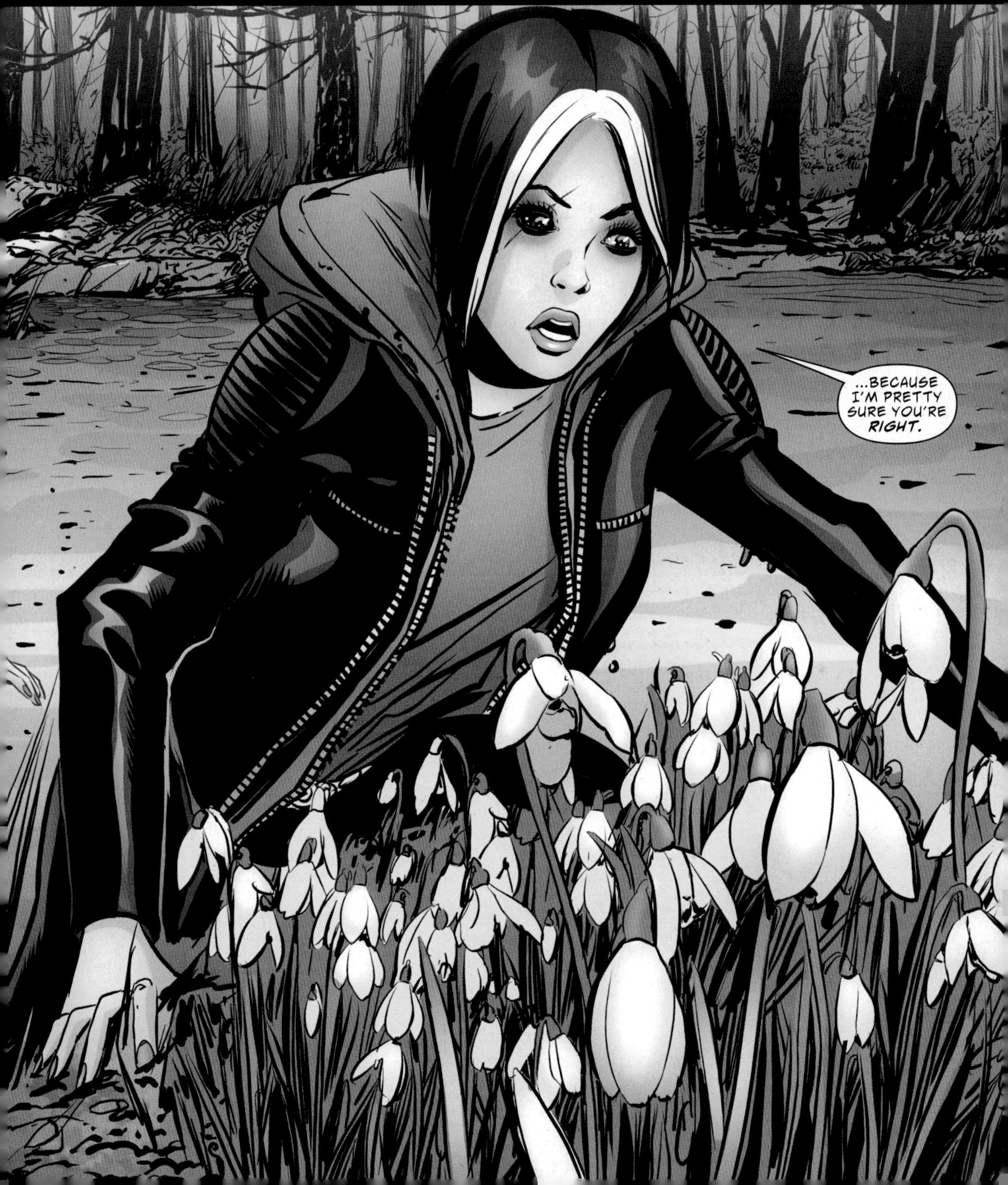
...BECAUSE I'M PRETTY SURE YOU'RE RIGHT.

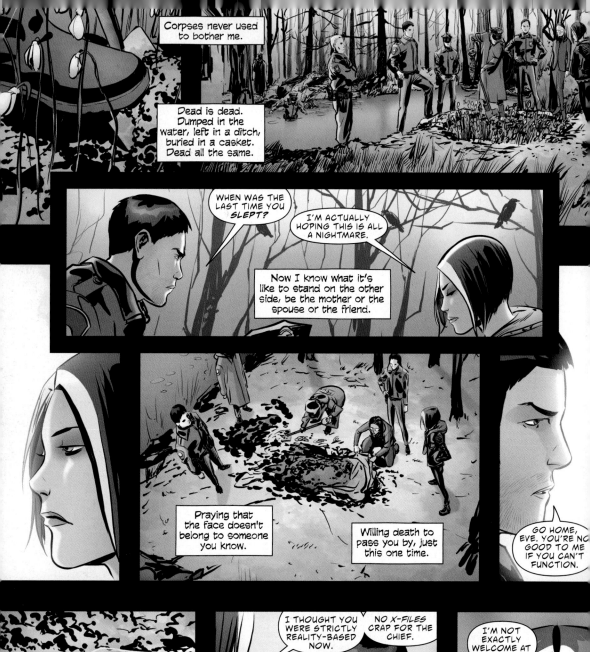

Corpses never used to bother me.

Dead is dead. Dumped in the water, left in a ditch, buried in a casket. Dead all the same.

WHEN WAS THE LAST TIME YOU *SLEPT?*

I'M ACTUALLY HOPING THIS IS ALL A NIGHTMARE.

Now I know what it's like to stand on the other side, be the mother or the spouse or the friend.

Praying that the face doesn't belong to someone you know.

Willing death to pass you by, just this one time.

GO HOME, EVE. YOU'RE NO GOOD TO ME IF YOU CAN'T FUNCTION.

I THOUGHT YOU WERE STRICTLY REALITY-BASED NOW.

NO *X-FILES* CRAP FOR THE CHIEF.

I AM. DOESN'T CHANGE THE FACT WHAT'S GOING ON ISN'T. SO I NEED YOU *SHARP.*

GET SOME REST. I'LL CALL YOU WHEN WE KNOW WHO SHE IS.

I'M NOT EXACTLY WELCOME AT HOME...

BUT NO WORRIES, *CHIEF.* I CAN TAKE CARE OF MYSELF.

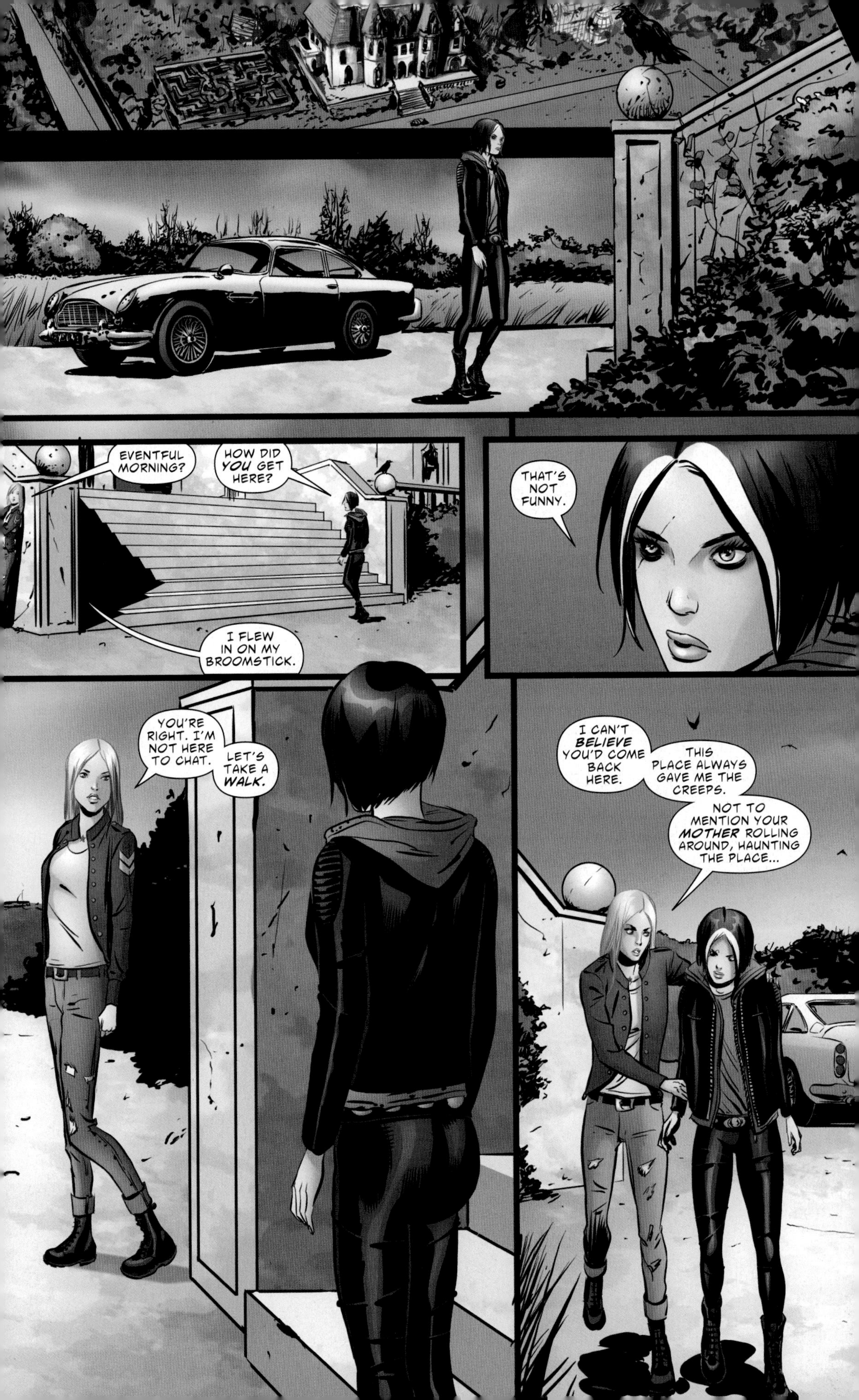
EVENTFUL MORNING?
HOW DID YOU GET HERE?
I FLEW IN ON MY BROOMSTICK.
THAT'S NOT FUNNY.
YOU'RE RIGHT. I'M NOT HERE TO CHAT.
LET'S TAKE A WALK.
I CAN'T BELIEVE YOU'D COME BACK HERE.
THIS PLACE ALWAYS GAVE ME THE CREEPS.
NOT TO MENTION YOUR MOTHER ROLLING AROUND, HAUNTING THE PLACE...

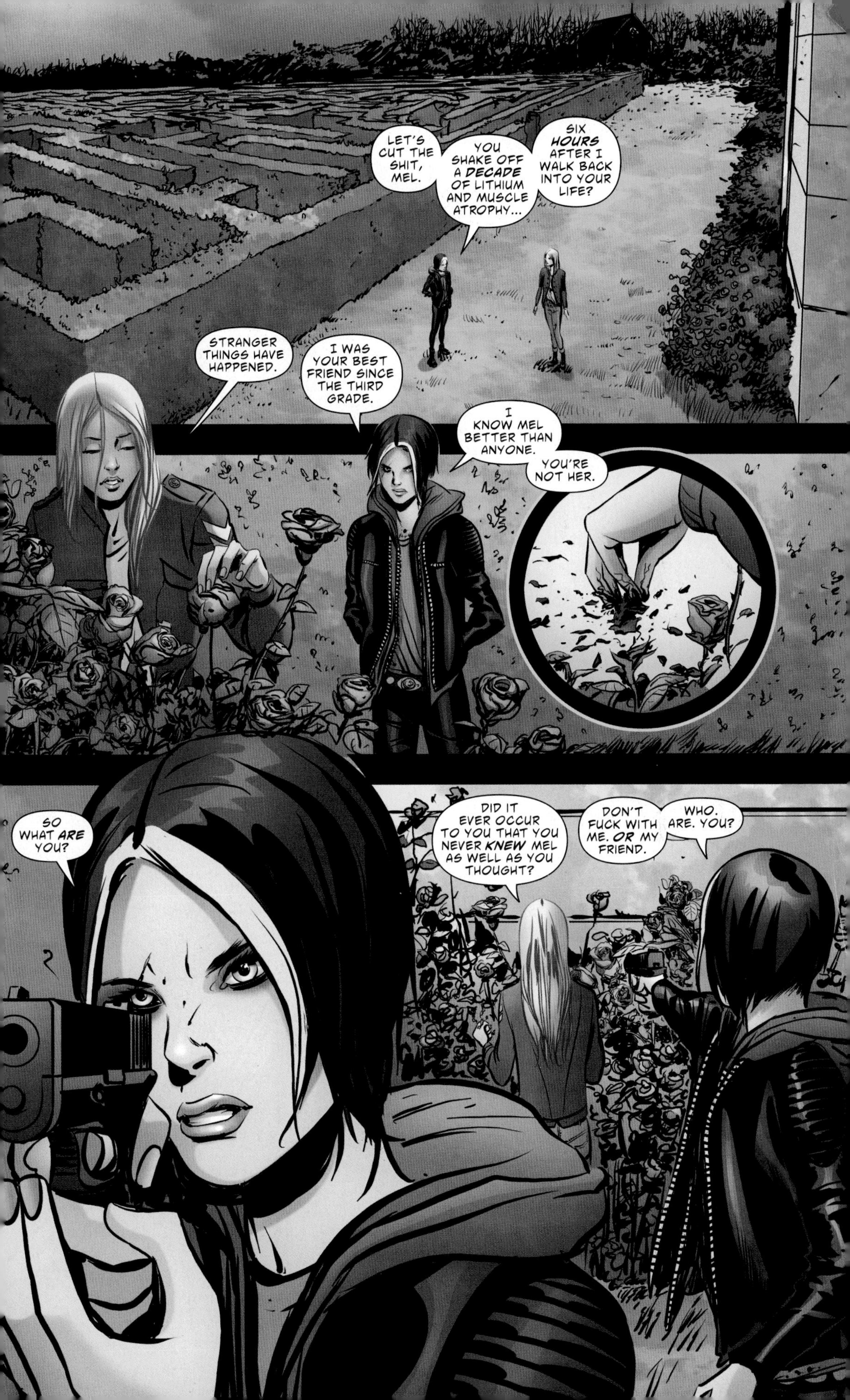
LET'S CUT THE SHIT, MEL.
YOU SHAKE OFF A DECADE OF LITHIUM AND MUSCLE ATROPHY...
SIX HOURS AFTER I WALK BACK INTO YOUR LIFE?
STRANGER THINGS HAVE HAPPENED.
I WAS YOUR BEST FRIEND SINCE THE THIRD GRADE.
I KNOW MEL BETTER THAN ANYONE.
YOU'RE NOT HER.
SO WHAT ARE YOU?
DID IT EVER OCCUR TO YOU THAT YOU NEVER KNEW MEL AS WELL AS YOU THOUGHT?
DON'T FUCK WITH ME. OR MY FRIEND.
WHO. ARE. YOU?

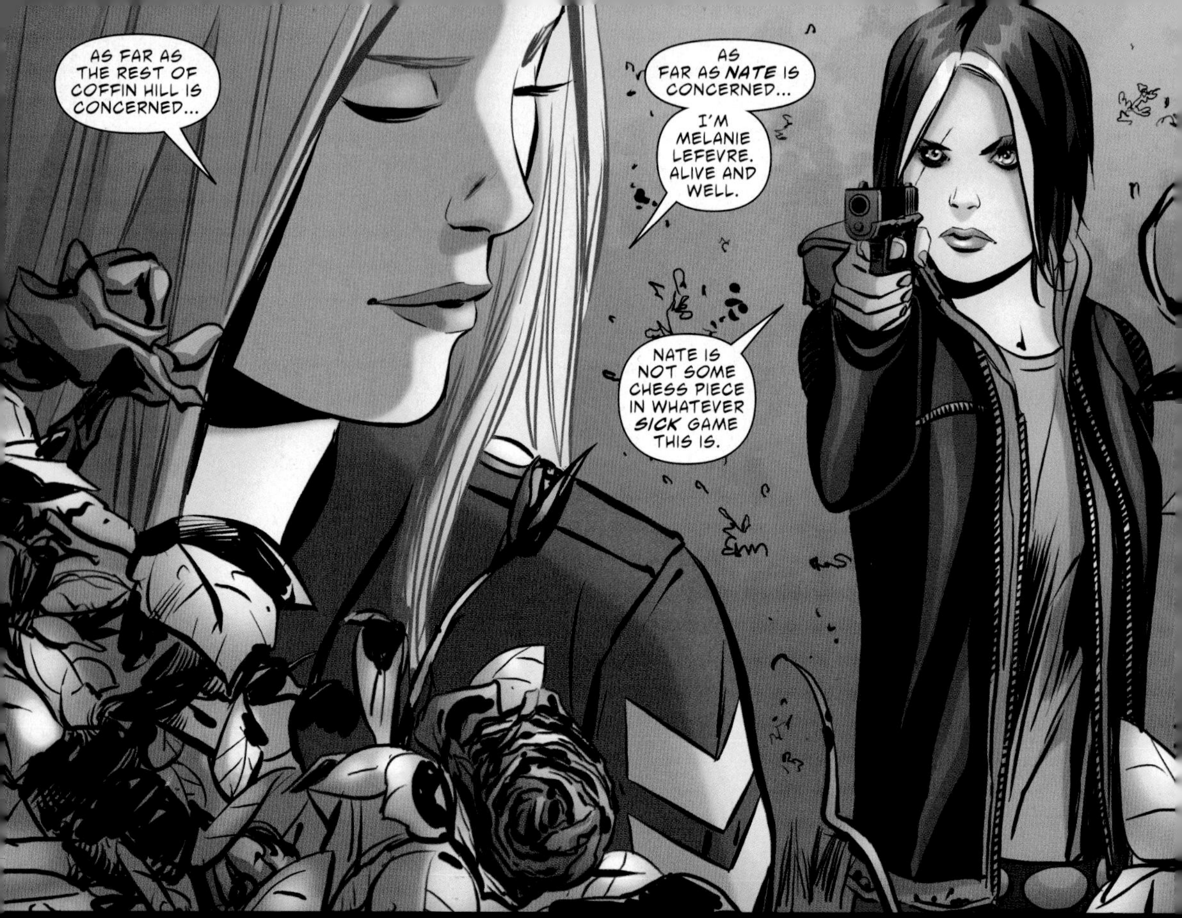
AS FAR AS THE REST OF COFFIN HILL IS CONCERNED...
AS FAR AS NATE IS CONCERNED...
I'M MELANIE LEFEVRE. ALIVE AND WELL.
NATE IS NOT SOME CHESS PIECE IN WHATEVER SICK GAME THIS IS.

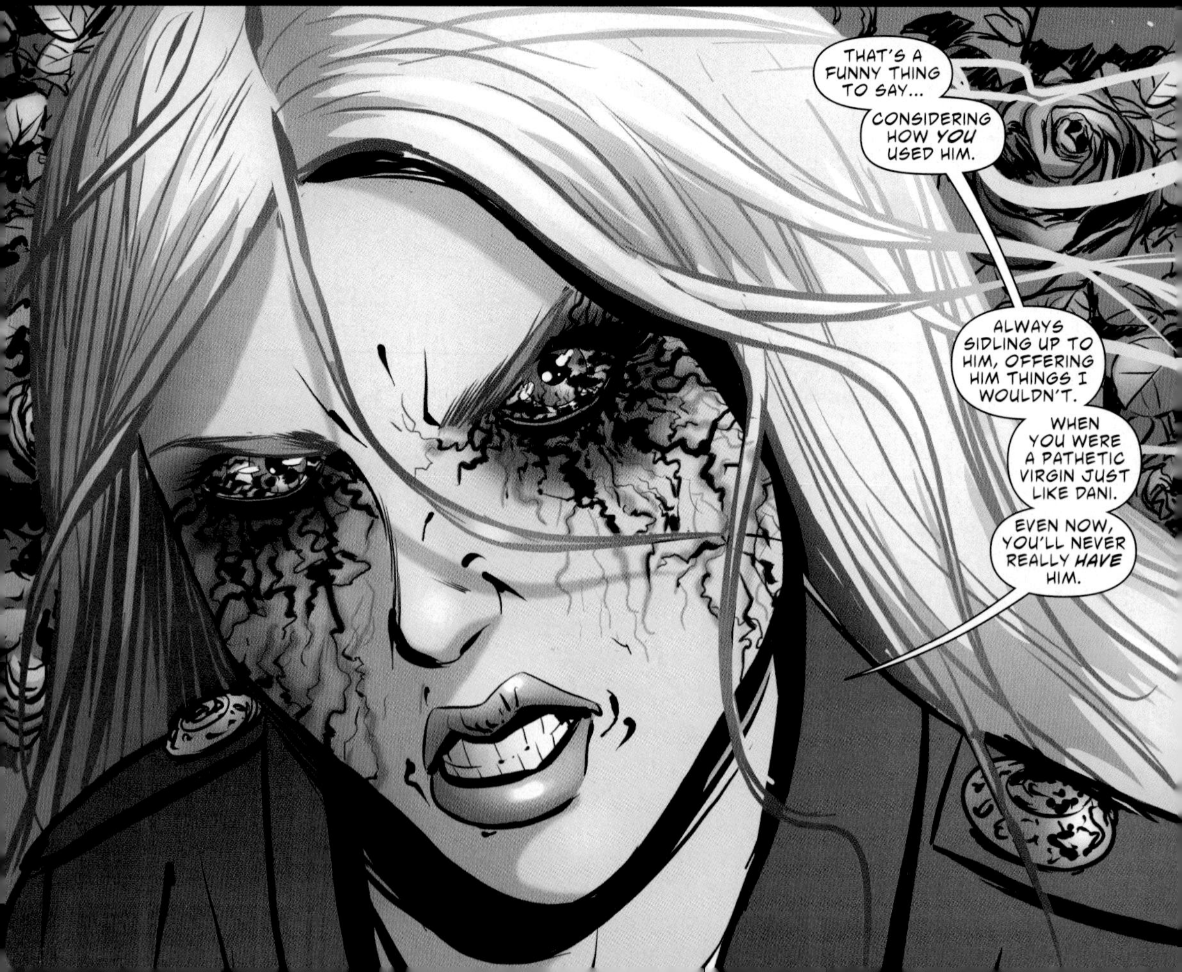
THAT'S A FUNNY THING TO SAY...
CONSIDERING HOW YOU USED HIM.
ALWAYS SIDLING UP TO HIM, OFFERING HIM THINGS I WOULDN'T.
WHEN YOU WERE A PATHETIC VIRGIN JUST LIKE DANI.
EVEN NOW, YOU'LL NEVER REALLY HAVE HIM.

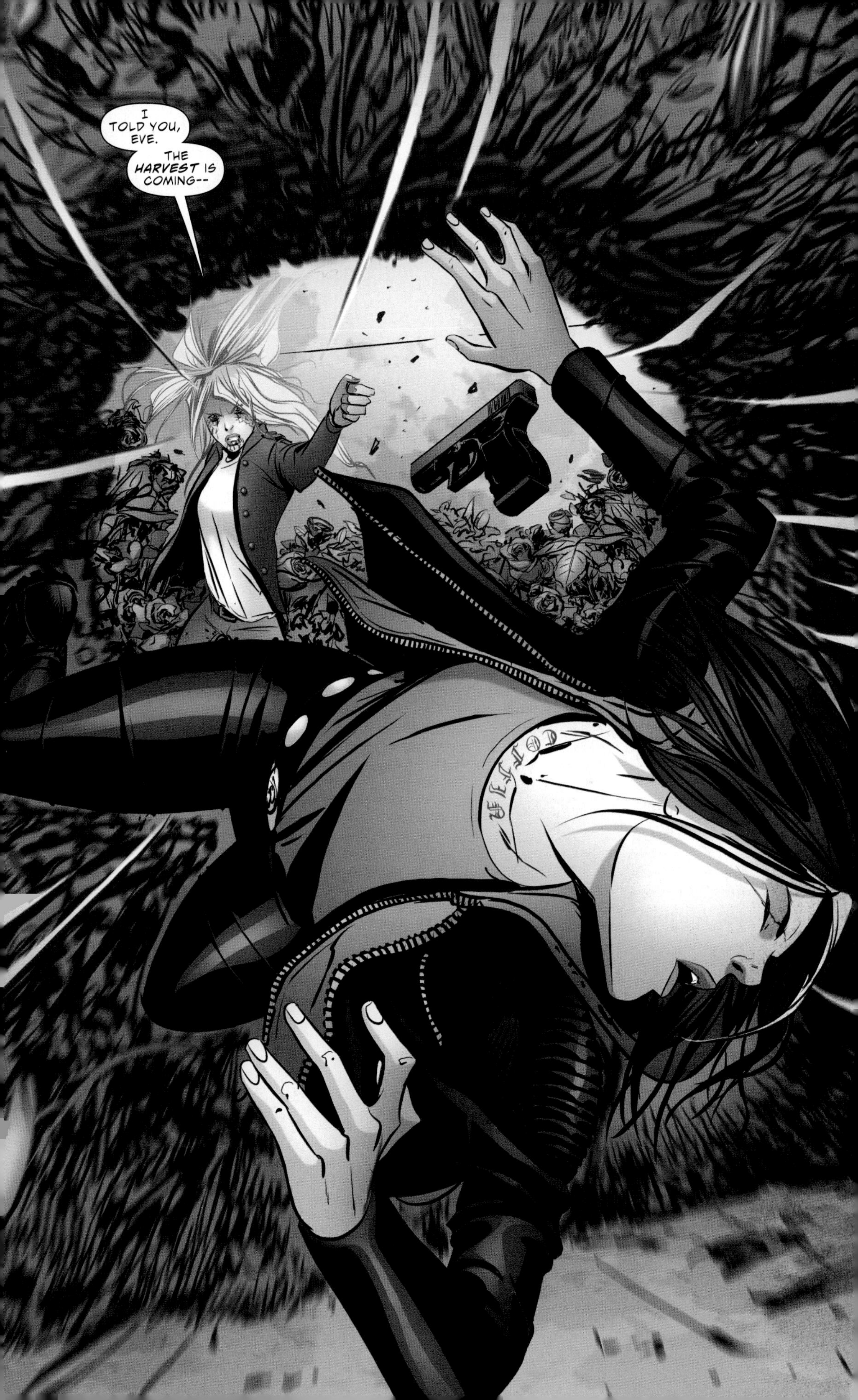
I TOLD YOU, EVE.
THE *HARVEST* IS COMING--

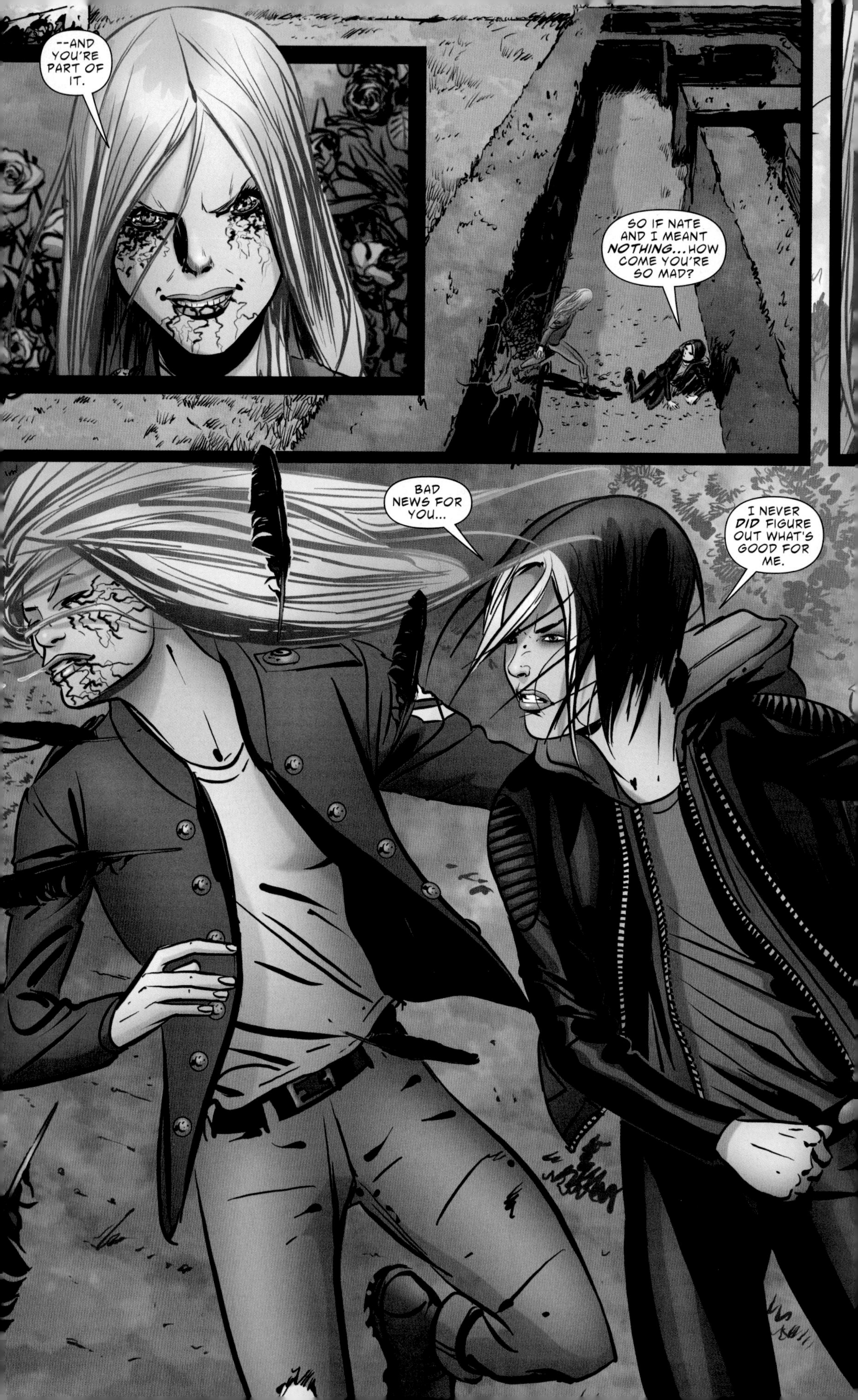
--AND YOU'RE PART OF IT.
SO IF NATE AND I MEANT NOTHING... HOW COME YOU'RE SO MAD?
BAD NEWS FOR YOU...
I NEVER DID FIGURE OUT WHAT'S GOOD FOR ME.

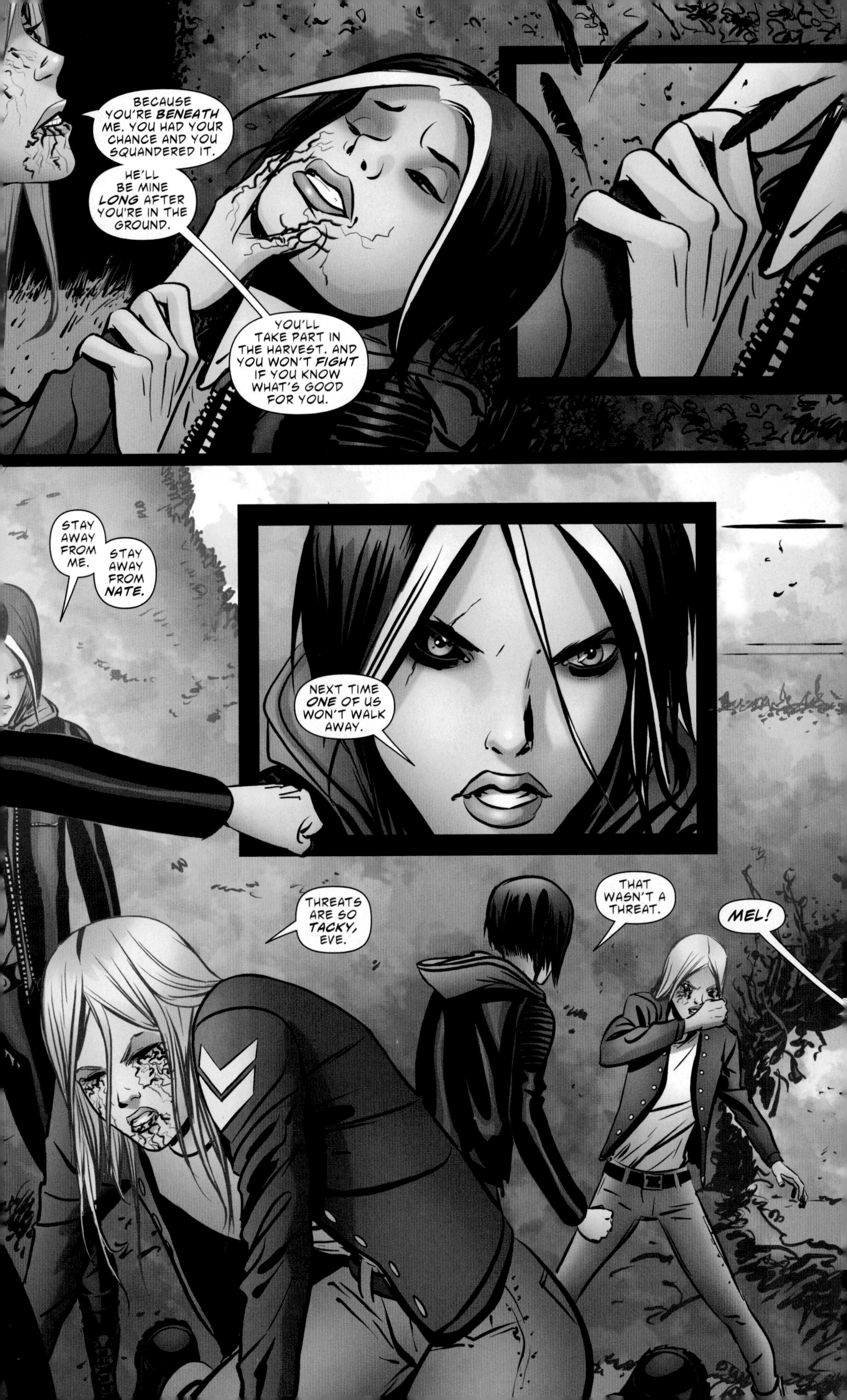
BECAUSE YOU'RE **BENEATH** ME. YOU HAD YOUR CHANCE AND YOU SQUANDERED IT.
HE'LL BE MINE **LONG** AFTER YOU'RE IN THE GROUND.
YOU'LL TAKE PART IN THE HARVEST. AND YOU WON'T **FIGHT** IF YOU KNOW WHAT'S GOOD FOR YOU.
STAY AWAY FROM ME.
STAY AWAY FROM **NATE.**
NEXT TIME **ONE** OF US WON'T WALK AWAY.
THREATS ARE SO **TACKY,** EVE.
THAT WASN'T A THREAT.
MEL!

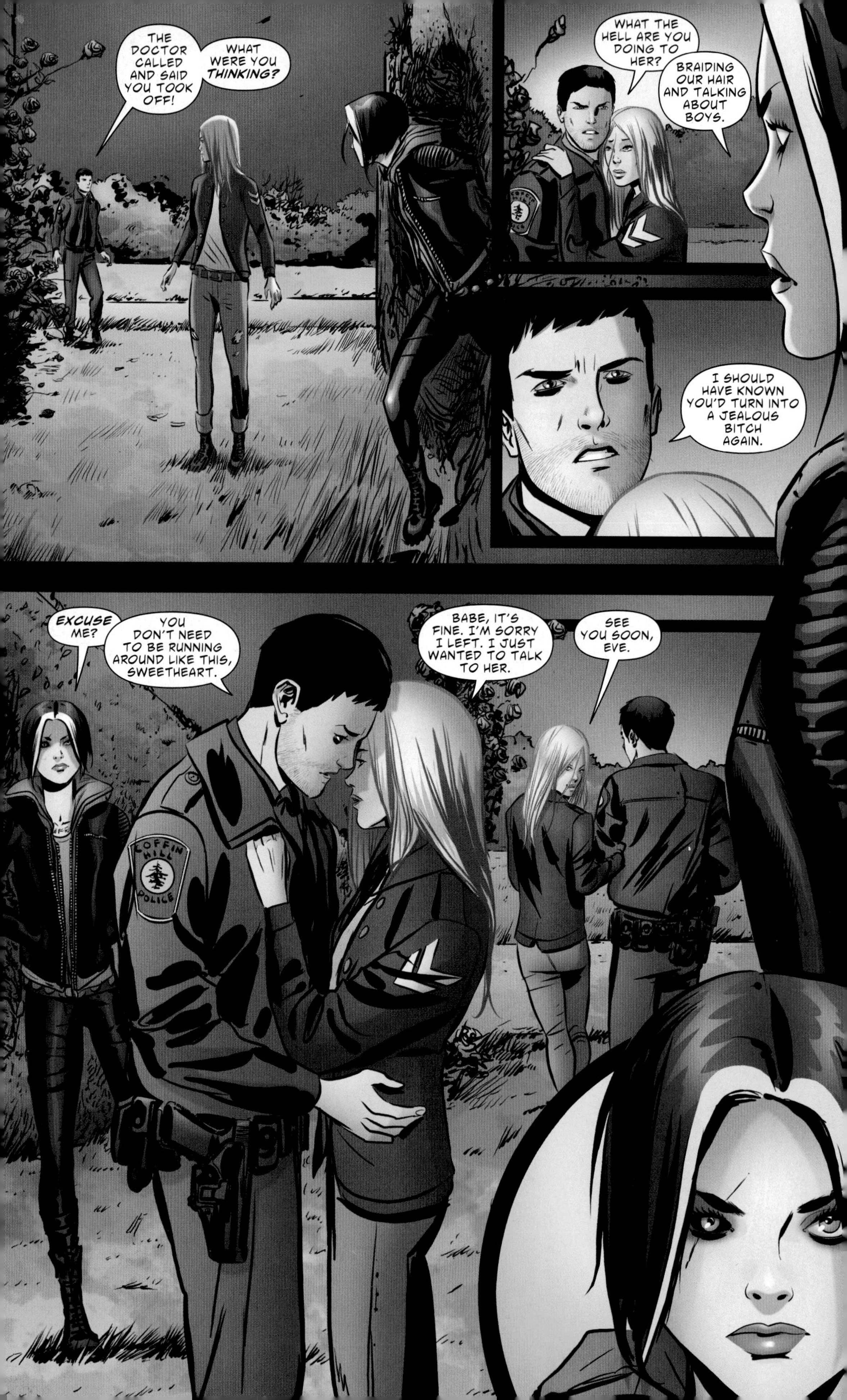
THE DOCTOR CALLED AND SAID YOU TOOK OFF!
WHAT WERE YOU *THINKING?*
WHAT THE HELL ARE YOU DOING TO HER?
BRAIDING OUR HAIR AND TALKING ABOUT BOYS.
I SHOULD HAVE KNOWN YOU'D TURN INTO A JEALOUS BITCH AGAIN.
EXCUSE ME?
YOU DON'T NEED TO BE RUNNING AROUND LIKE THIS, SWEETHEART.
BABE, IT'S FINE. I'M SORRY I LEFT. I JUST WANTED TO TALK TO HER.
SEE YOU SOON, EVE.
COFFIN HILL POLICE

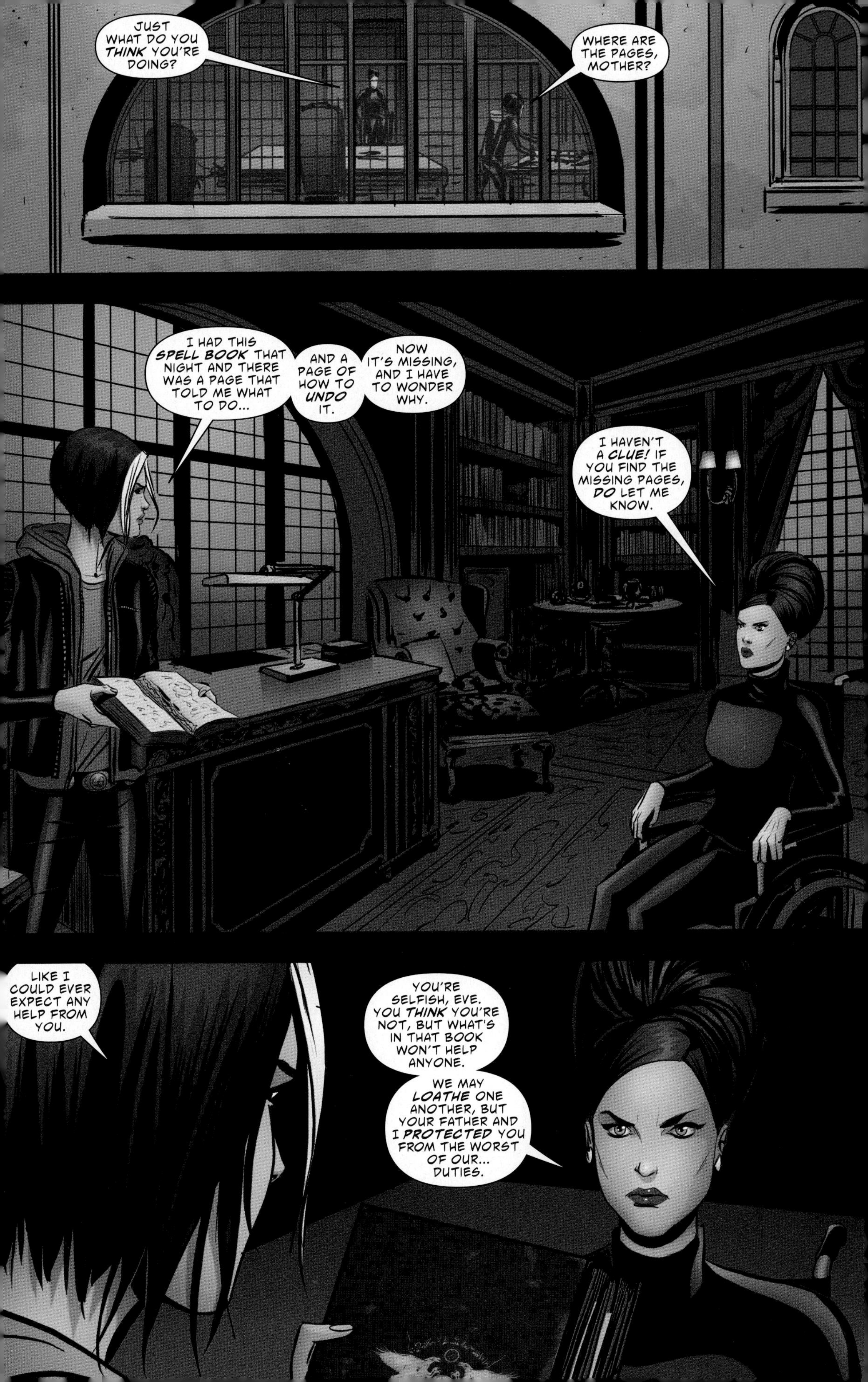
JUST WHAT DO YOU THINK YOU'RE DOING?
WHERE ARE THE PAGES, MOTHER?
I HAD THIS SPELL BOOK THAT NIGHT AND THERE WAS A PAGE THAT TOLD ME WHAT TO DO...
AND A PAGE OF HOW TO UNDO IT.
NOW IT'S MISSING, AND I HAVE TO WONDER WHY.
I HAVEN'T A CLUE! IF YOU FIND THE MISSING PAGES, DO LET ME KNOW.
LIKE I COULD EVER EXPECT ANY HELP FROM YOU.
YOU'RE SELFISH, EVE. YOU THINK YOU'RE NOT, BUT WHAT'S IN THAT BOOK WON'T HELP ANYONE.
WE MAY LOATHE ONE ANOTHER, BUT YOUR FATHER AND I PROTECTED YOU FROM THE WORST OF OUR... DUTIES.

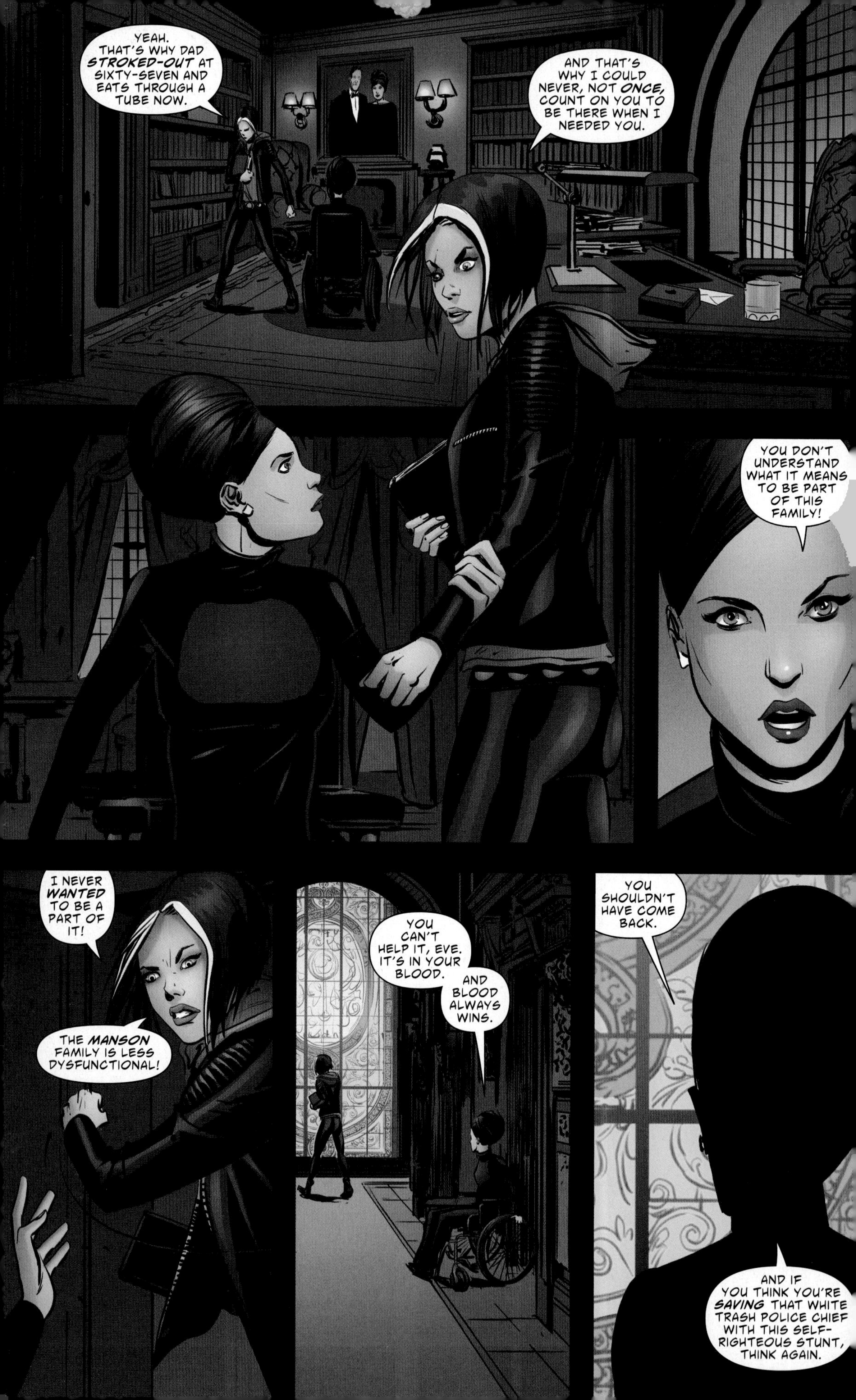
YEAH. THAT'S WHY DAD STROKED-OUT AT SIXTY-SEVEN AND EATS THROUGH A TUBE NOW.
AND THAT'S WHY I COULD NEVER, NOT ONCE, COUNT ON YOU TO BE THERE WHEN I NEEDED YOU.
YOU DON'T UNDERSTAND WHAT IT MEANS TO BE PART OF THIS FAMILY!
I NEVER WANTED TO BE A PART OF IT!
THE MANSON FAMILY IS LESS DYSFUNCTIONAL!
YOU CAN'T HELP IT, EVE. IT'S IN YOUR BLOOD.
AND BLOOD ALWAYS WINS.
YOU SHOULDN'T HAVE COME BACK.
AND IF YOU THINK YOU'RE SAVING THAT WHITE TRASH POLICE CHIEF WITH THIS SELF-RIGHTEOUS STUNT, THINK AGAIN.

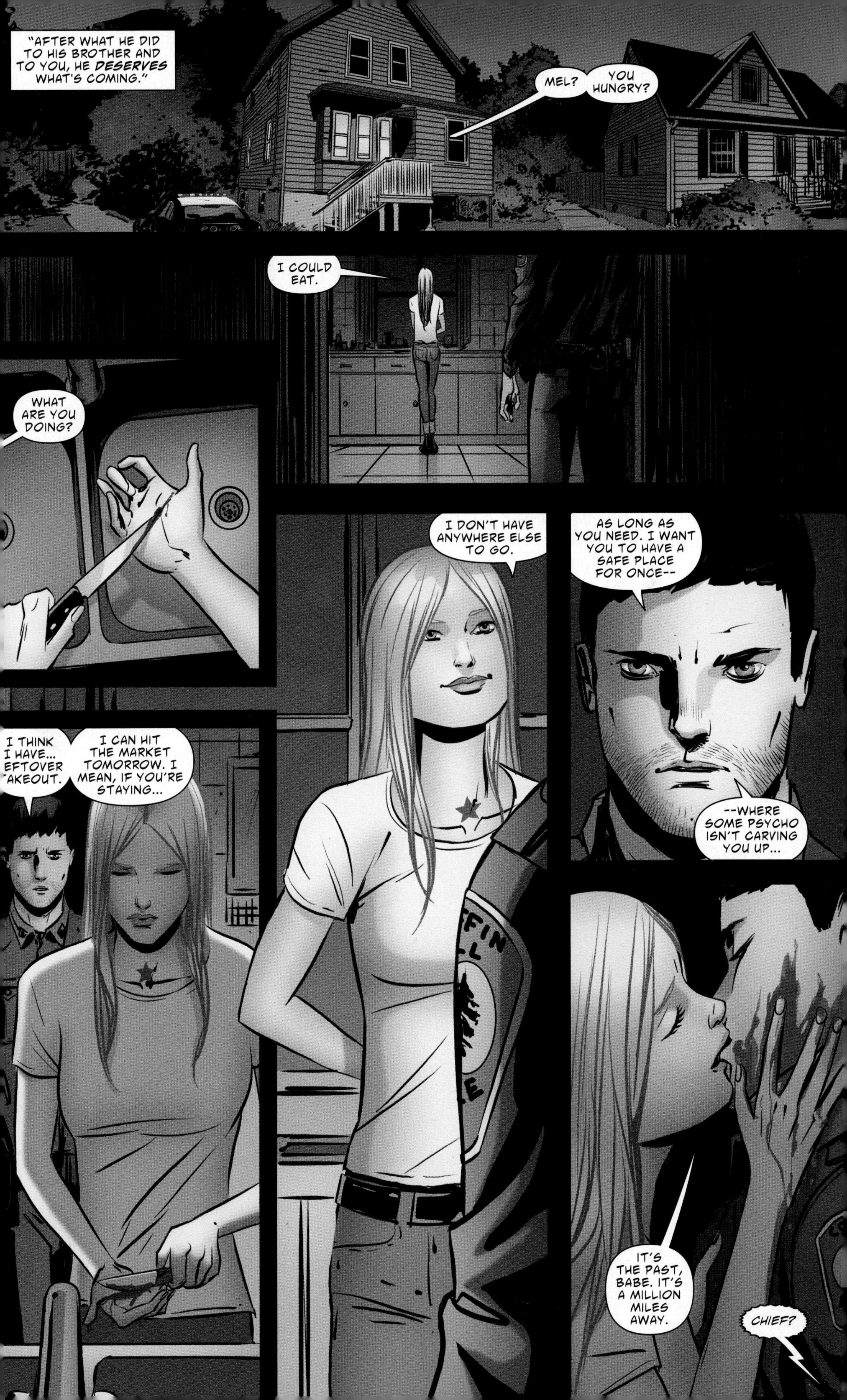
"AFTER WHAT HE DID TO HIS BROTHER AND TO YOU, HE DESERVES WHAT'S COMING."
MEL?
YOU HUNGRY?
I COULD EAT.
WHAT ARE YOU DOING?
I THINK I HAVE... EFTOVER AKEOUT.
I CAN HIT THE MARKET TOMORROW. I MEAN, IF YOU'RE STAYING...
I DON'T HAVE ANYWHERE ELSE TO GO.
AS LONG AS YOU NEED. I WANT YOU TO HAVE A SAFE PLACE FOR ONCE--
--WHERE SOME PSYCHO ISN'T CARVING YOU UP...
IT'S THE PAST, BABE. IT'S A MILLION MILES AWAY.
CHIEF?

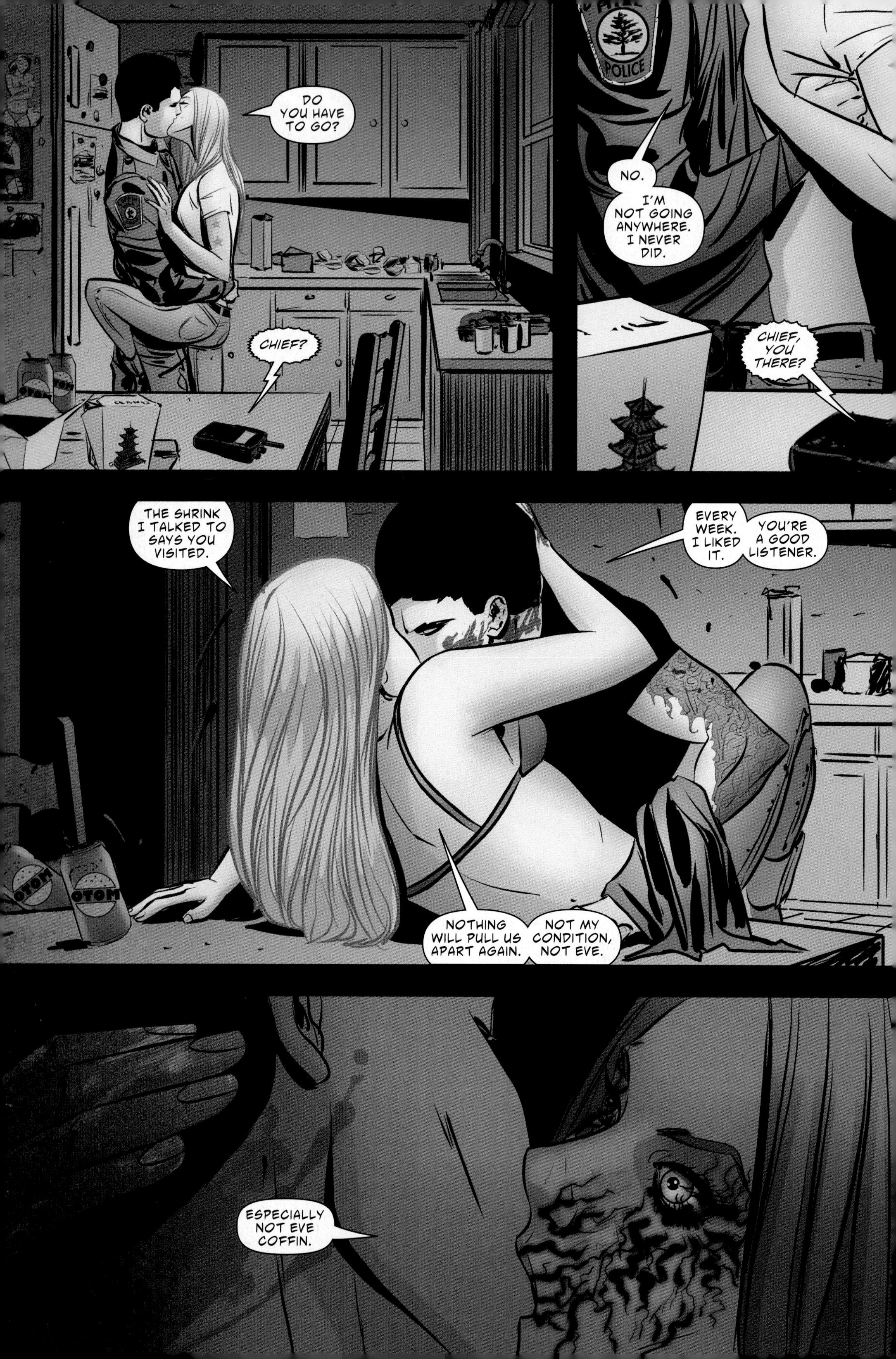
DO YOU HAVE TO GO?
CHIEF?
POLICE
NO.
I'M NOT GOING ANYWHERE. I NEVER DID.
CHIEF, YOU THERE?
THE SHRINK I TALKED TO SAYS YOU VISITED.
EVERY WEEK. I LIKED IT.
YOU'RE A GOOD LISTENER.
NOTHING WILL PULL US APART AGAIN.
NOT MY CONDITION, NOT EVE.
ESPECIALLY NOT EVE COFFIN.

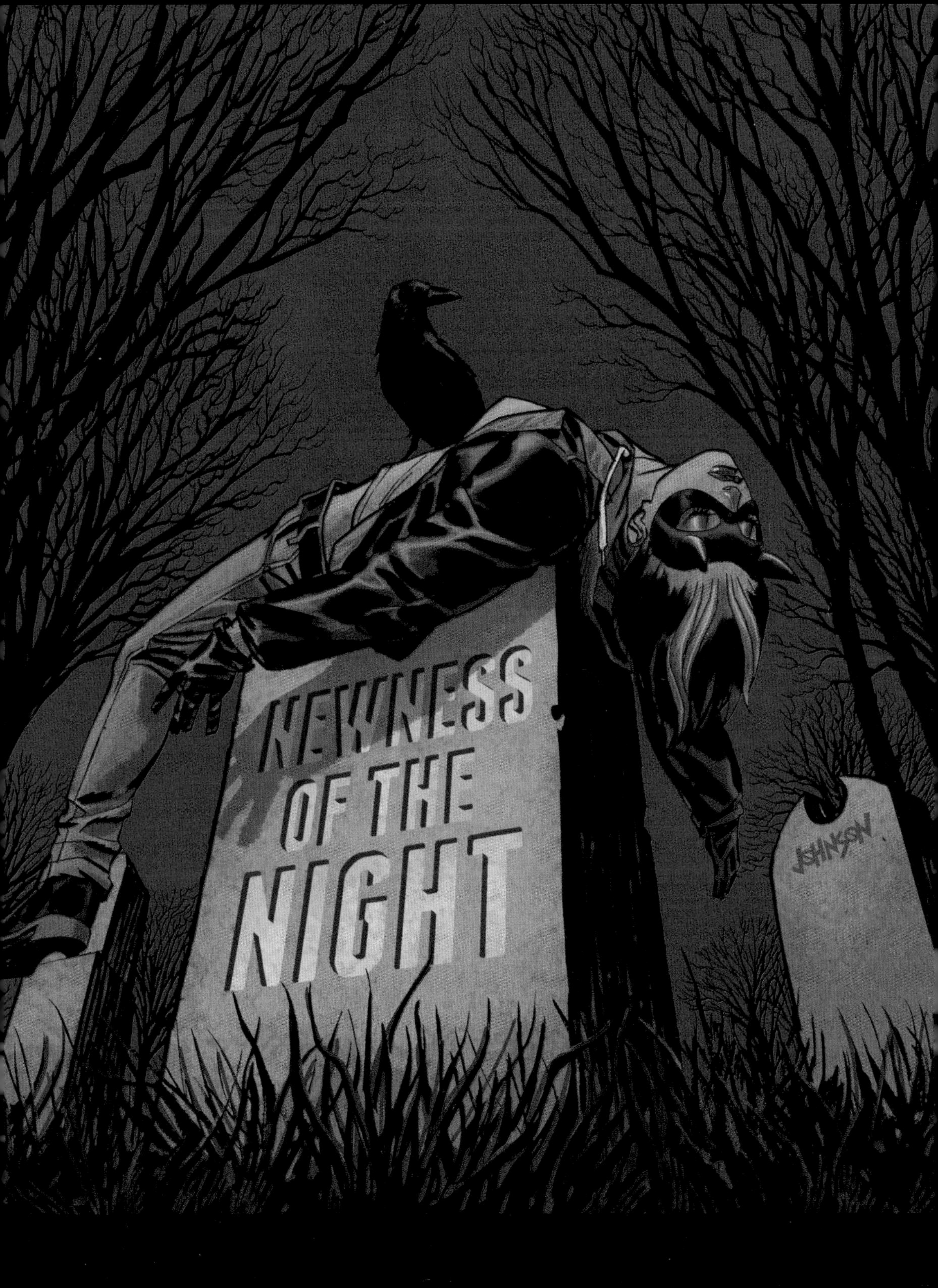
NEWNESS OF THE NIGHT
JOHNSON

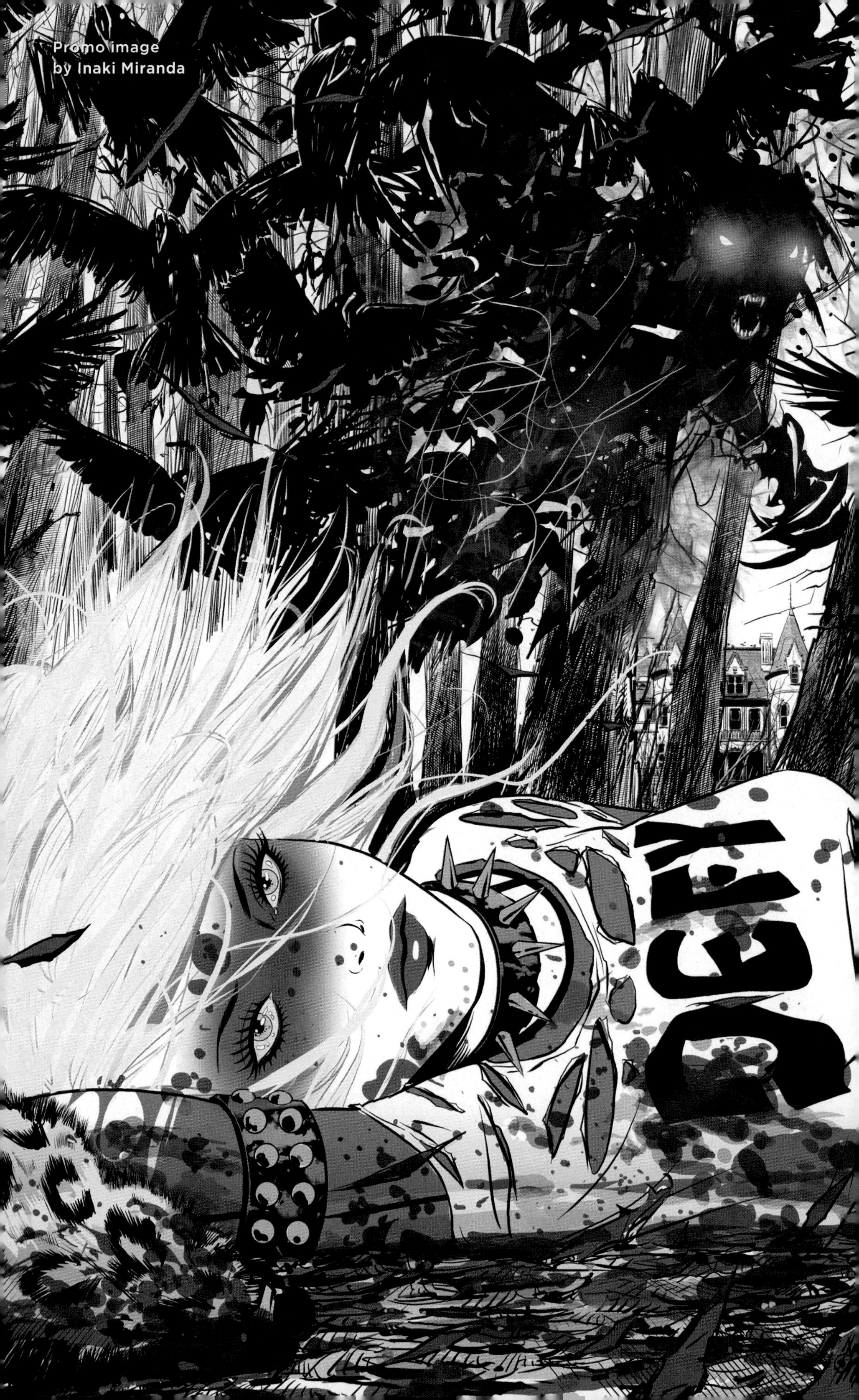

Promo image
by Inaki Miranda

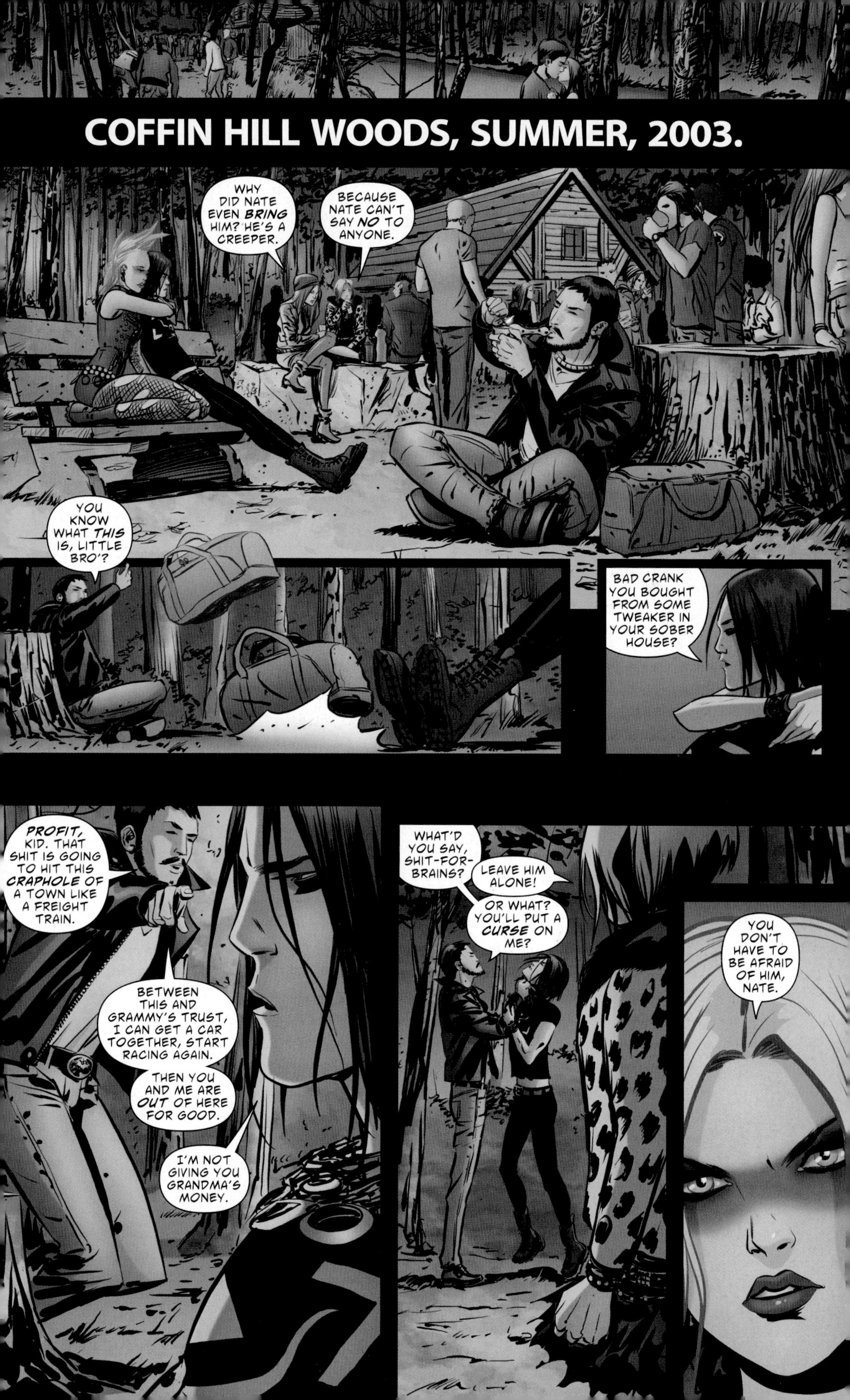
COFFIN HILL WOODS, SUMMER, 2003.
WHY DID NATE EVEN BRING HIM? HE'S A CREEPER.
BECAUSE NATE CAN'T SAY NO TO ANYONE.
YOU KNOW WHAT THIS IS, LITTLE BRO'?
BAD CRANK YOU BOUGHT FROM SOME TWEAKER IN YOUR SOBER HOUSE?
PROFIT, KID. THAT SHIT IS GOING TO HIT THIS CRAPHOLE OF A TOWN LIKE A FREIGHT TRAIN.
BETWEEN THIS AND GRAMMY'S TRUST, I CAN GET A CAR TOGETHER, START RACING AGAIN.
THEN YOU AND ME ARE OUT OF HERE FOR GOOD.
I'M NOT GIVING YOU GRANDMA'S MONEY.
WHAT'D YOU SAY, SHIT-FOR-BRAINS?
LEAVE HIM ALONE!
OR WHAT? YOU'LL PUT A CURSE ON ME?
YOU DON'T HAVE TO BE AFRAID OF HIM, NATE.

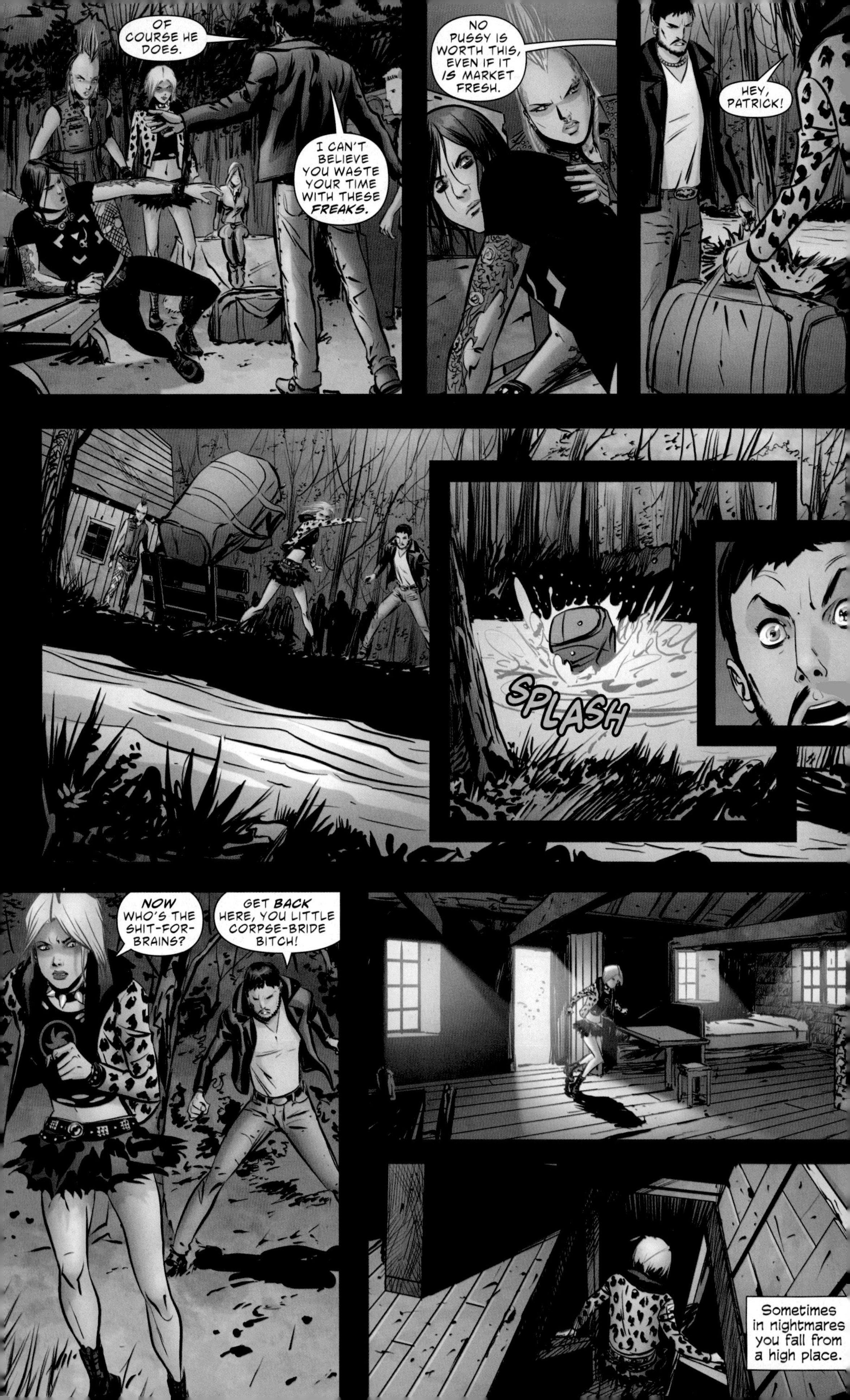
OF COURSE HE DOES.
I CAN'T BELIEVE YOU WASTE YOUR TIME WITH THESE FREAKS.
NO PUSSY IS WORTH THIS, EVEN IF IT IS MARKET FRESH.
HEY, PATRICK!
SPLASH
NOW WHO'S THE SHIT-FOR-BRAINS?
GET BACK HERE, YOU LITTLE CORPSE-BRIDE BITCH!
Sometimes in nightmares you fall from a high place.

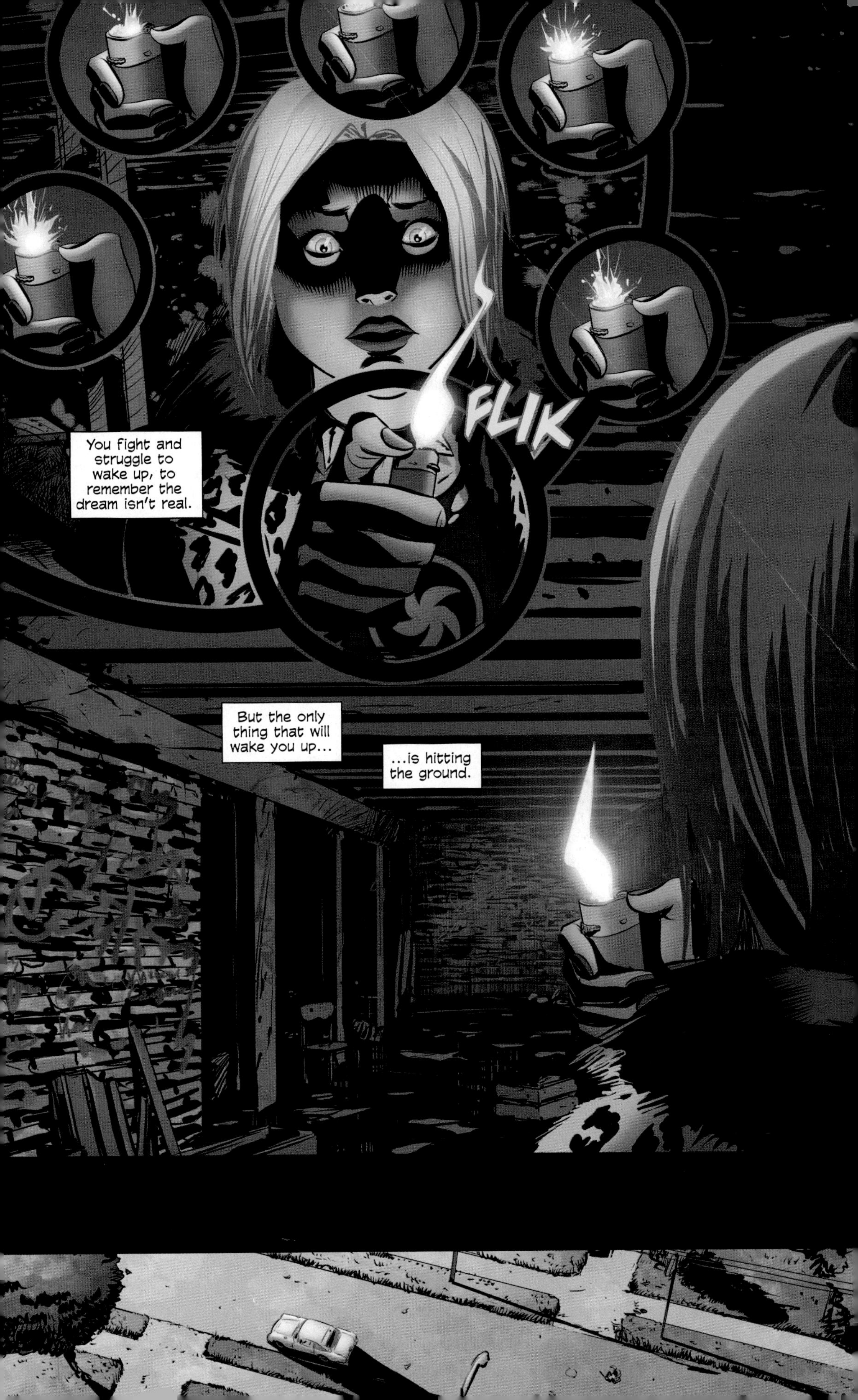
FLIK
You fight and struggle to wake up, to remember the dream isn't real.
But the only thing that will wake you up...
...is hitting the ground.

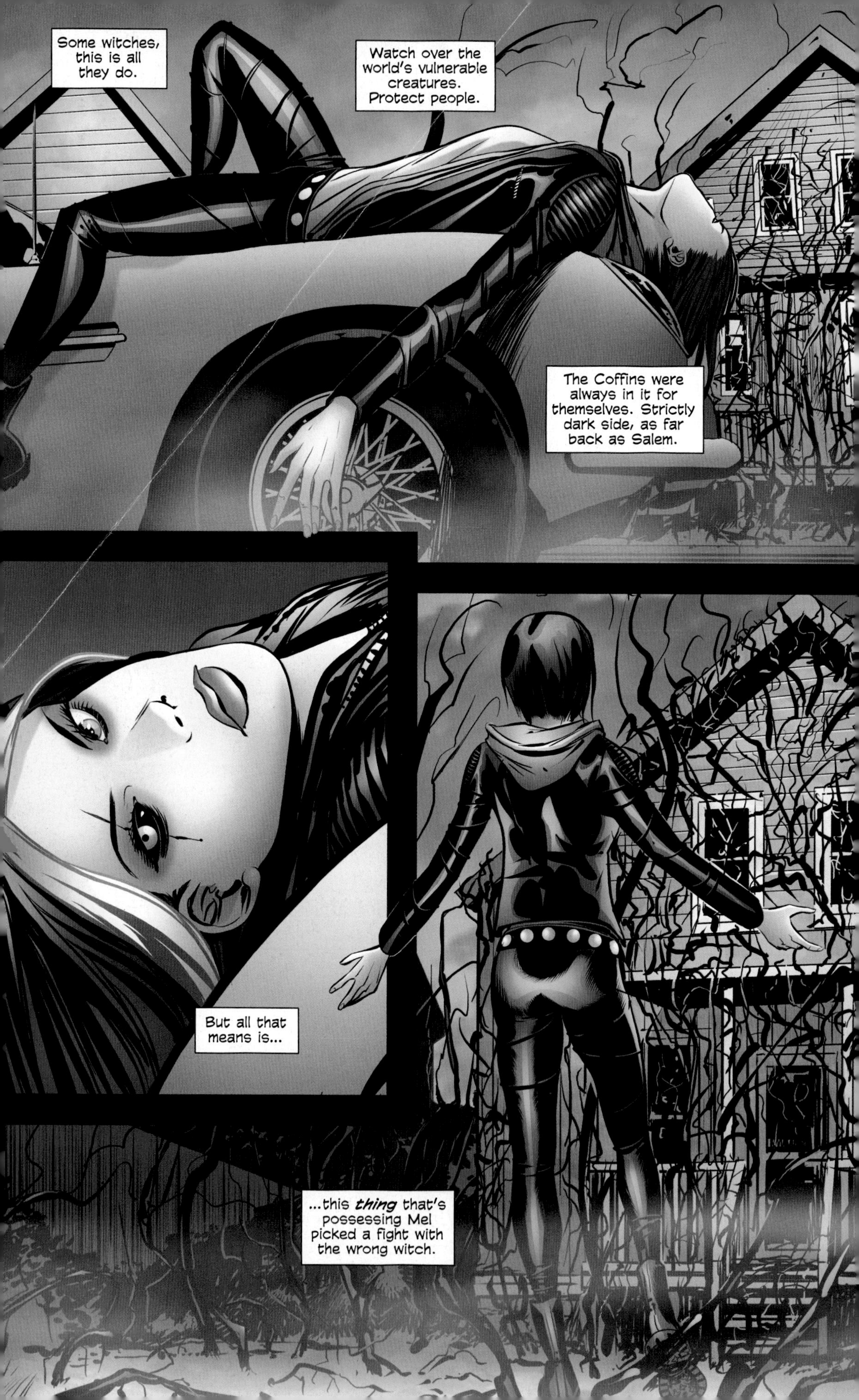
Some witches, this is all they do.
Watch over the world's vulnerable creatures. Protect people.
The Coffins were always in it for themselves. Strictly dark side, as far back as Salem.
But all that means is...
...this *thing* that's possessing Mel picked a fight with the wrong witch.

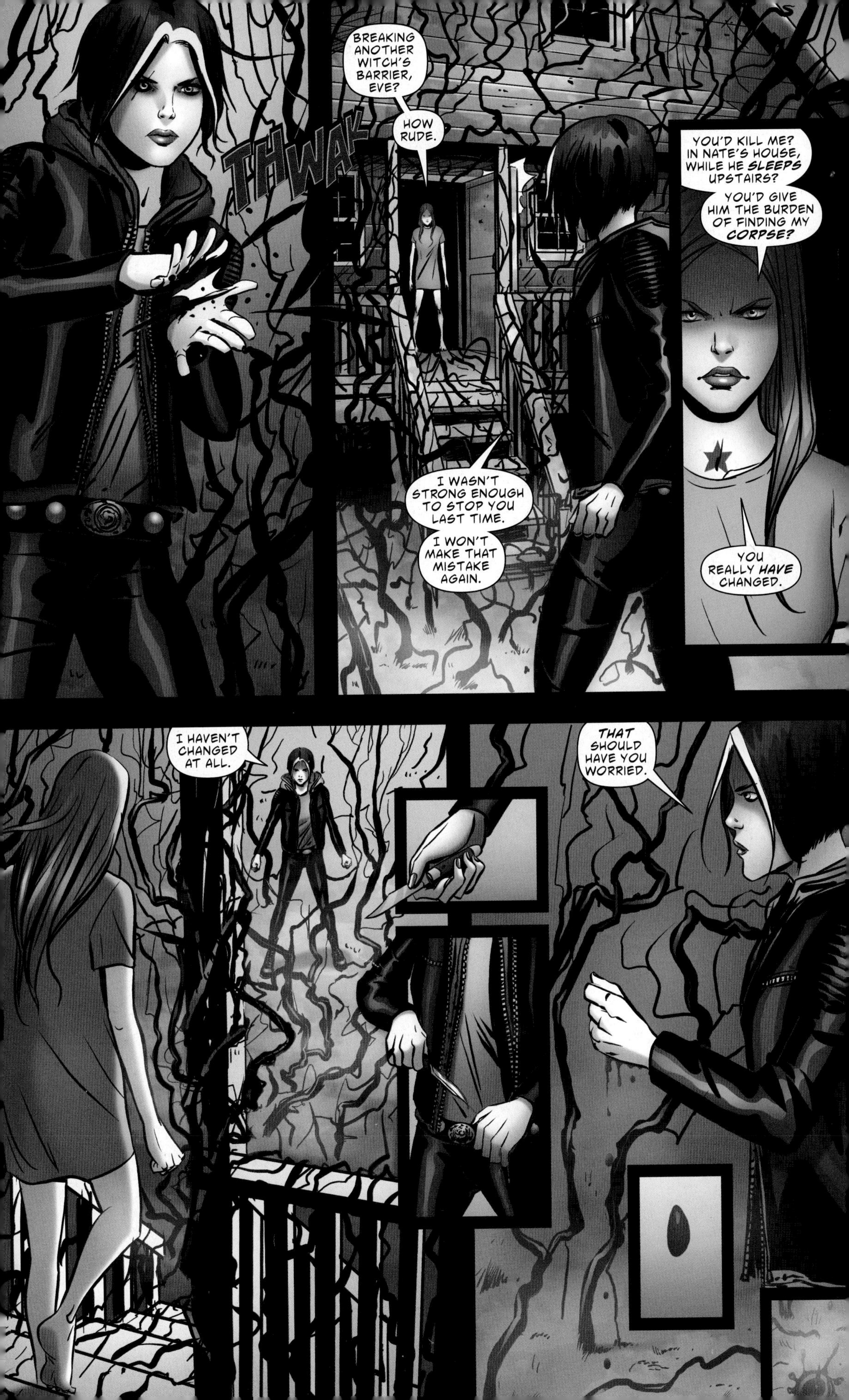
THWAK
BREAKING ANOTHER WITCH'S BARRIER, EVE?
HOW RUDE.
YOU'D KILL ME? IN NATE'S HOUSE, WHILE HE SLEEPS UPSTAIRS?
YOU'D GIVE HIM THE BURDEN OF FINDING MY CORPSE?
I WASN'T STRONG ENOUGH TO STOP YOU LAST TIME.
I WON'T MAKE THAT MISTAKE AGAIN.
YOU REALLY HAVE CHANGED.
I HAVEN'T CHANGED AT ALL.
THAT SHOULD HAVE YOU WORRIED.

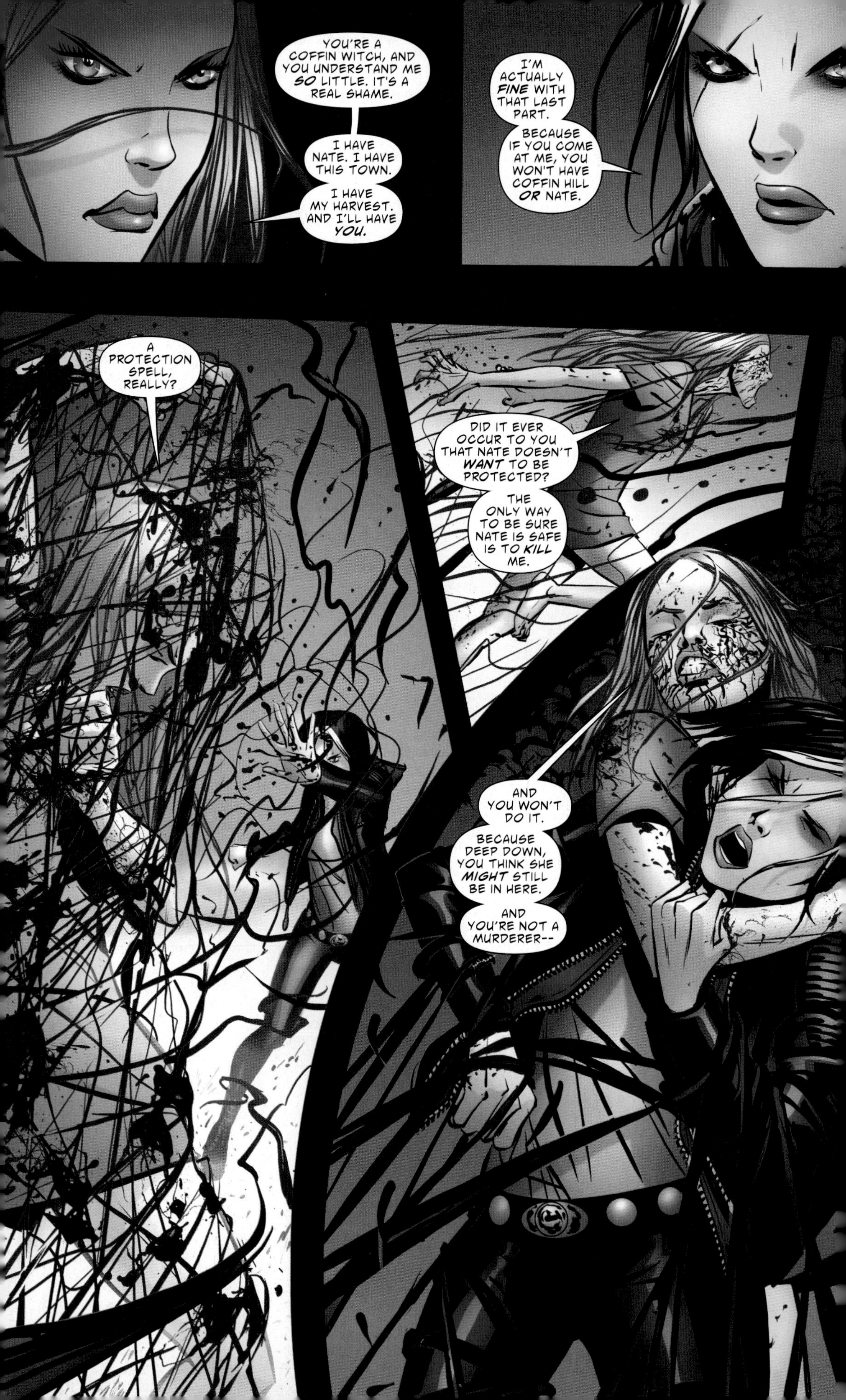

YOU'RE A COFFIN WITCH, AND YOU UNDERSTAND ME SO LITTLE. IT'S A REAL SHAME.
I HAVE NATE. I HAVE THIS TOWN.
I HAVE MY HARVEST. AND I'LL HAVE YOU.
I'M ACTUALLY FINE WITH THAT LAST PART.
BECAUSE IF YOU COME AT ME, YOU WON'T HAVE COFFIN HILL OR NATE.
A PROTECTION SPELL, REALLY?
DID IT EVER OCCUR TO YOU THAT NATE DOESN'T WANT TO BE PROTECTED?
THE ONLY WAY TO BE SURE NATE IS SAFE IS TO KILL ME.
AND YOU WON'T DO IT.
BECAUSE DEEP DOWN, YOU THINK SHE MIGHT STILL BE IN HERE.
AND YOU'RE NOT A MURDERER--

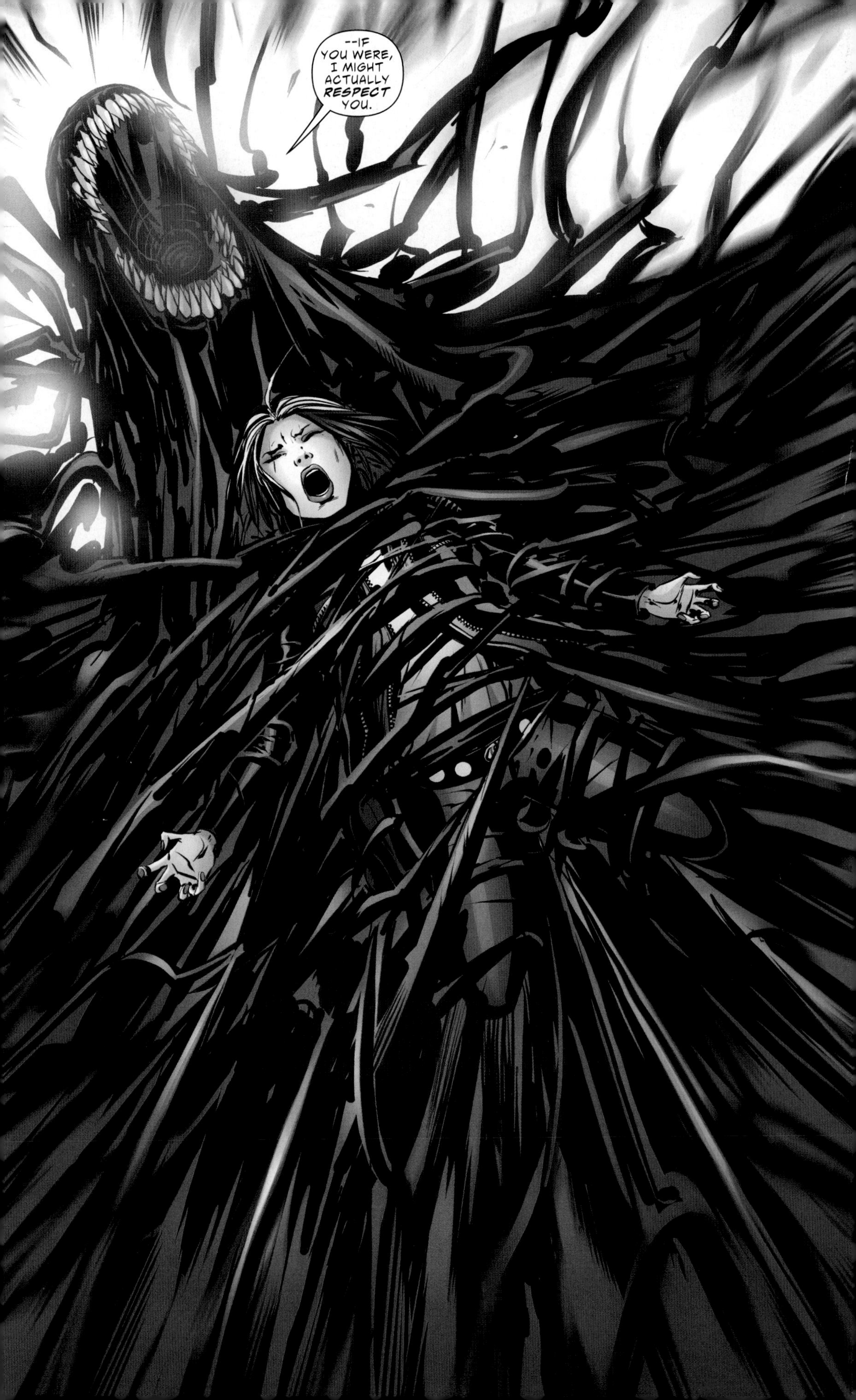
--IF YOU WERE, I MIGHT ACTUALLY RESPECT YOU.

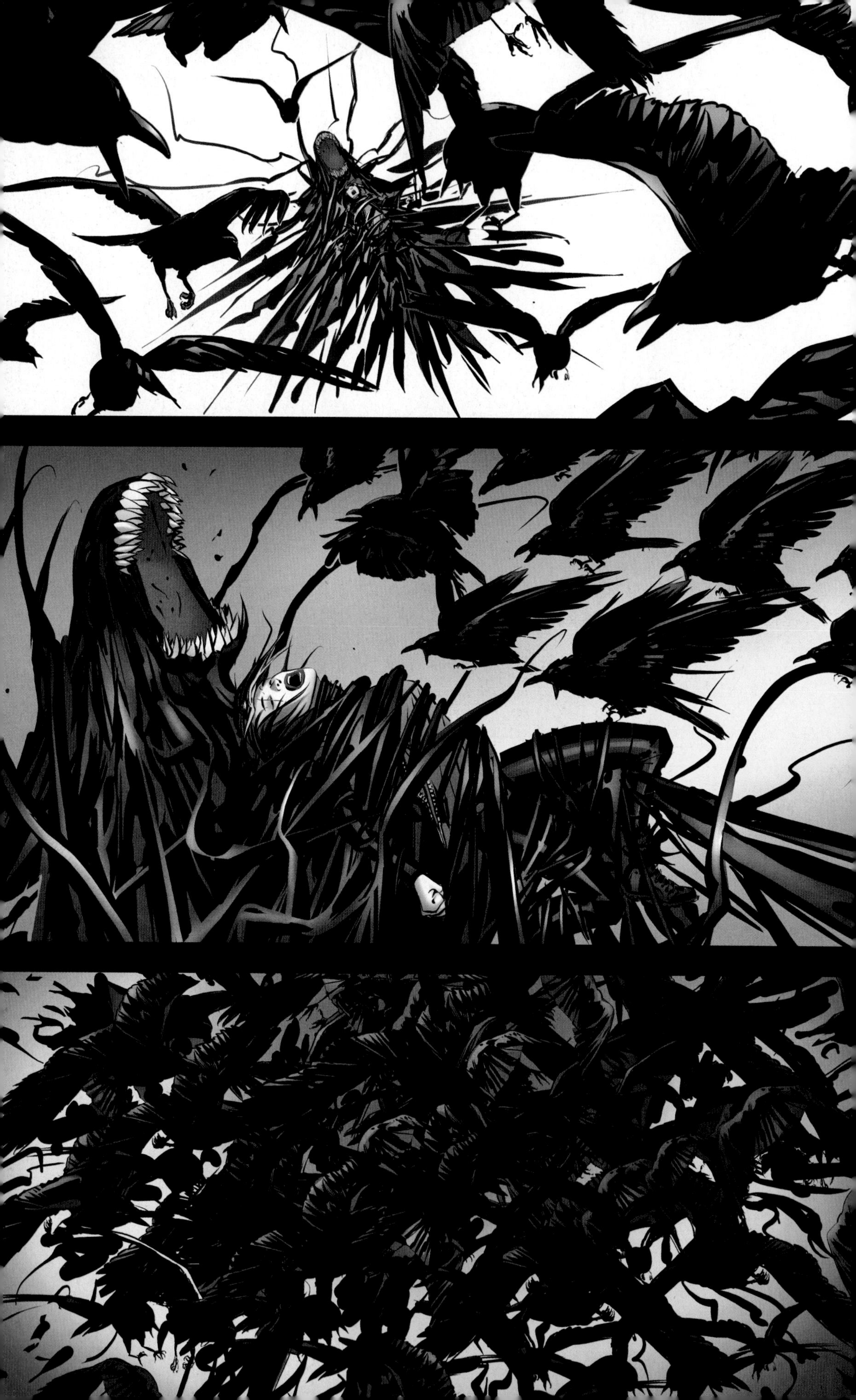

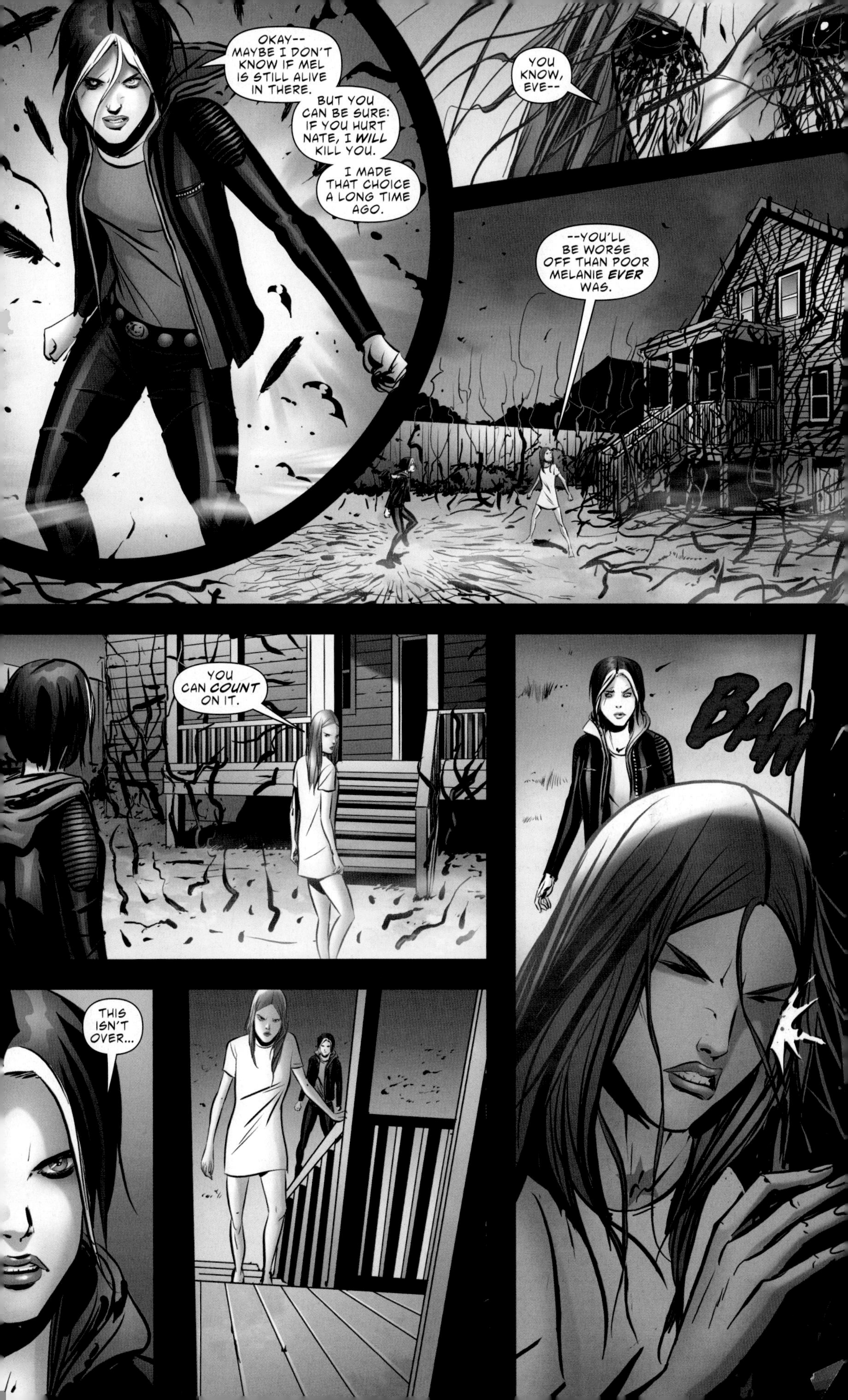
OKAY-- MAYBE I DON'T KNOW IF MEL IS STILL ALIVE IN THERE.
BUT YOU CAN BE SURE: IF YOU HURT NATE, I WILL KILL YOU.
I MADE THAT CHOICE A LONG TIME AGO.
YOU KNOW, EVE--
--YOU'LL BE WORSE OFF THAN POOR MELANIE EVER WAS.
YOU CAN COUNT ON IT.
BAM
THIS ISN'T OVER...

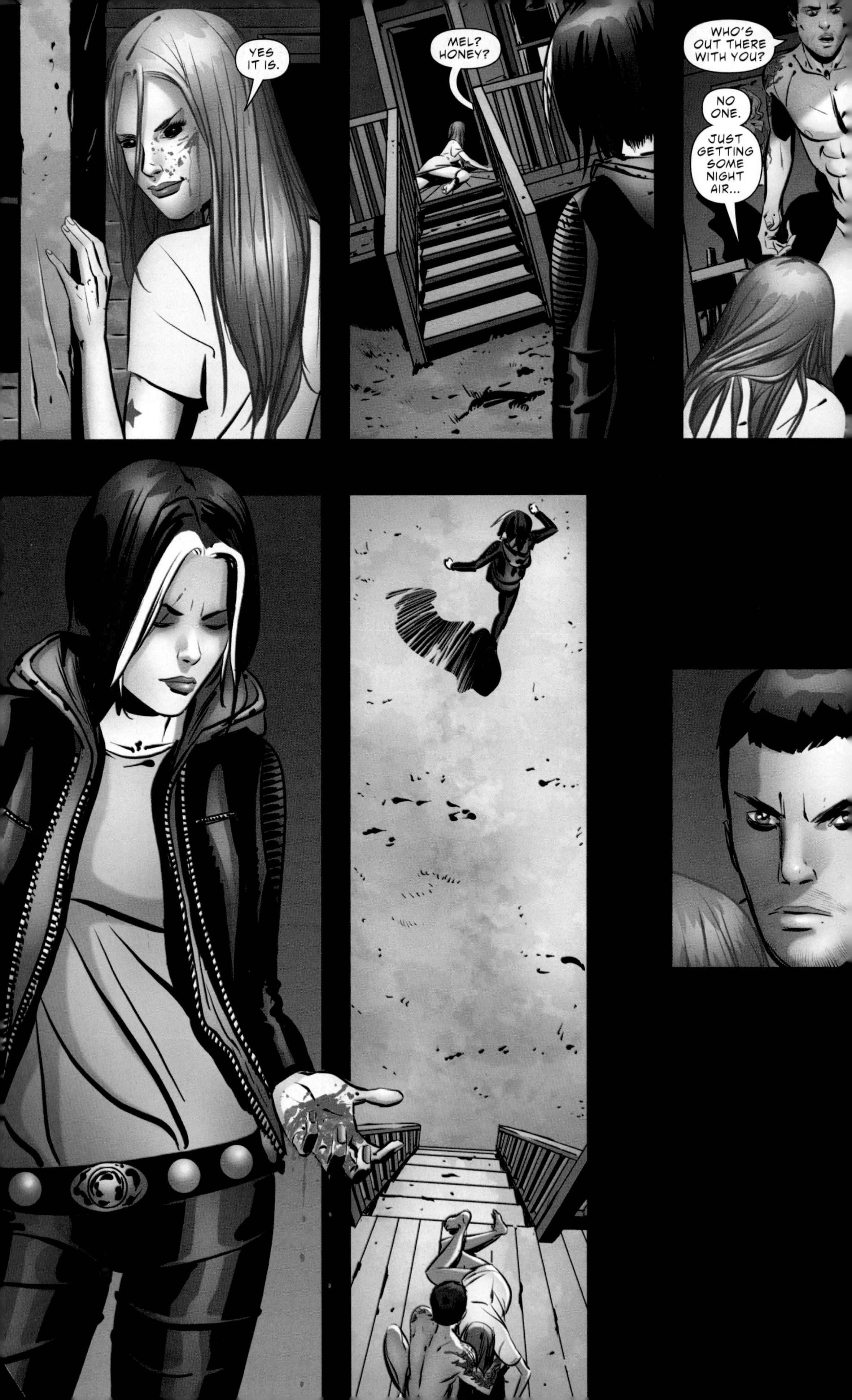
YES IT IS.
MEL? HONEY?
WHO'S OUT THERE WITH YOU?
NO ONE.
JUST GETTING SOME NIGHT AIR...

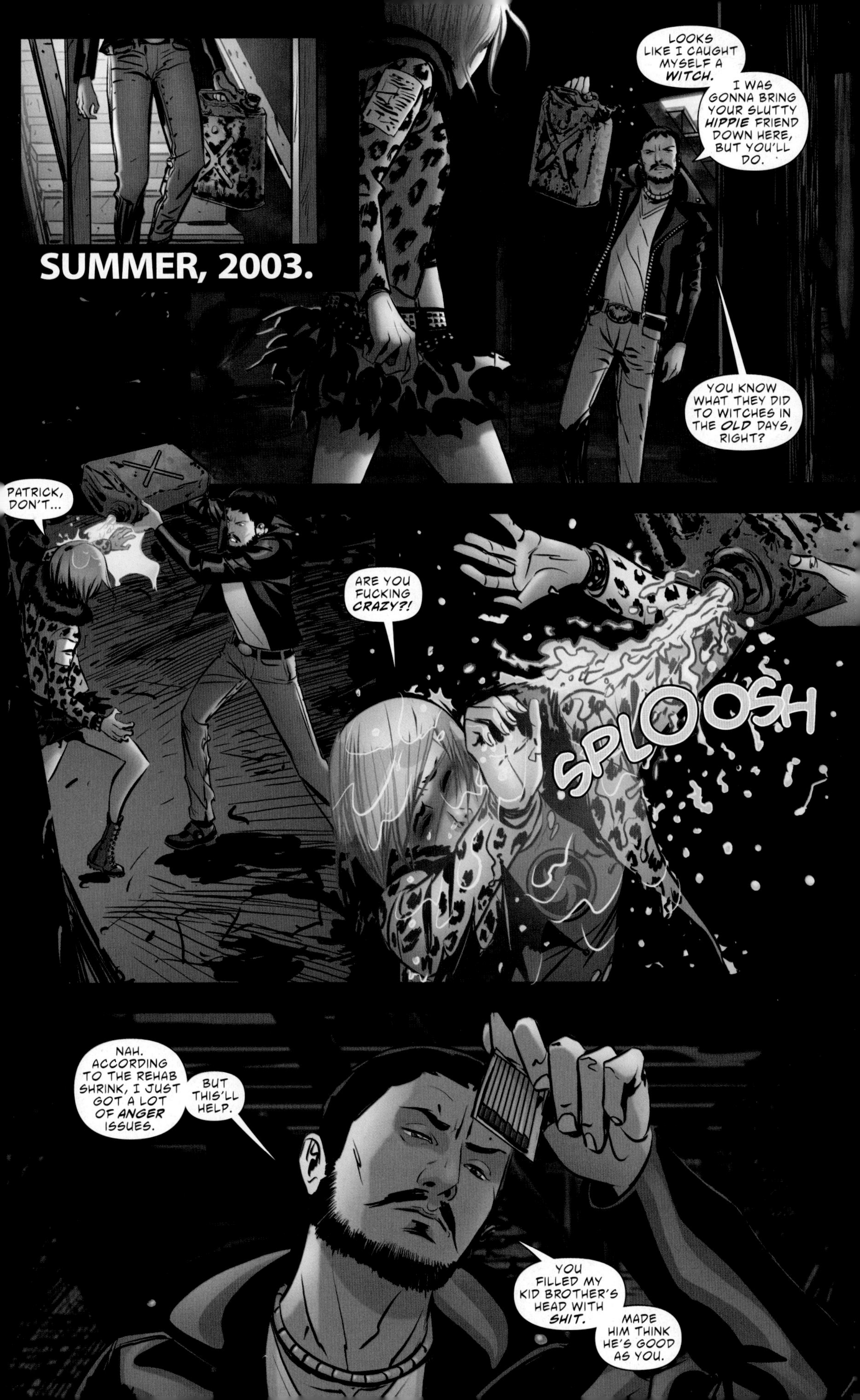
SUMMER, 2003.
LOOKS LIKE I CAUGHT MYSELF A WITCH.
I WAS GONNA BRING YOUR SLUTTY HIPPIE FRIEND DOWN HERE, BUT YOU'LL DO.
YOU KNOW WHAT THEY DID TO WITCHES IN THE OLD DAYS, RIGHT?
PATRICK, DON'T...
ARE YOU FUCKING CRAZY?!
SPLOOSH
NAH. ACCORDING TO THE REHAB SHRINK, I JUST GOT A LOT OF ANGER ISSUES.
BUT THIS'LL HELP.
YOU FILLED MY KID BROTHER'S HEAD WITH SHIT.
MADE HIM THINK HE'S GOOD AS YOU.

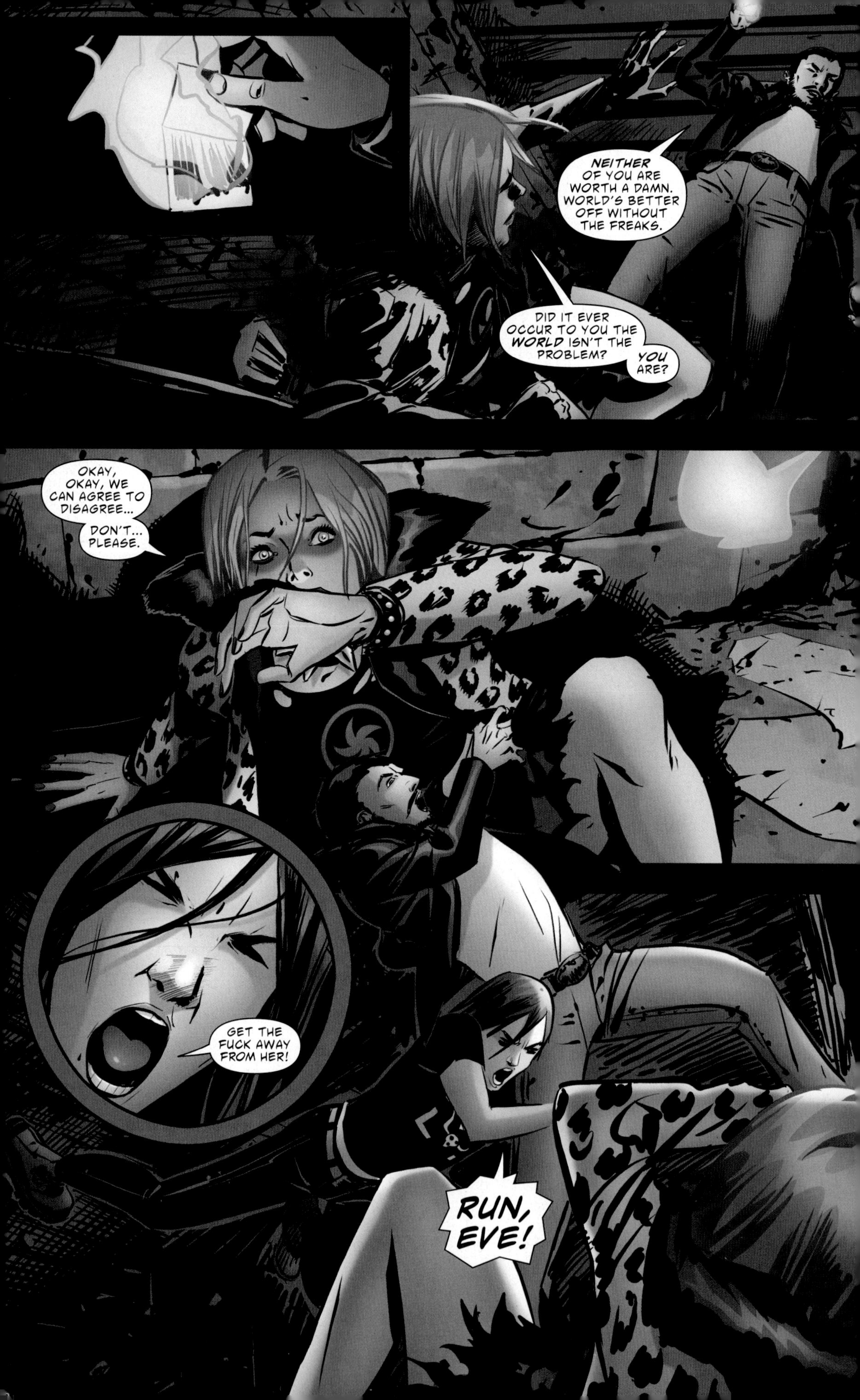
NEITHER OF YOU ARE WORTH A DAMN. WORLD'S BETTER OFF WITHOUT THE FREAKS.
DID IT EVER OCCUR TO YOU THE WORLD ISN'T THE PROBLEM?
YOU ARE?
OKAY, OKAY, WE CAN AGREE TO DISAGREE...
DON'T... PLEASE.
GET THE FUCK AWAY FROM HER!
RUN, EVE!

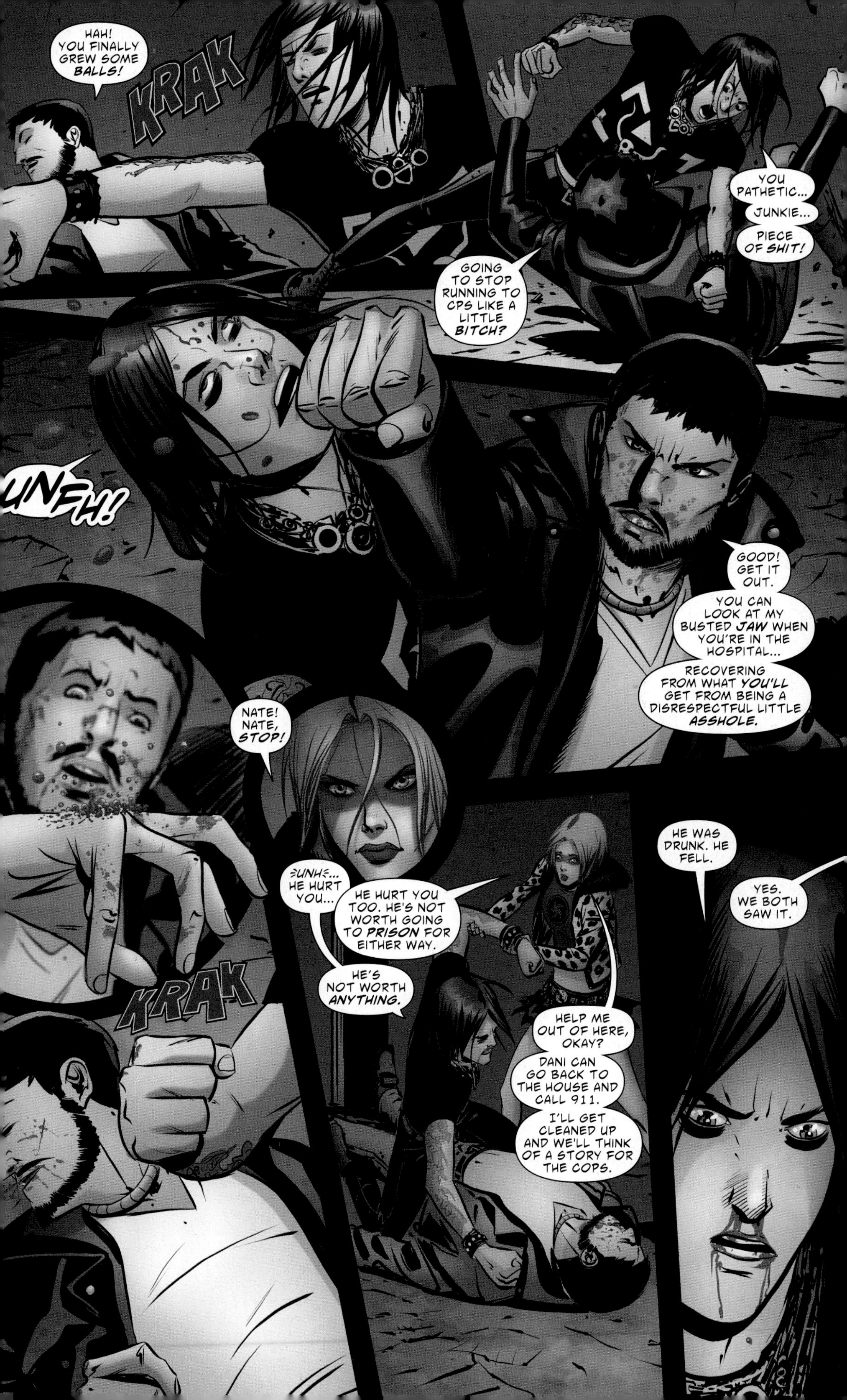
HAH! YOU FINALLY GREW SOME BALLS!
KRAK
YOU PATHETIC...
JUNKIE...
PIECE OF SHIT!
GOING TO STOP RUNNING TO CPS LIKE A LITTLE BITCH?
UNFH!
GOOD! GET IT OUT.
YOU CAN LOOK AT MY BUSTED JAW WHEN YOU'RE IN THE HOSPITAL...
RECOVERING FROM WHAT YOU'LL GET FROM BEING A DISRESPECTFUL LITTLE ASSHOLE.
NATE! NATE, STOP!
KRAK
UNH... HE HURT YOU...
HE HURT YOU TOO. HE'S NOT WORTH GOING TO PRISON FOR EITHER WAY.
HE'S NOT WORTH ANYTHING.
HELP ME OUT OF HERE, OKAY?
DANI CAN GO BACK TO THE HOUSE AND CALL 911.
I'LL GET CLEANED UP AND WE'LL THINK OF A STORY FOR THE COPS.
HE WAS DRUNK. HE FELL.
YES. WE BOTH SAW IT.

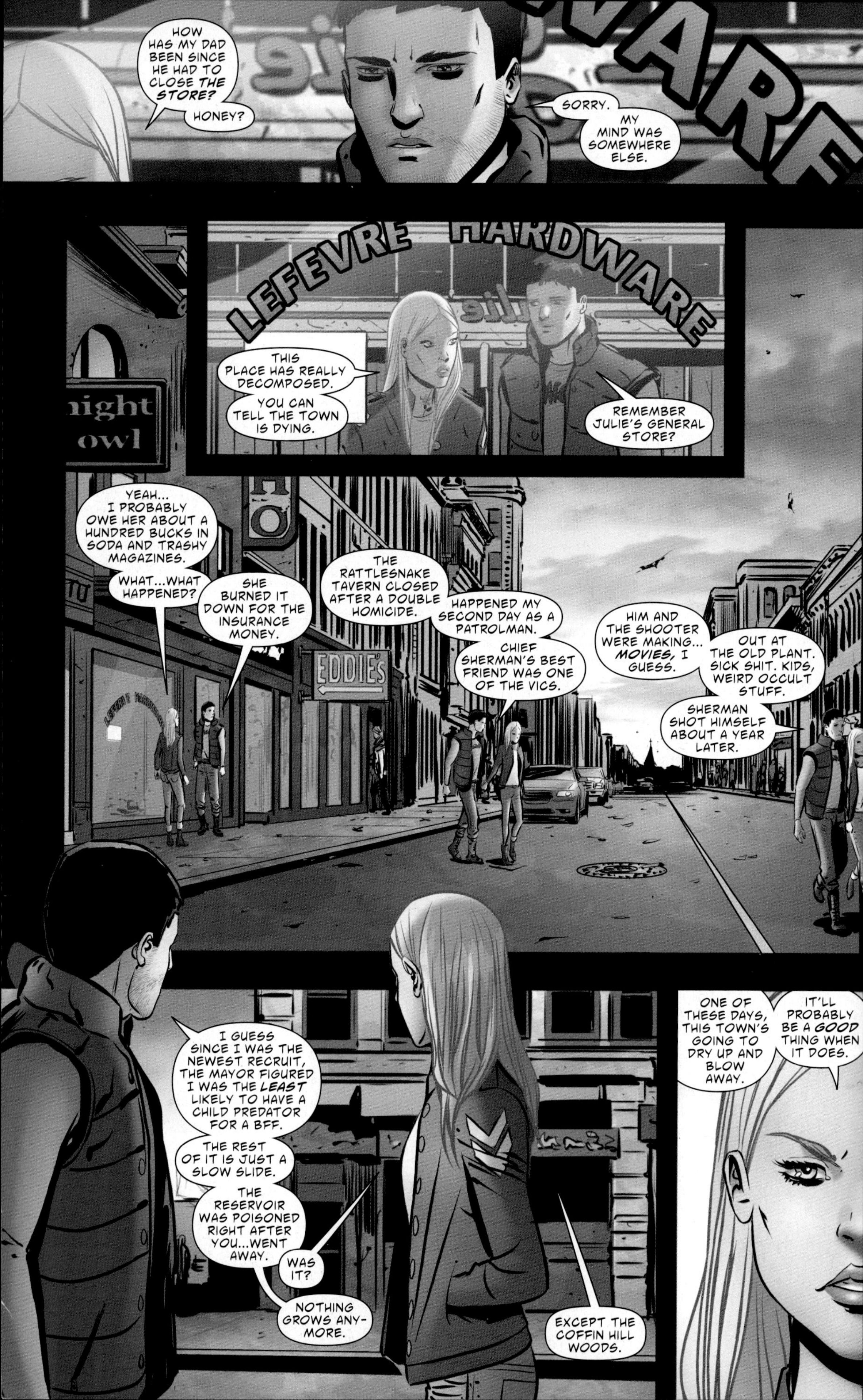

HOW HAS MY DAD BEEN SINCE HE HAD TO CLOSE *THE STORE?*
HONEY?
SORRY.
MY MIND WAS SOMEWHERE ELSE.
LEFEVRE HARDWARE
THIS PLACE HAS REALLY DECOMPOSED.
YOU CAN TELL THE TOWN IS DYING.
REMEMBER JULIE'S GENERAL STORE?
night owl
YEAH... I PROBABLY OWE HER ABOUT A HUNDRED BUCKS IN SODA AND TRASHY MAGAZINES.
WHAT...WHAT HAPPENED?
SHE BURNED IT DOWN FOR THE INSURANCE MONEY.
EDDIE'S
THE RATTLESNAKE TAVERN CLOSED AFTER A DOUBLE HOMICIDE.
HAPPENED MY SECOND DAY AS A PATROLMAN.
CHIEF SHERMAN'S BEST FRIEND WAS ONE OF THE VICS.
HIM AND THE SHOOTER WERE MAKING... *MOVIES,* I GUESS.
OUT AT THE OLD PLANT. SICK SHIT. KIDS, WEIRD OCCULT STUFF.
SHERMAN SHOT HIMSELF ABOUT A YEAR LATER.
I GUESS SINCE I WAS THE NEWEST RECRUIT, THE MAYOR FIGURED I WAS THE *LEAST* LIKELY TO HAVE A CHILD PREDATOR FOR A BFF.
THE REST OF IT IS JUST A SLOW SLIDE.
THE RESERVOIR WAS POISONED RIGHT AFTER YOU...WENT AWAY.
WAS IT?
NOTHING GROWS ANY-MORE.
EXCEPT THE COFFIN HILL WOODS.
ONE OF THESE DAYS, THIS TOWN'S GOING TO DRY UP AND BLOW AWAY.
IT'LL PROBABLY BE A *GOOD* THING WHEN IT DOES.

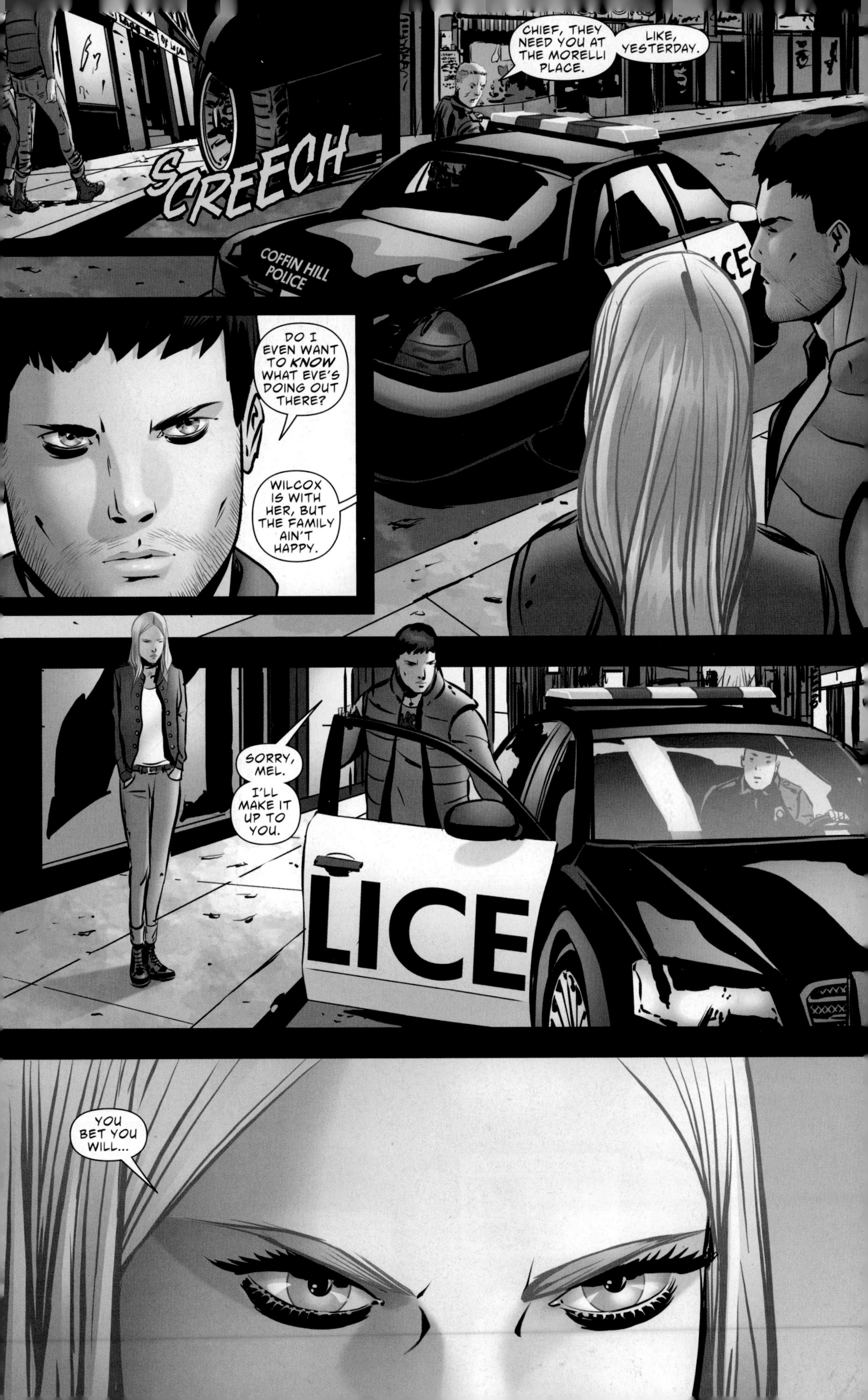
CHIEF, THEY NEED YOU AT THE MORELLI PLACE.
LIKE, YESTERDAY.
SCREECH
COFFIN HILL POLICE
DO I EVEN WANT TO KNOW WHAT EVE'S DOING OUT THERE?
WILCOX IS WITH HER, BUT THE FAMILY AIN'T HAPPY.
SORRY, MEL.
I'LL MAKE IT UP TO YOU.
LICE
YOU BET YOU WILL...

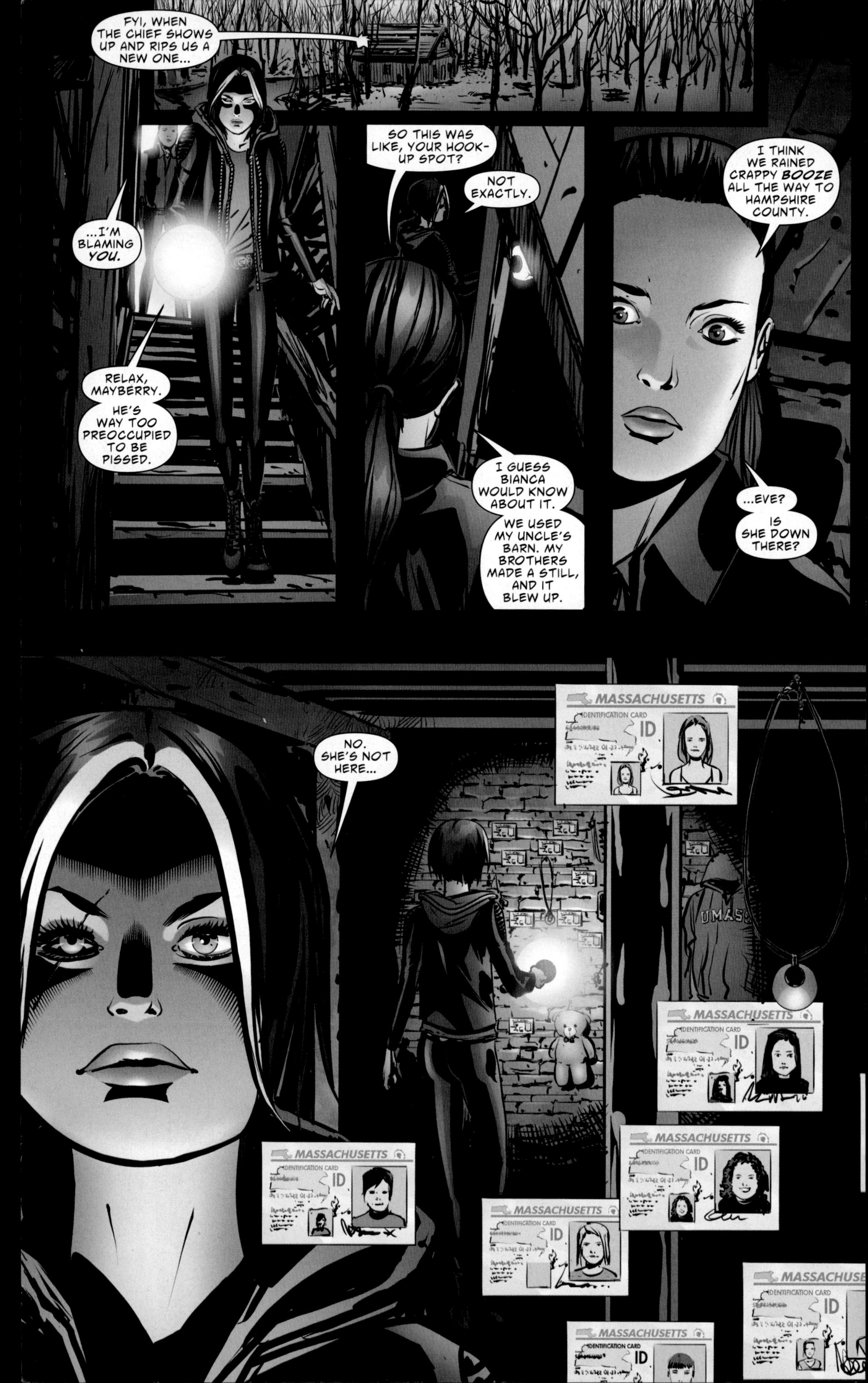

FYI, WHEN THE CHIEF SHOWS UP AND RIPS US A NEW ONE...
...I'M BLAMING *YOU.*
RELAX, MAYBERRY.
HE'S WAY TOO PREOCCUPIED TO BE PISSED.
SO THIS WAS LIKE, YOUR HOOK-UP SPOT?
NOT EXACTLY.
I GUESS BIANCA WOULD KNOW ABOUT IT.
WE USED MY UNCLE'S BARN. MY BROTHERS MADE A STILL, AND IT BLEW UP.
I THINK WE RAINED CRAPPY *BOOZE* ALL THE WAY TO HAMPSHIRE COUNTY.
...EVE?
IS SHE DOWN THERE?
NO. SHE'S NOT HERE...
MASSACHUSETTS
IDENTIFICATION CARD
ID
UMASS

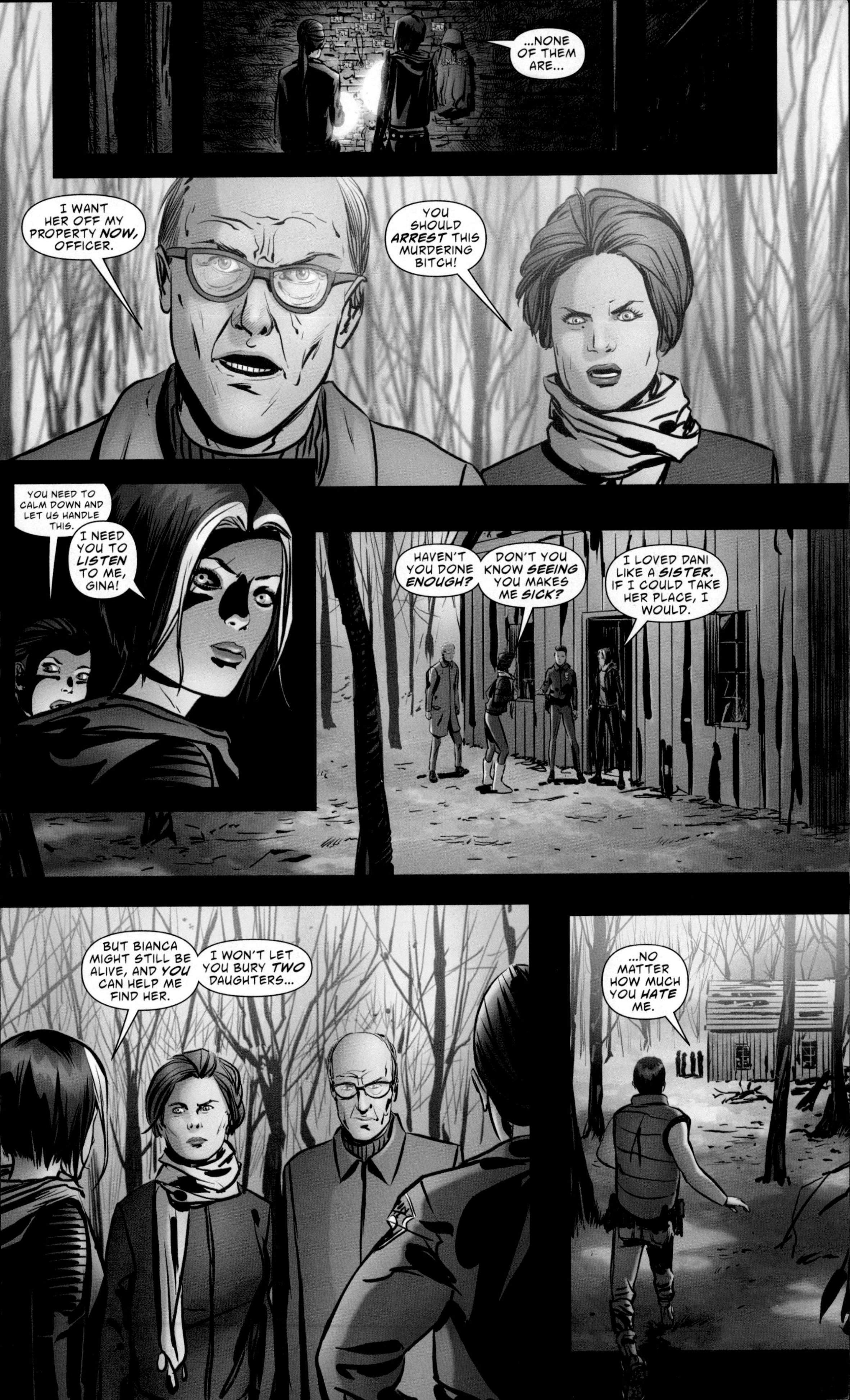
...NONE OF THEM ARE...
I WANT HER OFF MY PROPERTY NOW, OFFICER.
YOU SHOULD ARREST THIS MURDERING BITCH!
YOU NEED TO CALM DOWN AND LET US HANDLE THIS.
I NEED YOU TO LISTEN TO ME, GINA!
HAVEN'T YOU DONE ENOUGH?
DON'T YOU KNOW SEEING YOU MAKES ME SICK?
I LOVED DANI LIKE A SISTER. IF I COULD TAKE HER PLACE, I WOULD.
BUT BIANCA MIGHT STILL BE ALIVE, AND YOU CAN HELP ME FIND HER.
I WON'T LET YOU BURY TWO DAUGHTERS...
...NO MATTER HOW MUCH YOU HATE ME.

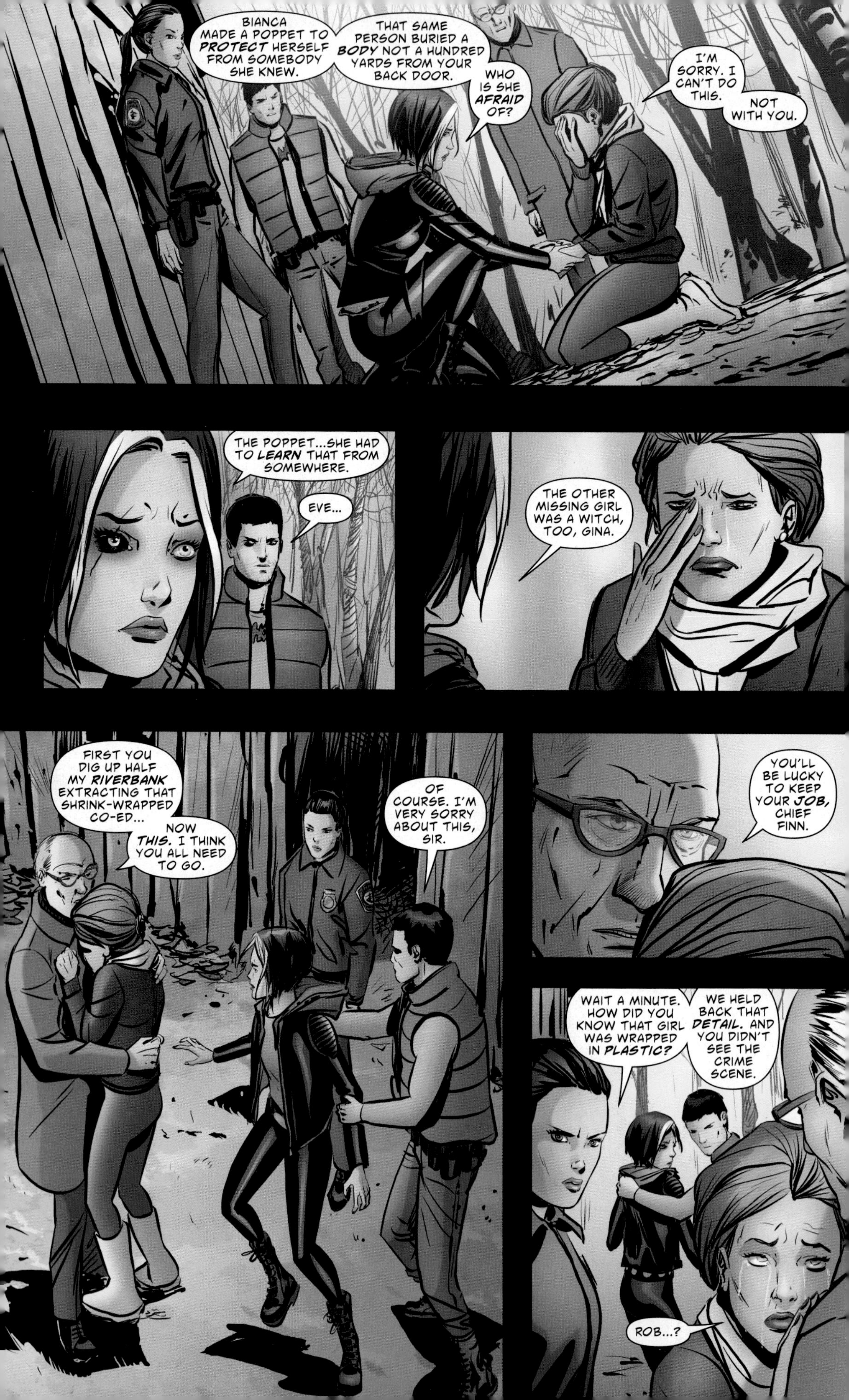
BIANCA MADE A POPPET TO PROTECT HERSELF FROM SOMEBODY SHE KNEW.
THAT SAME PERSON BURIED A BODY NOT A HUNDRED YARDS FROM YOUR BACK DOOR.
WHO IS SHE AFRAID OF?
I'M SORRY. I CAN'T DO THIS.
NOT WITH YOU.
THE POPPET...SHE HAD TO LEARN THAT FROM SOMEWHERE.
EVE...
THE OTHER MISSING GIRL WAS A WITCH, TOO, GINA.
FIRST YOU DIG UP HALF MY RIVERBANK EXTRACTING THAT SHRINK-WRAPPED CO-ED...
NOW THIS. I THINK YOU ALL NEED TO GO.
OF COURSE. I'M VERY SORRY ABOUT THIS, SIR.
YOU'LL BE LUCKY TO KEEP YOUR JOB, CHIEF FINN.
WAIT A MINUTE. HOW DID YOU KNOW THAT GIRL WAS WRAPPED IN PLASTIC?
WE HELD BACK THAT DETAIL. AND YOU DIDN'T SEE THE CRIME SCENE.
ROB...?

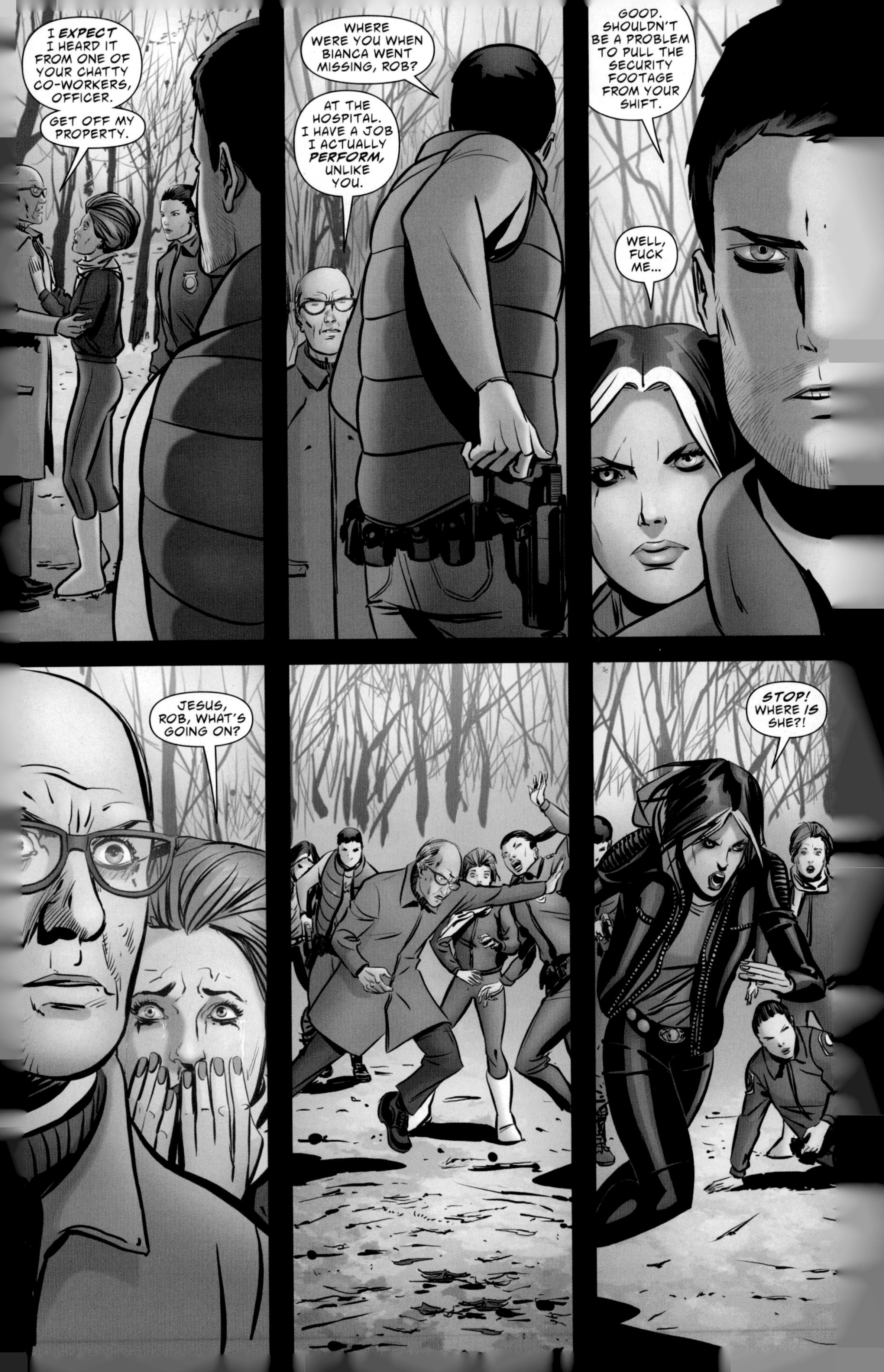
I EXPECT I HEARD IT FROM ONE OF YOUR CHATTY CO-WORKERS, OFFICER.
GET OFF MY PROPERTY.
WHERE WERE YOU WHEN BIANCA WENT MISSING, ROB?
AT THE HOSPITAL. I HAVE A JOB I ACTUALLY PERFORM, UNLIKE YOU.
GOOD. SHOULDN'T BE A PROBLEM TO PULL THE SECURITY FOOTAGE FROM YOUR SHIFT.
WELL, FUCK ME...
JESUS, ROB, WHAT'S GOING ON?
STOP! WHERE IS SHE?!

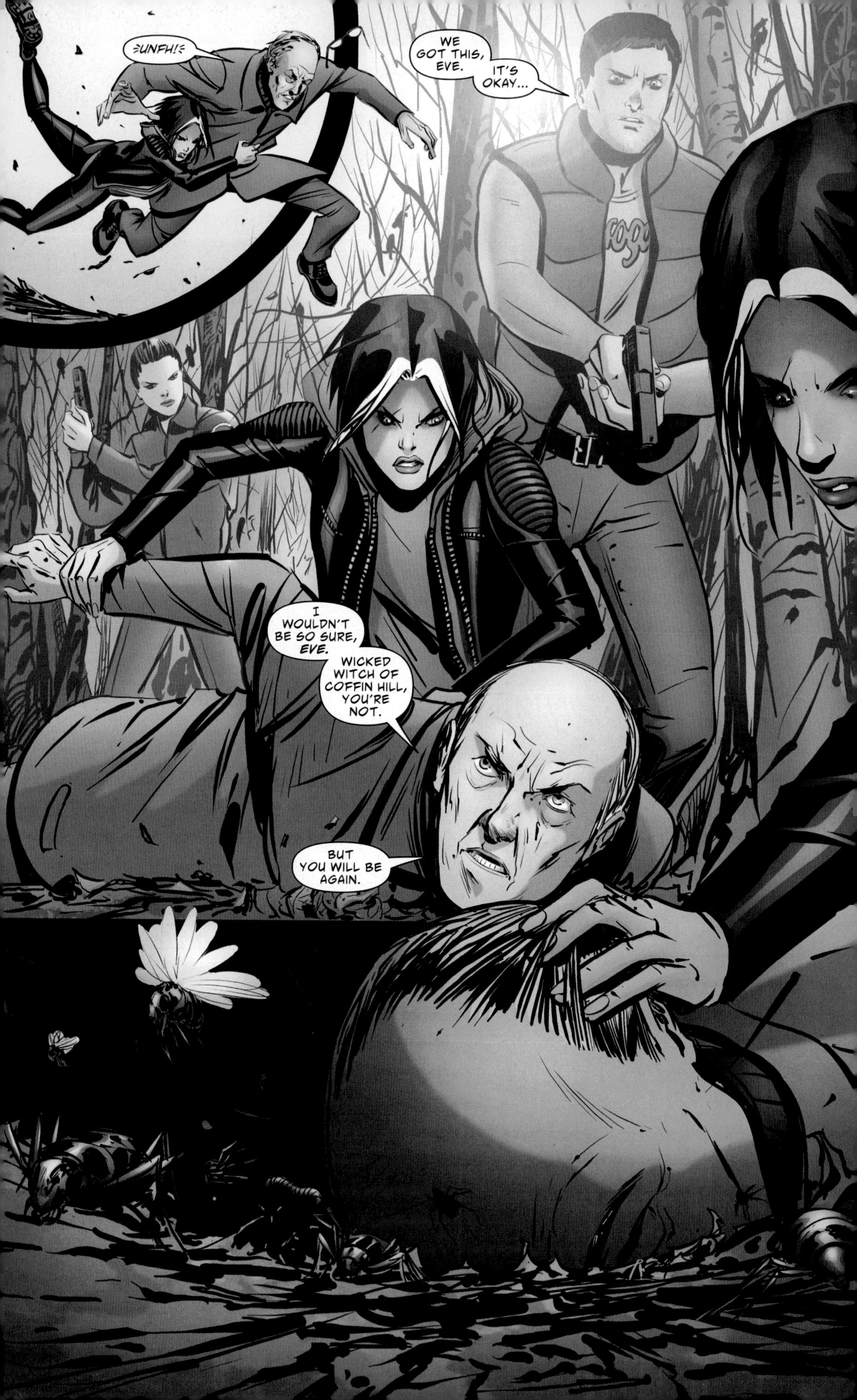

UNFH!
WE GOT THIS, EVE.
IT'S OKAY...
I WOULDN'T BE SO SURE, EVE.
WICKED WITCH OF COFFIN HILL, YOU'RE NOT.
BUT YOU WILL BE AGAIN.

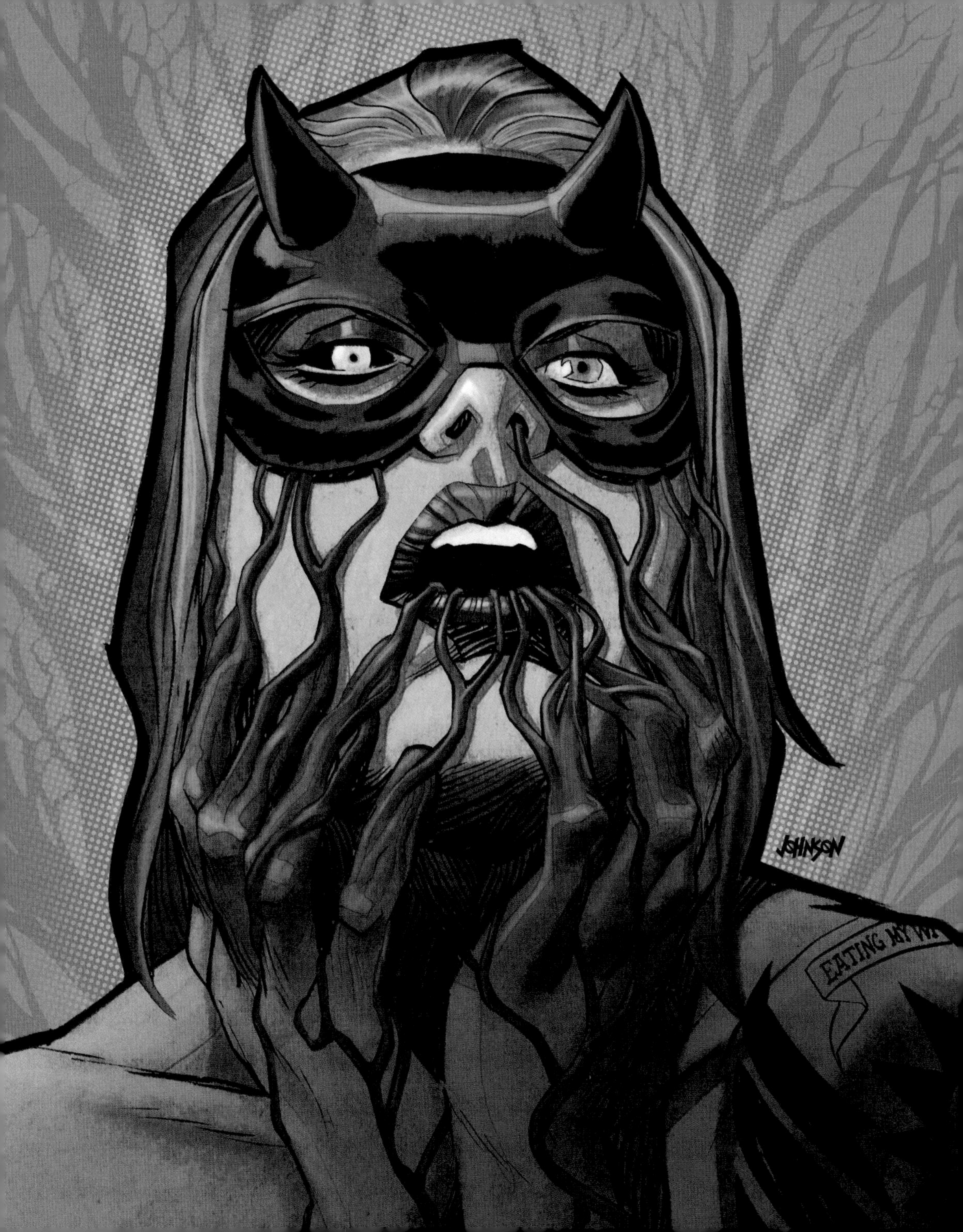
JOHNSON
EATING MY

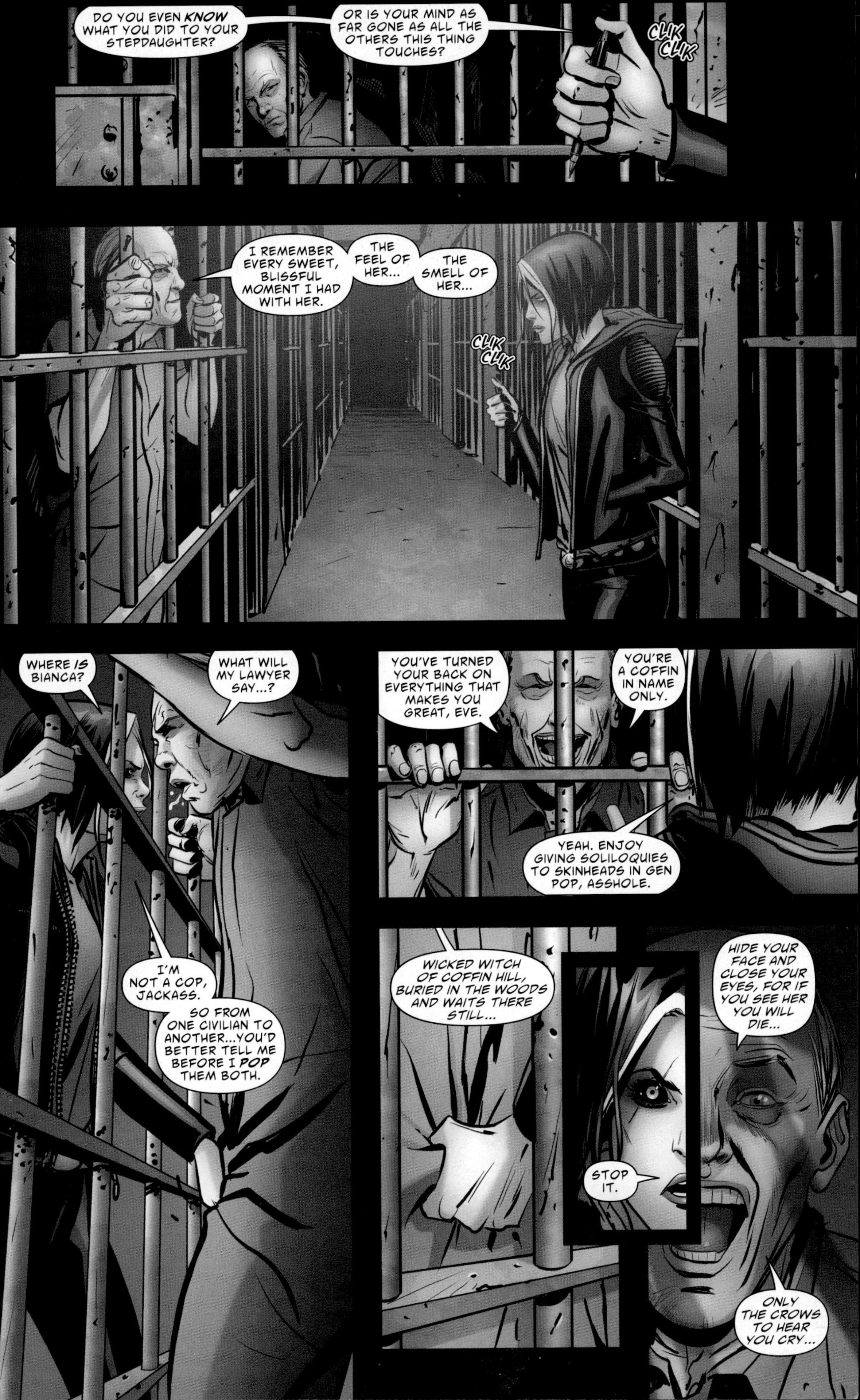
DO YOU EVEN KNOW WHAT YOU DID TO YOUR STEPDAUGHTER?
OR IS YOUR MIND AS FAR GONE AS ALL THE OTHERS THIS THING TOUCHES?
CLIK CLIK
I REMEMBER EVERY SWEET, BLISSFUL MOMENT I HAD WITH HER.
THE FEEL OF HER...
THE SMELL OF HER...
CLIK CLIK
WHERE IS BIANCA?
WHAT WILL MY LAWYER SAY...?
I'M NOT A COP, JACKASS.
SO FROM ONE CIVILIAN TO ANOTHER...YOU'D BETTER TELL ME BEFORE I POP THEM BOTH.
YOU'VE TURNED YOUR BACK ON EVERYTHING THAT MAKES YOU GREAT, EVE.
YOU'RE A COFFIN IN NAME ONLY.
YEAH. ENJOY GIVING SOLILOQUIES TO SKINHEADS IN GEN POP, ASSHOLE.
WICKED WITCH OF COFFIN HILL, BURIED IN THE WOODS AND WAITS THERE STILL...
HIDE YOUR FACE AND CLOSE YOUR EYES, FOR IF YOU SEE HER YOU WILL DIE...
STOP IT.
ONLY THE CROWS TO HEAR YOU CRY...

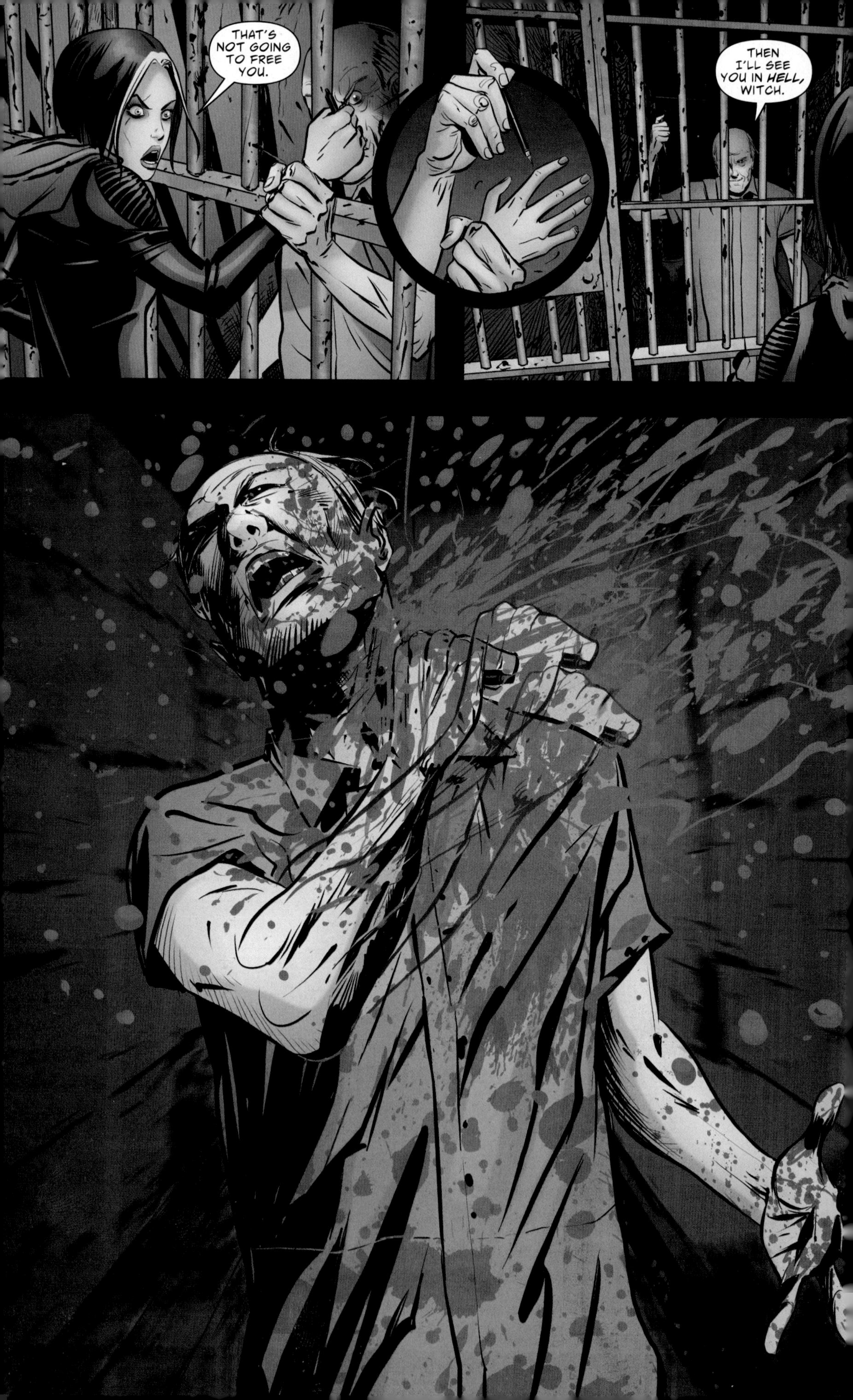
THAT'S NOT GOING TO FREE YOU.
THEN I'LL SEE YOU IN HELL, WITCH.

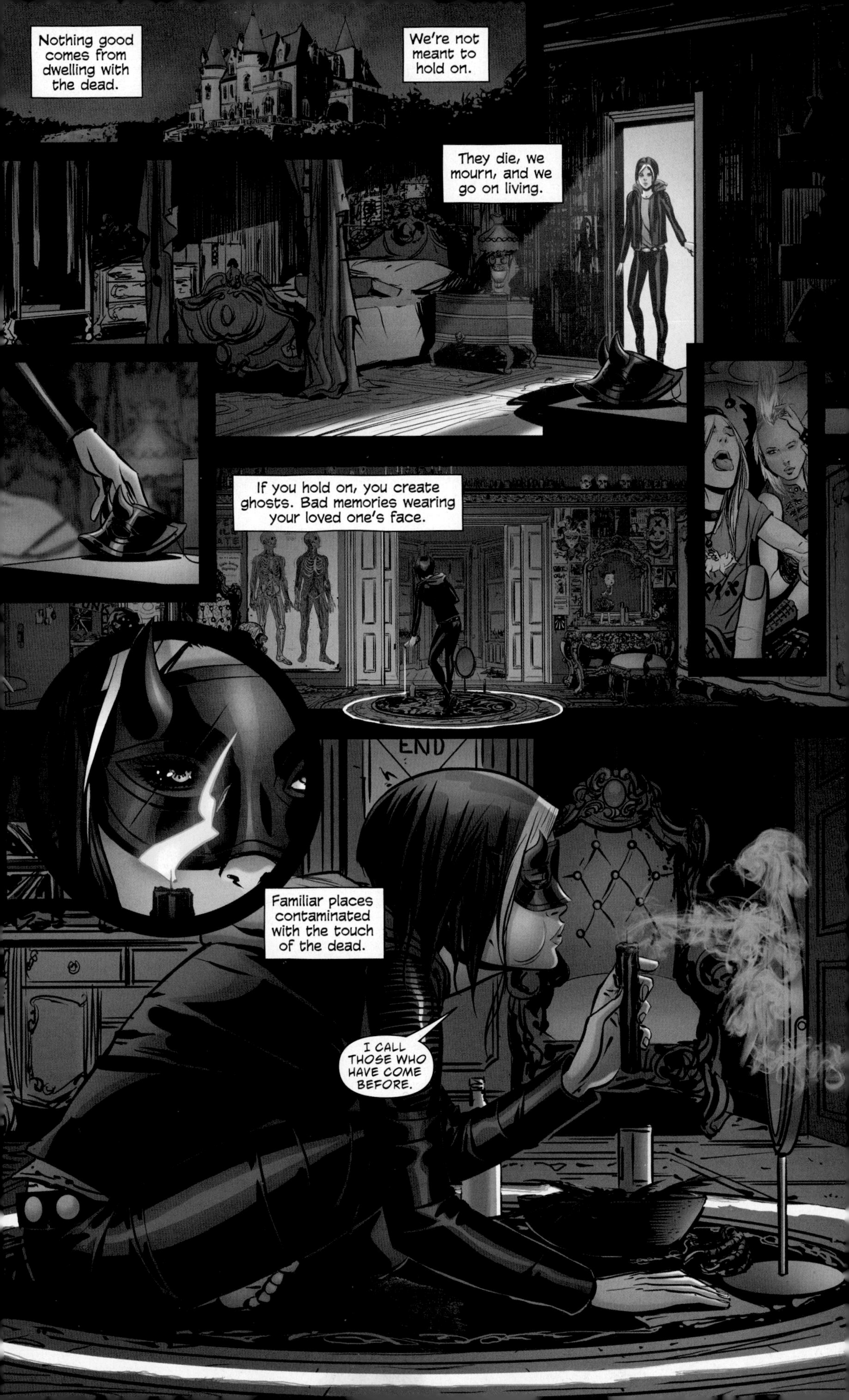

Nothing good comes from dwelling with the dead.
We're not meant to hold on.
They die, we mourn, and we go on living.
If you hold on, you create ghosts. Bad memories wearing your loved one's face.
END
Familiar places contaminated with the touch of the dead.
I CALL THOSE WHO HAVE COME BEFORE.

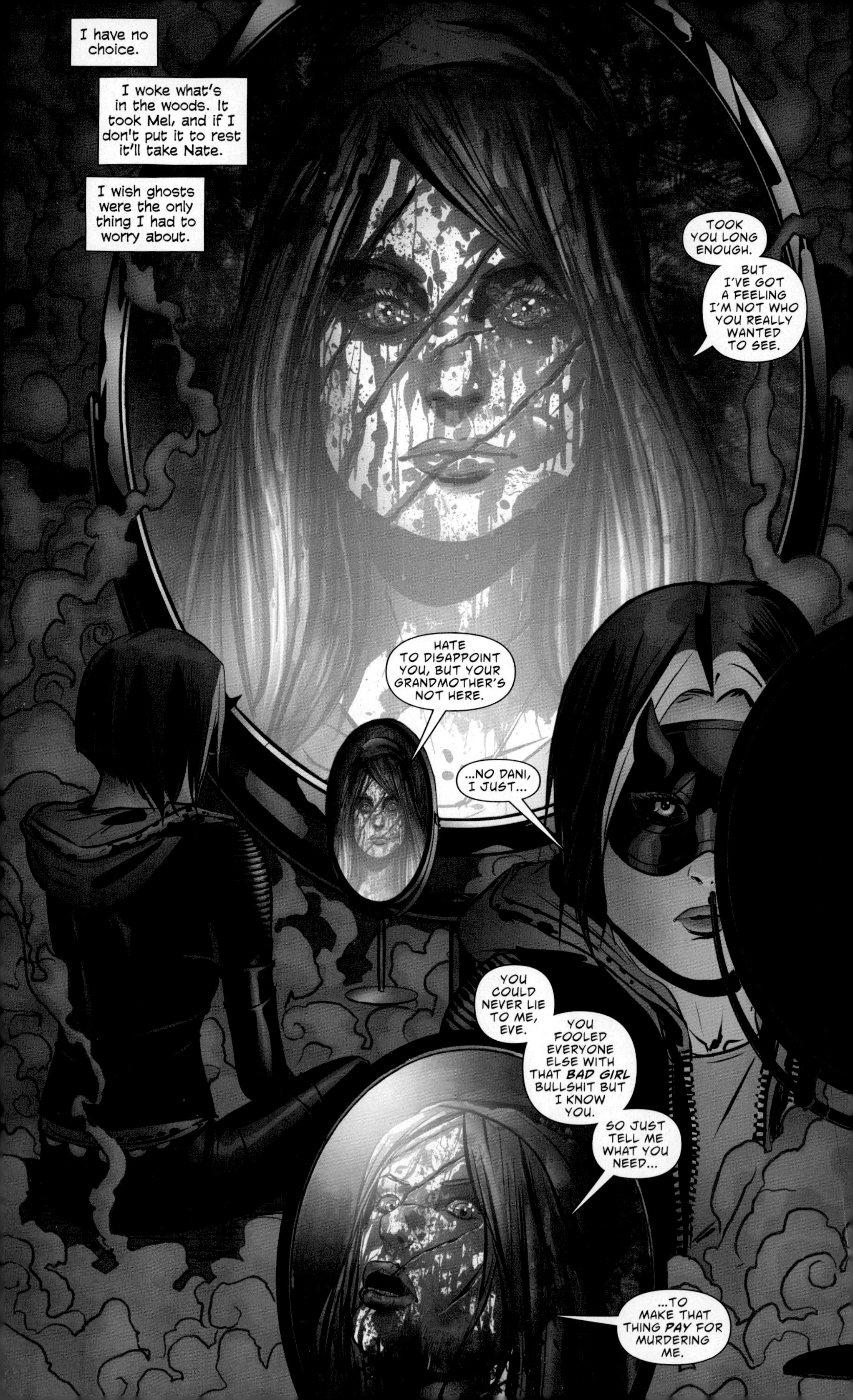
I have no choice.
I woke what's in the woods. It took Mel, and if I don't put it to rest it'll take Nate.
I wish ghosts were the only thing I had to worry about.
TOOK YOU LONG ENOUGH.
BUT I'VE GOT A FEELING I'M NOT WHO YOU REALLY WANTED TO SEE.
HATE TO DISAPPOINT YOU, BUT YOUR GRANDMOTHER'S NOT HERE.
...NO DANI, I JUST...
YOU COULD NEVER LIE TO ME, EVE.
YOU FOOLED EVERYONE ELSE WITH THAT *BAD GIRL* BULLSHIT BUT I KNOW YOU.
SO JUST TELL ME WHAT YOU NEED...
...TO MAKE THAT THING *PAY* FOR MURDERING ME.

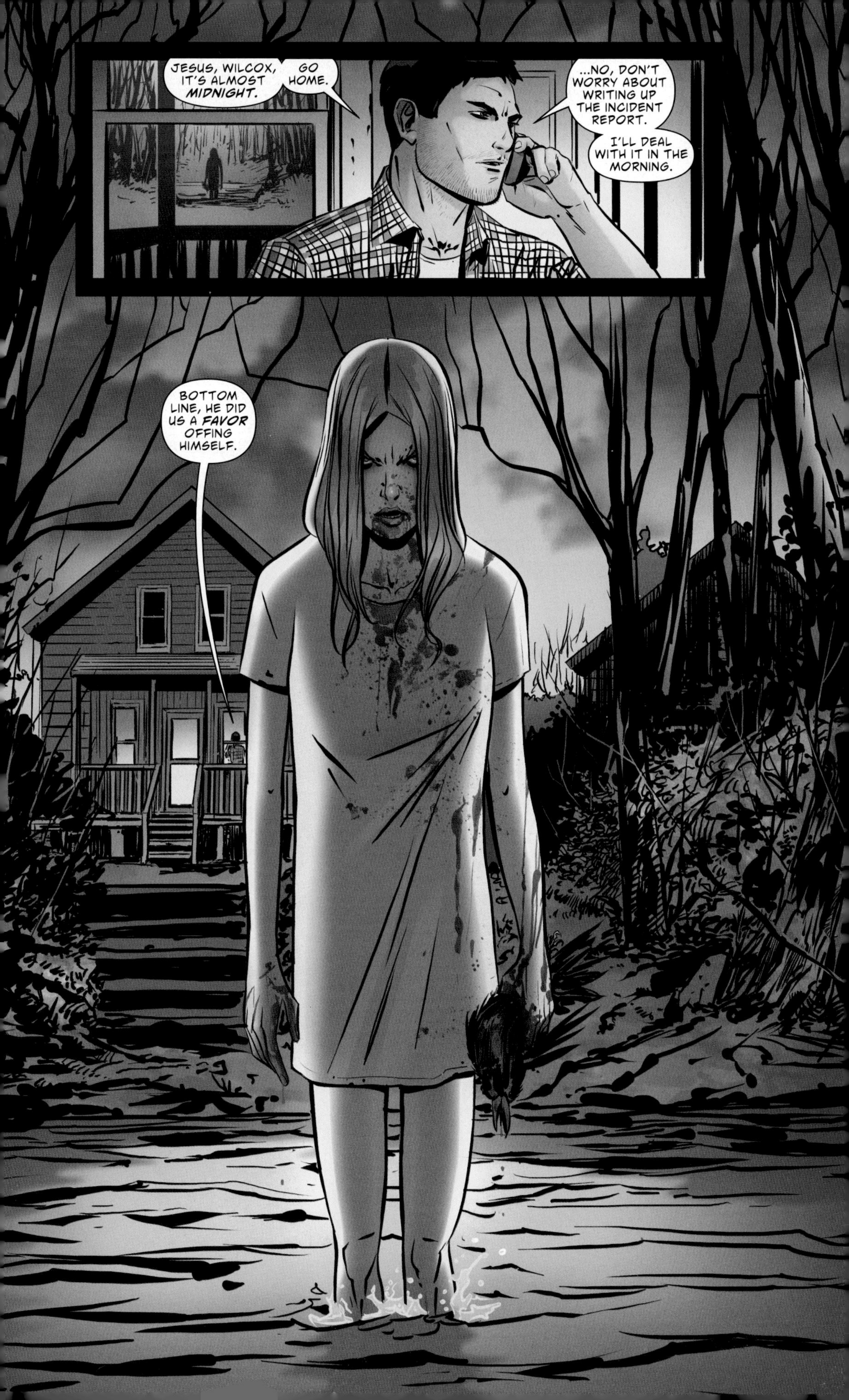
JESUS, WILCOX, IT'S ALMOST MIDNIGHT.
GO HOME.
...NO, DON'T WORRY ABOUT WRITING UP THE INCIDENT REPORT.
I'LL DEAL WITH IT IN THE MORNING.
BOTTOM LINE, HE DID US A FAVOR OFFING HIMSELF.

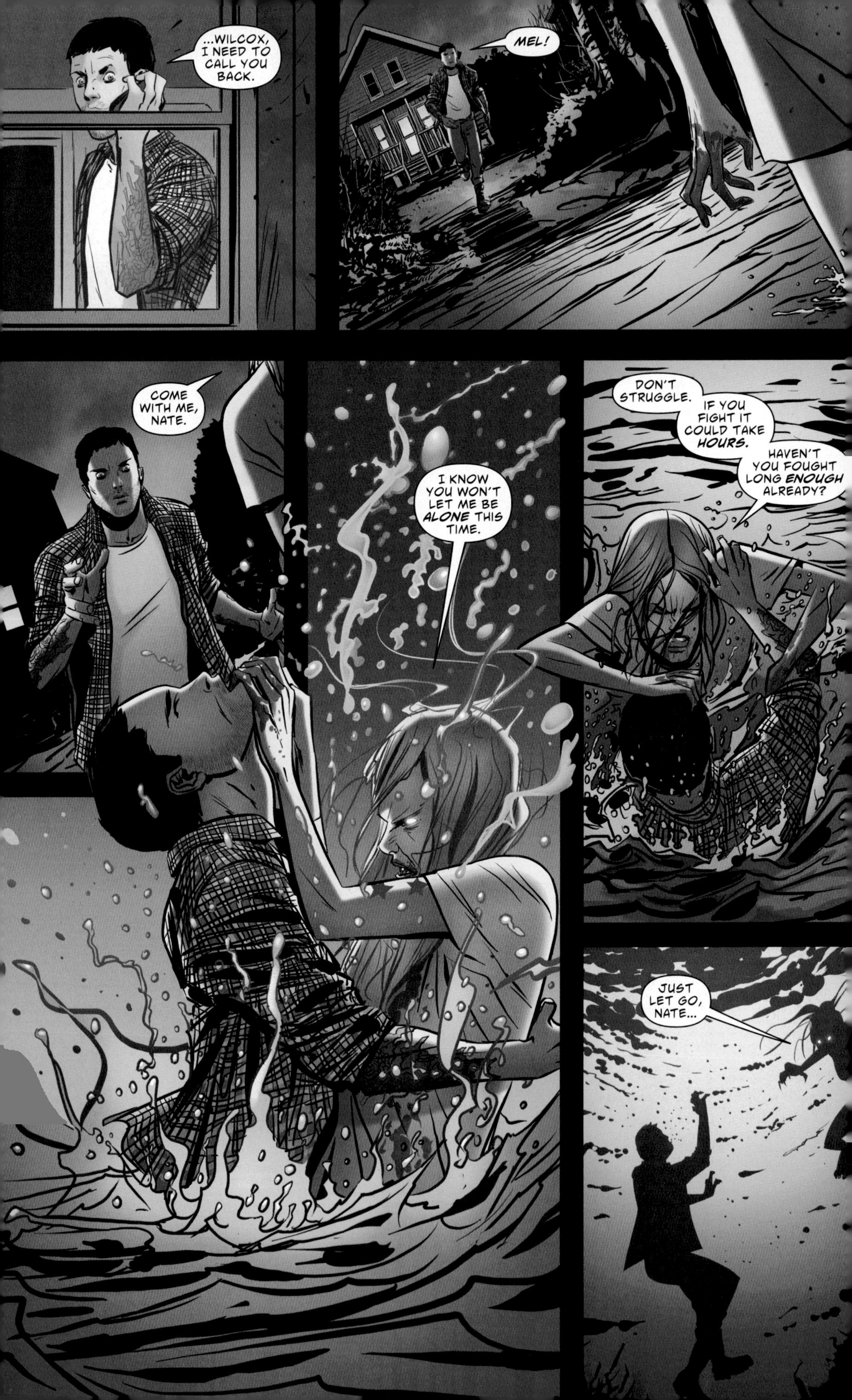
...WILCOX, I NEED TO CALL YOU BACK.
MEL!
COME WITH ME, NATE.
I KNOW YOU WON'T LET ME BE ALONE THIS TIME.
DON'T STRUGGLE.
IF YOU FIGHT IT COULD TAKE HOURS.
HAVEN'T YOU FOUGHT LONG ENOUGH ALREADY?
JUST LET GO, NATE...

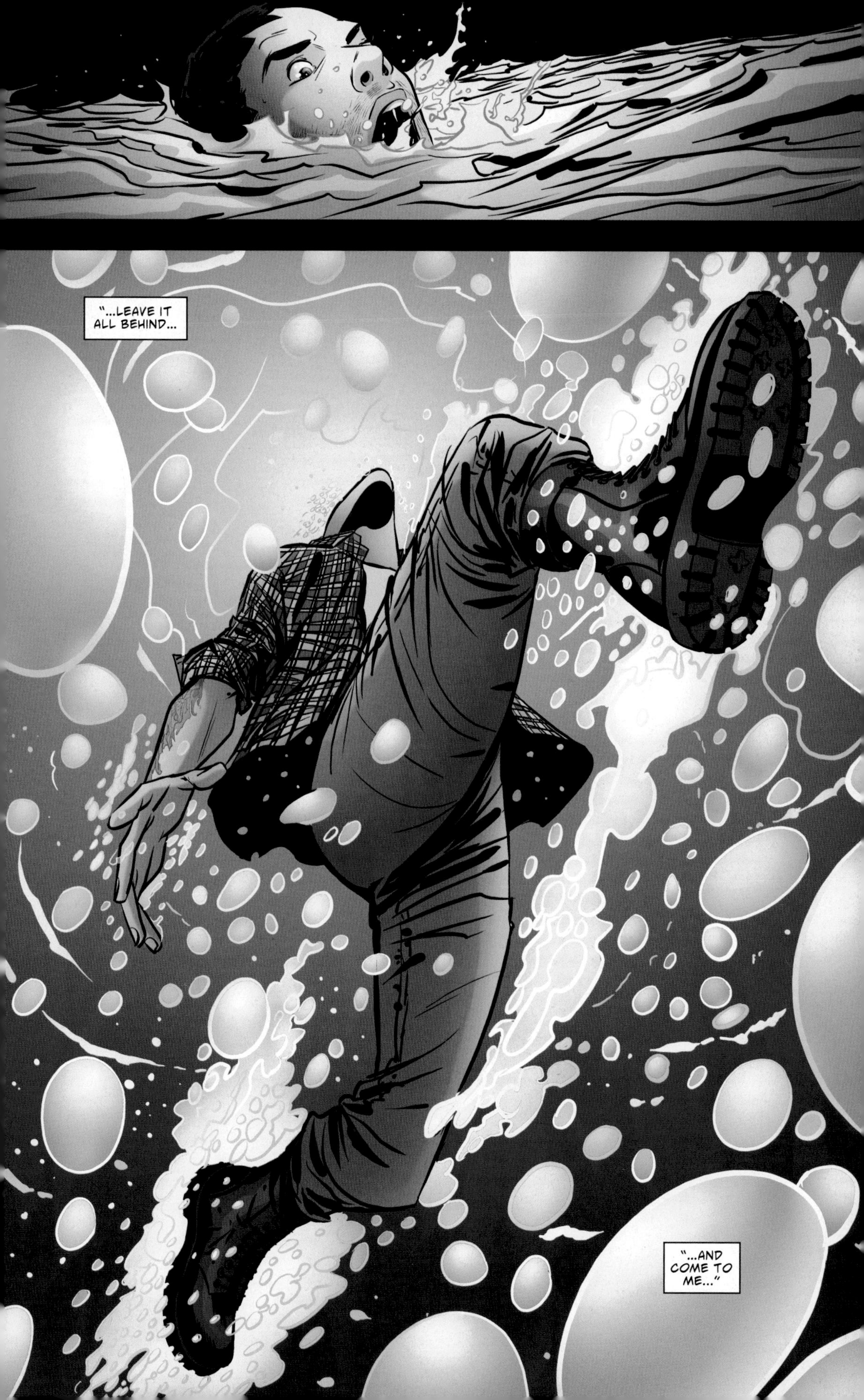
"...LEAVE IT ALL BEHIND...
"...AND COME TO ME..."

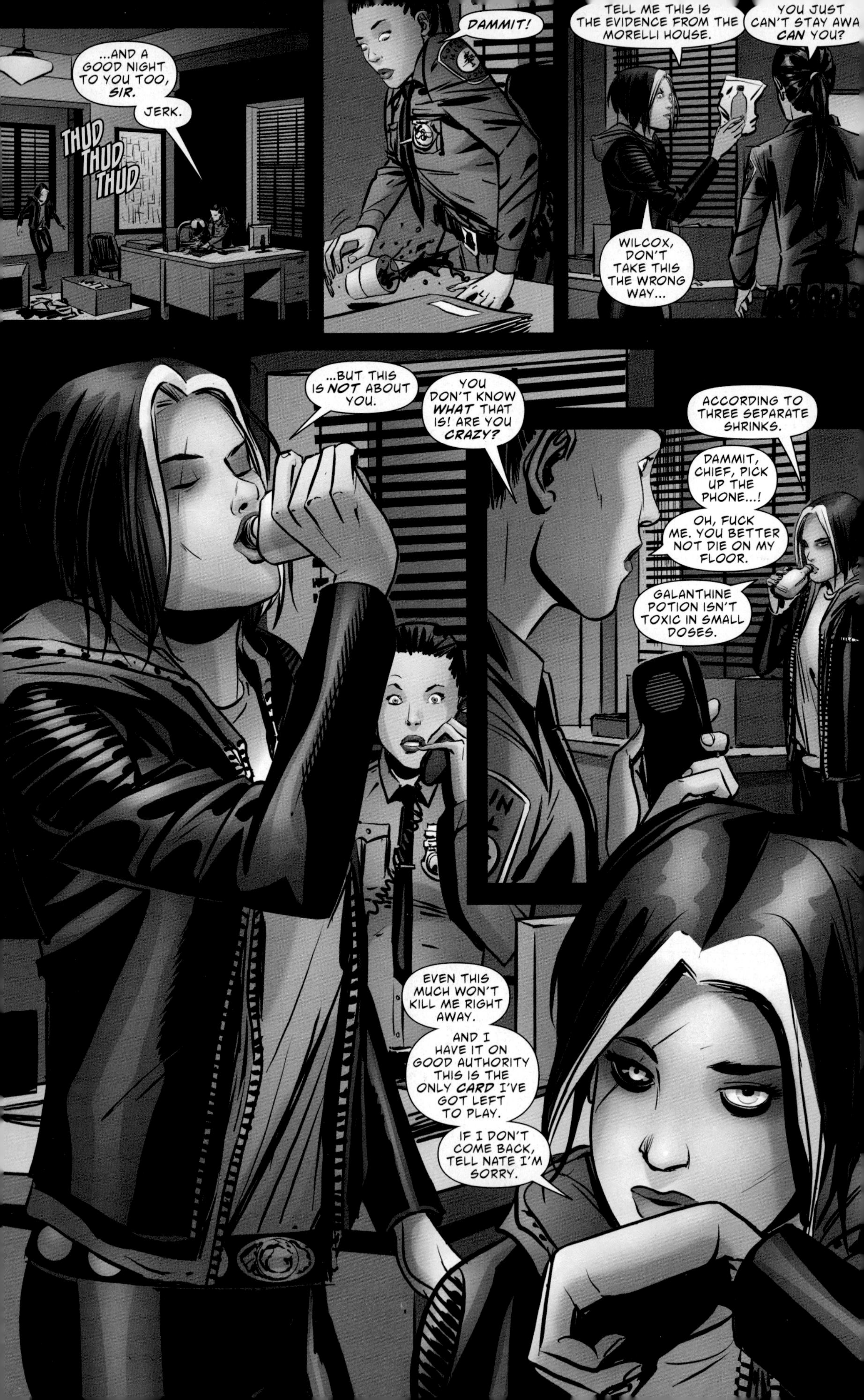
...AND A GOOD NIGHT TO YOU TOO, SIR.
JERK.
THUD THUD THUD
DAMMIT!
TELL ME THIS IS THE EVIDENCE FROM THE MORELLI HOUSE.
YOU JUST CAN'T STAY AWA
CAN YOU?
WILCOX, DON'T TAKE THIS THE WRONG WAY...
...BUT THIS IS NOT ABOUT YOU.
YOU DON'T KNOW WHAT THAT IS! ARE YOU CRAZY?
ACCORDING TO THREE SEPARATE SHRINKS.
DAMMIT, CHIEF, PICK UP THE PHONE...!
OH, FUCK ME. YOU BETTER NOT DIE ON MY FLOOR.
GALANTHINE POTION ISN'T TOXIC IN SMALL DOSES.
EVEN THIS MUCH WON'T KILL ME RIGHT AWAY.
AND I HAVE IT ON GOOD AUTHORITY THIS IS THE ONLY CARD I'VE GOT LEFT TO PLAY.
IF I DON'T COME BACK, TELL NATE I'M SORRY.

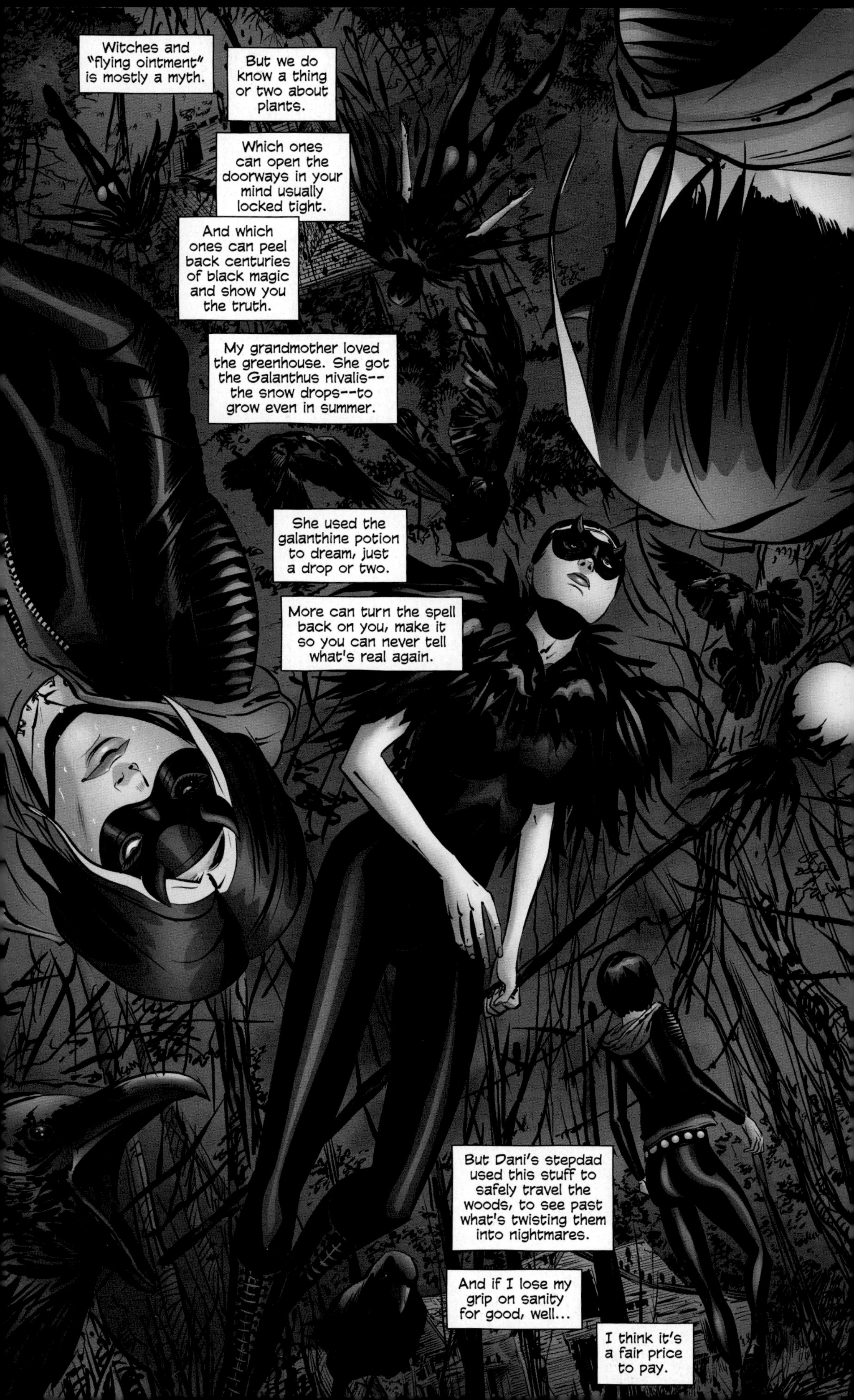
Witches and "flying ointment" is mostly a myth.
But we do know a thing or two about plants.
Which ones can open the doorways in your mind usually locked tight.
And which ones can peel back centuries of black magic and show you the truth.
My grandmother loved the greenhouse. She got the Galanthus nivalis--the snow drops--to grow even in summer.
She used the galanthine potion to dream, just a drop or two.
More can turn the spell back on you, make it so you can never tell what's real again.
But Dani's stepdad used this stuff to safely travel the woods, to see past what's twisting them into nightmares.
And if I lose my grip on sanity for good, well...
I think it's a fair price to pay.

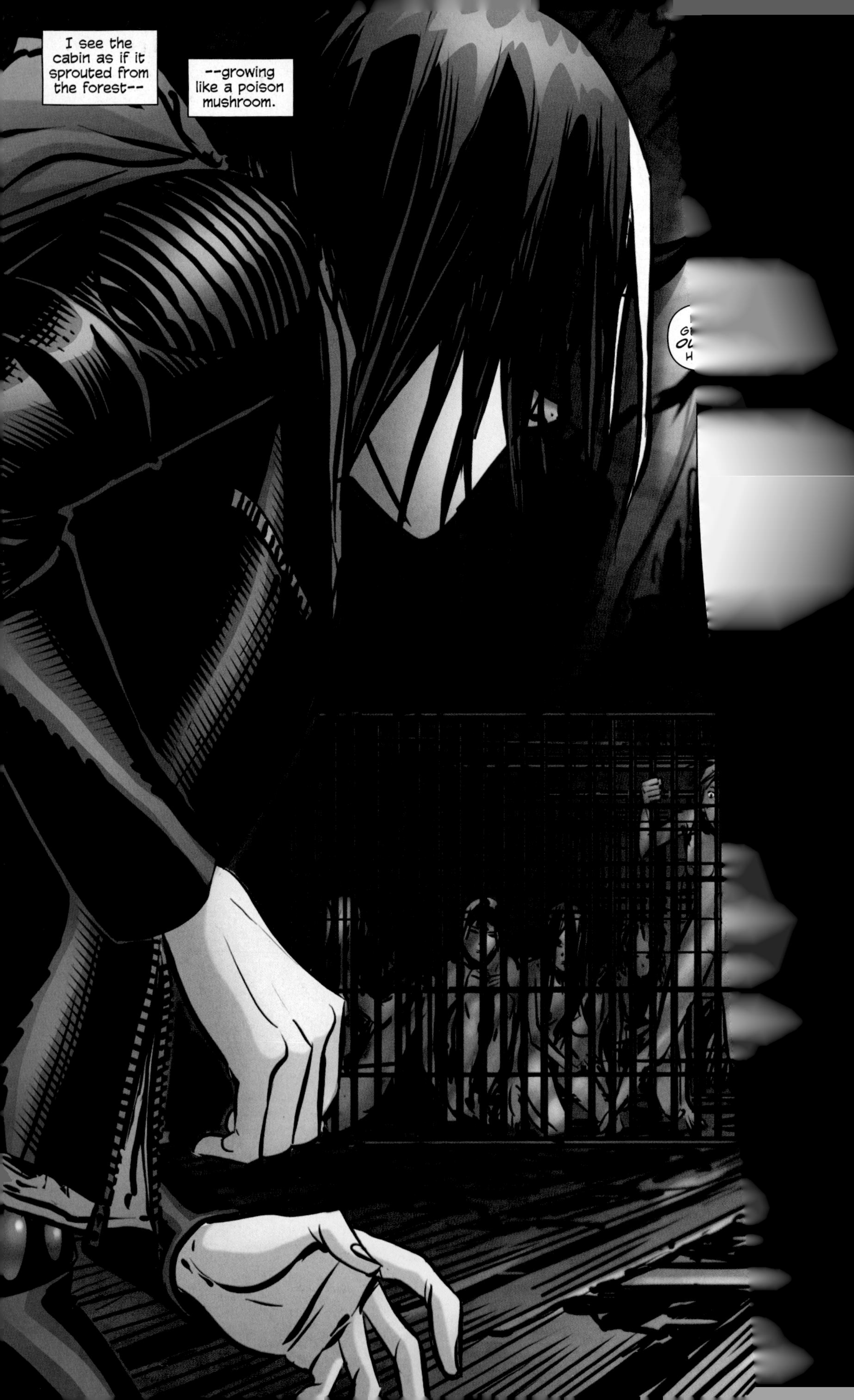
I see the cabin as if it sprouted from the forest--
--growing like a poison mushroom.

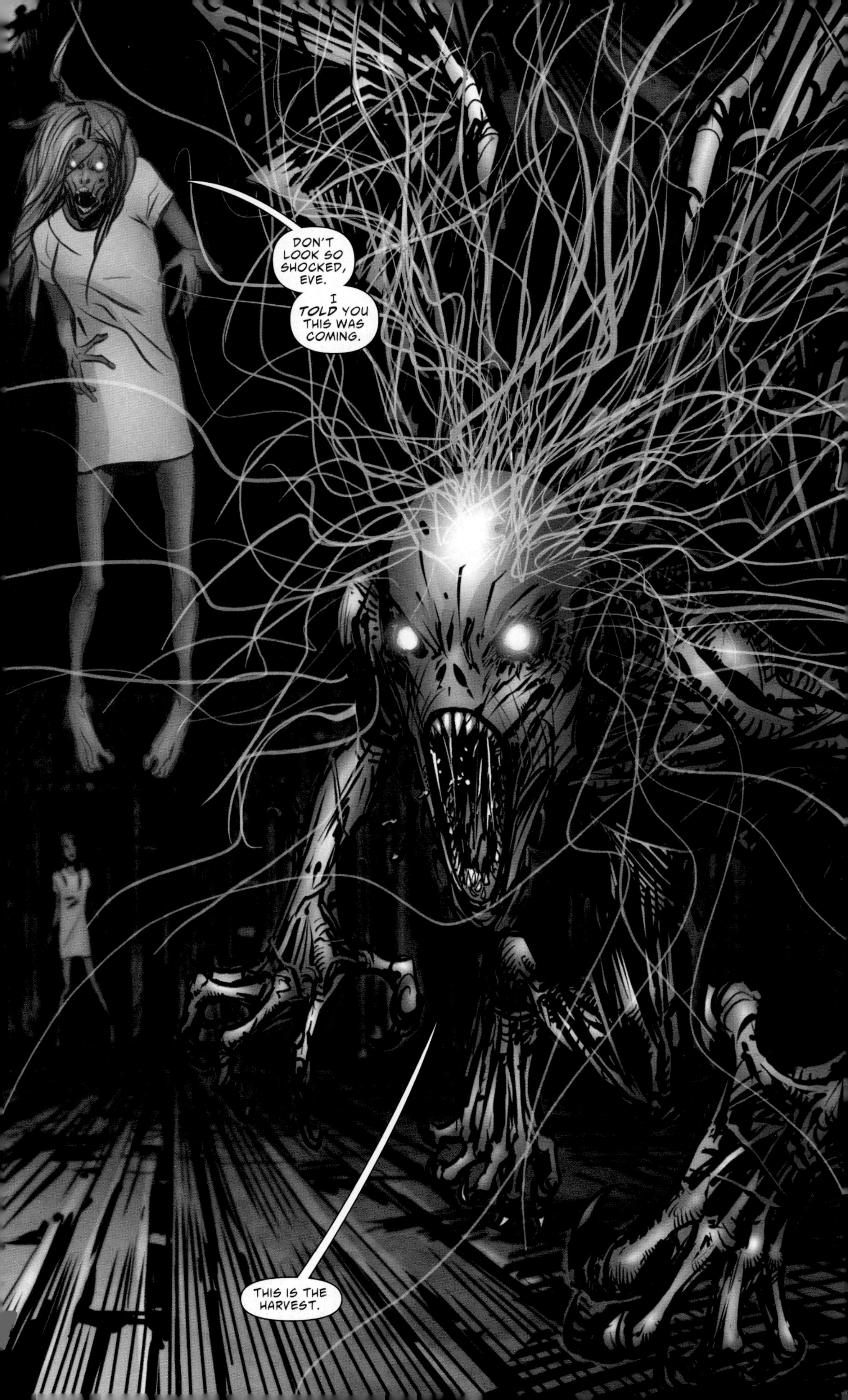
DON'T LOOK SO SHOCKED, EVE.
I *TOLD* YOU THIS WAS COMING.
THIS IS THE HARVEST.

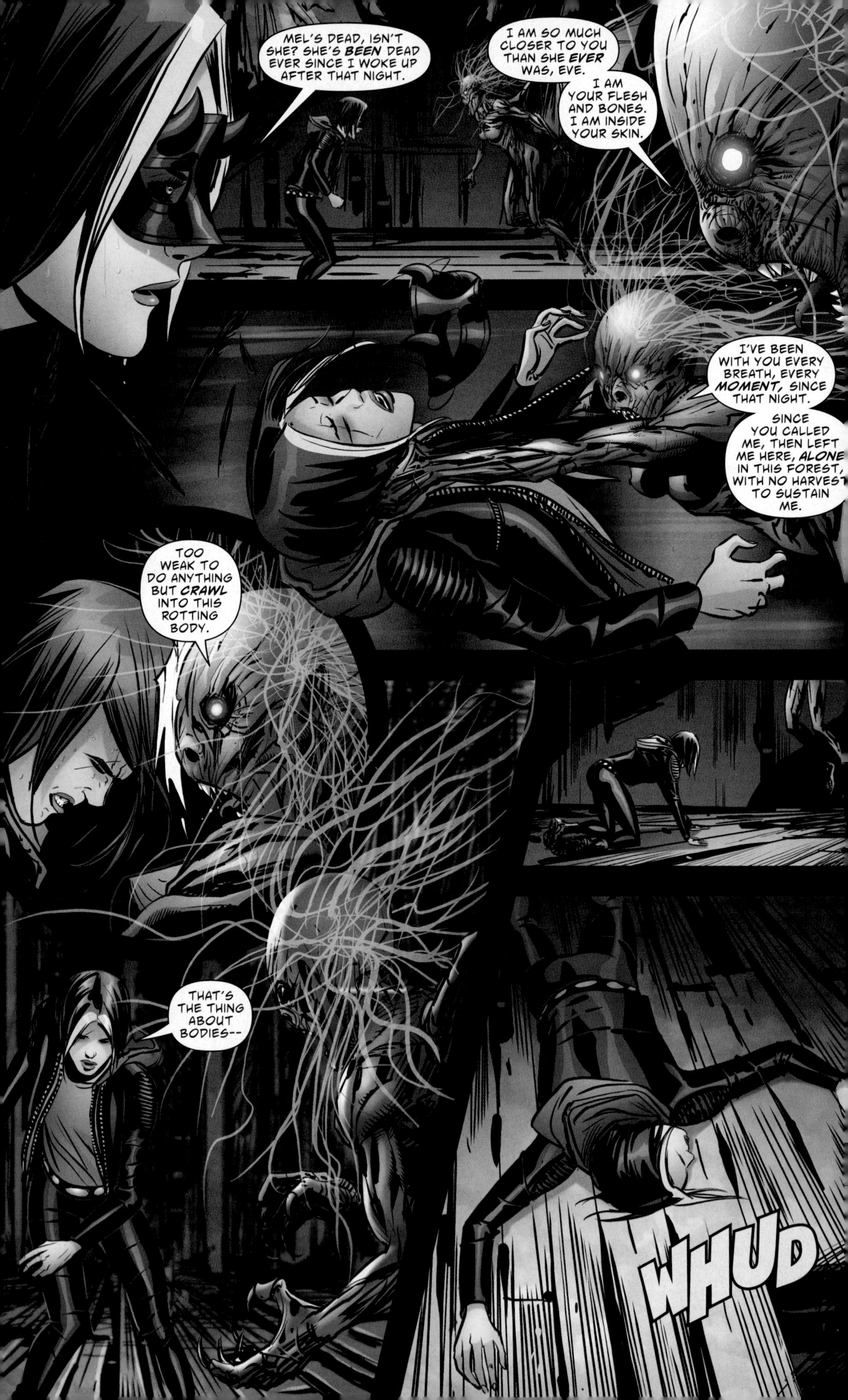
MEL'S DEAD, ISN'T SHE? SHE'S BEEN DEAD EVER SINCE I WOKE UP AFTER THAT NIGHT.
I AM SO MUCH CLOSER TO YOU THAN SHE EVER WAS, EVE.
I AM YOUR FLESH AND BONES. I AM INSIDE YOUR SKIN.
I'VE BEEN WITH YOU EVERY BREATH, EVERY MOMENT, SINCE THAT NIGHT.
SINCE YOU CALLED ME, THEN LEFT ME HERE, ALONE IN THIS FOREST, WITH NO HARVEST TO SUSTAIN ME.
TOO WEAK TO DO ANYTHING BUT CRAWL INTO THIS ROTTING BODY.
THAT'S THE THING ABOUT BODIES--
WHUD

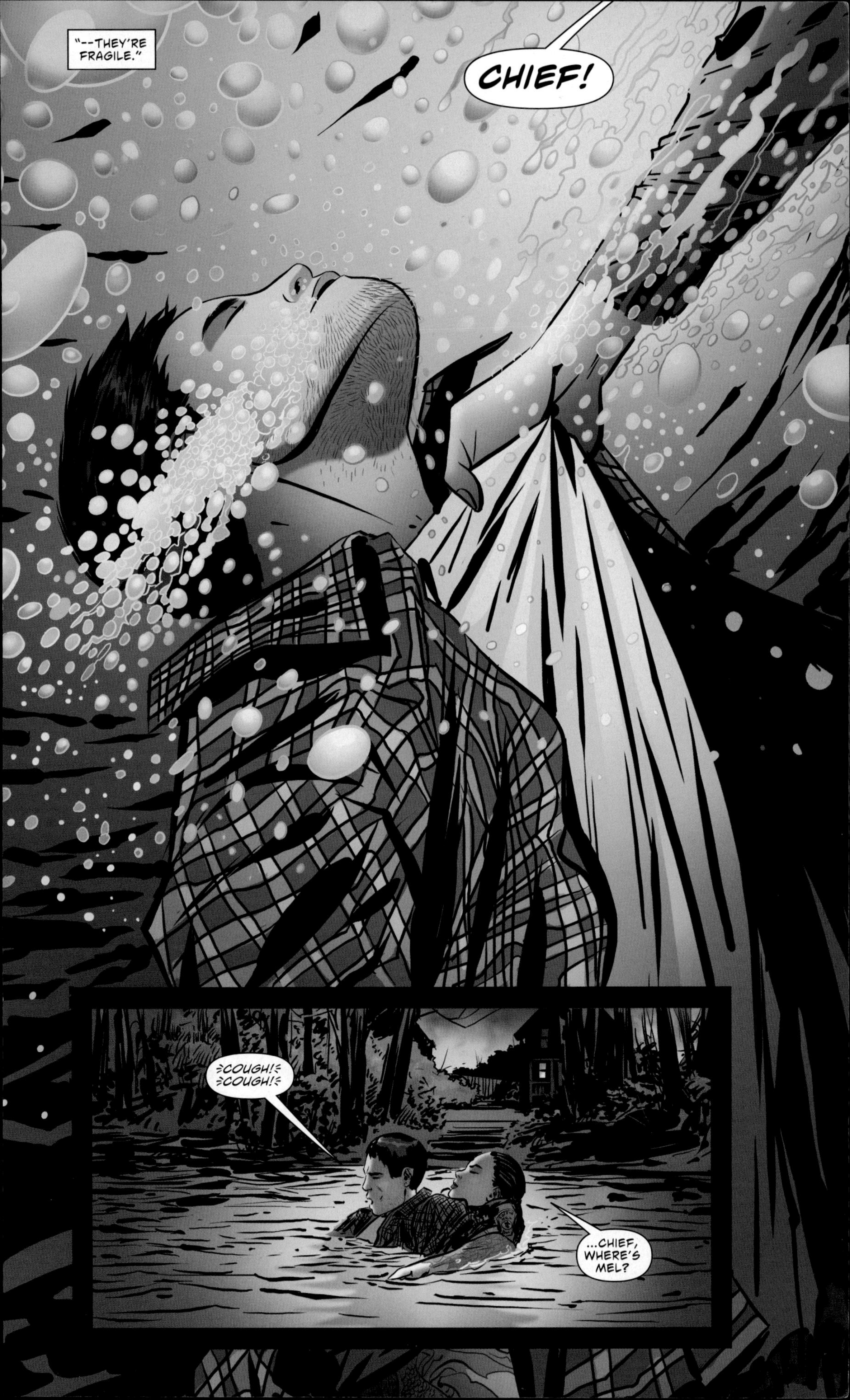
"--THEY'RE FRAGILE."
CHIEF!
COUGH! COUGH!
...CHIEF, WHERE'S MEL?

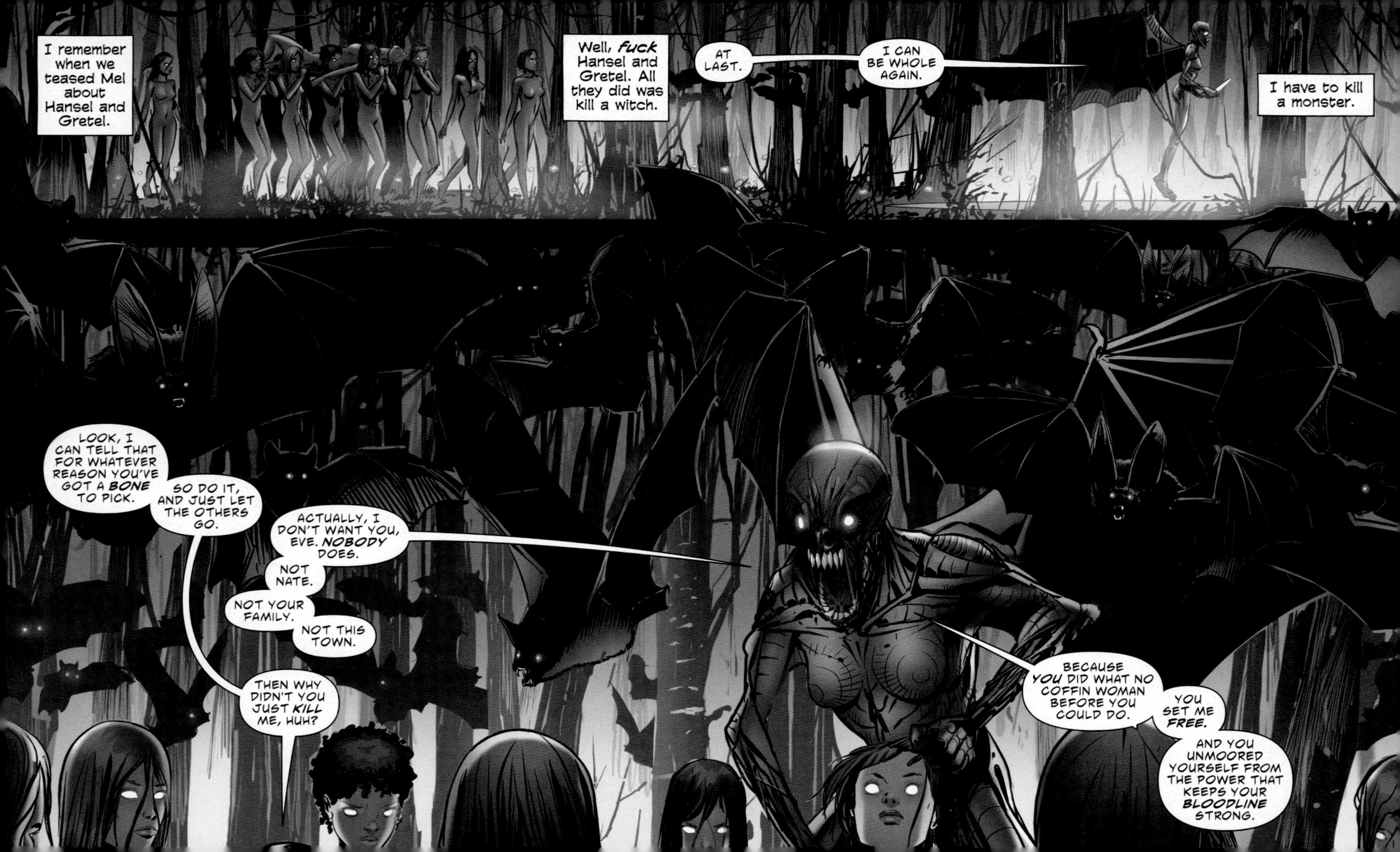
I remember when we teased Mel about Hansel and Gretel.
Well, *fuck* Hansel and Gretel. All they did was kill a witch.
AT LAST.
I CAN BE WHOLE AGAIN.
I have to kill a monster.
LOOK, I CAN TELL THAT FOR WHATEVER REASON YOU'VE GOT A *BONE* TO PICK.
SO DO IT, AND JUST LET THE OTHERS GO.
ACTUALLY, I DON'T WANT YOU, EVE. *NOBODY* DOES.
NOT NATE.
NOT YOUR FAMILY.
NOT THIS TOWN.
THEN WHY DIDN'T YOU JUST *KILL* ME, HUH?
BECAUSE *YOU* DID WHAT NO COFFIN WOMAN BEFORE YOU COULD DO.
YOU SET ME *FREE.*
AND YOU UNMOORED YOURSELF FROM THE POWER THAT KEEPS YOUR *BLOODLINE* STRONG.

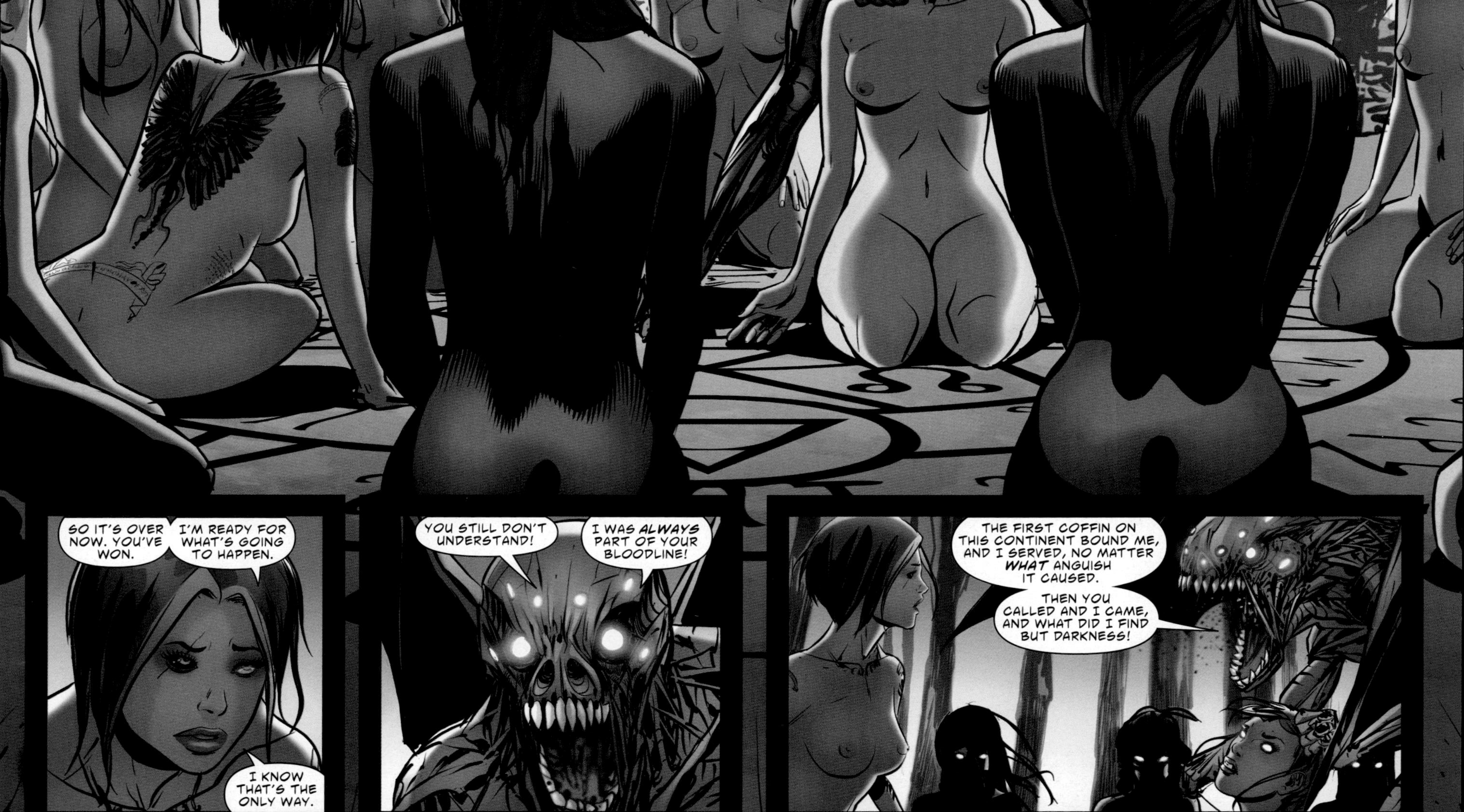
SO IT'S OVER NOW. YOU'VE WON.
I'M READY FOR WHAT'S GOING TO HAPPEN.
I KNOW THAT'S THE ONLY WAY.
YOU STILL DON'T UNDERSTAND!
I WAS *ALWAYS* PART OF YOUR BLOODLINE!
THE FIRST COFFIN ON THIS CONTINENT BOUND ME, AND I SERVED, NO MATTER ***WHAT*** ANGUISH IT CAUSED.
THEN YOU CALLED AND I CAME, AND WHAT DID I FIND BUT DARKNESS!

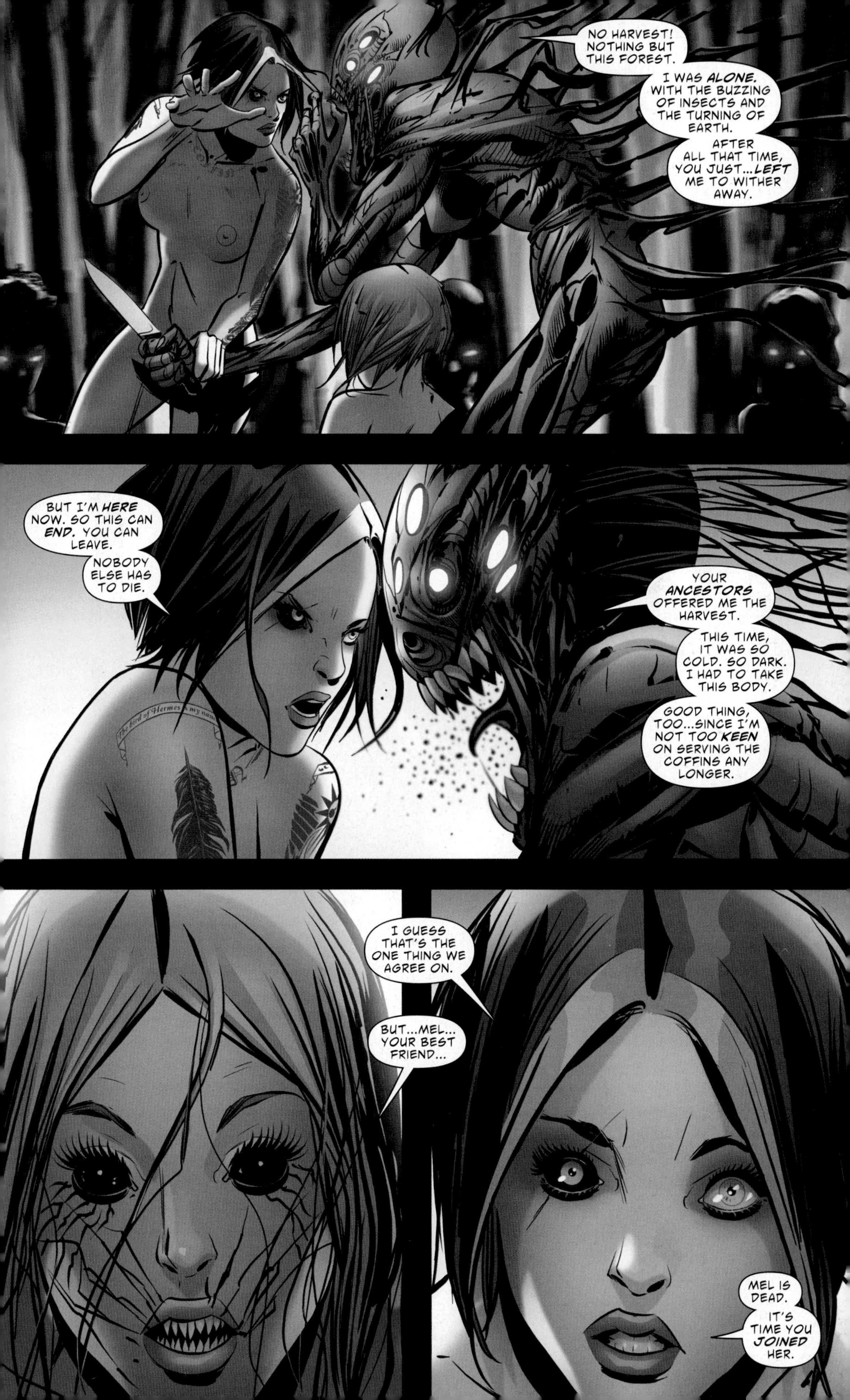
NO HARVEST! NOTHING BUT THIS FOREST.
I WAS ALONE. WITH THE BUZZING OF INSECTS AND THE TURNING OF EARTH.
AFTER ALL THAT TIME, YOU JUST...LEFT ME TO WITHER AWAY.
BUT I'M HERE NOW. SO THIS CAN END. YOU CAN LEAVE.
NOBODY ELSE HAS TO DIE.
YOUR ANCESTORS OFFERED ME THE HARVEST.
THIS TIME, IT WAS SO COLD. SO DARK. I HAD TO TAKE THIS BODY.
GOOD THING, TOO...SINCE I'M NOT TOO KEEN ON SERVING THE COFFINS ANY LONGER.
I GUESS THAT'S THE ONE THING WE AGREE ON.
BUT...MEL... YOUR BEST FRIEND...
MEL IS DEAD.
IT'S TIME YOU JOINED HER.

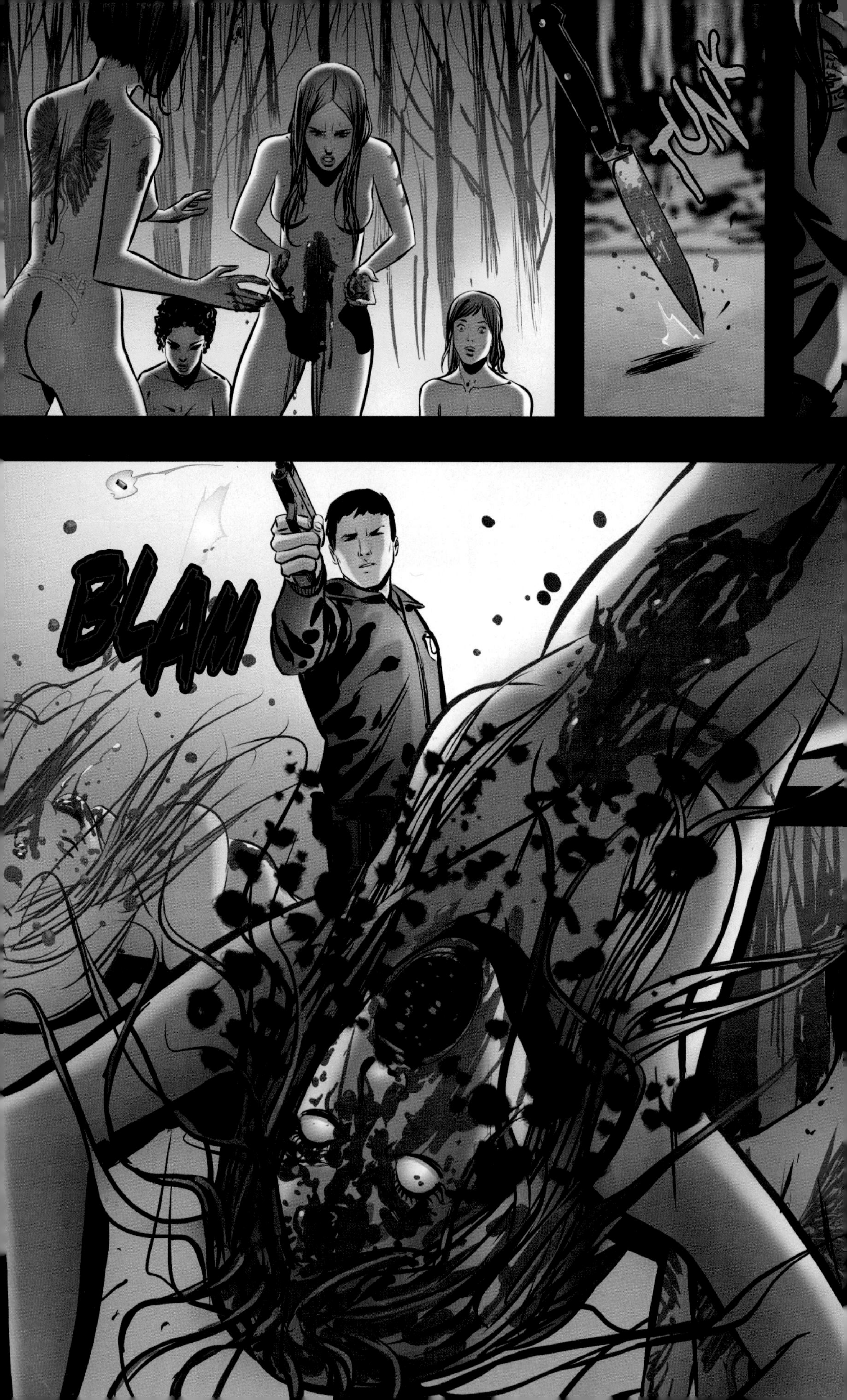
TUNK
BLAM

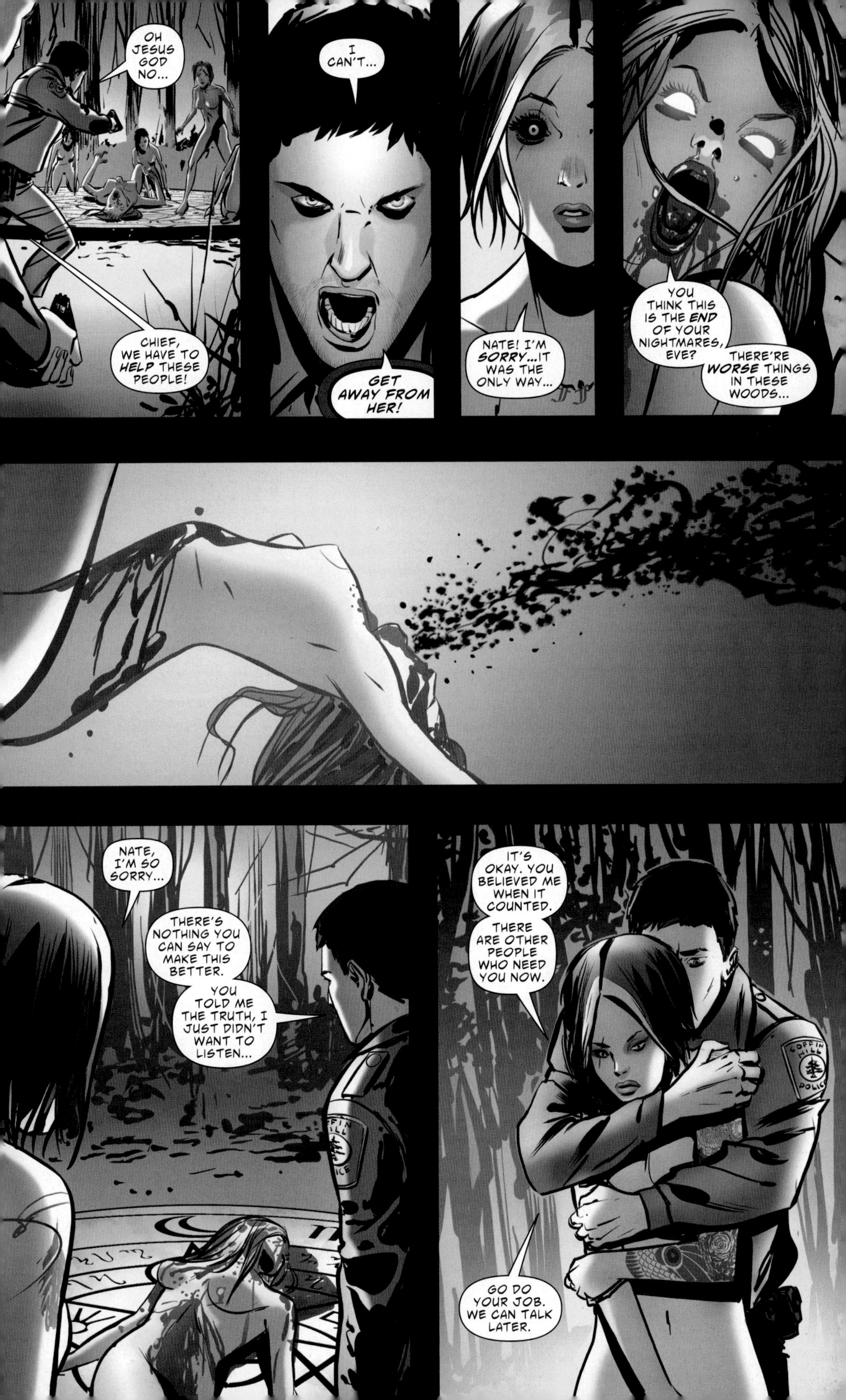
OH JESUS GOD NO...
CHIEF, WE HAVE TO HELP THESE PEOPLE!
I CAN'T...
GET AWAY FROM HER!
NATE! I'M SORRY...IT WAS THE ONLY WAY...
YOU THINK THIS IS THE END OF YOUR NIGHTMARES, EVE?
THERE'RE WORSE THINGS IN THESE WOODS...
NATE, I'M SO SORRY...
THERE'S NOTHING YOU CAN SAY TO MAKE THIS BETTER.
YOU TOLD ME THE TRUTH, I JUST DIDN'T WANT TO LISTEN...
IT'S OKAY. YOU BELIEVED ME WHEN IT COUNTED.
THERE ARE OTHER PEOPLE WHO NEED YOU NOW.
GO DO YOUR JOB. WE CAN TALK LATER.

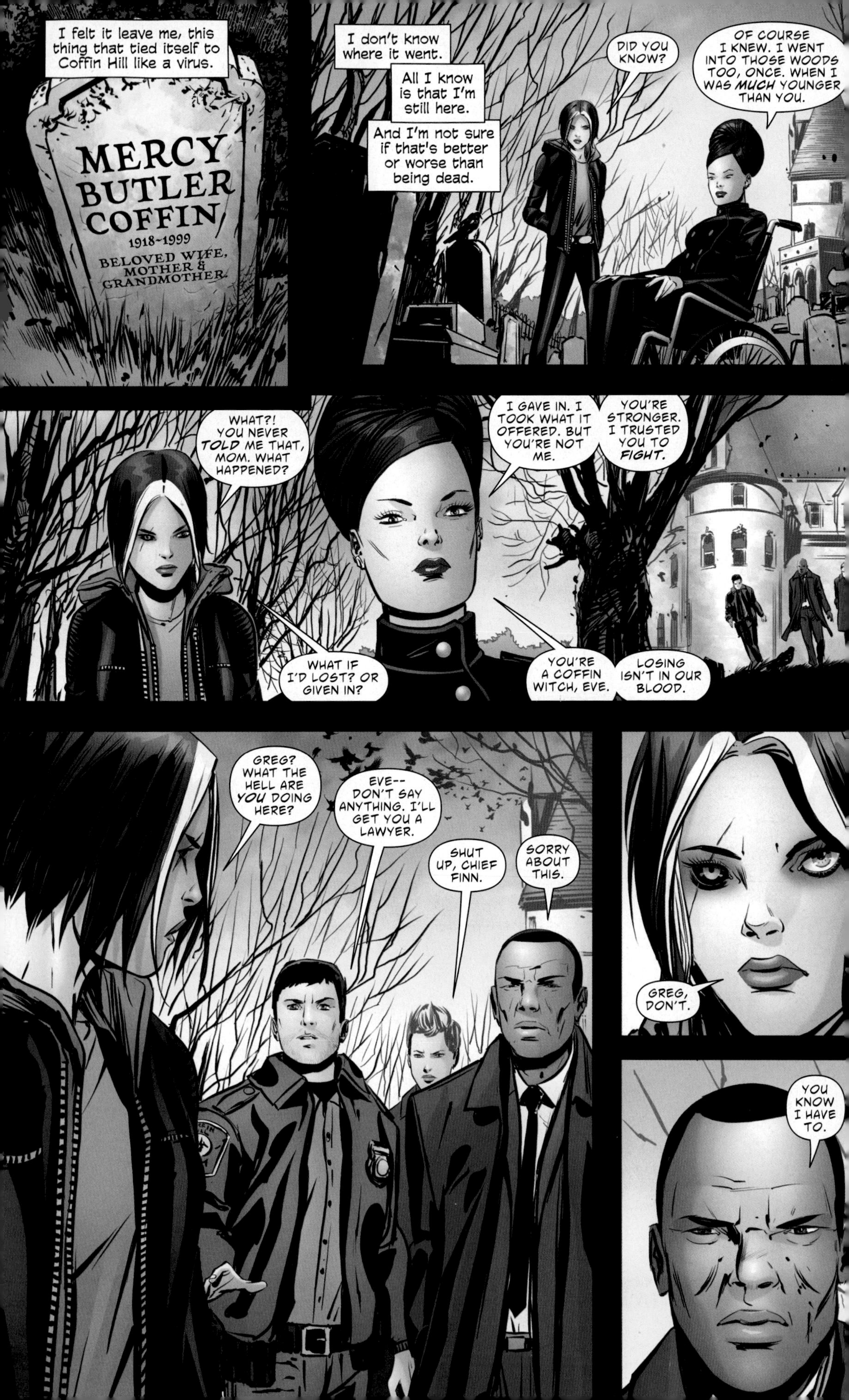
I felt it leave me, this thing that tied itself to Coffin Hill like a virus.
MERCY BUTLER COFFIN
1918~1999
BELOVED WIFE, MOTHER & GRANDMOTHER
I don't know where it went.
All I know is that I'm still here.
And I'm not sure if that's better or worse than being dead.
DID YOU KNOW?
OF COURSE I KNEW. I WENT INTO THOSE WOODS TOO, ONCE. WHEN I WAS MUCH YOUNGER THAN YOU.
WHAT?! YOU NEVER TOLD ME THAT, MOM. WHAT HAPPENED?
I GAVE IN. I TOOK WHAT IT OFFERED. BUT YOU'RE NOT ME.
YOU'RE STRONGER. I TRUSTED YOU TO FIGHT.
WHAT IF I'D LOST? OR GIVEN IN?
YOU'RE A COFFIN WITCH, EVE.
LOSING ISN'T IN OUR BLOOD.
GREG? WHAT THE HELL ARE YOU DOING HERE?
EVE-- DON'T SAY ANYTHING. I'LL GET YOU A LAWYER.
SHUT UP, CHIEF FINN.
SORRY ABOUT THIS.
GREG, DON'T.
YOU KNOW I HAVE TO.

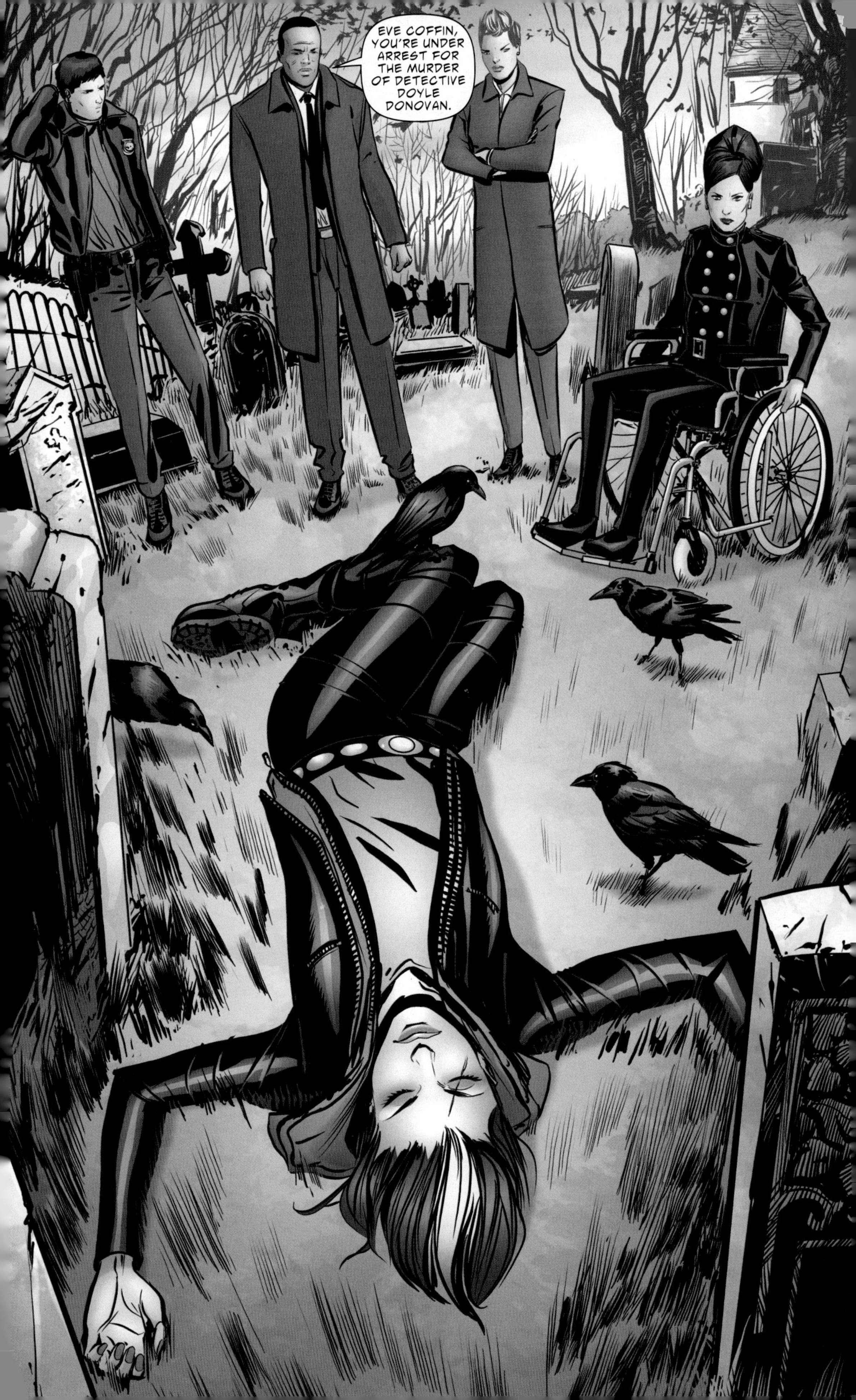
EVE COFFIN, YOU'RE UNDER ARREST FOR THE MURDER OF DETECTIVE DOYLE DONOVAN.

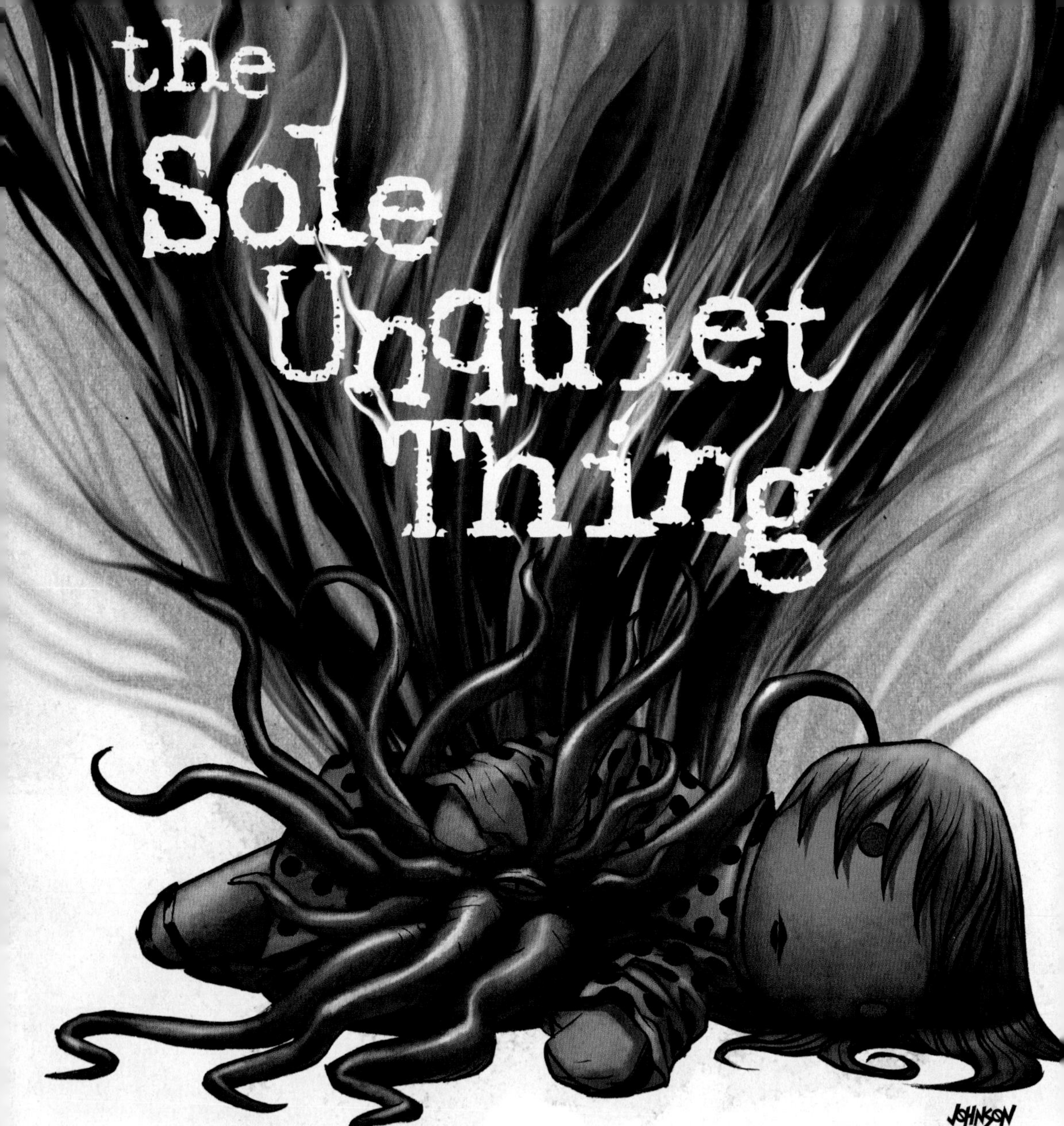
the Sole Unquiet Thing
JOHNSON

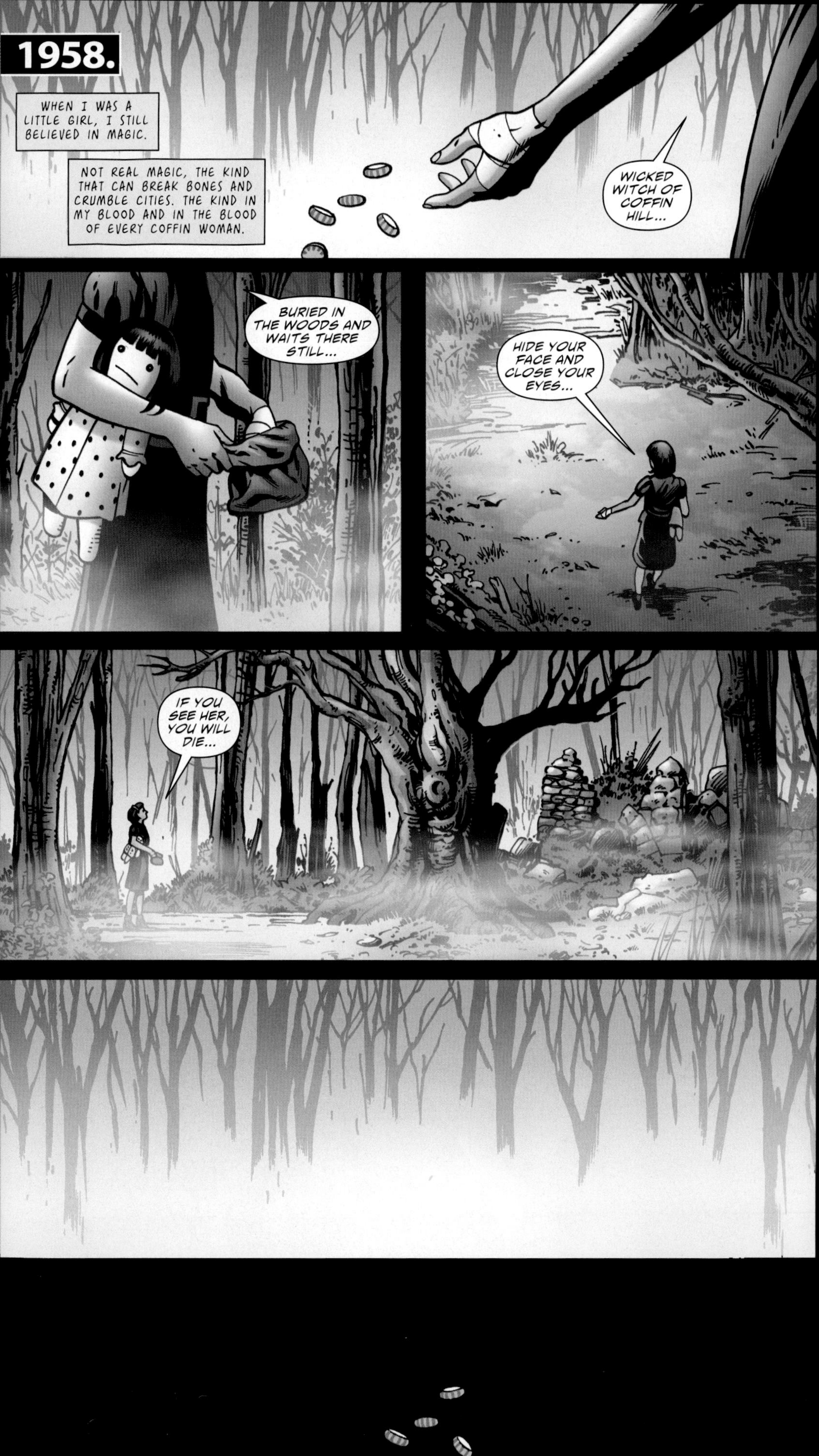
1958.
WHEN I WAS A LITTLE GIRL, I STILL BELIEVED IN MAGIC.
NOT REAL MAGIC, THE KIND THAT CAN BREAK BONES AND CRUMBLE CITIES. THE KIND IN MY BLOOD AND IN THE BLOOD OF EVERY COFFIN WOMAN.
WICKED WITCH OF COFFIN HILL...
BURIED IN THE WOODS AND WAITS THERE STILL...
HIDE YOUR FACE AND CLOSE YOUR EYES...
IF YOU SEE HER, YOU WILL DIE...

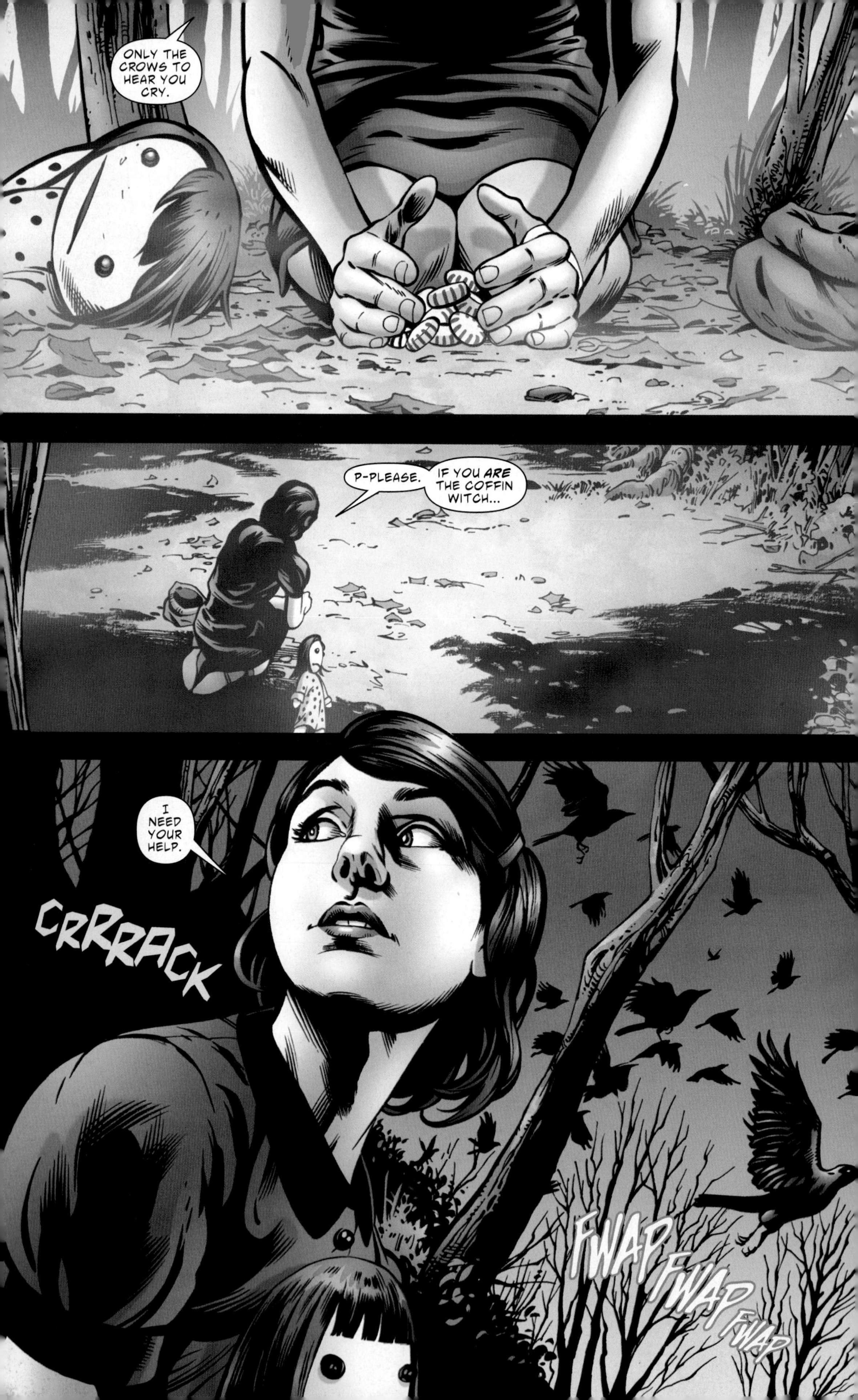
ONLY THE CROWS TO HEAR YOU CRY.
P-PLEASE.
IF YOU ARE THE COFFIN WITCH...
I NEED YOUR HELP.
CRRRACK
FWAP FWAP FWAP

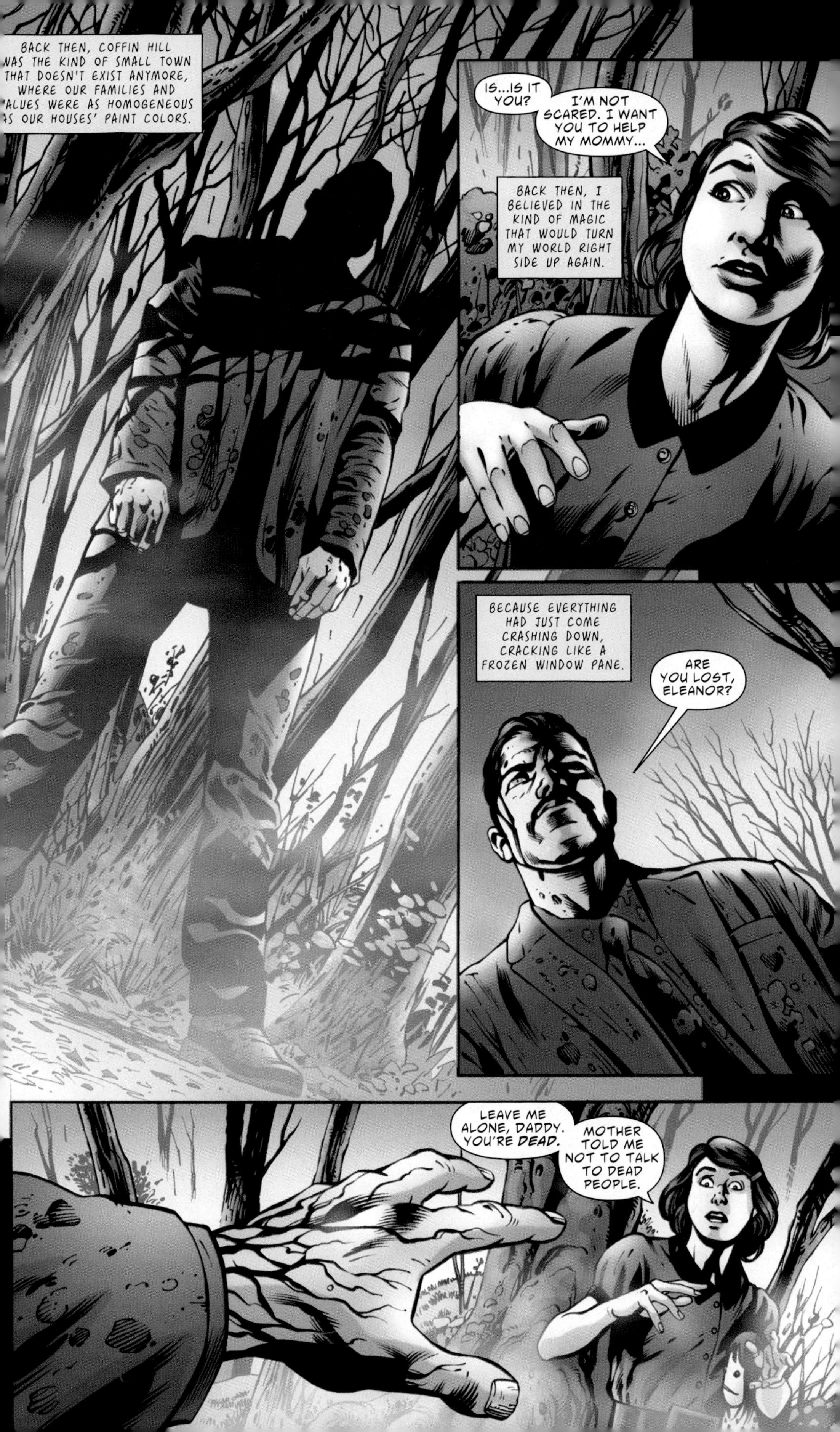
BACK THEN, COFFIN HILL WAS THE KIND OF SMALL TOWN THAT DOESN'T EXIST ANYMORE, WHERE OUR FAMILIES AND VALUES WERE AS HOMOGENEOUS AS OUR HOUSES' PAINT COLORS.
IS...IS IT YOU?
I'M NOT SCARED. I WANT YOU TO HELP MY MOMMY...
BACK THEN, I BELIEVED IN THE KIND OF MAGIC THAT WOULD TURN MY WORLD RIGHT SIDE UP AGAIN.
BECAUSE EVERYTHING HAD JUST COME CRASHING DOWN, CRACKING LIKE A FROZEN WINDOW PANE.
ARE YOU LOST, ELEANOR?
LEAVE ME ALONE, DADDY. YOU'RE *DEAD*.
MOTHER TOLD ME NOT TO TALK TO DEAD PEOPLE.

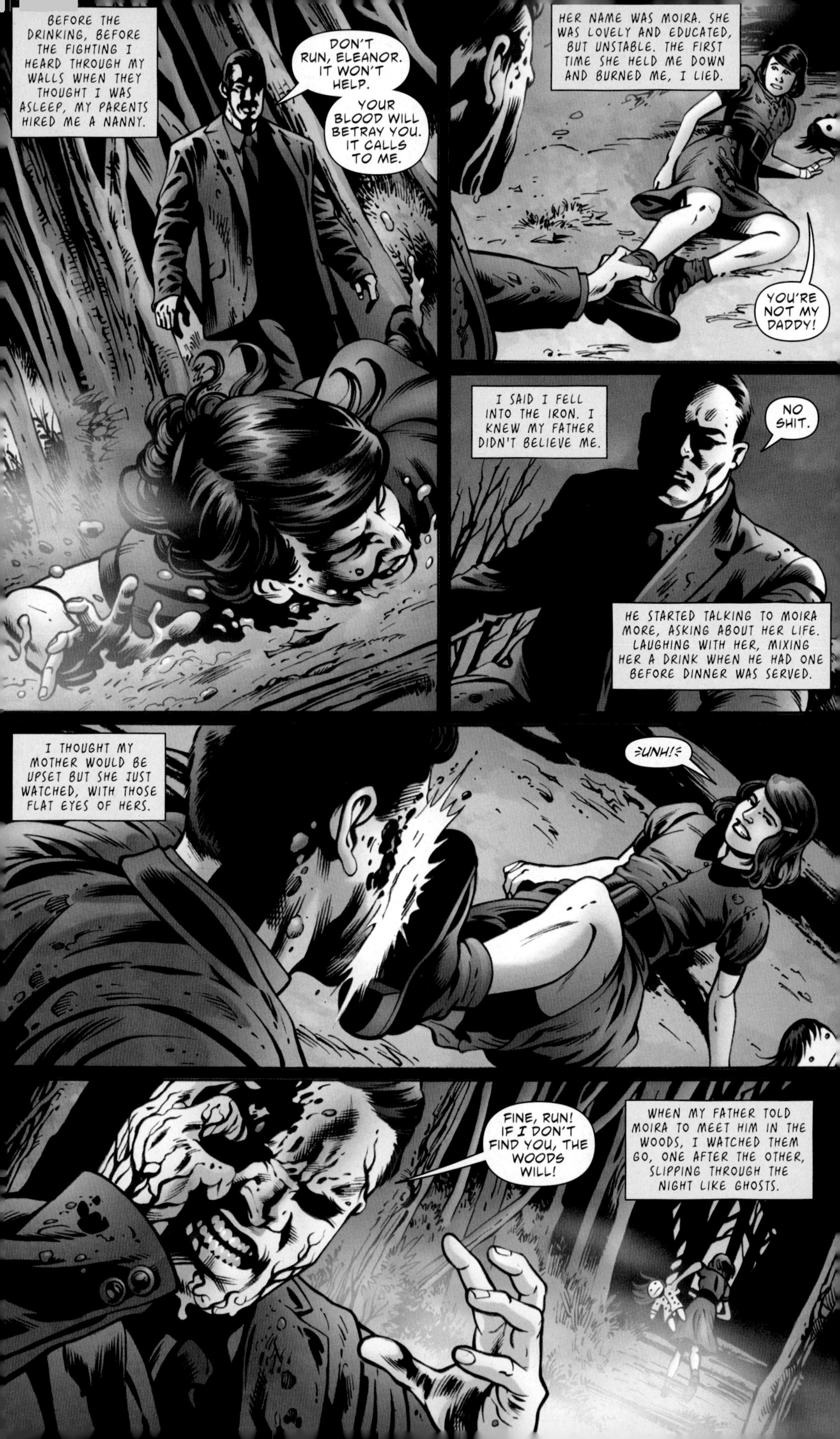

BEFORE THE DRINKING, BEFORE THE FIGHTING I HEARD THROUGH MY WALLS WHEN THEY THOUGHT I WAS ASLEEP, MY PARENTS HIRED ME A NANNY.
DON'T RUN, ELEANOR. IT WON'T HELP.
YOUR BLOOD WILL BETRAY YOU. IT CALLS TO ME.
HER NAME WAS MOIRA. SHE WAS LOVELY AND EDUCATED, BUT UNSTABLE. THE FIRST TIME SHE HELD ME DOWN AND BURNED ME, I LIED.
YOU'RE NOT MY DADDY!
I SAID I FELL INTO THE IRON. I KNEW MY FATHER DIDN'T BELIEVE ME.
NO SHIT.
HE STARTED TALKING TO MOIRA MORE, ASKING ABOUT HER LIFE. LAUGHING WITH HER, MIXING HER A DRINK WHEN HE HAD ONE BEFORE DINNER WAS SERVED.
I THOUGHT MY MOTHER WOULD BE UPSET BUT SHE JUST WATCHED, WITH THOSE FLAT EYES OF HERS.
UNH!
FINE, RUN! IF I DON'T FIND YOU, THE WOODS WILL!
WHEN MY FATHER TOLD MOIRA TO MEET HIM IN THE WOODS, I WATCHED THEM GO, ONE AFTER THE OTHER, SLIPPING THROUGH THE NIGHT LIKE GHOSTS.

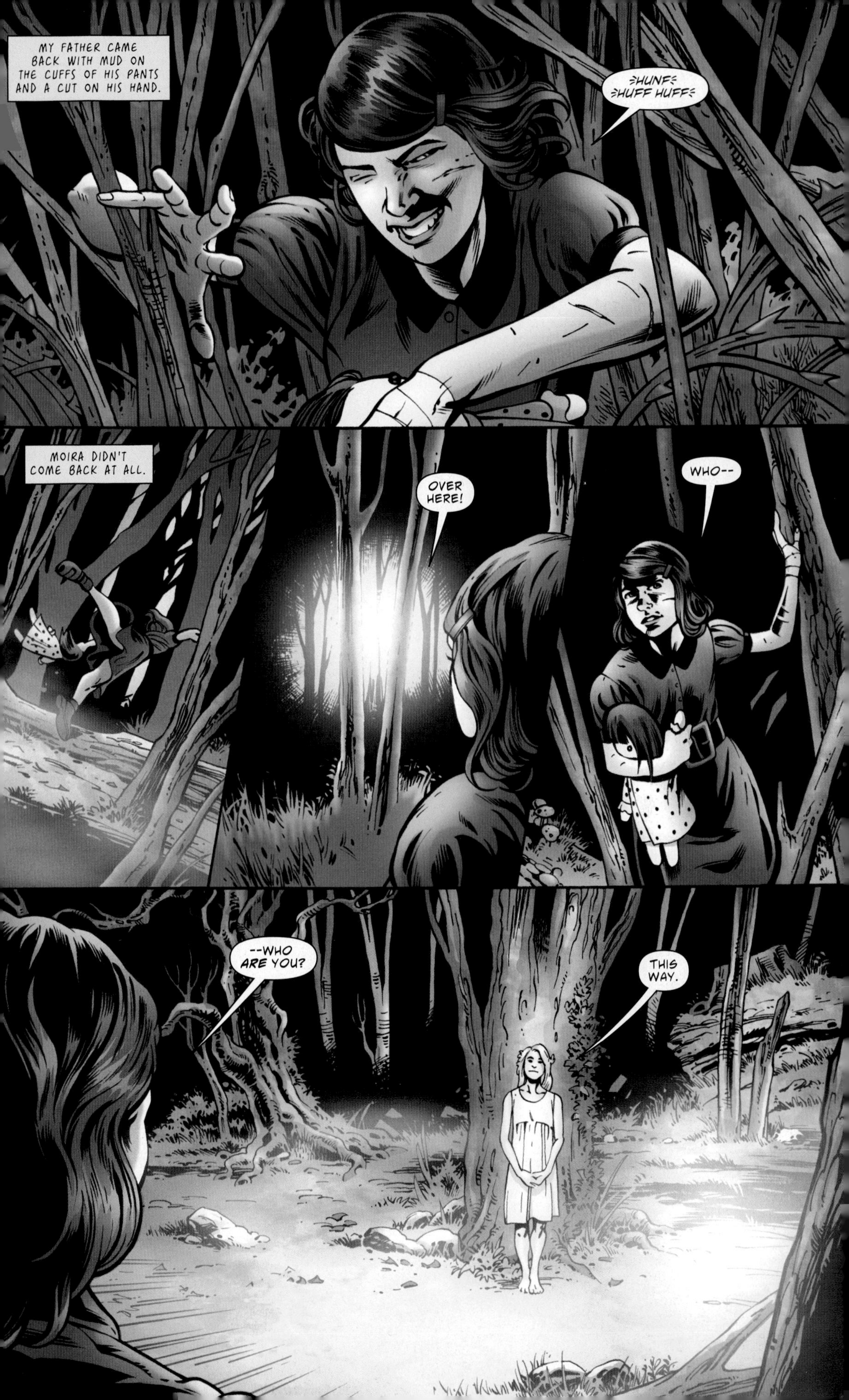
MY FATHER CAME BACK WITH MUD ON THE CUFFS OF HIS PANTS AND A CUT ON HIS HAND.
HUNF HUFF HUFF
MOIRA DIDN'T COME BACK AT ALL.
OVER HERE!
WHO--
--WHO ARE YOU?
THIS WAY.

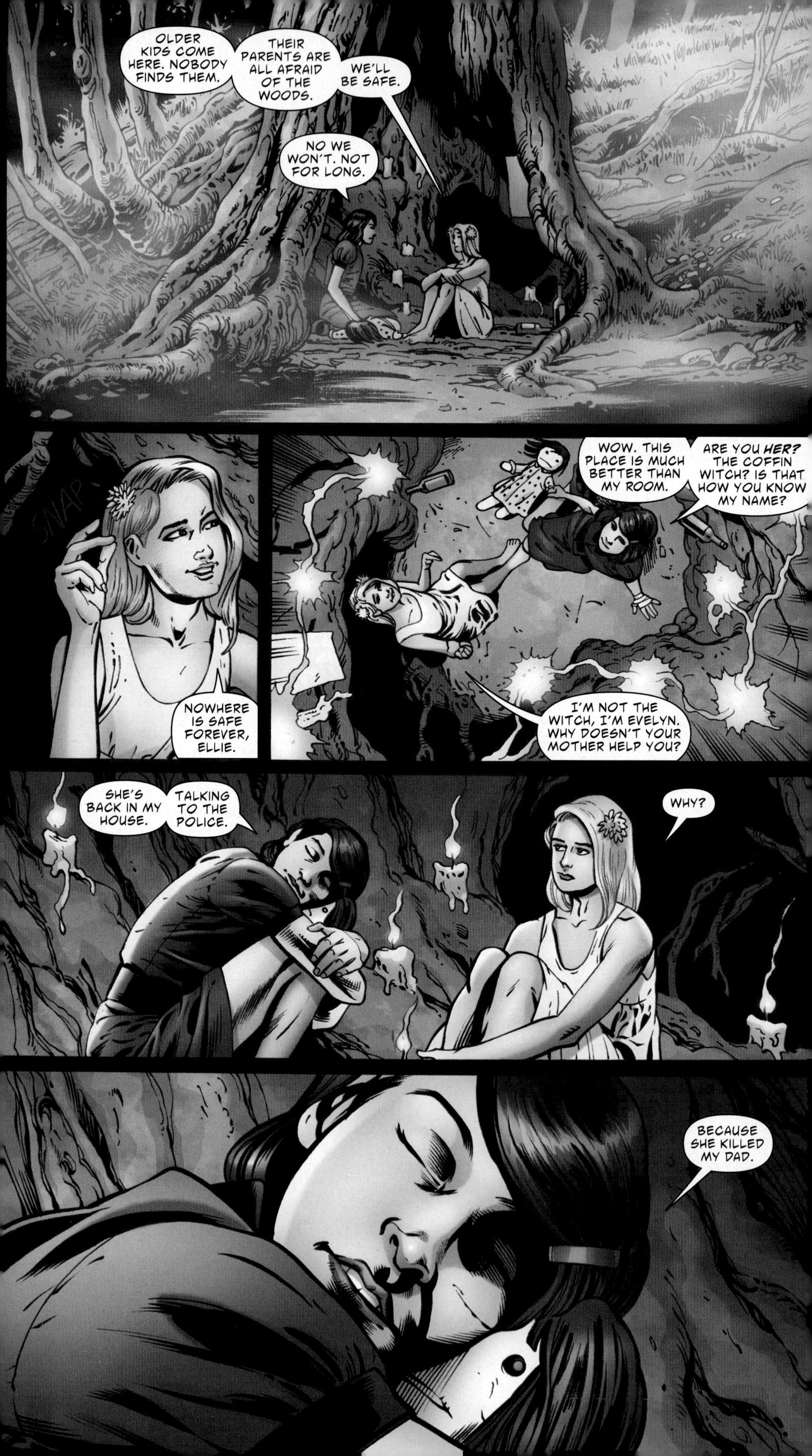
OLDER KIDS COME HERE. NOBODY FINDS THEM.
THEIR PARENTS ARE ALL AFRAID OF THE WOODS.
WE'LL BE SAFE.
NO WE WON'T. NOT FOR LONG.
SNAP
NOWHERE IS SAFE FOREVER, ELLIE.
WOW. THIS PLACE IS MUCH BETTER THAN MY ROOM.
ARE YOU *HER?* THE COFFIN WITCH? IS THAT HOW YOU KNOW MY NAME?
I'M NOT THE WITCH, I'M EVELYN. WHY DOESN'T YOUR MOTHER HELP YOU?
SHE'S BACK IN MY HOUSE.
TALKING TO THE POLICE.
WHY?
BECAUSE SHE KILLED MY DAD.

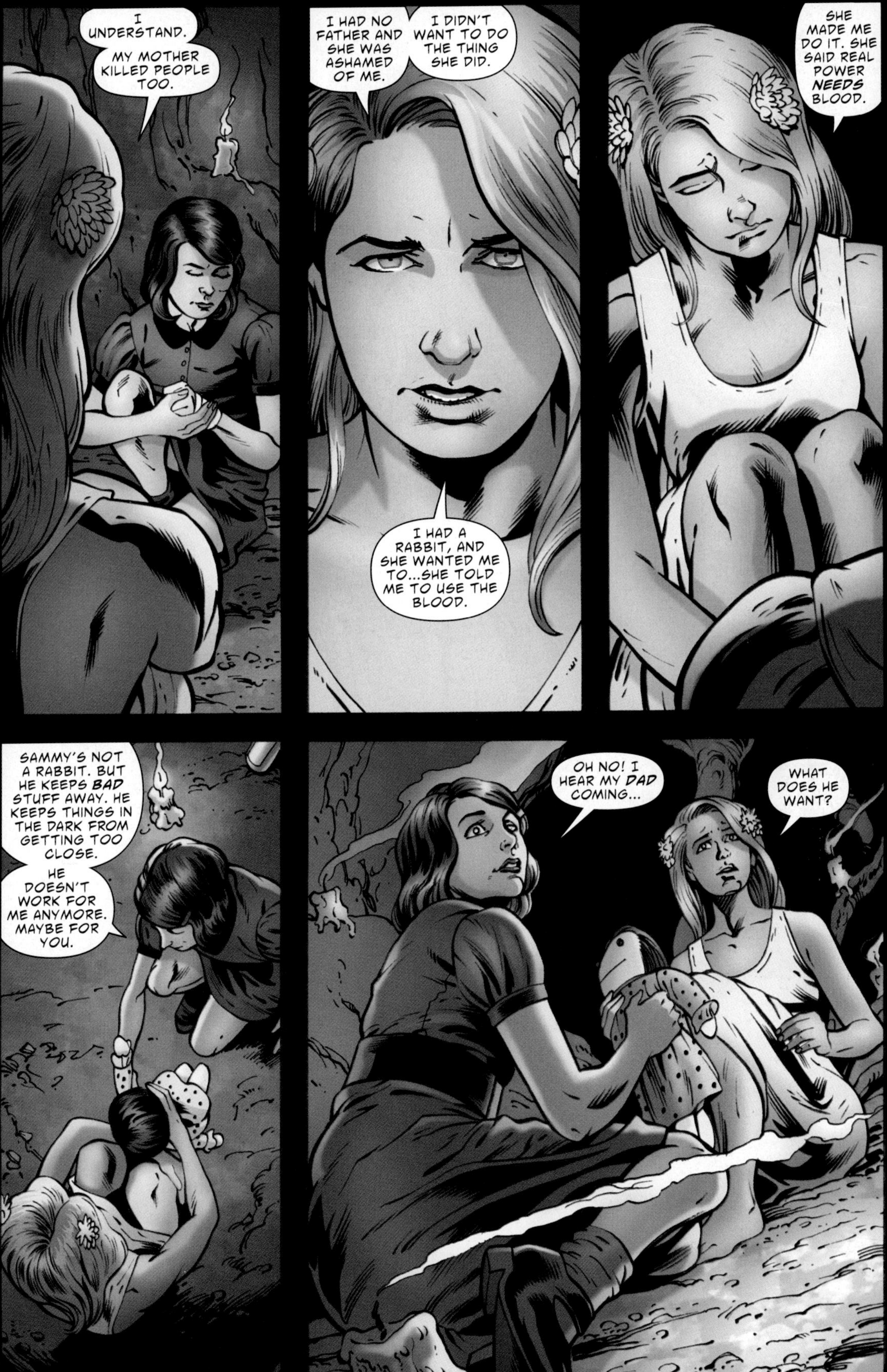
I UNDERSTAND.
MY MOTHER KILLED PEOPLE TOO.
I HAD NO FATHER AND SHE WAS ASHAMED OF ME.
I DIDN'T WANT TO DO THE THING SHE DID.
I HAD A RABBIT, AND SHE WANTED ME TO...SHE TOLD ME TO USE THE BLOOD.
SHE MADE ME DO IT. SHE SAID REAL POWER NEEDS BLOOD.
SAMMY'S NOT A RABBIT. BUT HE KEEPS BAD STUFF AWAY. HE KEEPS THINGS IN THE DARK FROM GETTING TOO CLOSE.
HE DOESN'T WORK FOR ME ANYMORE. MAYBE FOR YOU.
OH NO! I HEAR MY DAD COMING...
WHAT DOES HE WANT?

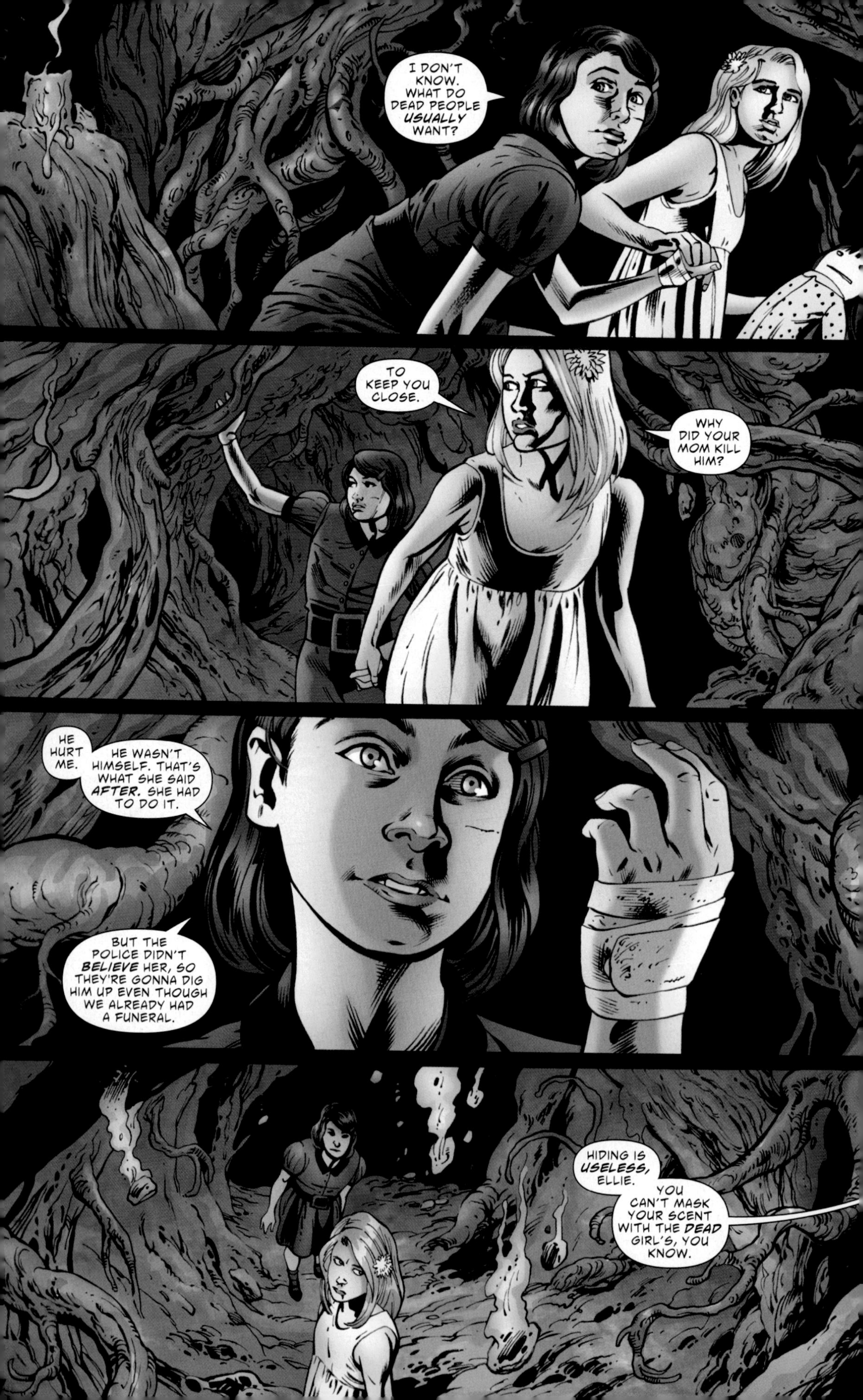
I DON'T KNOW. WHAT DO DEAD PEOPLE USUALLY WANT?
TO KEEP YOU CLOSE.
WHY DID YOUR MOM KILL HIM?
HE HURT ME.
HE WASN'T HIMSELF. THAT'S WHAT SHE SAID AFTER. SHE HAD TO DO IT.
BUT THE POLICE DIDN'T BELIEVE HER, SO THEY'RE GONNA DIG HIM UP EVEN THOUGH WE ALREADY HAD A FUNERAL.
HIDING IS USELESS, ELLIE.
YOU CAN'T MASK YOUR SCENT WITH THE DEAD GIRL'S, YOU KNOW.

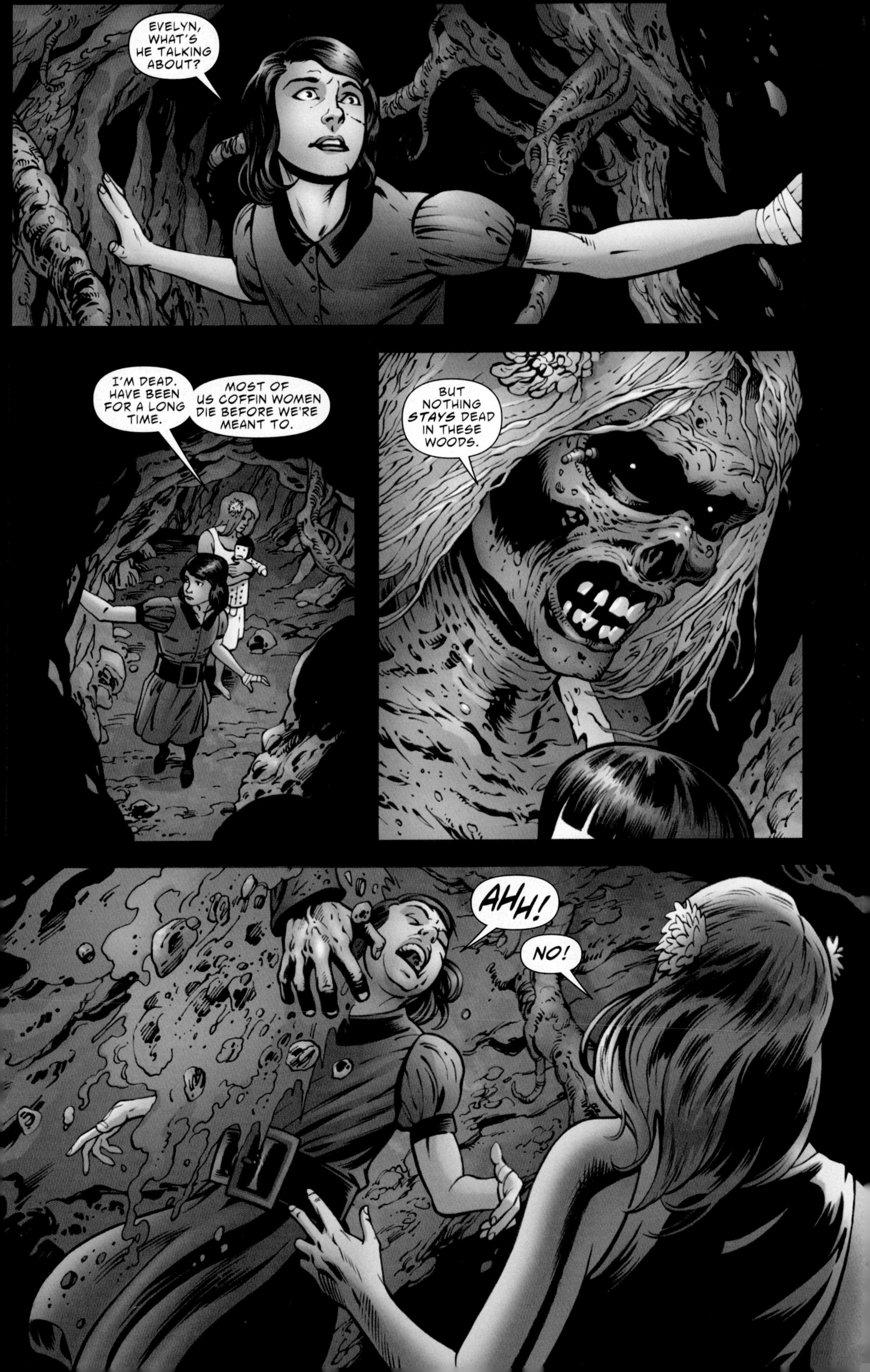
EVELYN, WHAT'S HE TALKING ABOUT?
I'M DEAD. HAVE BEEN FOR A LONG TIME.
MOST OF US COFFIN WOMEN DIE BEFORE WE'RE MEANT TO.
BUT NOTHING STAYS DEAD IN THESE WOODS.
AHH!
NO!

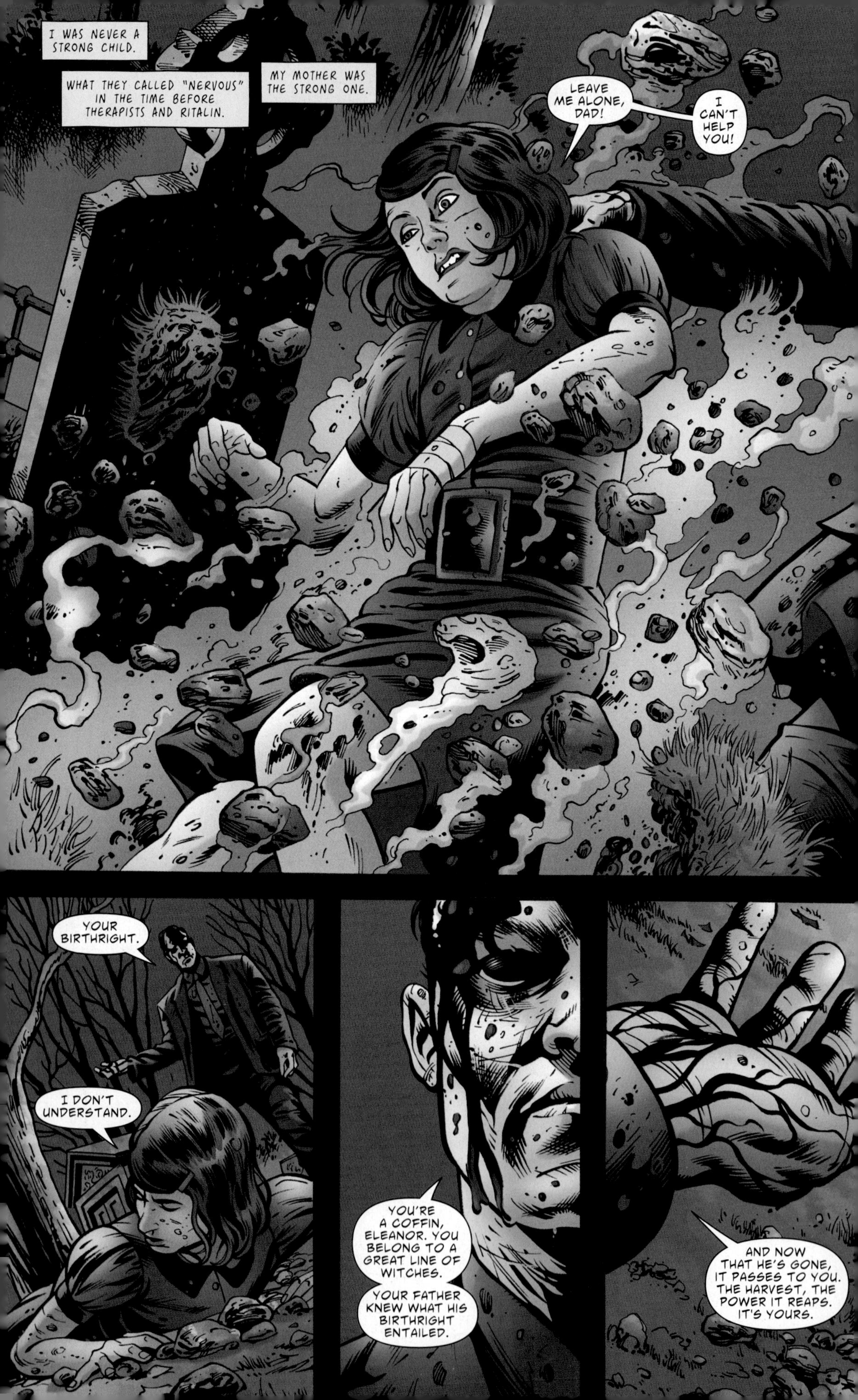
I WAS NEVER A STRONG CHILD.
WHAT THEY CALLED "NERVOUS" IN THE TIME BEFORE THERAPISTS AND RITALIN.
MY MOTHER WAS THE STRONG ONE.
LEAVE ME ALONE, DAD!
I CAN'T HELP YOU!
YOUR BIRTHRIGHT.
I DON'T UNDERSTAND.
YOU'RE A COFFIN, ELEANOR. YOU BELONG TO A GREAT LINE OF WITCHES.
YOUR FATHER KNEW WHAT HIS BIRTHRIGHT ENTAILED.
AND NOW THAT HE'S GONE, IT PASSES TO YOU. THE HARVEST, THE POWER IT REAPS. IT'S YOURS.

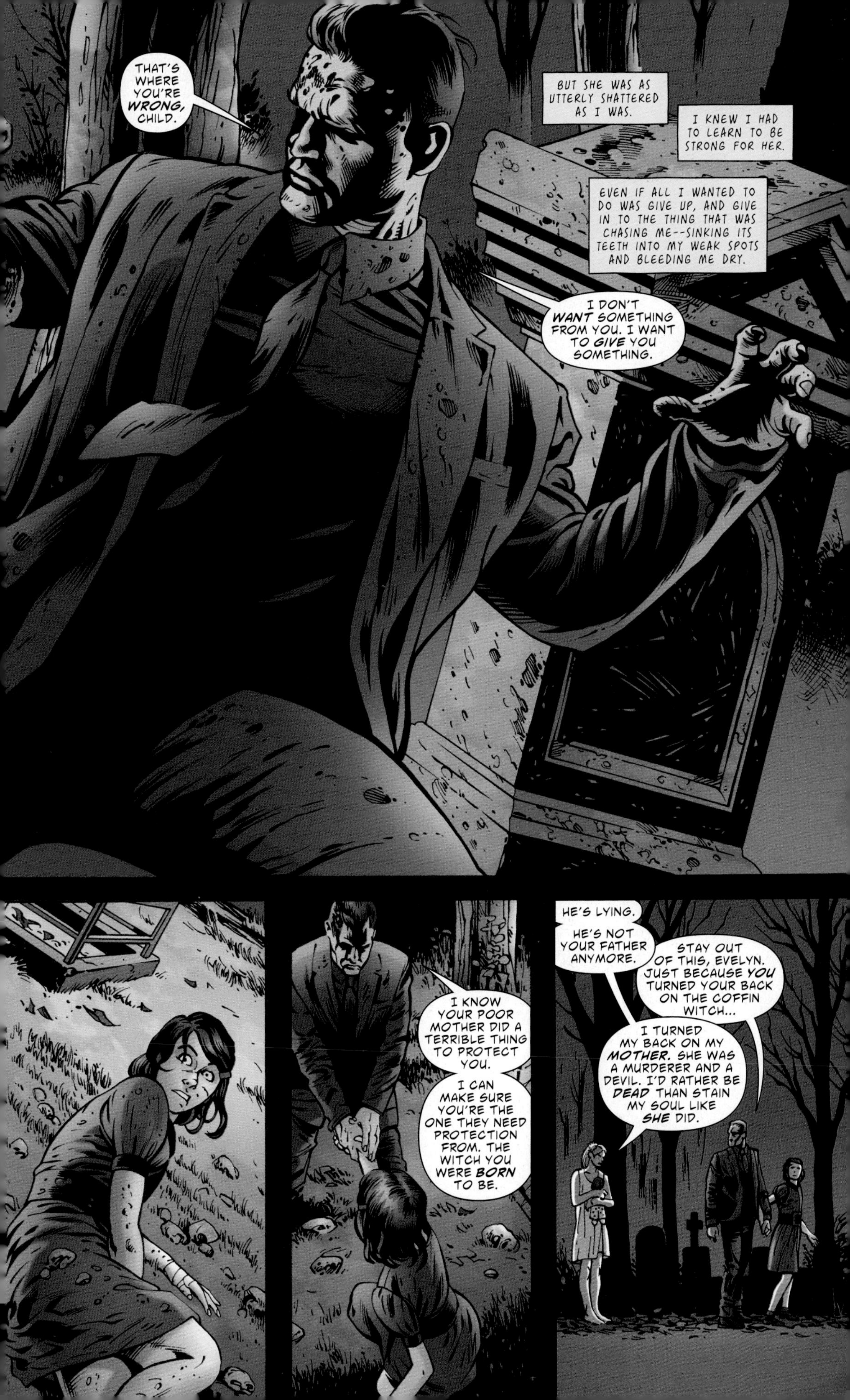

THAT'S WHERE YOU'RE WRONG, CHILD.
BUT SHE WAS AS UTTERLY SHATTERED AS I WAS.
I KNEW I HAD TO LEARN TO BE STRONG FOR HER.
EVEN IF ALL I WANTED TO DO WAS GIVE UP, AND GIVE IN TO THE THING THAT WAS CHASING ME--SINKING ITS TEETH INTO MY WEAK SPOTS AND BLEEDING ME DRY.
I DON'T WANT SOMETHING FROM YOU. I WANT TO GIVE YOU SOMETHING.
I KNOW YOUR POOR MOTHER DID A TERRIBLE THING TO PROTECT YOU.
I CAN MAKE SURE YOU'RE THE ONE THEY NEED PROTECTION FROM. THE WITCH YOU WERE BORN TO BE.
HE'S LYING.
HE'S NOT YOUR FATHER ANYMORE.
STAY OUT OF THIS, EVELYN. JUST BECAUSE YOU TURNED YOUR BACK ON THE COFFIN WITCH...
I TURNED MY BACK ON MY MOTHER. SHE WAS A MURDERER AND A DEVIL. I'D RATHER BE DEAD THAN STAIN MY SOUL LIKE SHE DID.

A MONTH EARLIER.

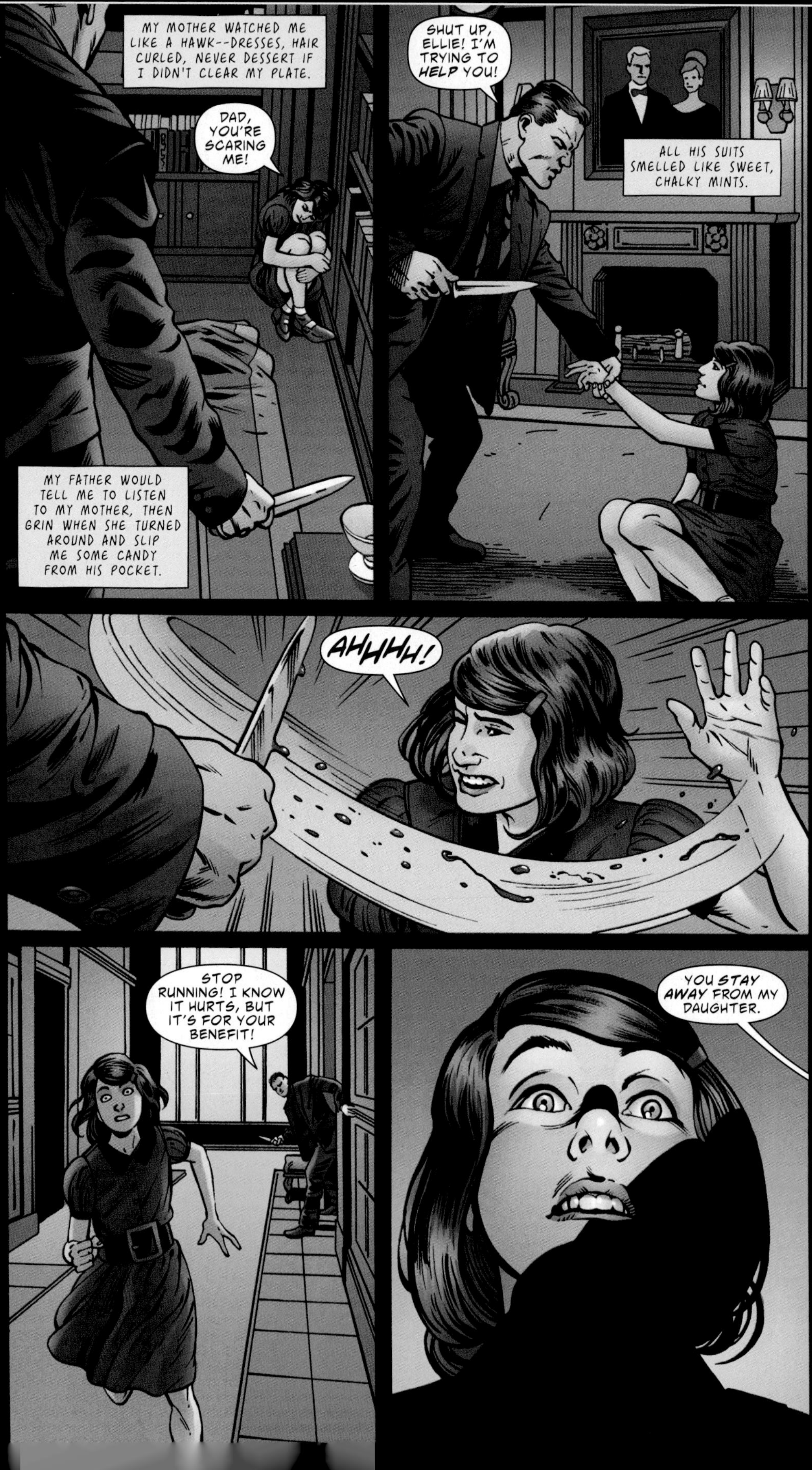
MY MOTHER WATCHED ME LIKE A HAWK--DRESSES, HAIR CURLED, NEVER DESSERT IF I DIDN'T CLEAR MY PLATE.
DAD, YOU'RE SCARING ME!
MY FATHER WOULD TELL ME TO LISTEN TO MY MOTHER, THEN GRIN WHEN SHE TURNED AROUND AND SLIP ME SOME CANDY FROM HIS POCKET.
SHUT UP, ELLIE! I'M TRYING TO HELP YOU!
ALL HIS SUITS SMELLED LIKE SWEET, CHALKY MINTS.
AHHHH!
STOP RUNNING! I KNOW IT HURTS, BUT IT'S FOR YOUR BENEFIT!
YOU STAY AWAY FROM MY DAUGHTER.

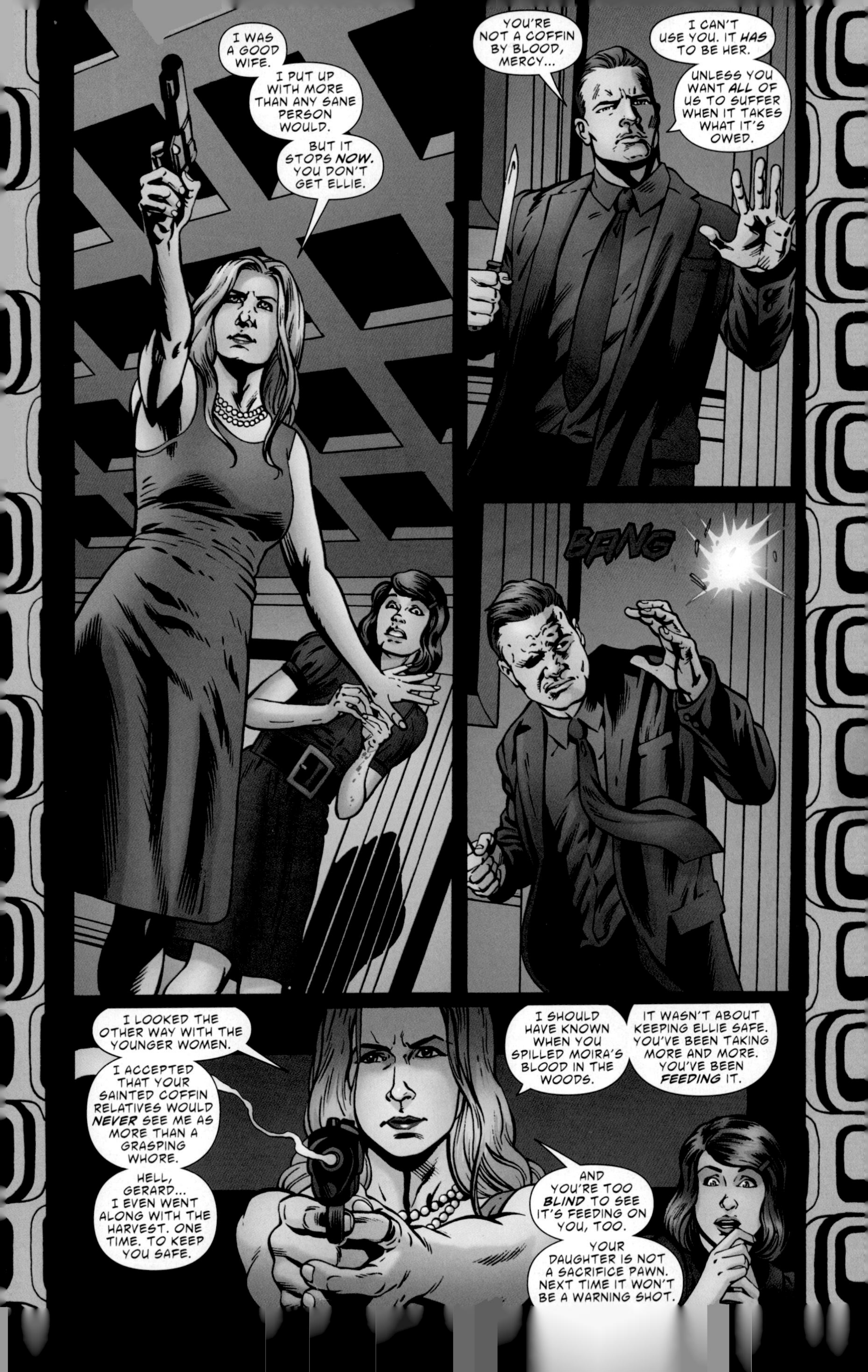
I WAS A GOOD WIFE.
I PUT UP WITH MORE THAN ANY SANE PERSON WOULD.
BUT IT STOPS NOW. YOU DON'T GET ELLIE.
YOU'RE NOT A COFFIN BY BLOOD, MERCY...
I CAN'T USE YOU. IT HAS TO BE HER.
UNLESS YOU WANT ALL OF US TO SUFFER WHEN IT TAKES WHAT IT'S OWED.
BANG
I LOOKED THE OTHER WAY WITH THE YOUNGER WOMEN.
I ACCEPTED THAT YOUR SAINTED COFFIN RELATIVES WOULD NEVER SEE ME AS MORE THAN A GRASPING WHORE.
HELL, GERARD... I EVEN WENT ALONG WITH THE HARVEST. ONE TIME. TO KEEP YOU SAFE.
I SHOULD HAVE KNOWN WHEN YOU SPILLED MOIRA'S BLOOD IN THE WOODS.
IT WASN'T ABOUT KEEPING ELLIE SAFE. YOU'VE BEEN TAKING MORE AND MORE. YOU'VE BEEN FEEDING IT.
AND YOU'RE TOO BLIND TO SEE IT'S FEEDING ON YOU, TOO.
YOUR DAUGHTER IS NOT A SACRIFICE PAWN. NEXT TIME IT WON'T BE A WARNING SHOT.

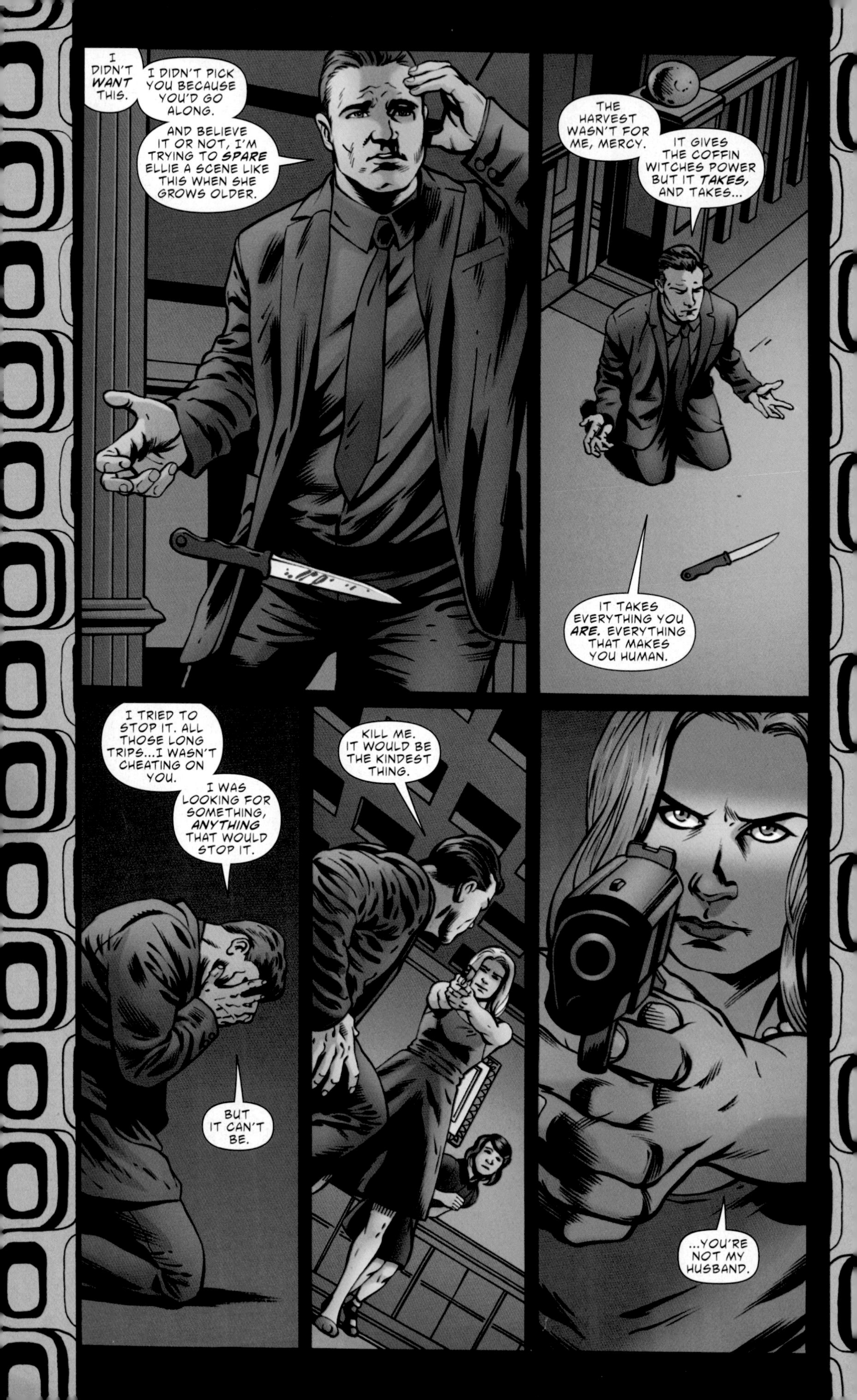
I DIDN'T WANT THIS.
I DIDN'T PICK YOU BECAUSE YOU'D GO ALONG.
AND BELIEVE IT OR NOT, I'M TRYING TO SPARE ELLIE A SCENE LIKE THIS WHEN SHE GROWS OLDER.
THE HARVEST WASN'T FOR ME, MERCY.
IT GIVES THE COFFIN WITCHES POWER BUT IT TAKES, AND TAKES...
IT TAKES EVERYTHING YOU ARE. EVERYTHING THAT MAKES YOU HUMAN.
I TRIED TO STOP IT. ALL THOSE LONG TRIPS...I WASN'T CHEATING ON YOU.
I WAS LOOKING FOR SOMETHING, ANYTHING THAT WOULD STOP IT.
BUT IT CAN'T BE.
KILL ME. IT WOULD BE THE KINDEST THING.
...YOU'RE NOT MY HUSBAND.

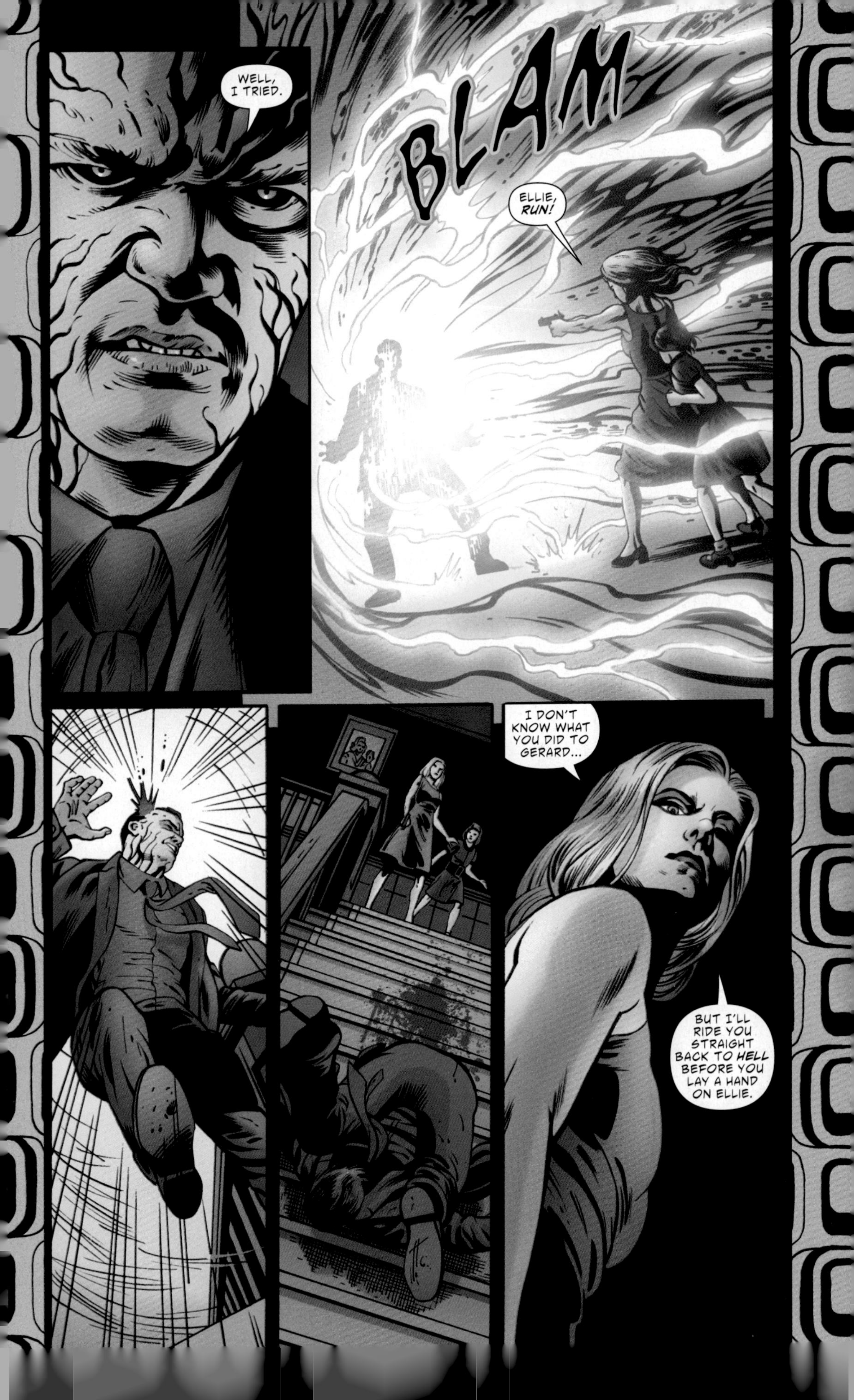
WELL, I TRIED.
BLAM
ELLIE, RUN!
I DON'T KNOW WHAT YOU DID TO GERARD...
BUT I'LL RIDE YOU STRAIGHT BACK TO HELL BEFORE YOU LAY A HAND ON ELLIE.

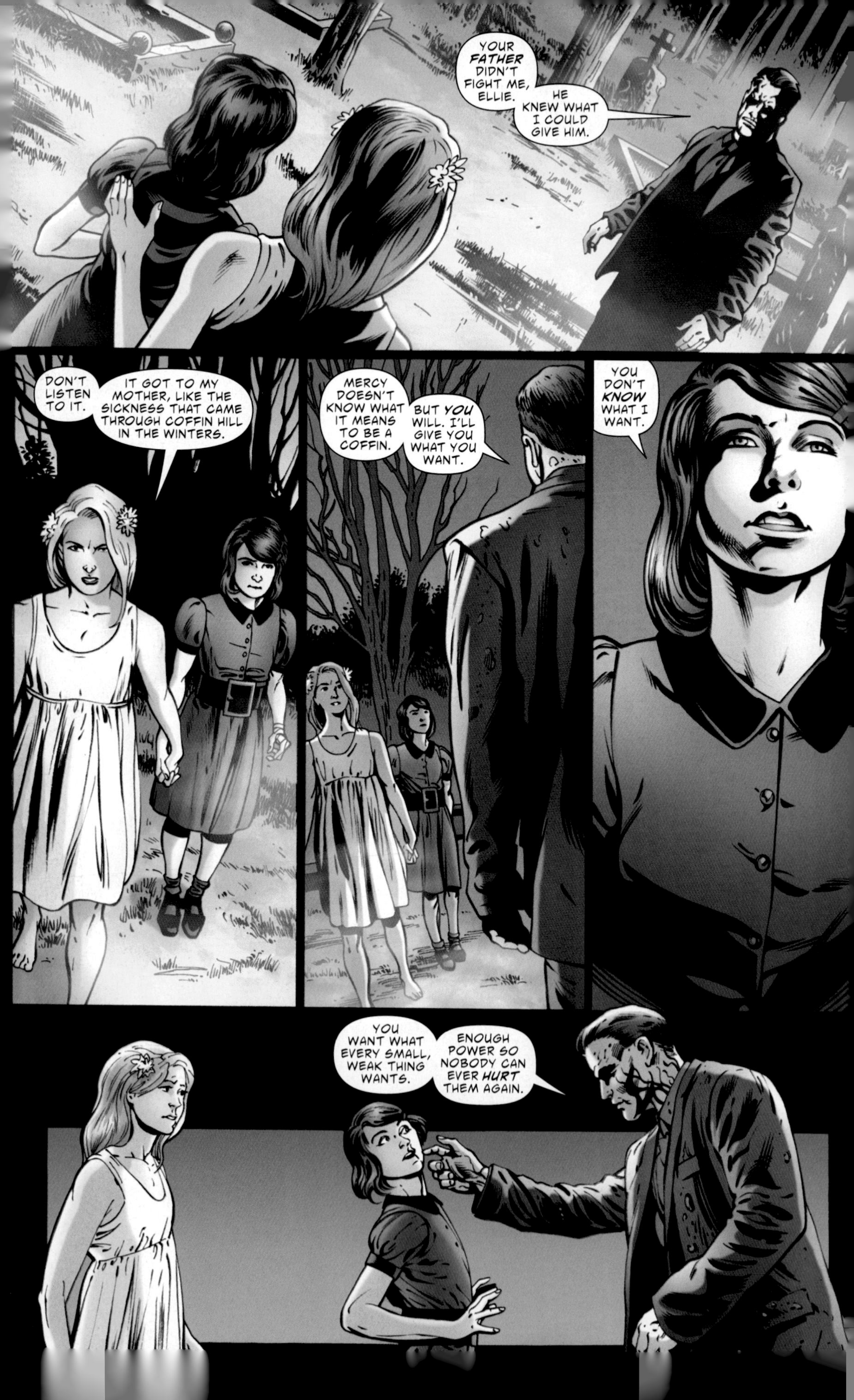
YOUR FATHER DIDN'T FIGHT ME, ELLIE.
HE KNEW WHAT I COULD GIVE HIM.
DON'T LISTEN TO IT.
IT GOT TO MY MOTHER, LIKE THE SICKNESS THAT CAME THROUGH COFFIN HILL IN THE WINTERS.
MERCY DOESN'T KNOW WHAT IT MEANS TO BE A COFFIN.
BUT YOU WILL. I'LL GIVE YOU WHAT YOU WANT.
YOU DON'T KNOW WHAT I WANT.
YOU WANT WHAT EVERY SMALL, WEAK THING WANTS.
ENOUGH POWER SO NOBODY CAN EVER HURT THEM AGAIN.

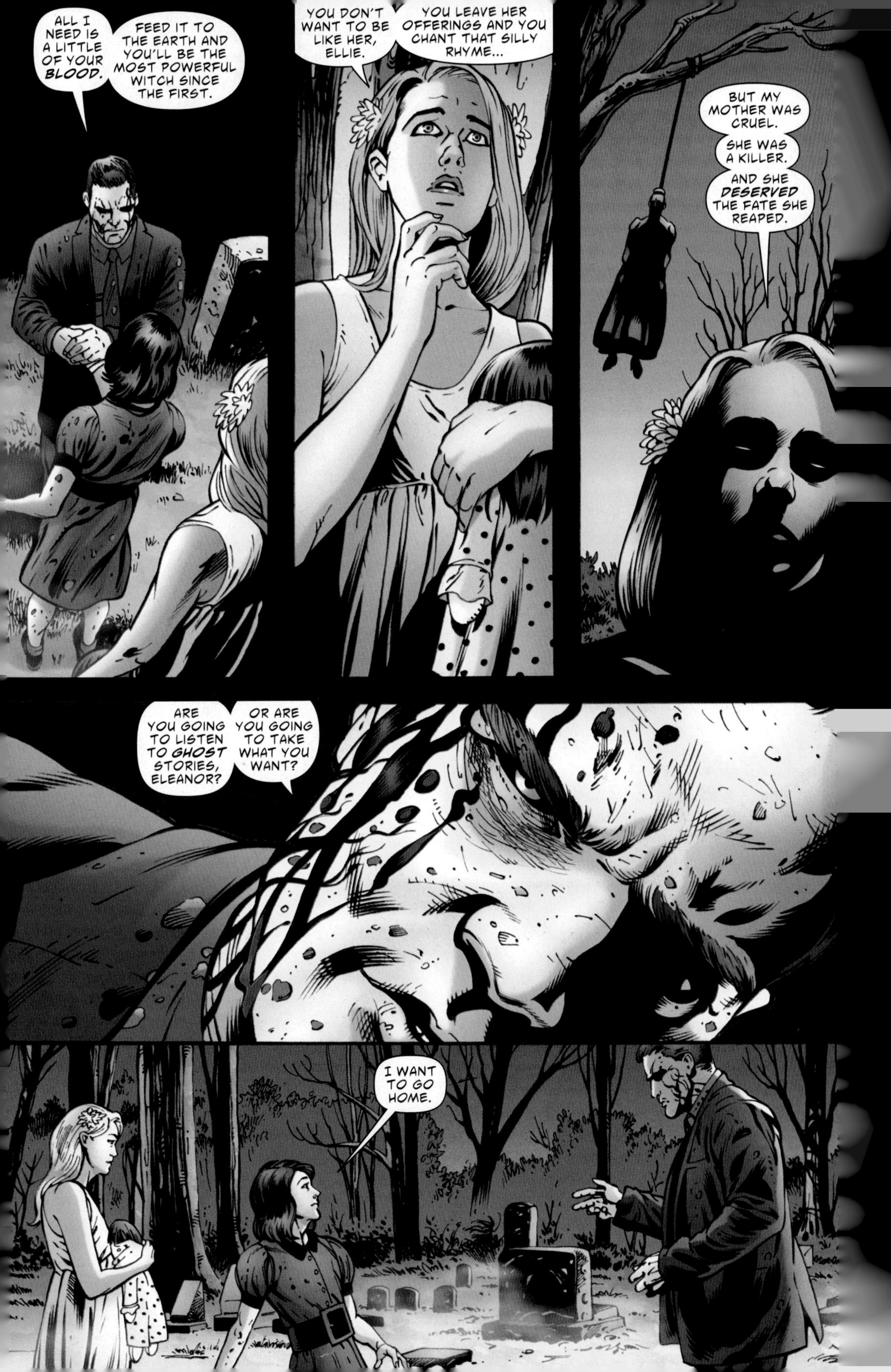
ALL I NEED IS A LITTLE OF YOUR BLOOD.
FEED IT TO THE EARTH AND YOU'LL BE THE MOST POWERFUL WITCH SINCE THE FIRST.
YOU DON'T WANT TO BE LIKE HER, ELLIE.
YOU LEAVE HER OFFERINGS AND YOU CHANT THAT SILLY RHYME...
BUT MY MOTHER WAS CRUEL.
SHE WAS A KILLER.
AND SHE DESERVED THE FATE SHE REAPED.
ARE YOU GOING TO LISTEN TO GHOST STORIES, ELEANOR?
OR ARE YOU GOING TO TAKE WHAT YOU WANT?
I WANT TO GO HOME.

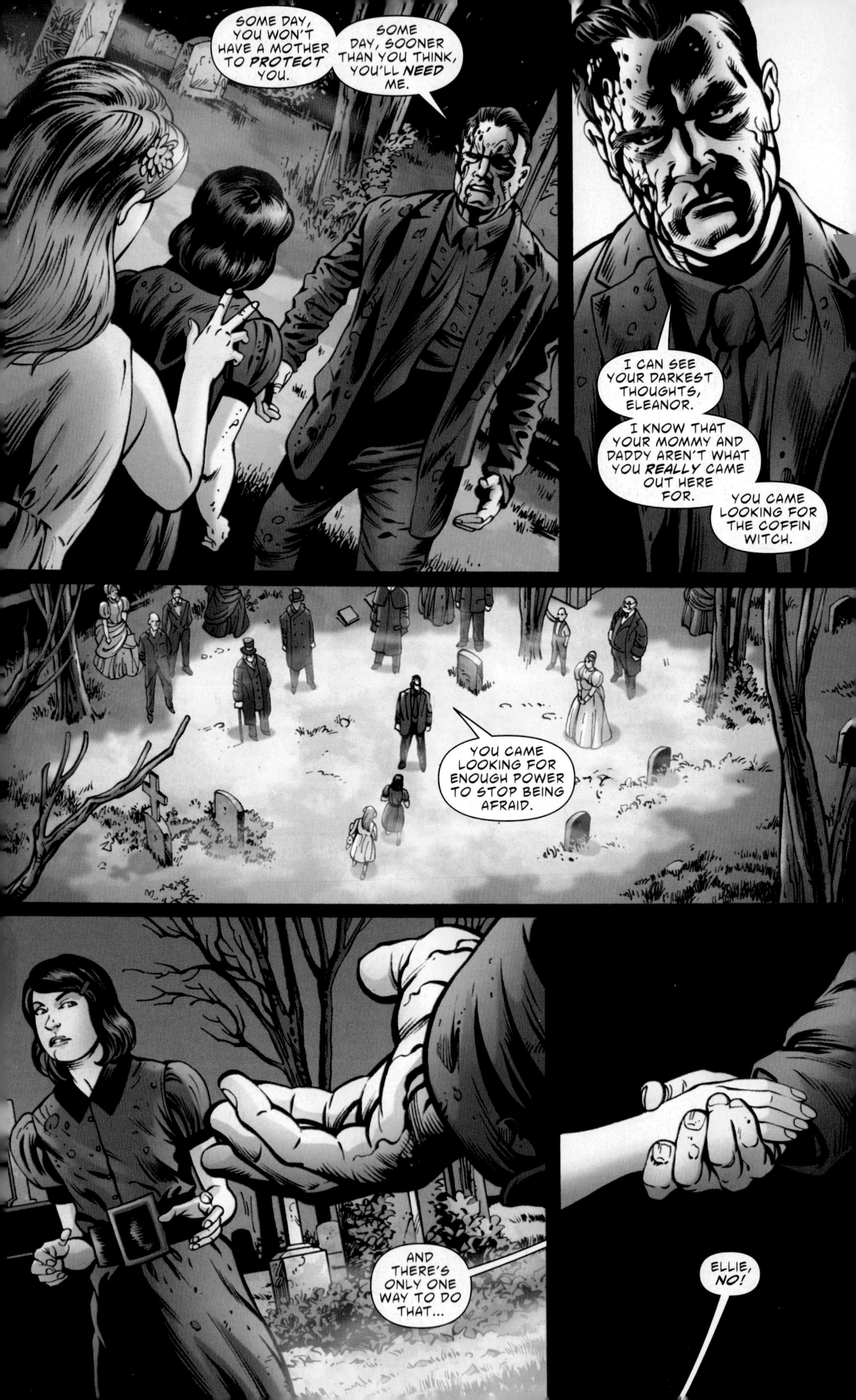
SOME DAY, YOU WON'T HAVE A MOTHER TO PROTECT YOU.
SOME DAY, SOONER THAN YOU THINK, YOU'LL NEED ME.
I CAN SEE YOUR DARKEST THOUGHTS, ELEANOR.
I KNOW THAT YOUR MOMMY AND DADDY AREN'T WHAT YOU REALLY CAME OUT HERE FOR.
YOU CAME LOOKING FOR THE COFFIN WITCH.
YOU CAME LOOKING FOR ENOUGH POWER TO STOP BEING AFRAID.
AND THERE'S ONLY ONE WAY TO DO THAT...
ELLIE, NO!

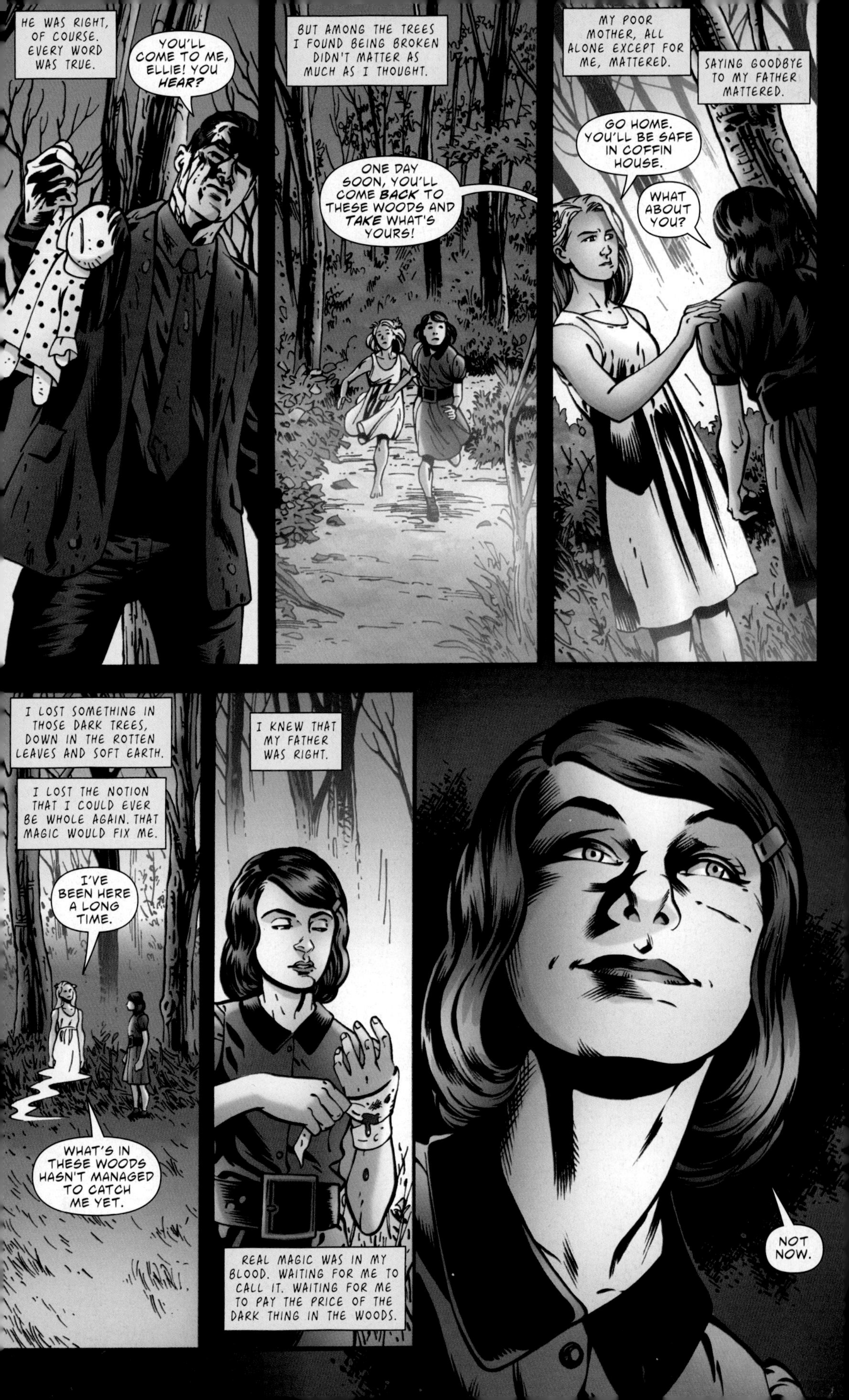
HE WAS RIGHT, OF COURSE. EVERY WORD WAS TRUE.
YOU'LL COME TO ME, ELLIE! YOU HEAR?
BUT AMONG THE TREES I FOUND BEING BROKEN DIDN'T MATTER AS MUCH AS I THOUGHT.
ONE DAY SOON, YOU'LL COME BACK TO THESE WOODS AND TAKE WHAT'S YOURS!
MY POOR MOTHER, ALL ALONE EXCEPT FOR ME, MATTERED.
SAYING GOODBYE TO MY FATHER MATTERED.
GO HOME. YOU'LL BE SAFE IN COFFIN HOUSE.
WHAT ABOUT YOU?
I LOST SOMETHING IN THOSE DARK TREES, DOWN IN THE ROTTEN LEAVES AND SOFT EARTH.
I LOST THE NOTION THAT I COULD EVER BE WHOLE AGAIN. THAT MAGIC WOULD FIX ME.
I'VE BEEN HERE A LONG TIME.
WHAT'S IN THESE WOODS HASN'T MANAGED TO CATCH ME YET.
I KNEW THAT MY FATHER WAS RIGHT.
REAL MAGIC WAS IN MY BLOOD. WAITING FOR ME TO CALL IT. WAITING FOR ME TO PAY THE PRICE OF THE DARK THING IN THE WOODS.
NOT NOW.

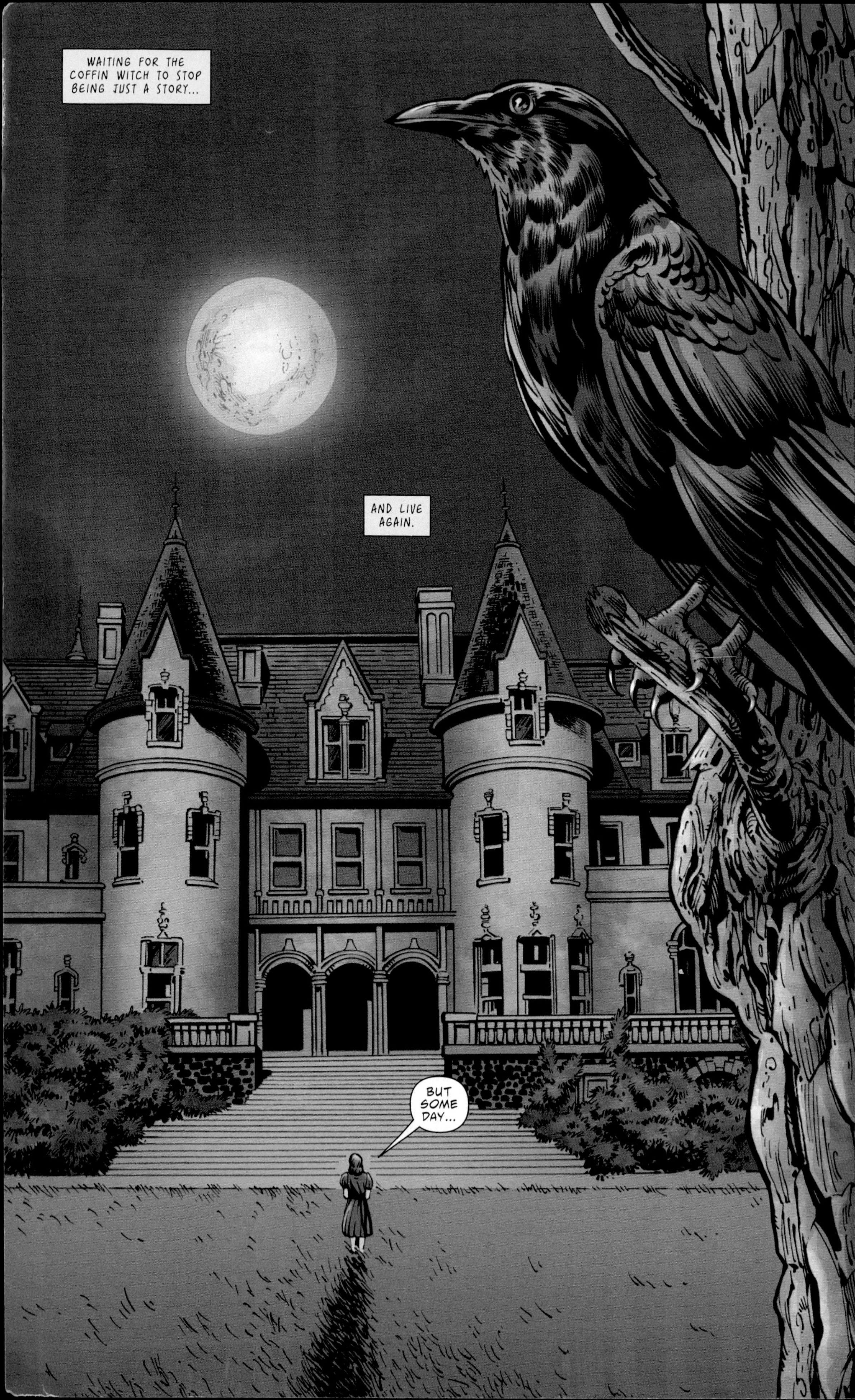
WAITING FOR THE COFFIN WITCH TO STOP BEING JUST A STORY...
AND LIVE AGAIN.
BUT SOME DAY...

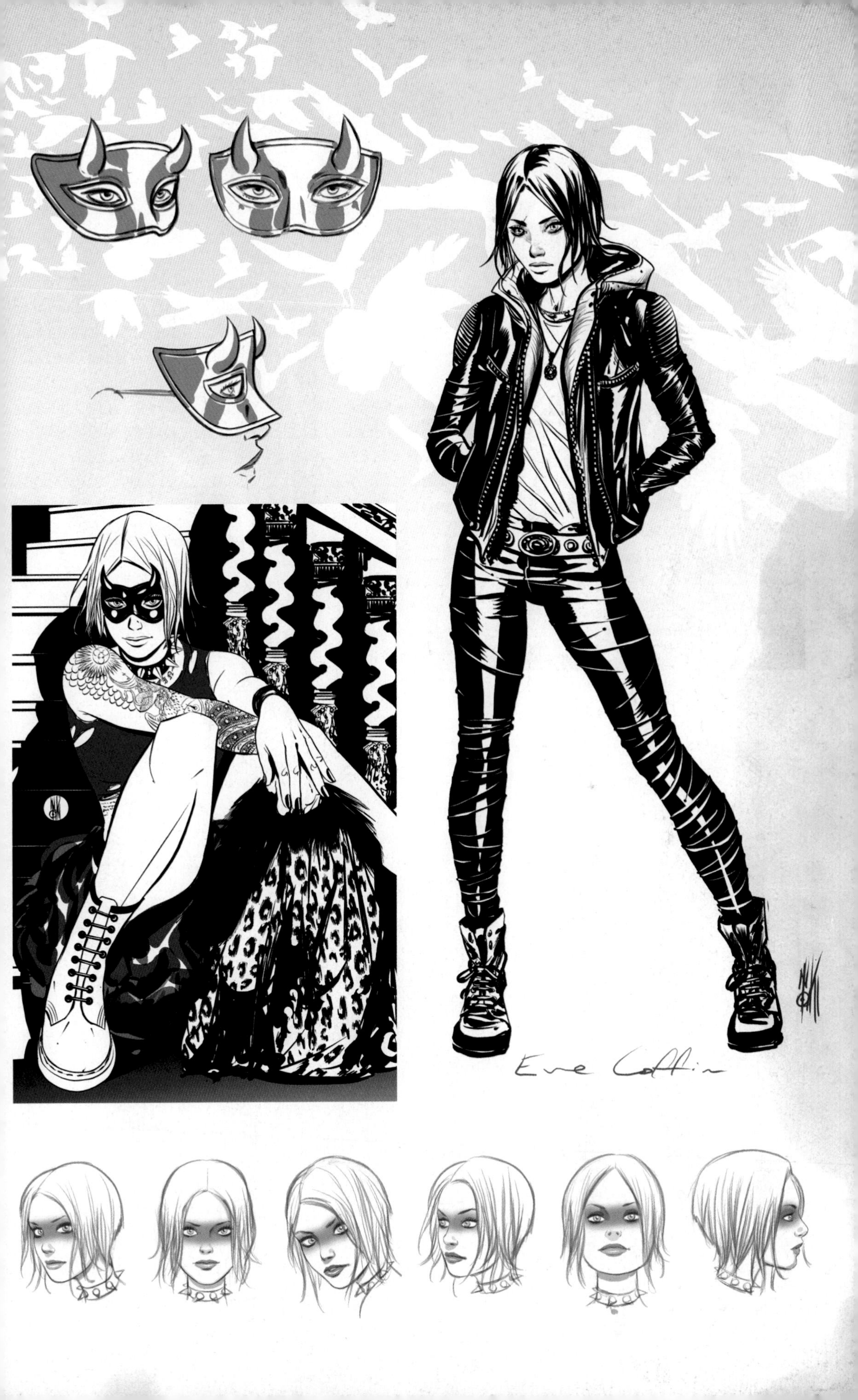
Eve Coffin

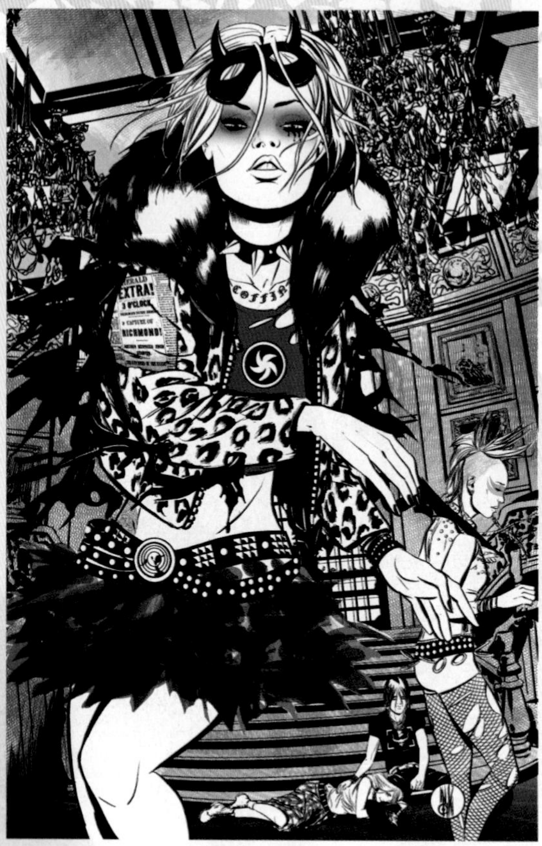
EXTRA!
RICHMOND!

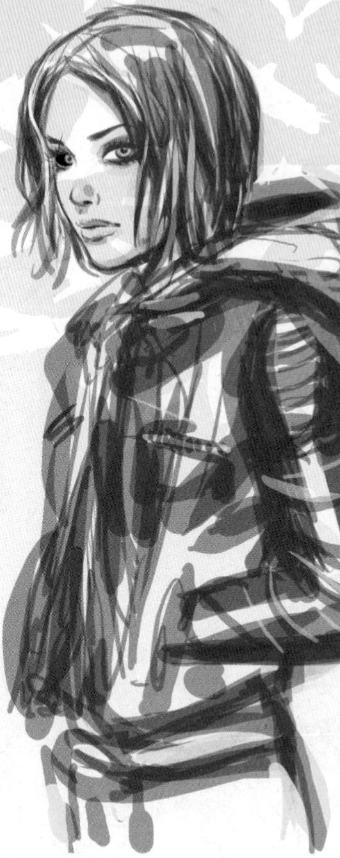

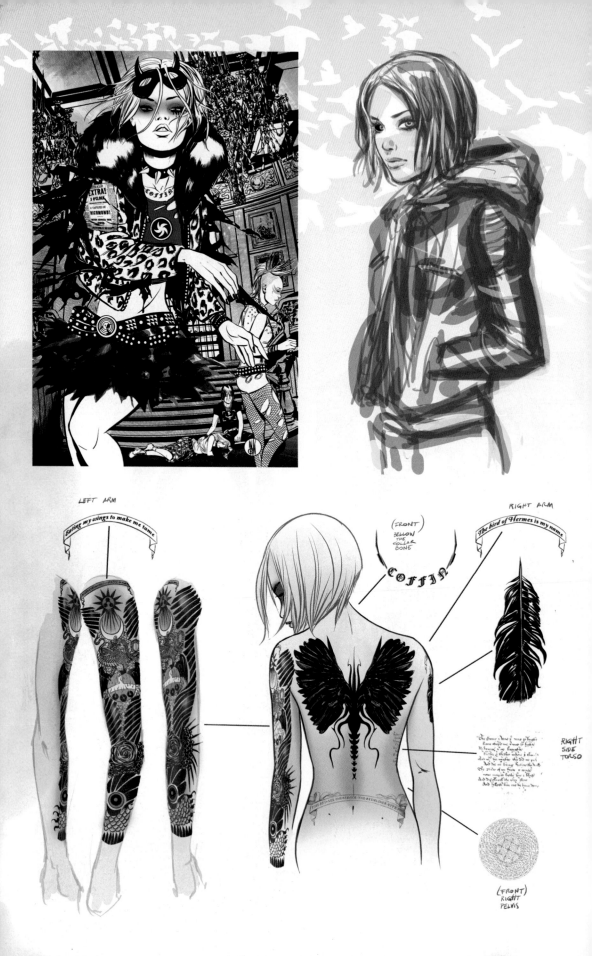

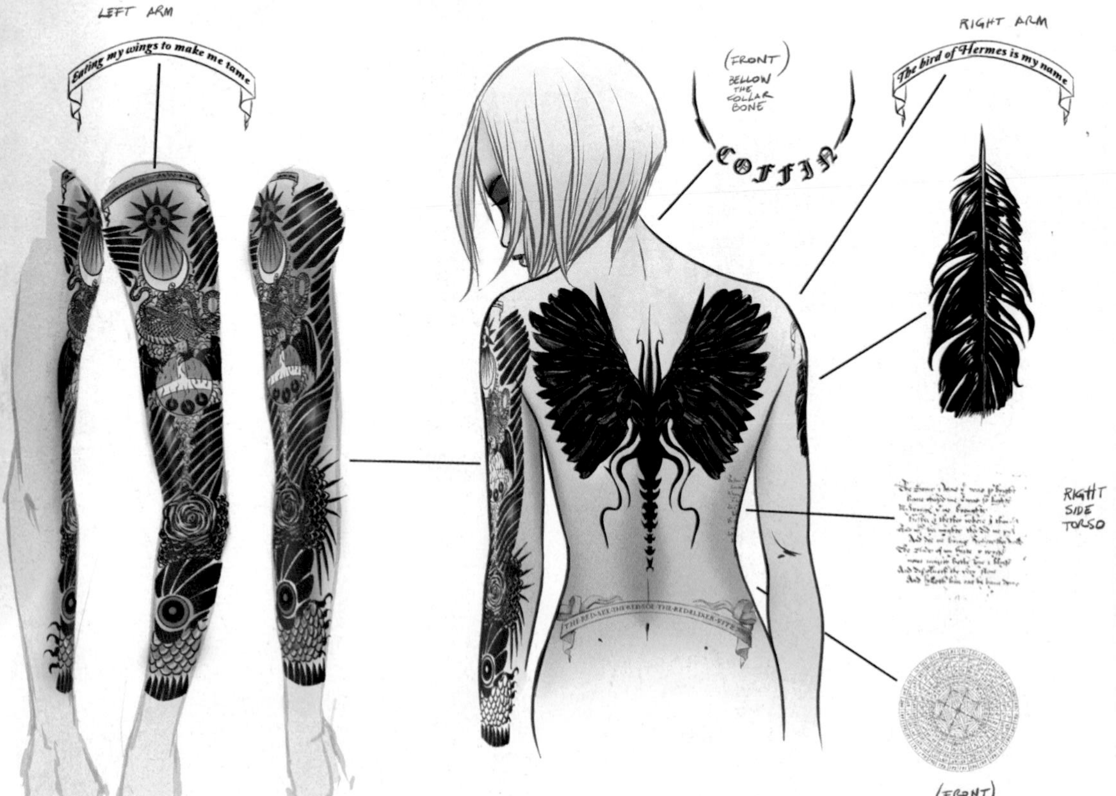
LEFT ARM
Eating my wings to make me tame
RIGHT ARM
The bird of Hermes is my name
(FRONT) BELLOW THE COLLAR BONE
COFFIN
RIGHT SIDE TORSO
(FRONT) RIGHT PELVIS

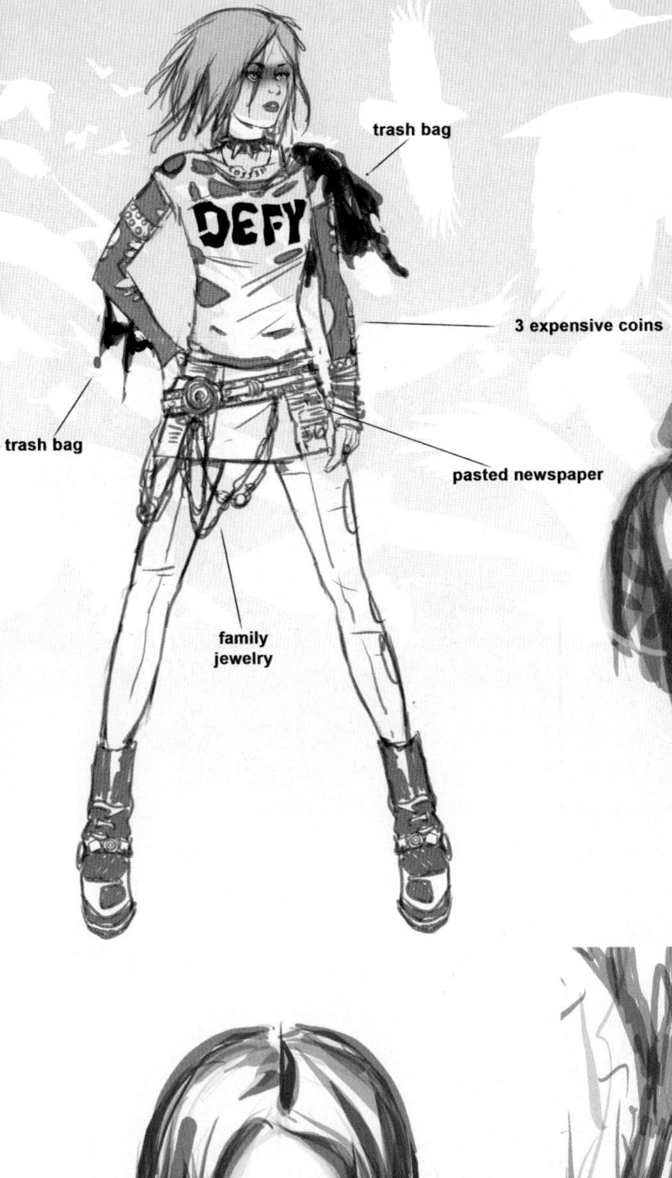
trash bag
DEFY
3 expensive coins
trash bag
pasted newspaper
family jewelry

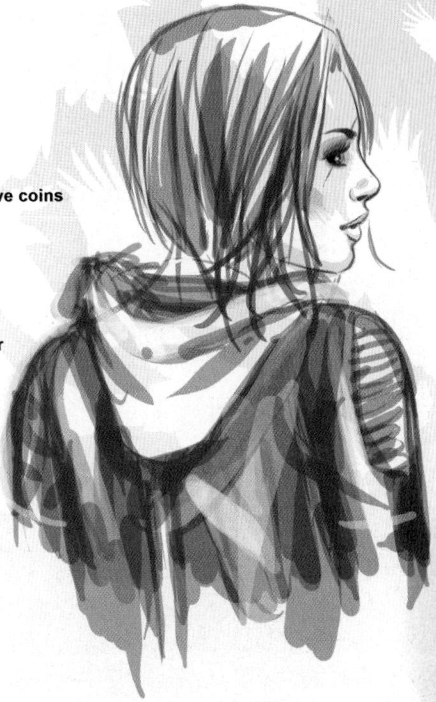

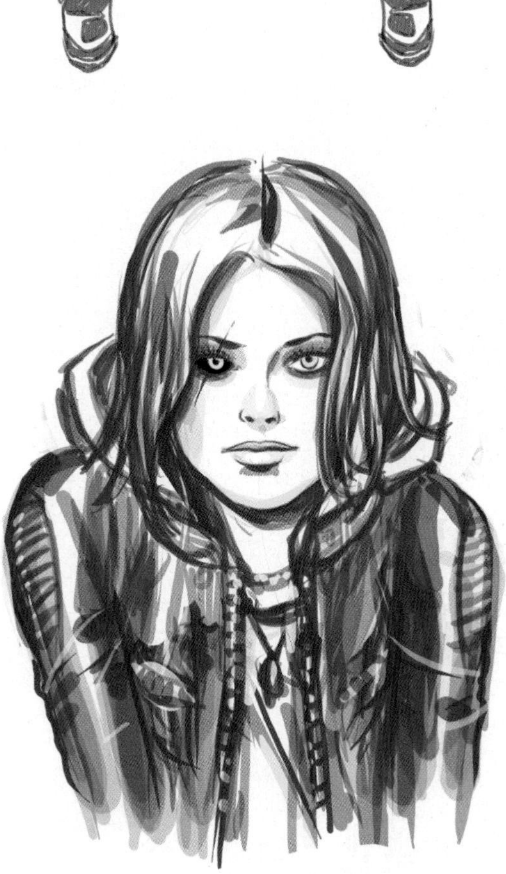

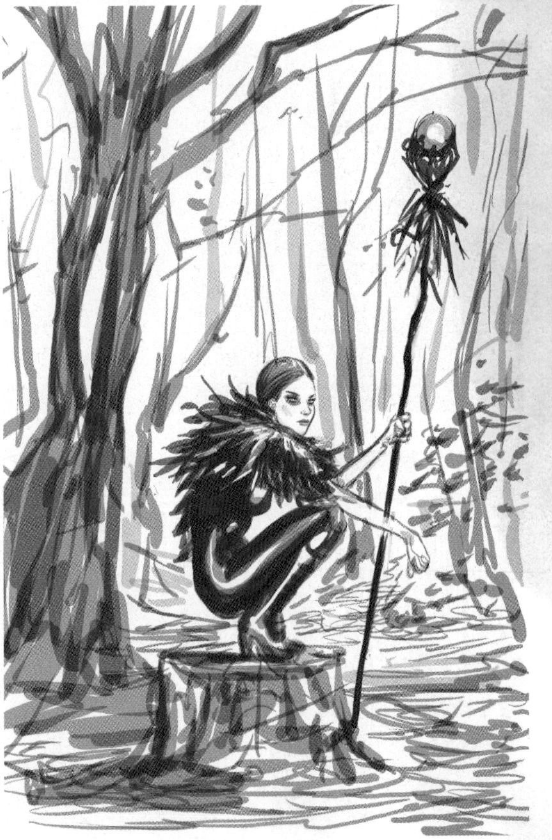

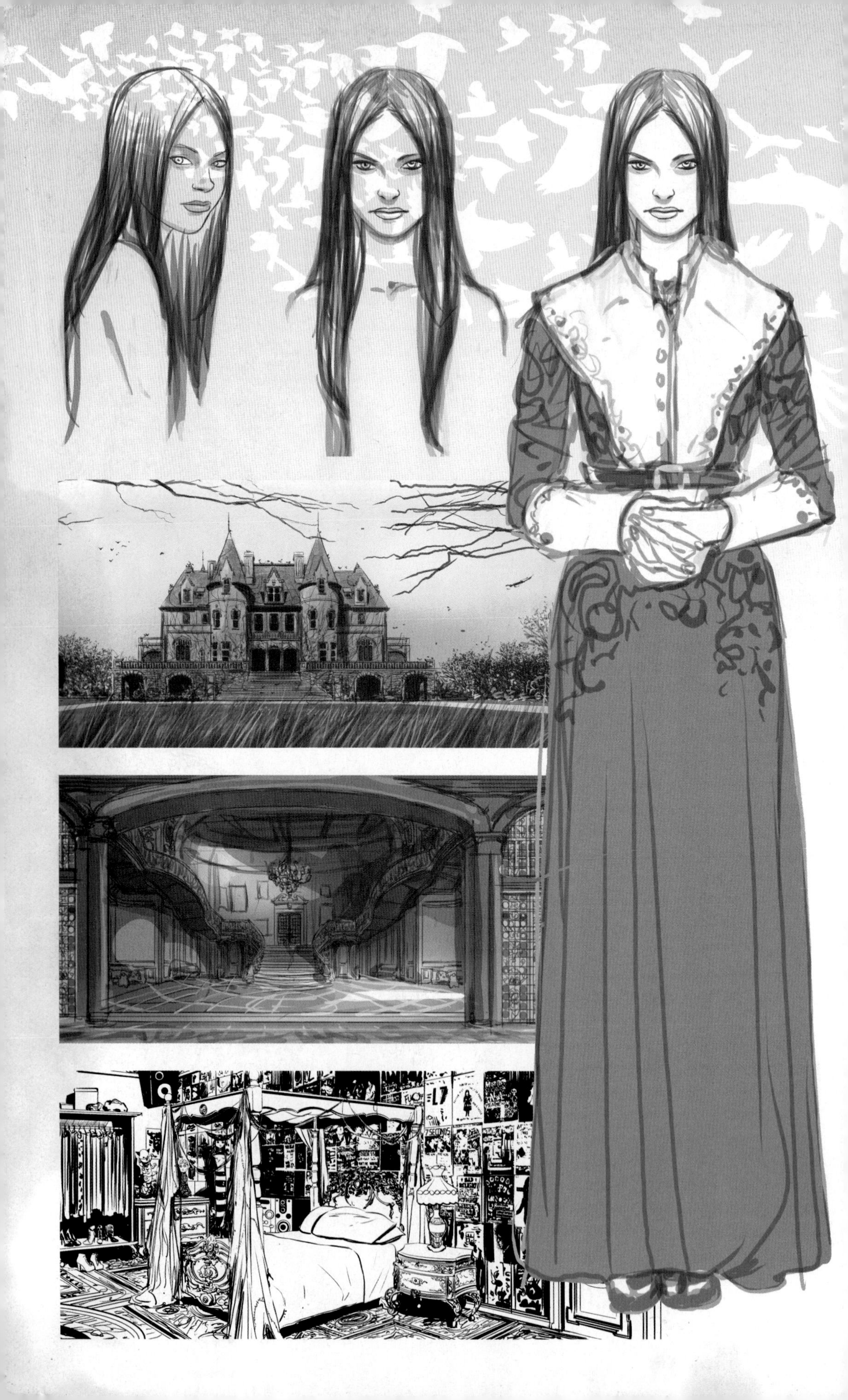

L7
7SECONDS